# CREATING SAFE, EQUITABLE, ENGAGING SCHOOLS

A Comprehensive, Evidence-Based
Approach to Supporting Students

Edited by
**David Osher**
**Deborah Moroney**
**Sandra Williamson**

HARVARD EDUCATION PRESS
CAMBRIDGE, MASSACHUSETTS

Paperback ISBN 978-1-68253-262-1
Library Edition ISBN 978-1-68253-263-8

Library of Congress Cataloging-in-Publication Data

Names: Osher, David, editor. | Moroney, Deborah, editor. | Williamson, Sandra
    L., editor.
Title: Creating safe, equitable, engaging schools : a comprehensive,
    evidence-based approach to supporting students / edited by David Osher,
    Deborah Moroney, Sandra Williamson.
Description: Cambridge, Massachusetts : Harvard Education Press, [2018] |
    Includes bibliographical references and index.
Identifiers: LCCN 2018031193| ISBN 9781682532621 (pbk.) | ISBN 9781682532638
    (library edition)
Subjects: LCSH: Community and school—United States. | Home and
    school—United States. | School improvement programs—United States. |
    Educational leadership—United States. | Educational
    accountability—United States. | Educational change—United States.
Classification: LCC LB2822.82 .C77698 2018 | DDC 371.2/07—dc23 LC record available
    at https://lccn.loc.gov/2018031193

Published by Harvard Education Press,
an imprint of the Harvard Education Publishing Group

Harvard Education Press
8 Story Street
Cambridge, MA 02138

Cover Design: Wilcox Design
Cover Image: shuoshu/DigitalVision Vectors/Getty Images

The typefaces used in this book are ITC Legacy Serif and ITC Legacy Sans.

# Contents

## Part IV  Improve

# Introduction

*David Osher*

THINK OF YOUR FIRST DAYS at school, or at a new school. Maybe you arrived with high hopes, expectations, and excitement. Or perhaps, due to previous negative experiences, you felt wary. One way or the other, you felt alone—until you experienced something that gave you a sense of comfort and belonging. Maybe it was a principal or teacher meeting you at the front door, smiling, calling you by your name, and expressing happiness that you were there. If you were lucky, you soon felt safe and supported, were engulfed in learning, and felt that you belonged and that you could succeed. If you were particularly fortunate, these feelings characterized your entire school career: you experienced challenging and engaging educational opportunities and support for realizing them, and you could develop the skills, mindsets, and identity that helped you build a future.

This happens in some places, at some times, in some classes, for some students. But all too frequently, it does not happen for other students, who experience poor conditions for learning, have limited opportunities for deep learning and creativity, and realize poor or mediocre learning outcomes. Multiple sources of data outline the dimensions of this problem. These data document persistent disparities for students of color, English language learners, students with disabilities, students whose families and communities struggle with poverty, and students who experience trauma and other adversities.[1]

So how can schools routinely create a caring community that supports the social-emotional and academic needs of all students? How can schools realize equitable high standards and build and foster deeper learning and creativity while supporting the physical, emotional, and identity safety and engagement of every student? These are the questions that many educators try daily to answer. As we discuss in the next section, we now have a unique opportunity to address them successfully thanks to advances in science, lessons from practice, and recent legislative policy. We have compiled this volume to leverage this information and to provide a comprehensive resource of research-based practices, frameworks, and tools for school leaders and other professionals who support children and youth in and out of school. With contributions from experts in a variety of fields who serve as chapter coauthors, we have designed the book to help you, the professional educator, address these questions in a practical, strategic way. Our aim is to help you improve your school and district and accelerate equitable and quality outcomes—both in the short and long run—no matter how close or far you currently are from equity with excellence at scale.

This volume builds on a variety of reports and publications produced by the American Institutes for Research (AIR), notably the 2004 publication *Safe, Supportive, and Successful Schools Step by Step.*[2] It is also based on the editors' and coauthors' extensive experience, including our ongoing work with urban, suburban, rural, and frontier schools and with districts, states, and agencies in every US state and territory. Our experience includes both consultation and technical assistance with schools, districts, agencies, and states as well as evaluation research and synthesis activities to identify and apply what we know about supporting student, educator, school, and system capacity so that every student is engaged and thrives—both educationally and as a whole person. We have discovered a great need for a single resource that helps educators think strategically about what it takes to create schools that support deep learning and well-being for all students, that makes sense of all the existing programs and frameworks, and that provides a road map as well as recommended tools. This book intends to do exactly that.

## WHY THE OPPORTUNITY IS NOW
### Scientific Advances: Science-Based Principles for Learning and Development

Over the past decade, researchers working in neurobiology, learning science, developmental science, psychology, child and youth development, and education have learned much about the factors that enhance or impede learning and development for children and adolescents. This knowledge converges on practical science-based principles regarding learning and development that have been reviewed by leading scientists and practitioners.[3] These principles include the following:

- Relationships and stress drive and undermine learning.
- Social-emotional and academic skills interrelate and can be learned.
- Conditions for learning and teaching matter.
- The impacts of stress and adversity must and can be addressed, and resilience can be supported.
- Culture, identity, and subjective perceptions affect learning.
- Neurobiological and neurohormonal processes (e.g., the impact of cortisol) can support or undermine learning.
- Learning and development is both social and individual.
- Multiple factors within the individual and the individual's context contribute to results.
- New analytical techniques enable us to personalize instruction by addressing the multiple factors that contribute to results.

## Lessons from Practice: Successes and Failures

At the same time as scientific understanding has evolved, practice-based research and wisdom have accumulated. We have learned the following from the successes and failures of interventions and other initiatives intended to support children and youth:

- Evidence is necessary but not sufficient; readiness to implement, implementation quality, and context matter.
- Cultural competence and responsiveness are essential to realizing both equity and excellence.
- Academic pressure without student engagement and support does not work.
- Comprehensive approaches that align social-emotional, academic, and health supports can best address barriers to learning.
- Comprehensive approaches can be efficiently implemented through a relational, multitiered model (see figure I.1) with a robust foundation adapted to local needs.
- Data-informed planning and continuous improvement are necessary to drive change; these data should include stakeholder perceptions and concerns.

**Figure I.1** Work at three levels

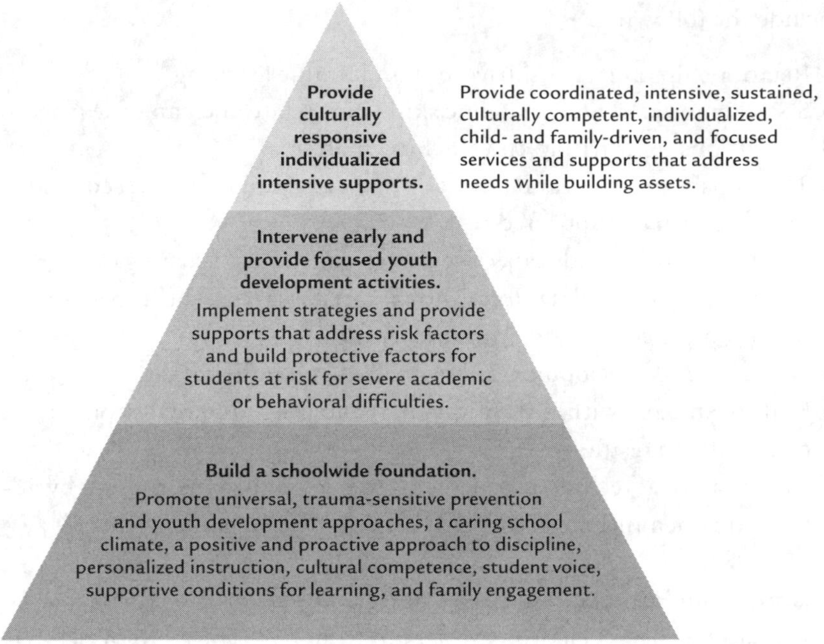

Provide culturally responsive individualized intensive supports.

Provide coordinated, intensive, sustained, culturally competent, individualized, child- and family-driven, and focused services and supports that address needs while building assets.

Intervene early and provide focused youth development activities.

Implement strategies and provide supports that address risk factors and build protective factors for students at risk for severe academic or behavioral difficulties.

Build a schoolwide foundation.

Promote universal, trauma-sensitive prevention and youth development approaches, a caring school climate, a positive and proactive approach to discipline, personalized instruction, cultural competence, student voice, supportive conditions for learning, and family engagement.

- Collaborative, strengths-based asset mapping enhances collaboration and efficiency.

## Legislative Policy: Implications of the Every Student Succeeds Act

This book comes at a fortuitous time, not only thanks to advances in knowledge from science and practice, but also because today's educators are being encouraged by policy makers, families, and communities to monitor the quality of their school climate and its effect on all students. The federal Every Student Succeeds Act (ESSA), passed in 2015, provides opportunities for school personnel to improve student academic progress by addressing the whole child and equity. The legislation's Title IV, Part A, grant program guidance states that education agencies may adopt strategies to support children's social-emotional development to meet the program's mandate to deliver a "well-rounded education." As part of its accountability system, ESSA requires a nonacademic "fifth indicator," which can relate to whole-child development, student engagement, or school climate. The act prioritizes equitable schools and opportunities for students to engage deeply in their academic experience. ESSA also emphasizes the use of data to continually inform state and local improvements.

## VOICES THAT INFORM OUR PERSPECTIVE

In addition to the sources of knowledge and policy just described, throughout this book we draw upon what we have learned from students, teachers, pupil services personnel, administrators, family members, and agency staff. We begin now with the voices of youth and teachers.

### Youth

In countless conversations in schools and in forums, youth have told us what they need from adults in order to thrive. These conversations have enriched our thinking and undergird much of the advice in this book. Here is some of what they say:

> You see me as you want to. If all you see is a stereotype, then you shall never know me, but you will forever know who I am not. (*Langston, an African American high school senior from New England*)

> You don't know me; you just see me. You don't even give me a chance. (*Melissa, a seventeen-year-old Caucasian high school student*)

> I am the one people expect less of, the underachiever, the dropout. No, I think not. But I am the one who had to go against all stereotypes, mean and dirty looks, and much worse. (*José, a Mexican American youth advocate who dropped out of a California high school*)

> Know students' names, and call them by their names; know what embarrasses them, and never embarrass them. (*Mexican American student activists from Texas, when asked what teachers can do to make classes work*)

> We are not afraid of challenge and hard work, because our teachers "have our backs." (*African American high school students responding to the question, "Are you ever pushed too hard?"*)

> We are happy when we have a sense of belonging. (*Caucasian 4-H youth when asked, "What makes you happy?"*)

### Teachers

Teachers, who work most directly with children and youth, have also informed this volume. Here is one teacher's story from Mary Cathryn D. Ricker, a National Board–certified teacher and executive vice president of the American Federation of Teachers. Mary's story, like many stories we have heard, illustrates the need for a comprehensive, systematic approach to supporting students:

When I was a new teacher hired to teach eighth-grade English, the middle school I joined had just completed a lengthy process of redefining itself as a middle school and adopting middle school philosophies and practices, including printing posters to be displayed in every classroom that began with "All students can learn."

It was an important, informal induction into my profession, which solidified three lessons from my teacher training program: approach everything with the belief that all students can learn; don't assume anyone knows you believe that if you haven't explicitly stated it; and if students aren't learning in your class, then do the work to uncover what barriers are preventing them from learning and remove them.

Initially, I believed the barriers were in the four walls of the classroom. I asked myself questions such as, "Did I need to reteach something? Were the definitions clear enough? Had I given enough time to the material? Did I provide interesting and relevant connections to create engaging lessons?" Looking back on my career in the classroom, I realized that these were surmountable obstacles to learning I could control—not that they weren't pernicious from time to time.

While those barriers existed and it was my primary job to look for and remove them, I noticed issues that didn't reflect on my inability to introduce a short story in an engaging way or had nothing to do with offering constructive feedback on a student's writing that was both clear and concise—for example, the student who was frequently late to class, the student who refused to sit in his new seat assignment, the student who put his head down on the desk and started sleeping shortly after class started, or the student who would come back from lunch crying and ask to go to the bathroom.

Initially, these situations elicited a superficial disciplinary response. Being marked tardy meant lunch detention. Refusing to sit down in a newly assigned seat like every other student meant a standoff that resulted in sending a student out of the classroom, while I felt my authority was challenged. The student who slept got nudged awake as often as needed so the principal wouldn't walk in and see a student sleeping in class and reprimand me (and how was I supposed to know if my lessons were engaging if a student wouldn't even try to engage with them?!). Maybe the student crying would have to use a pass to go to the bathroom.

However, none of these situations were what they seemed on the surface. After some investigation, I learned that the student who was frequently late to class had purposefully hung back in the classroom to avoid students who otherwise would bully her when they found her in the hallway. The student who refused to sit down told the social worker that the desk he was assigned would be too embarrassing to sit in because it had an attached chair and he was afraid he wouldn't fit in it; he was too embarrassed to tell me that. The student who slept in class had a part-time job at a local fast food restaurant and took only closing shifts so he could be home after school to watch his little sister. And all those students who returned to the classroom after lunch crying? (There were many more than one. A lot happens at lunch in middle school.) They all had their reasons, and when you are twelve or thirteen or fourteen and life happens, sometimes it's sad or it hurts. No teacher telling you, "It's time to learn now" is going to distract you from how sad you are or how hurt you feel.

In these cases, and countless others, students were lacking a safe environment, or maybe they didn't feel supported by the teacher or their school community. I realized there was something besides my teaching that wasn't engaging them or that there was a logic in their world outside of school that was more relevant, meaningful, or engaging to them and took precedence. In some cases, school was not a place where they felt successful because their success, sometimes just in that moment, was tied to something the school did not have a way to value.

The realization that a school community, and a teacher in that school community, had the responsibility to show students their lives had value extended into the other things I noticed or discovered were impediments to learning. For example, I had a student who was frequently absent after he turned thirteen. When his mom came to parent/ teacher conferences, she apologized profusely for his attendance, with him sitting right there, and went on to explain that she and her children were homeless and had moved from her car to a shelter to be just a little more comfortable; but now that her son was thirteen, he didn't get to stay in the "women's and children's" side anymore. He had to stay in the men's side. He wasn't getting much sleep, so he would sleep when he was with her. There was a student whose work started to drop off after a strong start to the school year. When I called home, I found out the student's older sister had recently been convicted of a crime and sent to jail. Her mom said they had all been struggling with the situation at home. One Monday, a student came to school and walked into homeroom with his wrist cupped in his opposite hand. He came up to me, showed me his wrist—which was blue, purple, black, and about three sizes larger than it should have been—and asked, "Ms. Ricker, my mom wanted me to ask you if I could see the nurse this morning to take a look at my thumb?" His family had no health insurance. His mother had kept him as comfortable as she could all weekend with ice, over-the-counter pain relievers, and her constant attention. The school nurse was his urgent care center.

How do we create school environments that support the learning and development of the whole child with these and other barriers to learning and development? What conditions need to be in place so that I can successfully meet the academic needs of students while being present and mindful of the social and emotional needs of students as well? How can we assure those professionals that they are not expected to do this alone and that there is an entire school community collaborating toward successfully meeting the needs of our students? That our talents in isolation may be impressive, but our talents in concert with those of our colleagues are unstoppable? How do we amplify the professional voices of those of us hired because of our expertise at meeting the needs of students? What are the most meaningful ways of collaborating with our students, their families, and our surrounding community to create safe and supportive spaces that engage learners and their families for the most successful outcomes possible?

We start this book featuring the voices of students and teachers because they are essential to driving equity with excellence and must be at the center of school improvement. We could also begin with pupil services personnel, who work hard to provide students with individual support, but often feel marginalized or overloaded by staff-to-student ratios, or by needing to spend time on documentation rather than on consultation and student support. Or we could begin with the visionary principals and superintendents we have met, who are committed to supporting both teachers and students and who envision schools that promote the success of all students, foster creativity and healthy development, and contribute to the wellness of their entire community. We could also start with family members, who, like teachers, balance multiple jobs and roles. They support their children 24/7, and experience their children's strengths and needs as a whole—not as a set of service silos. Or, we could start with culturally competent agency staff who employ strengths-based, family- and child-driven approaches to supporting children and youth. We have written about all of these groups elsewhere, and include their perspectives throughout this book.[4]

For these reasons, this book purposely employs the word *you* for our intended readers—superintendents, principals, teachers, out-of-school educators, paraprofessionals, pupil service professionals, student leaders, family members, board members, and agency staff. This book is designed to help *you*, and other members of your school or district community, realize your goals and aspirations by leveraging the assets and addressing the challenges of fostering educational equity with excellence in a way that includes social and emotional learning (SEL) and deeper learning for all students. We know this work is hard and has many elements. However, it is made harder by ineffective, underaligned, incoherent solutions that address only part of the problem and may add to the burden on students, families, teachers, and leaders. This book will help you by:

- naming and explaining problems and their interconnectedness;
- strengthening your school's capacity to assess needs, identify solutions, plan implementation, and roll out your plan in a way that maximizes engagement and support;
- showing how you can identify, adapt, and align interventions that will work in your context;
- providing tools to assess and develop readiness to implement these interventions and to monitor, assess, and continually improve what you do;
- supplying links to other tools and resources; and
- documenting examples of schools, districts, and communities that have experienced success with a comprehensive, systematic approach.

## HOW THIS BOOK IS ORGANIZED

The chapters in this volume are organized in four parts focusing on activities that will enable you to create schools that support the social-emotional and academic needs of all students and produce excellence with equity. Although each chapter can be read as a stand-alone resource, the parts are organized in a logical, iterative order and the chapters are interdependent, with specific chapters describing certain issues and practices in depth. Links to all of the major tools and other resources mentioned in the chapters can be found in appendix B. For direct access to the tools and resources referenced throughout this volume, you can go to www.air.org/SafeEquitableEngaging.

### Part I: Build Capacity

Chapters 1 through 5 address building the capacity of the school and its staff to lead and implement the work with passion, enthusiasm, and efficiency. This involves building skills, structures, and motivation, including organizational incentives, to do the work; fostering leadership qualities and teams that work well; and conducting needs assessments and developing strategies and action plans that include the right interventions. Topics by chapter are as follows:

- Developing individual and organizational readiness and capacity (chapter 1)
- Leading schools and school improvement through effective leadership and key teams (chapter 2)
- Implementing needs assessment and asset mapping, identifying doable and sustainable interventions that produce short-term gains while addressing the root causes of problems and challenges, developing an action plan and indicators for monitoring, and securing stakeholder input and investment (chapter 3)
- Becoming a critical consumer ready to select the right programs, practices, strategies, approaches, curricula, and policies for your specific context and concerns, and understanding the challenges of implementation and adaptation (chapter 4)
- Identifying, leveraging, and coordinating resources that can support whole-child education and development, including blending and braiding funding and redeploying resources (chapter 5)

## Part II: Engage

Chapters 6 through 10 focus on engaging and harnessing the strengths of the school's undertapped stakeholders. You will learn the following:

- How and why to implement culturally competent and responsive approaches (chapter 6)
- Strategies for engaging students and employing youth development approaches (chapter 7)
- Ways to effectively engage families in a culturally responsive and family-driven way to maximize partnership, equity, and excellence (chapter 8)
- Methods to effectively engage and collaborate with the community (chapter 9)
- Techniques for leveraging community-based, expanded learning and support (chapter 10)

## Part III: Act

Chapters 11 through 19 address approaches to creating safe, supportive, engaging, academically robust, and equitable schools. They cover these activities:

- Building a foundation for equity with excellence through the lens of a generalized three-tiered model to support the success of all students (chapter 11)
- Building and restoring school communities through relational and restorative practices (chapter 12)
- Creating respectful, trauma-sensitive, and inclusive schools with intentional programing to address and prevent the effects of adversity and marginalization (chapter 13)
- Using multitiered systems of support (MTSS) to coordinate and align academic and behavioral goals (chapter 14)
- Employing selective intervention strategies to address the needs of students who are at some elevated risk of academic, social-emotional, and/or behavioral problems (chapter 15)
- Employing intensive, indicated interventions to address the needs of students who are at a highly elevated risk of academic, social-emotional, and/or behavioral problems (chapter 16)
- Employing effective approaches to leverage the power of universal SEL skill-building programs (chapter 17)

- Building conditions for teaching so that teachers feel supported and equipped to address the needs of all of their students (chapter 18)
- Addressing learning challenges in a way that accounts for the individualized and culturally grounded nature of learning, does not stigmatize students or create negative identities, and scaffolds skill development and engagement in deeper learning (chapter 19)

## Part IV: Improve

The concluding chapter underscores the importance of continuous improvement—specifically, progress monitoring and formative and summative assessment techniques—for creating and maintaining safe, equitable, and engaging school cultures (chapter 20).

Building equity with excellence is important for our children, our communities, and ourselves. It is not an easy task. But it can be and is being done. This book is intended to help you do this work in a sustainable manner—collaboratively, respectfully, and strategically.

# PART ONE

# Build Capacity

# ONE

# Building Readiness and Capacity

*David Osher*

BUILDING SAFE, SUPPORTIVE, engaging, and academically robust schools that support equity with excellence is no simple task. It depends upon the capacity and readiness of students, teachers, and other school staff, as well as the school as a whole, to meet the demands of teaching and learning and to engage in the work of school improvement. All members of the school community need the social-emotional and cognitive skills to do their work.

## DEFINING CAPACITY

Capacity is more than a skill—it is produced by the combination of (1) technical and social-emotional competence, and (2) supportive conditions. For example, if we want educators to succeed, we must do more than hire teachers with the right skills. We must provide them with professional development and scaffolding so that they can attune to, support, and engage their students. In the case of schools, capacity includes efficient systems and relational trust.

## DEFINING READINESS

In addition to sufficient capacity, another ingredient is required for teachers, school staff, and students to produce desired results: motivation. Readiness is the combination of capacity and motivation.[1] Because readiness is necessary for successful implementation of all of the activities in this book, in this first chapter we define it, explain its importance, illustrate how it shapes the work described in the rest of the book, and discuss how it can be built, amplified (or attenuated), and assessed.

Readiness is a dynamic property that can be developed or lost. Heuristically, it is the mathematical product of three distinct sets of factors: motivation, general organizational capacity, and intervention-specific capacity. While each factor is important by itself, they combine to maximize or limit success, hence the formula: Readiness = Motivation × General Capacity × Intervention-Specific Capacity ($R = MC^2$).[2] When any one of these three factors is low, success is limited or cannot be realized at all. You realize your best outcomes when all the relevant participants want to do something, have the necessary skills to do it, and are in an environment that supports doing it.

## Motivation
### Individual motivation
Individual motivation is a psychological process that varies with the task or intervention. It affects whether people begin tasks, persist at them, and invest their hopes and efforts in implementation.[3] Motivation involves beliefs, values, interests, goals, drives, needs, reinforcements from others, and how people view themselves.[4] When people are intrinsically motivated, acting fulfills a personal interest or provides meaning. Intrinsic motivation results in deeper investment of energy as well as focus, creativity, confidence, and achievement.[5] Believing you can do something affects motivation. Motivation in turn may be affected by past experiences with similar tasks, perceptions of support, and/or the supports and risks of failure. People are pressed for time, and have finite physical and emotional resources and cognitive bandwidth. Although they may not be conscious of it, they usually make return-on-investment (ROI) calculations, which influence how much effort and hope they put into something. These calculations include beliefs about the need for the task or intervention, its desirability, the anticipated outcomes, and its potential benefits. These calculations may be affected by scarcity of money or time, or even by the ability to invest hope. Behavioral economists suggest that this scarcity can contribute to *tunneling*, where people focus only on what they need now, not some future benefit.[6]

*Organizational motivation*

Organizational motivation is systemic rather than psychological. While it includes both the individual and collective motivation of the members of the school community, it also includes legal mandates and policy incentives and disincentives. Policy constraints may exist at the federal, state, or district level, and even when principals and staff—functioning as "street-level bureaucrats"—interpret policy and put it into practice.[7] For example, a superintendent may prioritize social and emotional learning (SEL), but principals may feel pressure to increase test performance and worry about losing time to programs that interfere with test preparation. Organizational motivation is also affected by strategic plans and overarching goals, and by collective experience with change in general and types of innovation in particular (e.g., "we tried that and it made things worse," or "they never support us").

*Components of motivation*

As mentioned earlier, motivation may be affected by time horizons and intuitive (unconscious) or explicit analyses of the expected ROIs. Different stakeholder groups and organizations, and different members of each stakeholder group (or of an organization), may have different time horizons. Take an academic intervention for struggling students: school board members may have a two-year time horizon, principals a one-year horizon, willing teachers a four-month horizon, and parents or students and skeptical teachers even shorter time horizons. Similarly, you may need to address the fact that people and organizations vary in their calculation of the benefits of taking action. For example, when implementing a student support program, people may weigh the following against the potential benefits of the program:

- The risk of the program having bad effects
- The "costs" of implementing or participating in the program, including:
  - Expenditure of time (e.g., instructional time)
  - Emotional resources (e.g., hoping for something that may not work)
  - Money (e.g., baby-sitting costs for a parent)
  - The opportunity cost versus doing something else (e.g., academic tutoring)

These estimates are often subjective, so during your planning and evaluation of a task or intervention you may want to do a formal cost–benefit analysis or formal ROI analysis of the different components of motivation (see table 1.1), where you monetize benefits and costs and then use this information to address stakeholder concerns and/or modify your strategy.

## General Capacity

General capacity consists of the features necessary for an organization to function efficiently. Schools and districts are dynamic systems, where many actors directly or indirectly influence the ability to do something easily and successfully. There are five interactive components: human and material resources; leadership; systems, structures, linkages, and networks; culture and climate; and social capital and slack (see table 1.2).

**Table 1.1** Components of motivation

| COMPONENT | DEFINITION |
| --- | --- |
| Doability | Degree to which the task or intervention is perceived as relatively difficult to understand and use |
| Intrinsic motivation | Degree to which individuals want to do something |
| Observability and visibility | Degree to which individual performance or outcomes that result from the intervention are visible to others |
| Priority | Extent to which the intervention is regarded as more important than other interventions or actions |
| Risk | Perceived consequences of failure |
| Relative advantage | Degree to which a particular intervention is perceived as being better than what it is being compared against; can include perceptions of anticipated outcomes |
| Compatibility | Degree to which the task or intervention is perceived as being consistent with existing values, cultural norms, experiences, and the needs of potential users |
| Trialability | Degree to which an intervention can be tested in a pilot fashion before going to scale |

*Sources:* Jonathan Scaccia et al., "A Practical Implementation Science Heuristic for Organizational Readiness: R = MC2," *Journal of Community Psychology* 43, no. 4 (2015): 484–501, doi:10.1002/jcop.21698; Allison Dymnicki et al., *Willing, Able, Ready: Basics and Policy Implications of Readiness as a Key Component for Implementation of Evidence-Based Practices* (Washington, DC: Office of the Assistant Secretary for Planning and Evaluation, Office of Human Services Policy, 2014); Paul Flaspohler et al., "Unpacking Prevention Capacity: The Intersection of Research to Practice Models and Community-Centered Models," *American Journal of Community Psychology* 41, no. 3–4 (2008): 182–96.

**Table 1.2** Components of general capacity

| COMPONENT | DEFINITION |
| --- | --- |
| Human and material resources | Resource utilization (resources available to do a job) and staff capacity (general skills, education, dispositions, and expertise that staff possess) |
| Leadership | The nature of school leadership and how it articulates and supports organizational activities |
| Systems, structures, linkages, and networks | Processes that influence how well an organization functions on a day-to-day basis |
| Culture and climate | Expectations about how things are done in the school, how it functions, and organizational innovativeness (general receptiveness toward change—the organizational learning environment); how members of the school community individually and collectively perceive, appraise, and feel about the school and work environment that they experience |
| Social capital and slack | Social relationships that can be drawn upon or leveraged to meet needs or address goals; planned or available resources that are left untapped, which provide elasticity in responding to an unanticipated need |

*Sources:* Jonathan Scaccia et al., "A Practical Implementation Science Heuristic for Organizational Readiness: R = MC2," *Journal of Community Psychology* 43, no. 4 (2015): 484–501, doi:10.1002/jcop.21698; Allison Dymnicki et al., *Willing, Able, Ready: Basics and Policy Implications of Readiness as a Key Component for Implementation of Evidence-Based Practices* (Washington, DC: Office of the Assistant Secretary for Planning and Evaluation, Office of Human Services Policy, 2014); James S. Coleman, "Social Capital in the Creation of Human Capital," *American Journal of Sociology* 94 (1988): S95–S120; Sendhil Mullainathan and Eldar Shafir, *Scarcity: Why Having Too Little Means So Much* (London: Allen Lane, 2013).

Before beginning a new intervention or program, it's important to assess and build a school's general capacity to implement the intervention or program. We find the following set of questions valuable for school leaders to assess and build general capacity.

### What human and material resources are available, and are they adequate for the task or intervention?

Human resources include staffing ratios; the experience, knowledge, and technical competency of staff in their areas of work; staff social-emotional and cultural competency; and, when appropriate, staff knowledge of child development. Human resources are allocated according to the school's capacity to provide staff development and support. The human resources deployed are constrained by the amount of time staff have available to develop new skills and, in some districts, by a lack of resources to compensate teachers for staff development time that takes place outside of the school day. Material resources include budgetary resources and the amount and adaptability of space.

### How is the school led, and how does its leadership affect the ability to act?

Team *leadership* in this context encompasses many elements. It involves the nature, quality, and stability of leadership as well as the extent to which it is distributed. It includes the supports for leaders; the capacity of leaders to ensure effective execution and follow-through of policies and interventions; and the extent to which leadership is strategic, responsive, adaptive, and coherent to stakeholders. It also refers to the degree to which leadership supports staff capacity and wellness, builds a sense of common mission, and creates a strong organizational culture. Finally, this feature includes the extent to which leadership encourages innovation and fosters an environment that promotes both individual and collective accountability and a commitment to continuous improvement.

### What systems, structures, linkages, and networks are in place to get things done, and how efficient are they?

What are the protocols and procedures that are in place? Are they synergistic? Do they help or hinder the process of getting work done? Are administrative efforts aligned and coherent? What about programmatic efforts? Finally, how do the nature and quality of formal and informal networks and communication affect the ability to get things done?

### How does the school climate and culture affect people's willingness and ability to engage in tasks and interventions?

How do the members of the school community experience the school and their role? Do they feel safe emotionally and physically? Do they feel connected to the school and supported in their role? And do they feel listened to and engaged in what they do? These feelings can both reflect and be affected by the school's culture—including its norms, goals, and values, as well as the degree of relational trust across the school community. (See "The Importance of Relational Trust in Schools" for more on this topic.)

### The Importance of Relational Trust in Schools

Relational trust is a key component of school climate and culture. Tony Bryk and Barbara Schneider describe trust (based on their analysis of trust in Chicago schools) as "the connective tissue that holds improving schools together."[8] They suggest that "a broad base of trust across a school community lubricates much of a school's day-to-day functioning and is a critical resource as local leaders embark on ambitious improvement plans."[9] For example, when relational trust was high, teachers were more likely to experiment with new practices and collaborate with parents, and this resulted in gains in student learning. Where it was weak, there was less collaboration and experimentation, and no discernable improvement in their reading or mathematics scores.

*Do members of the school community extend each other's social capital?*
Are there support networks in the community that can be leveraged to support interventions? Are there budgetary cushions that can be leveraged to address unanticipated exigencies? Are there efficient ways of handling unanticipated demands for staff time without compromising programming?

## Intervention-Specific Capacity

As members of the education community, we have many roles, each of which involves a set of tasks, and schools perform many functions as well. Ideally, we are able to execute these actions as reflective practitioners, with ease, grace, and adaptability, and without undue stress or cognitive burden, and schools have the capacity to support all school-relevant tasks. Intervention-specific capacity includes the human, technical, and fiscal conditions necessary for successfully implementing interventions with quality. These skills are *both* technical and social-emotional. A teacher we met while researching SEL in Anchorage provides an example.[10] He applies collaborative techniques to math instruction. His ability to do this successfully depends on his pedagogical, relational, and social-emotional skills, as well as the conditions for learning in the classroom, which are supported by his school's commitment to SEL.

Table 1.3 presents global constructs associated with intervention-specific capacity; each new task, program, practice, or policy has its own set of knowledge and skills required to implement it with quality.

**Table 1.3** Components of intervention-specific capacity

| COMPONENT | DEFINITION |
| --- | --- |
| Intervention-specific knowledge, skills, and abilities | Knowledge, skills, and abilities needed for an intervention, such as an understanding of the evidence-based intervention's theory of change or skills being taught in curricula |
| Program champion(s) | Key stakeholder(s) who support an intervention through connections, knowledge, expertise, and social influence |
| Specific implementation climate supports | Extent to which the intervention is supported; presence of strong, convincing, informed, and demonstrable management support |
| Interorganizational relationships | Relationships between (1) providers and the training and technical assistance support system and (2) different provider organizations that are used to facilitate implementation |

*Sources:* Jonathan Scaccia et al., "A Practical Implementation Science Heuristic for Organizational Readiness: R = MC2," *Journal of Community Psychology* 43, no. 4 (2015): 484–501, doi:10.1002/jcop.21698; Allison Dymnicki et al., *Willing, Able, Ready: Basics and Policy Implications of Readiness as a Key Component for Implementation of Evidence-Based Practices* (Washington, DC: Office of the Assistant Secretary for Planning and Evaluation, Office of Human Services Policy, 2014).

## ASSESSING READINESS

Readiness is a dynamic property that represents the confluence of intra-individual factors, collective and individual factors, and organizational factors. It can be developed, or diminished, as a product of individual experiences, organizational learning, and organizational change.

Readiness can be assessed and supported at an individual and an organizational level. Tools for assessment include surveys and focus groups. The information collected can inform planning and continuous improvement, along with the efforts described in the remaining chapters.

## BUILDING CAPACITY AND PLANNING FOR READINESS: AN EXAMPLE

Cleveland Metropolitan School District (CMSD), in Ohio, chose the Promoting Alternative Thinking Strategies (PATHS) program as part of a strategic, comprehensive plan to implement universal, early, and intensive interventions—which the district called "Humanware"—to improve conditions for learning (CFL) and student outcomes. This work was done in a manner consistent with the recommendations in the next four chapters. The Humanware team, the district equivalent of the student support team (SST; see chapter 2), selected PATHS after conducting a strategic planning process (chapter 3) and using appropriate selection criteria (chapter 4). PATHS is a research-based curriculum for grades K–6 that has been found to prevent or reduce behavioral and emotional problems in similar urban populations by facilitating emotional literacy, self-control, social competence, positive peer relations, and interpersonal problem-solving skills.[11] The team also leveraged short-term economic recovery resources to build long-term capacity through teacher training in PATHS, a creative approach consistent with chapter 5's recommendations.

After an independent audit found that CMSD's conditions for learning were generally poor and that this contributed to poor academic and behavior outcomes, rather than jumping straight to implementation, CMSD undertook a strategic, comprehensive planning process to build the capacity needed to deliver and support PATHS and other interventions—increasing the chances that their efforts would improve CFL.[12]

First and foremost, CMSD set about building leadership support for PATHS among department heads and district administrators. "Prior to the PATHS teachers' training, we had weekly Humanware executive committee meetings with representatives from major departments in the district talking about what this would look like," explains Bill Stencil, school psychologist and Humanware partner with CMSD. "We shared the PATHS language, concepts, and plans. We needed to let our upper-level administrators share with our principals that we were going to be using PATHS and how we would support their efforts. We explained that training would follow and teachers would be supplied with all the materials they needed."

Only after gaining their buy-in did CMSD train all preK–5 teachers who would be implementing PATHS. "Training is critical, and we chose PATHS because it has trainers available," says Kevin Dwyer, the lead consultant to CMSD from American Institutes for Research. "It is a well-researched curriculum that was an important component of SEL initiatives that CMSD implemented. The twelve-hour training covered important topics such as: How do teachers best teach the PATHS curriculum with modeling and practice? . . . It was a well-planned process." Follow-up research determined that when teachers were well trained, they were more likely to implement PATHS with quality, which in turn was associated with improved student and school outcomes.[13]

Additionally, the district provided awareness training for all other school staff—including school psychologists and counselors, nurses, security officers, and food service staff—since PATHS lessons were not just delivered in the classroom, but also on buses, playgrounds, and anywhere else students would be. The awareness training reduced resistance and increased staff motivation.

CMSD continued to hold Humanware executive committee meetings to plan the rollout. The meetings always involved teacher union officials as a critical partner in the planning. Dwyer explains, "The teacher union buy-in was critical, and was facilitated by that intensive involvement in those weekly meetings." To further build readiness among teachers, teachers who were successful with implementation spoke at monthly staff meetings to share best practices and lessons learned with their colleagues.

Dwyer believes that planning for readiness and building capacity were critical to the success of PATHS in CMSD. "Building this entire process was very intentional. We were looking for a program that started in the preK level and built on each successive school year. As a result, each year our students become stronger in SEL."

## TAKEAWAYS

- Competence is both a technical and social-emotional skill.
- Capacity is a product of both competence and supportive conditions.
- Readiness is the product of motivation × general capacity × innovation-specific capacity.
- Readiness can be assessed and developed.

# TWO

# Leading, Coordinating, and Managing for Equity with Excellence

*Catherine Barbour, Kevin Dwyer,*
*and David Osher*

BUILDING SAFE, SUPPORTIVE, engaging, and academically robust schools that support equity with excellence requires transforming mindsets and practices. This, in turn, requires transformational district and school leadership that models and builds commitment to the social-emotional and academic development and success—including emotional and cognitive engagement and deep learning—of every student.[1] Successful implementation of school improvement efforts hinges on leaders' ability to model this commitment and engage stakeholders in visioning and enacting change; build teams to share leadership; distribute ownership; develop readiness; understand and address the affective and relational components of change; set clear expectations; provide support to meet these expectations; and foster dialogue, problem solving, and continuous improvement. The lessons of school reform across the country suggest that unless line professionals and staff—the street-level bureaucrats—are engaged, even powerful reforms will have "shallow roots."[2]

School leaders have the authority to implement changes to build conditions for equity, engagement, and improved learning. Although authority is important, it is insufficient. As we discuss in this chapter, successful implementation of transformative change requires individual and collective leadership as well as the effective use of teams.

## INDIVIDUAL AND COLLECTIVE LEADERSHIP

Effective leaders know how to support the development of a collective vision to guide change and how to distribute leadership. They understand that change must be both top-down and bottom-up—what Michael Fullan has called a "change sandwich"—and that it is realized by individuals working with support from others.[3] These leaders build readiness and relational trust and ensure that implementers on the ground:

- understand the goals;
- identify the challenges they face in realizing the goals;
- collaborate in realizing the goals; and
- receive the necessary support.

School improvement requires changing practice, which is hard and often disruptive. Successful leaders are socially, emotionally, and politically skilled; they understand that change causes unease and, potentially, "innovation fatigue."[4] They also know and address the lessons of lasting reform and successful innovation: new programs and change efforts will succeed and develop strong roots only if they are implemented well and for a sufficient amount of time to become institutionalized—culturally ("this is how we do business"), procedurally (i.e., embedded in protocols that range from standards and assessment to human resource policy), and in terms of relational practices between and among members of the school community.

## EFFECTIVE USE OF TEAMS

Change is a marathon, not a sprint, and it must be sustainable. Successful leaders know that although they must be relentless, they cannot do it alone. Leaders can use teams to distribute leadership and build organizational capacity that outlives them.

In our experience, schools and districts that are successful in implementing change employ a small number of teams with clearly defined roles and responsibilities. We suggest that schools employ two core teams. The first, the *schoolwide team*, addresses the school's entire ecology and its overall performance with a focus on strategy, planning, monitoring for implementation, and evaluation. The second, the *student support team* (SST), focuses on identifying and implementing interventions designed to address individual student needs. Both teams are necessary to ensure that every student learns and thrives and that the school and its staff support equity, deeper learning, and healthy development.

The schoolwide team and SST should coordinate and communicate regularly to ensure that (1) universal school approaches are sufficiently robust and realized to prevent students from falling through the cracks, and (2) the SST has the capacity to work with teachers, students, and families to identify individualized interventions, consult on their use, and provide monitoring of how they are working. Collaboration and coordination between the two teams maximizes clear, coherent communication with staff and alignment of initiatives to district and school improvement goals. To facilitate this collaboration, a minimum of three people—the principal, a teacher, and a mental health specialist such as a school counselor, school social worker, school psychologist, or behavior specialist—should serve on both teams (see figure 2.1).

It's important to note, however, that schools can have too many teams. Although multiple teams provide opportunities for participation, they can also waste precious time and work against a coordinated effort. Avoid redundant teams; when additional teams are necessary, consider creating time-limited task forces to engage staff. If your school has several teams, each focused on different academic, behavioral, and community components, consider

**Figure 2.1** Linkage between schoolwide and student support teams

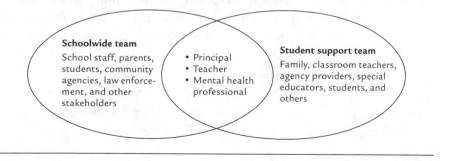

Schoolwide team
School staff, parents, students, community agencies, law enforcement, and other stakeholders

• Principal
• Teacher
• Mental health professional

Student support team
Family, classroom teachers, agency providers, special educators, students, and others

combining those that have overlapping functions related to student support, schoolwide management, and any change initiative. However, before you do this, develop a respectful strategy that remembers that team members and their leaders may have a stake in continuing their work as a separate team.

You may have teams that already function or could function as schoolwide teams and SSTs. The schoolwide team may be called the *school management team*, *school leadership team*, or *school improvement team*. The SST may be known as the *child study team* or the *student assistance team*. You can develop a schoolwide team by expanding an existing team, such as one that addresses academic performance, climate, discipline, safety, and family involvement; or, in the case of the SST, you can build upon similar teams that focus on student-level interventions. Piggybacking on and expanding an existing team to align efforts can foster collaborative and efficient work. When teams already exist, they have formal and informal operational rules, as well as personal interest in what they do. New roles and members will require time to establish trust and acceptance. If the principal or a student support specialist or teacher is a member of the existing schoolwide team or student-level team, this may ease the integration.

Next, we'll look in a bit more detail at what each team does.

## The Schoolwide Team

The schoolwide team has six functions: (1) identify and assess what needs to be improved and what school assets already exist to help support improvement, (2) determine goals and objectives that align with the school vision, (3) align all school reform efforts and community initiatives, (4) select and implement interventions to realize goals and objectives, (5) coordinate and monitor implementation, and (6) evaluate the effect of the interventions. The schoolwide team works with administrators, teams, and task forces to plan, coordinate, and monitor all short- and long-term school improvement efforts. This work involves social-emotional, behavioral, and academic matters and includes community engagement, needs assessment, and strategic planning. The schoolwide team supports the establishment and communication of the school vision, plans and uses continuous improvement to monitor implementation, and ensures that staff have support in realizing new approaches, systems, and practices. (For an example of an effective schoolwide team, see "Distributing Leadership to Implement SEL.")

## Distributing Leadership to Implement SEL

In chapter 1, we provided an overview of the Cleveland Metropolitan School District's implementation of the PATHS program. One important component of that effort was that it involved district and union leaders in every step of capacity building and planning. To help bolster the success of PATHS and realize the vision of universal SEL programming, CMSD worked to maintain leaders' enduring support during the curriculum's early implementation stages. CMSD administrators engaged as true partners with the PATHS teams in each school (principals, select teachers, and union representatives), as well as community organizations that worked in the schools (school-based mental health providers and organizations that delivered afterschool programming). The schoolwide team and community partners provided the infrastructure and logistical support for teacher training and coaching, and helped design a plan for implementation across the district. Without those necessary supports, teachers would not have the skills, time, or materials needed to implement PATHS. Similarly, principals from each participating school in the district created the structure and opportunities at the building level for PATHS to be woven into the school day, and encouraged all staff to adopt PATHS language and principles.

## The Student Support Team

The SST focuses on students who exhibit early warning signs (ranging from academic failure to violence) as well as students who are at more elevated levels of risk—students who in a three-tiered model could benefit from selective interventions (see chapter 15) or indicated interventions (see chapter 16). Intervention requires a referral process that can respond to student needs in a timely, coordinated, and effective manner. The team meets regularly to discuss students' academic, behavioral, and emotional needs and problems, and may require more personnel or time if the schoolwide foundation is weak and there are too many referrals. The SST should respond to students' problems promptly to address warning signs and help students succeed and achieve in school. (See "Student Support Team Protocol" for guidelines on doing so.)

SST referrals can be made by a student's teacher, another staff member, an external agency partner, a parent, a principal, or the student. Implementation

## Student Support Team Protocol

The SST protocol for meetings follows these guidelines:

1. Assess the problem, review the collected information, and identify and prioritize referral concerns to develop appropriate intervention strategies.
2. Inventory and prioritize student strengths with the goal of employing a positive approach that uses appropriate incentives to increase the likelihood that a student accepts and engages with the intervention strategies.
3. Review baseline data related to the target behavior or difficulty and define the concern in observable/measurable terms (e.g., days absent, instances tardy, analysis of grades over time).
4. Set the goals and spell out the process for monitoring the student's progress.
5. Design the intervention(s) and designate who will implement it (e.g., bus aide, teacher), specifying what the intervention is, where it is to be used, how often it will take place, and its target success rate or level. Provide the *Intervention Tracking Form* to the individual implementing the intervention. This is to be completed regularly during the intervention.
6. Establish a method for measuring and summarizing the case to ensure that stakeholders are clear on the individual roles and intervention plan, reviewing the procedures for evaluating the intervention (method of determining success), and selecting a date for a follow-up meeting, if necessary.

of SST plans may require coordinating with community agencies and redeploying district specialists to maximize their ability to support these school-based teams.

### Selecting team members

Your SST needs five assets to be effective: knowledge, perspective, technical skills, personal skills, and legitimacy. Team members should be knowledgeable about your school community, and at least some of them should be knowledgeable about school safety, student support, student engagement, cultural competence and responsiveness, pedagogy, mental health, and school reform. Team members should reflect the perspectives of the stakeholders who make up your school community. Some team members should have the technical skills, such as data analysis, that are necessary to carry out your team's tasks. All team members should possess the interpersonal skills that are important for smooth team functioning. Finally, they should be individuals who are respected by the school community for who they are and how they were selected. Consider members of existing school improvement teams, as well as members of other school community groups whose participation will consolidate the team's knowledge and influence.

### Engaging representatives from the broader community

Include family and community representatives who can enhance planning and champion the SST's work, identify and access community partners and resources, and spread the word to build community support. Engage individuals who will be affected by school improvement and student support plans—such as underrepresented community groups, who are all too frequently left out. Examine your community's characteristics and make sure that representative groups are included, and that their effective participation is supported. Support may include scheduling meetings at convenient times, providing transportation, and addressing child-care needs.

Identify organizations or agencies (e.g., community mental health agencies) whose involvement will be necessary in implementing part or all of the individual student support plan. Look first at the individuals and organizations that already partner with your school. In larger schools, existing partnerships may not be obvious, so you may need to survey staff to identify all organizations that work with the school. Examples, along with the Community Assessment Form, can be found in *Safe, Supportive, and Successful Schools Step by Step.*[5]

## Team Functioning

Determining schoolwide and SST team member roles and responsibilities and team size will ensure that the team is able to function smoothly. Group sizes of eight to twelve work the most efficiently, providing an opportunity for a diverse set of stakeholders that can effectively distribute roles and work as a highly productive team. Assigning roles and responsibilities helps ensure that key duties are performed and logistical tasks are addressed. Your team's division of labor should attend to the day-to-day assignments that keep the team working efficiently. For example, does everyone know who schedules the meetings, secures the meeting resources for the team, records and disseminates the minutes, and publishes progress reports for the superintendent, school board, or key stakeholders? In all cases, team members should be clear about who has or shares responsibility for tasks. Common roles and responsibilities include the following:

- **Formal leadership.** Teams require leadership. The principal may function (or designate someone to serve) as the team leader to ensure authority for planning, budgeting, and delegating responsibilities.
- **Operational leadership.** Day-to-day scheduling of meetings and planning are necessary and may be delegated to an assistant leader.
- **Facilitation.** Facilitation requires specific skills and knowledge of team decision-making and group processes. A designated facilitator can help the team stay focused, adhere to team norms, focus on agenda items, ensure input from all team members, and use protocols for decision making.
- **Data analysis.** At least one team member should be comfortable with collecting, monitoring, and analyzing data and helping others understand its meaning.
- **Recording.** A team recorder should keep a record of all meeting action steps and key decisions.
- **Archiving.** The recorder should also collect and archive team materials.
- **Work groups.** Methods should be established to allow members to work together or with other members of the school community between formal meetings to prepare or follow up on agenda items.
- **Communication and liaison.** One or more team members should serve as the ongoing liaison with the administration, teachers, support staff, paraprofessionals, and community groups to report frequently on progress and to learn about challenges. This will contribute to coherence, improvement, and buy-in.

## TAKEAWAYS

- Equity with excellence requires transformative leadership.
- Successful change is a journey that requires a top-down/bottom-up process and distributed leadership.

- Leadership can be efficiently distributed and coordinated through two teams, the schoolwide team and the SST, which have some overlapping members.
- Avoid too many teams. Consolidate teams and create task forces when necessary.
- Teams should be representative of the school community and collectively possess the necessary technical skills.

# THREE

# Guiding and Planning Improvement for Equity with Excellence

*Catherine Barbour, R. Jason LaTurner,*
*and David Osher*

CHANGE IS A JOURNEY, and you must determine where you want to go, what you need to get there, and how you will know that you are making progress toward your goal.[1] You will need to identify the gaps between where you want to be (your vision) and where you are currently in practice. The best way to do this is to specify how you will know when your vision is realized, what the indicators of success are, and how they can be measured. Once you have done this, you can examine your current capacities, needs, and outcomes to determine what you need to change to realize your vision. You can then develop the necessary strategies to build capacity, address needs, and improve outcomes. These decisions drive the development of implementation and continuous improvement plans. In this chapter, we discuss the importance of having a vision, as well as the role of needs assessments, strategic planning, implementation planning, and continuous improvement, keeping in mind the human side of change and the ever-present challenges of engagement.

## DEFINING A VISION

Humans crave meaning, so an effective vision should frame and provide meaning to your improvement or transformation efforts. The visioning process supports commitment, provides purpose, and frames planning, implementation, monitoring, and evaluation. Develop (or revitalize) and communicate *a vivid and clear vision* of (a) what the school(s) and classrooms should look like, and (b) what the experiences of students, families, and educators will be, when the vision is realized.[2] Members of the school community need to be able to envision the change, have congruent images of their role in that change, and understand how the change will affect them. This requires a common language and even grammar—the basic elements underlying your thinking.[3] Stakeholders—particularly all leaders and staff—should understand what quality practice is (and is not), why it is important, and how changing practices can align with their daily work. If the vision is particular to a new initiative, it should align with the school's or district's mission and strategic plan. Ideally, everyone should embrace and understand the vision, although this will take time.

The vision statement (and its development) plays an important role in the change process. Ideally, the vision is codeveloped, actively shared, and committed to academic equity and excellence and to enabling all students to thrive. Leaders should engage members of the school community in a facilitated visioning process that aligns the present and the future. One way of doing this is to ask people about their hopes for their students' futures—for example, what their students will be like, and what they will be able to do, by the time they are thirty years old—and then "back-plan" to figure out what needs to happen in students' school experience to support this goal. What learning opportunities, experiences, and supports would students need to experience at school? What should they not experience? This initial visioning (thinking about students at the age of thirty) can often help to emotionally connect and align diverse stakeholders before they drill down to areas where it may be harder to reach agreement. Say Yes to Education successfully employed this process of visioning and back-planning to develop its school- and community-wide monitoring and intervention system, which informs its personalized, data-driven continuous improvement processes. They started out with a vision of their students as successful adults at thirty and back-planned from there, all the way to first grade. As an example of what they did, consider math. Success at thirty is facilitated by college access and completion, which, along with access to tech careers, has been tied to success in Algebra II. This, in turn, has been associated with success in Algebra I in eighth grade, which in turn has been linked to math success in lower grades.[4]

Identify the best ways *to engage and get meaningful input from all stakeholders*, in a manner that builds their ownership in the process and results, and contributes to shared understanding and long-term collaboration. Focus groups and town hall meetings, along with online surveys, are effective strategies to gather input and feedback and to generate investment in the planning. Ensure the participation of staff with diverse points of view, including union leadership, as well as culturally and linguistically diverse students, families, and community members.

Create and implement a communication and engagement plan that identifies outreach and engagement strategies for different stakeholders to help them understand and apply the vision, and to focus feedback so that it can support implementation quality, planning, and progress toward goals. Getting and making use of input from everyone involved is one of the most valuable aspects of working to define a vision.

An Alabama district provides a useful example of successfully engaging in a collaborative (rather than top-down) approach with key stakeholders to define a vision for change. The district was implementing the state's Strategic Teaching framework, which focused on standards, lesson planning, and instructional strategies. Although the district had provided training on the framework, there had been very little follow-up, and implementation varied among schools. In response to this situation, district leaders and teachers discussed and dissected the framework, defining in greater detail what all stakeholders should be doing as they implemented the framework in the classroom. The group then presented the description to school principals, who provided support and guidance on possible modifications that might be necessary in each school setting. Adopting this collaborative approach with key stakeholders provided staff with clear, specific, and shared expectations for the implementation of the framework, a timeline for the process of implementation, and a description of how implementation would be monitored. The result was a clear and thorough understanding of the framework and expectations. Because stakeholders at all levels had helped define the vision, they felt more ownership and became advocates for the framework. Finally, because everyone had a clear idea of how teachers should be using the framework, administrators charged with overseeing implementation said their classroom walk-throughs had greater focus and purpose.

## PLANNING AND CONDUCTING A NEEDS ASSESSMENT

Once you have identified where you want to go, you can determine what you need and what you must do to get there. Ideally, the schoolwide team will lead the school needs assessment and conduct it over one school term. If planning is districtwide, it will likely take two terms or even the entire year. The team(s) will want to meet regularly to review findings and discuss results.

The needs assessment involves four steps:

1. Identify the gaps between where you want to be (your vision) and where you currently are.
2. Identify the problems (needs) and available resources.
3. Analyze the problems and their root and systemic causes.
4. Identify potential strategies to address the problems and gaps, while leveraging assets and opportunities.

### Identify Gaps, Problems, and Available Resources

Based on the needs assessment process, or other available information, the schoolwide team should define the problem (or problems) to be addressed, agree on its scope and severity, and identify the resources available to address it. The problem identification process should capture the gaps between your vision and your current capacities, needs, and outcomes. Quantitative and qualitative data can illuminate unidentified challenges and resources. For example, you may use a questionnaire to determine how safe or engaged children feel, as Cleveland has done since 2008 through an annual (and now semiannual) Conditions for Learning Survey, the results of which are examined school- and districtwide. Or you may interview teachers to determine their training needs for supporting emotional and identity safety. The schoolwide team can do this work, or create a workgroup (or workgroups), perhaps led by team members. Workgroups spread the workload and engage other members of the school community, while still remaining part of the core improvement team. Through this process, the team should identify not only needs and resource gaps, but also assets and strengths, because these provide the toeholds for change.

Assessing characteristics without substantial objective data may mean that schools or districts overlook some problems and focus resources on inadequate interventions. Fortunately, schools collect data that can be used to identify strengths and determine problems. Information about students' grades, attendance, mobility, and reading and math achievement scores; discipline; class size; faculty qualifications; school climate; and staff satisfaction or turnover should be available. Identify what data your school and district collect. Determine which data will contribute to your needs assessment, planning, monitoring, and evaluation efforts. Remember to look at community data as well. In addition, you will want to assess existing resources.

Key questions for a resource assessment are as follows:[5]

- What services and supports are currently available in the school and broader community?[6]
- Who specifically is providing them?
- When are they available?
- To whom are they being offered?

Community mapping can be helpful. For example, in terms of needs, a school can consider the number of children living in poverty, the number who are uninsured, the rates of mental health referrals, the number of students on probation, and community crime statistics. These data can be gathered through interagency cooperation and, in some cases, geomapped. Three useful websites for finding community information can be found in appendix B.

## Analyze the Problems and Their Causes

Don't just address symptoms of the problems you've identified. Dissect their possible causes and effects by asking who, what, where, when, and why questions. Look for root causes and systemic factors. A *root-cause analysis* provides a structured process for looking beyond symptoms to understand the underlying causes of a problem. If you can identify and eliminate root causes, you can eliminate the problem in a sustainable manner. This helps you to avoid doing something that is expedient but incomplete and inadequate. Root-cause analysis gets you past *putting out* fires and helps you instead find ways to *prevent* fires, such as chronic absenteeism or limited participation in AP/IB classes, by addressing systemic causes.

Schools are complex and dynamic systems, so your analysis should go beyond a single root cause. Some root causes also may not be immediately apparent, so remember to look for the whole story. For example, root and systemic causes may not be evident if you examine only one data set (e.g., disciplinary data). Your analyses will most likely reveal several root causes or clusters of causes. For example, root causes of high suspensions or of racial disproportionalities in suspensions may be educator and administrator stress, a lack of support for educator understanding of student behavior, educators' need for skill building to prevent and address troubling behaviors that evoke punitive responses, explicit or implicit biases, or the lack of staff skills in using positive approaches and de-escalation techniques. Critical issues such as these can surface when you ask the right questions, take time for deep and honest conversations, conduct surveys and interviews, and gather input from a wide range of stakeholders in the school, district, and community.[7]

### Identify Potential Strategies to Address the Problems and Gaps, While Leveraging Assets and Opportunities

As the final step in the needs assessment process, you'll examine needs, capacities, and assets (e.g., current activities that support your goals), and develop strategies to address the problems and gaps you've identified in the previous steps. You can identify potential strategies through brainstorming, or, in more complex cases, through research. Strategies will need to be thoughtfully planned out and implemented. Some strategies will produce short-term results (i.e., those needed within the school year). Others strategies may take multiple years to realize, requiring training of staff, shoulder-to-shoulder coaching, and possibly structural adjustments to the school, such as longer class periods or reassigning of teachers to different teams or grade levels. The important thing is to "go slow to go fast"—that is, take the time needed to find the most sustainable interventions that have been proven to address the problems you've identified in terms of school climate and student needs. Keep in mind the danger of impatience and superficial solutions: "Reforms . . . fail because our attempts to solve problems are frequently superficial. Superficial solutions, introduced quickly in an atmosphere of crisis, normally make matters worse."[8]

## ENGAGING IN STRATEGIC PLANNING

Once the team (or workgroup) has developed a vision and conducted the needs assessment, it is time to identify and prioritize areas for improvement, establish goals for these priority areas, determine measurable objectives that will lead to the realization of these goals, identify solutions, and develop a plan for implementing the solutions. Areas could include a lack of family engagement, a lack of cultural responsiveness, or poor teacher morale. For each area, develop an implementation plan that builds on your school's resources and aligns your strategies with achieving your goals and objectives. Remember, school improvement efforts are often limited by diffuse objectives, a lack of technical skills, insufficient resources, or the inability to actively engage and listen to all stakeholders. Effective strategic planning has the following elements:[9]

- Clear goals and objectives
- Specific action steps to implement these objectives
- A plan for implementing each solution and coordinating the implementation of all solutions (including what is needed to do so)
- Realistic timelines
- Effective communication with the school community
- Staff engagement, development, and support
- Plans for continuous improvement that include:
  - Types of data that will be used for improvement
  - Benchmarks to indicate progress in implementing solutions
  - Standards that will be employed to evaluate efforts and measure success

The strategic planning process should ensure that goals and objectives are clear, realistic, and ambitious. It is useful to identify both short- and long-term outcomes. Goals should be SMART (specific, measurable, attainable, realistic, time-bound) and focused on the desired outcome.

## Identifying Strategies and Interventions

Clearly identifying what you are hoping to address, and analyzing the potential causes and effects of the problems you're concerned with or improvements that will contribute to realizing your vision, is essential before selecting and implementing interventions. This is also true for the capacities you need to change to realize your goals.

Consider your school's or district's needs, assets, and priorities, including its culture and its historical experience with addressing the problems. Identify effective current programs, which you will want to build upon, along with your school's experience (both positive and negative) with particular interventions or types of interventions. Be clear as to whether you are intervening to prevent something from happening, to address an existing problem, to enhance an approach that is working, or to maintain effects. You should know as well whether you are looking for an immediate effect or one over multiple years. You also want to determine the extent to which (a) you need to intervene universally across the school, a grade, or even (if you have community partners on board) the community, and (b) you need to intervene with children and youth who are at elevated levels of risk (selective interventions) and high levels of risk (indicated interventions). Ensure that the interventions you select are developmentally and culturally appropriate, address relevant risk and protective factors (see "Risk and Protective Factors"), and have worked within community contexts like your own.

## Assessing Readiness

Next, assess your school's readiness to implement specific strategies or interventions. Factors that you should consider include:

- specialized knowledge and skills required for implementing your strategy;
- the existence of implementation champions who can "own" and promote the work;[10]
- stakeholder buy-in;
- potential implementation partnerships (e.g., with the YMCA for an afterschool program);

---

### Risk and Protective Factors

A *risk factor* is any factor that increases the probability—not inevitability or likelihood—that a person will suffer harm. A *protective factor* is any factor that diminishes or prevents the potential harmful effect of a risk factor, either by preventing it or buffering its effects. These factors can be inherent in an individual (e.g., impulsivity) or in an environment (e.g., harsh discipline). Risk and protective factors have different effects at different stages of a person's development, and often cluster (e.g., a student who cannot read may also have a behavioral problem and associate with antisocial peers). Risk and protective factors often are relevant to multiple social outcomes (e.g., school dropout, delinquency, violence, and substance abuse). The more risk factors someone has, the more likely it is that the person will realize poor social and academic outcomes; the more protective factors and assets someone has, the more likely the person is to realize better outcomes.

- how the strategy fits with the values, norms, and needs of individuals in the school;
- how easy the strategy is to understand and use;
- the strategy's advantages over existing programs and practices;
- the potential to show some measurable indicator of benefit or progress toward a long-term benefit after six months of implementation;
- whether the strategy is a priority, compared to other programs and practices in the school; and
- whether the strategy is conducive to exploration or piloting before you make a longer-term commitment.[11]

## SUPPORTING IMPLEMENTATION PLANNING

School improvement requires staff to develop new skills, knowledge, strategies, practices, and, in many cases, attitudes and mindsets. Staff will need time to learn, try out, and master new skills and strategies, which means that *staff development* must involve more than one-shot training. Effective implementation of an intervention requires coaching from someone who has mastered the new practice or strategy, collaborative learning and problem solving among colleagues who are also implementing the solution, and booster sessions to renew skills and address new problems. Everybody who will be involved in the intervention—teachers, staff, administrators, and, in many cases, family members—should be trained. For example, teachers benefit from coaching, as well as discussions with other teachers, to support problem solving and let them know that their concerns are not unique. Teacher self-help is a powerful tool for implementing new practices and counters the isolation and alienation many teachers experience. Coaching and staff discussion bolster a problem-solving (rather than a problem-avoiding) mentality and help teachers focus on the new practice and expand their capacity to implement it.[12] Some schools, districts, and regional organizations employ professional development staff to do this coaching; other schools train individuals with appropriate expertise (e.g., school social workers or special educators) and release their time to perform this function.

Thinking beyond "adopt and train" and considering how staff will use a strategy is a key step in implementation planning for districts and schools at the initiating change stage. When expectations are clear and support is available, new practices have a greater chance of being adopted successfully, as we saw earlier in the Alabama example. Without clarity, individuals are left on their own (or within their own networks) to interpret training, decide what parts are most important to implement, and come up with a vision of what strong implementation looks like, which can undermine impact. At the same time, leadership might not learn about barriers to successful implementation and how to address them up front. This lack of understanding and feedback from implementers can frustrate leaders, who wonder why the training was not successful and why the program is not producing results as promised. Implementers need descriptions of implementation quality—including what are ideal, acceptable, and less desirable variations—rather than simply what *implementing* versus *not implementing* looks like. (Think about the qualities of good traffic directions—for example, telling you what to look for when making a turn, or how to know when you have gone too far.)

## Check In with Implementers to Ensure Engagement and Provide Encouragement

Address both the affective (emotional or sentimental) and technical concerns of the people doing the work. Effective leaders understand the *relational side of change* and elevate their personal connections during the transition from the mindset of "this is the way we have always done things" to "this is the new way we do things." Leaders may overlook people's discomfort with changing routines and practices and minimize the importance of the "letting go" phase of the change process. Rather than providing support to teachers, they instead focus all their energy on launch activities, such as training and preparation activities. Staff may respond to an initiative in a variety of ways, from resistance and stress to enthusiasm. Those who are less comfortable with a new team structure or innovation may express concern about how the innovation will affect them personally. Those who are more comfortable with and skilled in adapting to an innovation may focus on broader impacts, such as how the initiative will affect their students or their working relationships with colleagues.

Check in with implementers to ensure they not only understand the expectations but also are engaged in the change process, have the support they need, and are comfortable implementing something new. You can use surveys, focus groups, and interviews to get a snapshot of staff concerns and identify support needs. In providing support—which may include coaching, consulting, or follow-up actions such as small-group instruction or guidance—you can communicate encouragement and genuine concern for the individual or group, an appreciation of the challenges, and a willingness to help advance the change effort. This supportive facilitation style contributes to the development of a culture that is conducive to the change process, and it reflects a commitment to staff engagement in their journey toward improvement.

In the same way that teachers support, monitor, and respond to the needs of their students, leaders should assess and address the needs of their staff, facilitating and guiding them in their professional growth. Further, just as teachers should differentiate and customize support, so, too, should leaders. Undersupported and unmanaged changes make it more likely that implementation will go badly or produce minimal results.

### Attend to the Logistics

Don't forget the details! No matter how powerful and clear an intervention is, or how well staff members are trained, the nuts and bolts of implementing an intervention are also important to its success. Ensure necessary time, space, equipment, technology, and materials are available to implement the improvement. Outlets may need to be updated for a technology intervention, for example.

## EMPLOYING CONTINUOUS IMPROVEMENT THROUGH PROGRESS MONITORING AND EVALUATION

Developing an implementation plan with clear processes and procedures will help you sustain implementation over time. However, it's not easy to implement interventions—particularly new programs or practices that run counter to people's experiences or challenge their level of comfort—even if you have ensured that your organization has the capacity, and you have developed a clear implementation plan. You may face unforeseen barriers and resistance to change. For this reason, it is important to employ continuous improvement throughout implementation to identify and address potential implementation barriers (or any changes that may affect implementation), and to clearly communicate with—and maintain buy-in and support from—staff and stakeholders by keeping them informed and soliciting their feedback. (We recommend quarterly check-ins.) Chapter 20 will describe in more detail how continuous improvement practices can help you improve implementation or identify necessary adaptations.

Continuous improvement requires identifying indicators that provide evidence of a target you want to achieve and can measure—whether a long-term goal (e.g., academic achievement) or the results of a particular intervention (e.g., greater and more equitable success rates in eighth-grade Algebra I). Indicators are often employed in school and district planning. They can be based on: (a) one measure (e.g., a measure of student engagement); (b) a scale that combines many measures psychometrically (e.g., a survey scale on student engagement); or (c) an index that combines related measures, sometimes with weighting (e.g., combining attendance, extracurricular participation, and a survey scale on student engagement).

To realize equity with excellence, we recommend that your indicators include the following:

- Social-emotional and academic measures that address conditions for both learning and teaching.
- "Quick-win" indicators, which generate buy-in and progress toward full implementation of a solution that may take a longer time to realize (e.g., graduation rates).[13] Quick wins should alleviate stakeholder impatience while creating successes that strategically move the plan forward (improving conditions for learning), rather than being truly short-term outcomes (just moving "bubble" students to proficiency). Take the example of algebra being tied to college and tech success. If we want more students from diverse backgrounds to pass Algebra II, the solution is not just drilling down on those students who look like they are close to passing—the students on the bubble—and having them pass. Rather, the solution is to get more students ready to take and pass Algebra II and to maximize learning and engagement during Algebra I, which will contribute to more students taking and passing Algebra II.
- Leading and progress indicators to predict future outcomes and track ongoing process. Leading indicators signal early progress. They can help leaders make "more strategic and less reactive decisions about services and supports to improve student learning."[14] Progress indicators track ongoing execution and results (in terms of both implementation and implementation impact). If, for example, the school implemented an intervention to reduce suspensions (e.g., My Teaching Partner), is it being implemented as planned and are suspensions being reduced?[15]

## ROLLING OUT THE DRAFT PLAN

Present your draft plan to all the relevant stakeholders for their understanding and feedback. This gives you an opportunity to explain the logic of the plan while providing stakeholders with opportunities to ask questions, raise concerns, and endorse the plan. The process produces information that you can use to improve your plan as you finalize it and secures buy-in and investment in the plan. Communicate often about the plan and during the phases of implementation. Communication should address stakeholders' interests and concerns both during the plan rollout and through the stages of implementation.

## Gaining School Community Buy-in and Engagement

When providing information, you should address different levels of readiness and help boost individuals' understanding of and commitment to priorities for improvement (e.g., academic improvement, supportive environments, student mental health, equity, and school safety).

Informal discussions and structured focus groups can identify interests and concerns as well as individuals who will champion change and those who might resist it. Although "idea champions" should be seen as allies and recruited, it is just as important to elicit the questions and concerns of those who will not be your initial adopters.[16] Your communication efforts and implementation strategies should be sure to speak to those who have not yet bought in to the change. For example, a focus group discussion may uncover fears that must be addressed, such as "We did something like this before and I didn't receive any support." Focus groups can also unearth interests and other information to inform strategies to promote buy-in, by elevating naysayers' priorities or needed proof points. Although some initial adopters will fully commit to change based on the information you present, other individuals will give their full commitment only when they see results. Change takes time, and it is important to identify indicators that can both secure the buy-in of hesitant individuals and sustain the commitment of early advocates.

## Creating an Atmosphere and Context for Change

Because the very basis of school improvement involves changing the way the school and its staff approach their work, it is vital to create an environment where change is encouraged. A safe and collaborative atmosphere that promotes relational trust and problem solving is essential, as school staff must be comfortable learning new skills or ideas and taking risks to implement change. Undertaking a change process involves learning new content, new skills, and sometimes even new ways of thinking about education and the classroom. This means that each person involved in the reform must be regarded as a learner, including teachers, principals, administrators, parents, and students. By sharing responsibility and recasting everyone as learners, you help to create a critically important context for change and support the development of relational trust. As this new learning environment is created and nurtured, new instructional practices, organizational structures, and content can be introduced. It is important to reflect on each change and note which practices are working well and which are not. No matter how effective your efforts are, you will likely encounter some staff who are hesitant or unwilling to adopt new practices. Many individuals have experienced ill-conceived reform initiatives, a lack of logistical support for change, "strategies of the month," and silver bullets that did not work. Still others may suffer from "innovation fatigue." Cynicism and reluctance are understandable and, in most cases, can be addressed (see "Ten Things to Do About Resistance"). We have found that having a wide range of staff "at the table" early in the process creates a much higher chance of ownership and buy-in. The work will have been done *with* them, instead of *to* them.

## Ten Things to Do About Resistance[17]

1. **Acknowledge change as a process.** Change is not an isolated event, but a series of stages that requires time. Remember that the process of educational change is lengthy, and that it may take years to move from goal setting to stable establishment. Conflict and resistance are natural products of change, not automatic signs of failure.

2. **Empower stakeholders.** As critical components of innovation, stakeholders must be included as decision makers. Empowering people means creating mechanisms that provide them with genuine authority and responsibility; otherwise, change efforts become incoherent. Remember that real or perceived shifts in power can spark resistance among colleagues, administrators, or board members.

3. **Encourage all stakeholders.** Stakeholders must be active, invested participants throughout the change process. Often it is beneficial to focus directly on helping participants understand the innovation. Providing a variety of opportunities (for both individuals and groups) to vent concerns can also be effective.

4. **Set concrete goals.** Agreed-upon goals should form a shared agenda reached by consensus, creating a broad sense of ownership and strengthening communication among stakeholders. This step is criti-

cally important because if anything goes awry later in the change process, the stakeholders will be able to return to a shared agenda and refocus their intent and efforts.

5. **Show sensitivity.** Managing conflict means being aware of differences among individuals. Each stakeholder must genuinely feel that he or she is an equal and valued party throughout the change process, not just in the initial trust-building stage. All persons need to be treated with respect, sensitivity, and support as they struggle to redefine their roles and master new concepts.

6. **Model process skills.** Teaching the appropriate process skills and actions through modeling is fundamental to successful staff development initiatives. Staff developers may find, for example, that reflecting publicly and straightforwardly on their own doubts and resistance to change may help others. At the very least, honesty goes a long way toward building credibility. When staff developers model desirable behaviors, they give other stakeholders a chance to identify with someone going through the difficult process of change.

7. **Develop strategies for dealing with emotions.** All too often, educators concentrate on outcomes and neglect the emotional experiences of change, such as anxiety, fear, loss, and grief. Effective staff development programs include activities and strategies to address those emotions. Focus on questions such as: How will our lives be different with the changes? How do we feel about the changes? Is there anything that can or should be done to honor the past before we move on?

8. **Manage conflict.** Ideally, change is a negotiated process. Stakeholders should be invited to negotiate on issues that provoke their resistance. For example, an assistant principal may need to negotiate the needs of the whole school with faculty members who rank their departmental priorities higher.

9. **Communicate.** Openness in communication is a necessary component of collaborative problem solving. Communication that focuses on differences can move issues of concern out of the shadows.

10. **Monitor process dynamics.** The constant interplay between the various tensions within the change process must be monitored, and appropriate adjustments must be made. Evaluation begins with the original assessment of the need and readiness to change and remains a key factor throughout systemic reform. Reflection forms the scaffolding of the evaluation process, and ongoing assessments of progress serve as checkpoints on the reform journey.

## TAKEAWAYS

Members of the school community need to:

- envision the change, have congruent images of their role in that change, and understand how the change will affect them;
- collectively develop a vivid and clear vision;
- conduct an action-oriented needs assessment that also identifies assets;
- identify and address the root causes of problems;
- develop strategies to address the problems that use effective interventions and leverage opportunities;
- develop strategic plans that address readiness, implementation support and quality, and the relational aspects of change; and
- engage stakeholders in planning in a manner that enhances quality and investment.

# FOUR

# Selecting the Right Programs, Strategies, and Approaches

*David Osher and Allison Dymnicki*

THIS CHAPTER HELPS YOU identify and select interventions with a focus on implementation and sustainability. Selecting and implementing effective programs, curricula, practices, strategies, approaches, and school policies—what we will call "interventions"—involves these tasks: identifying appropriate interventions for your needs and adapting them, if necessary; ensuring a good fit between interventions and your school or community; and implementing the interventions with quality.

## IDENTIFYING AND ADAPTING INTERVENTIONS FOR YOUR NEEDS

Multiple sources of information can help you match the problem or gap you have identified with the pool of existing interventions. These include information on:

- evidence-based programs;
- kernels and discrete practices;
- broader strategies and approaches; and

- common elements of nurturing environments that prevent a host of psychological and behavioral problems.

## Evidence-Based Programs

Programs are usually packaged, multicomponent interventions that have been designed to address specific needs or problems. *Evidence-based programs* (EBPs) are grounded in theory and have a sound body of evidence demonstrating that they have produced positive results in particular settings. EBPs have sometimes been combined in order to enhance program effects. Ideally, although not always, the research specifies whom the program has been effective for and the contexts in which it has been effective. You access and compare many EBPs through curated lists, known as *registries*. Examples include several federal lists (e.g., the What Works Clearinghouse) and professional association lists (e.g., CASEL.org), which can be found in appendix B. Registries vary in the programs they include, how they define evidence, the depth of evidence they require, the criteria they use for classifying EBPs, and their area of focus. Some registries provide information on programs that meet a certain standard of evidence, while others report both programs with evidence of positive effects and those that have limited, mixed, or negative effects. While registries can also vary in how they categorize programs, most registries contain:

- descriptive information for each program listing;
- ratings of research quality;
- a description of the research rating methodology;
- a list of studies, implementation, and technical support materials reviewed; and
- contact information.

This information can help you identify programs that best meet your needs and have a body of vetted research behind them.

## Kernels and Discrete Practices

Researchers have started to systematically assess the components and features of individual programs in order to more effectively implement practices. Much of this work has been done in mental health and juvenile justice, and some has been incorporated into school-based treatments.[1] This adaptive approach may help to address the inability to replicate or scale up EBPs in schools, along with the costs and cognitive demands of new programs. This approach includes: (a) kernels or more fine-grained active ingredients of effective programs, (b) practices promoting skill development through daily interactions with students, (c) broader strategies associated with effective prevention and treatment programs, and (d) characteristics of nurturing environments that prevent a wide range of psychological and behavioral problems.

*Kernels* are low-cost, targeted strategies that may represent the essential active ingredients in effective programs.[2] They target a specific behavior and can be taught quickly; therefore, they are thought to be higher impact and more feasible to implement. Examples of kernels include verbal praise (a person or group receives recognition for demonstrating the desired behavior); peer-to-peer tutoring (groups of two or three people take turns asking questions, giving praise or points, and offering corrective feedback); and cooperative, structured peer play (planned activities during children's playtime that involve roles, turn taking, and social competence). Kernels may be integrated into daily practice or they can be used to enhance an existing EBT such as the Good Behavior Game.[3]

Teaching *practices* can support and reinforce skill development when educators incorporate specific strategies and structures regularly or as part of daily practice.[4] This type of teaching and reinforcement might occur through developing (a) routines, (b) training and support for all school staff, (c) support for adults' own skill development, and (d) standards for what students should be able to know and do with regard to social-emotional skills. Schools use many routines to keep things running smoothly and communicate expectations to students; however, using routines such as emotional regulation and conflict resolution strategies, games that hone attention skills, and class council meetings for resolving classroom issues reinforces skill development in different contexts. Focusing on strategies may facilitate teachers' abilities to generalize SEL strategies to new situations. It can also ease the cognitive burden posed by having to master an entire program and align it with other parts of the instructional day or period.

## Broader Strategies and Approaches

Some federal agencies and researchers have identified *broader strategies and approaches* that can be applied to prevent and treat behavioral issues such as violence and substance abuse. For example, the Centers for Disease Control and Prevention (CDC)—which defines a *strategy* as a "prevention direction or action to achieve the goal of preventing youth violence" and an *approach* as "the specific ways to advance the strategy"—outlines several strategies and accompanying approaches to prevent youth violence.[5] Specifically, the CDC advises: (a) strengthening youth's skills by implementing universal, school-based programs; (b) connecting youth to caring adults and activities through mentoring or afterschool programs; and (c) creating protective community environments by modifying the physical or social environment, reducing exposure to community-level risks, and providing street outreach and community norm change. As another example, the Department of Education's What Works Clearinghouse provides insight (e.g., on addressing behavior problems in elementary school classrooms) through its practice guides.[6] The Department of Education also provides information about effective strategies—for example, to prevent sexual harassment in high school—through its TA Centers' websites.[7]

## Common Elements of Nurturing Environments

Another approach that can be helpful is the identification of *critical characteristics of environments* that work to promote prosocial development and prevent a range of psychological and behavioral problems.[8] For example, Anthony Biglan and colleagues state that nurturing environments: (a) minimize biologically and psychologically toxic events; (b) teach, promote, and reinforce prosocial behaviors; (c) monitor and limit opportunities for problem behavior; and (d) foster the ability to be mindful of one's own thoughts and feelings.[9] Other examples of this approach can be found in reports from the National Academies of Sciences, Engineering, and Medicine (e.g., on youth development) and the American Educational Research Association (e.g., on bullying), and in work on the science of learning and development.[10]

## ENSURING A GOOD FIT

### Examining the Evidence as a Critical Consumer

Whether you select an evidence-based program or another strategy, you want to be confident that it is likely to work, and also know its limitations. When researching potential interventions to address your identified needs, it is helpful to remember that what has been demonstrated to work elsewhere will not necessarily work in your school or district with the types of children you want to serve.[11] Be a skeptical consumer and ask questions about evidence quality, outcomes, costs, contextual fit, adaptability, and external support.

*Quality and generalizability*

Rigorous research may help you develop a short list, but you cannot generalize findings about program effects to your own context without asking the following questions:

- **What outcomes were measured?** Do they match your outcome(s) of interest? Were the effects sizeable enough to warrant replication, and if so, what is the size of the effects?
- **How many times has the intervention been studied and in how many different contexts?** The more contexts, and thus the more replications, the more you can learn about where, when, and with whom an intervention can work.
- **Where did the evidence originate?** Did it come from an independent systematic review, an independent article in a peer-reviewed journal, research by the developer that was peer reviewed, or a vendor website?
- **What type of evidence is it, and what is its technical quality?** Is it a randomized control trial, single-case design, quasi-experimental design, or quantitative research synthesis? There are quality criteria for each type of evidence. A good starting point is the American Educational Research Association's Standards for Research Conduct.[12]
- **To what extent can you generalize the evidence to your school or district?** More specifically:
  - What was the sample size for the study/studies?
  - How representative was the population studied (e.g., who was included in the study/studies), and is it similar to your target population (e.g., in terms of age, gender, race, culture, disability status, and language spoken)?
  - Were the data disaggregated by subgroup to understand variation of outcomes by subgroup?
  
  The larger the sample, the more confidence you should have, but only if the population of the study is like your own.
- **What is the quality of implementation evidence?** Was the program implemented by an independent researcher and peer reviewed or vetted? Was fidelity measured? How feasible is it for you to replicate the program under the same conditions used in the original study?
- **What isn't measured?** Research is as good as the questions asked, the designs used, the measures and data employed, and the quality of the

analyses. Some things that are important are hard to measure—or at least to measure efficiently.[13]

## Outcomes

Ask whether the program can work with the types of students and staff that you have. What evidence shows that this program has worked in school communities similar to yours? With what types of students? Is there evidence of negative outcomes?

## Costs

Determine the monetary costs of implementing the intervention. Examples include the cost of materials, licenses, training, staffing, and overseeing.

## Contextual fit

Does the intervention align with your team's (or school's or district's) strategic plan; procedures; timelines; culture; and needs, strengths, skills, and resources? How could the intervention be affected by anticipatable, competing demands that could prevent successful implementation? The issue brief *The Importance of Contextual Fit When Implementing Evidence-Based Interventions*, by Rob Horner, Caryn Blitz, and Scott W. Ross, can help you think about fit and how to address it.[14] The Hexagon Tool, which outlines six contextual factors to help you evaluate your interventions, is another useful resource.[15]

## Adaptability

Differences in context, staff, and populations may require adaptations. While adaptations or modifications to the program may be necessary, it is important that you do not change the core components of the program. The key question to answer is how the changes you make when adapting the program will affect your desired outcomes. If your adaptations stray too far from an EBP's essence, your results will no longer be representative of that program. Therefore, if you are selecting an evidence-based program, it is essential that you consider what adaptations you will make, particularly for staffing and dosage/duration, and ensure that the fundamentals of the program are maintained.

Identify what key features of an intervention cannot be changed. Some program developers will provide information on these core components, or you can consult Karen Blase and Dean Fixsen's research brief *Core Interven-*

*tion Components* to determine whether you can successfully implement key components without alteration.[16] Examples might include number of minutes per day or staffing ratios.

If you need additional information to make an informed decision, you can reach out to the program developers, technical assistance providers, or others who have implemented or studied the program. When doing so, ask the following questions:

- How well did successful or unsuccessful implementers stick to the program? Did they implement as the research on the program suggested they should?
- How often was the program delivered and for how long? Did this dosage and exposure match the research recommendation?
- How well was the program delivered, and what was the innovation-specific capacity of the staff to implement the program?
- Were participants engaged by the program?

### External support

Implementing a new intervention may require support. Is support available from the developers, technical assistance centers, state department staff, regional or intermediate educational unit staff, district staff, or school staff who have been trained to implement the intervention?

## IMPLEMENTING THE INTERVENTIONS WITH QUALITY

Evidence is necessary, but not sufficient—the implementation context also must be right for you to implement your chosen intervention with quality. For example, Promoting Alternative Thinking Strategies (PATHS) aligned with the needs of the Cleveland Metropolitan School District (CMSD) because the program wanted to start upstream in elementary schools; it had an elaborated scope and sequence for grades K–6, which could be mastered more easily by teachers who were less ready for a more constructivist curriculum; it was backed by strong professional development support; and it was focused on particular social-emotional skills that were of interest to the district. In selecting interventions, identify what will work best for you, with your resources, and in your context, because evidence-based programs will not work the same for everyone. Consider your population, your capacity, and your structure to ensure that you can implement and sustain the program.

## Population

Because evidence-based programs may work differently with different populations, compare the populations studied with your target population and determine whether the program provides information to address variations in the impact across different individuals. Specifically, you should look at:

- how the program addresses a need for variation such as cultural or linguistic differences, and
- whether the data showed differences in the impact for different individuals or different subgroups.

## Capacity

To ensure that you will be able to sustain the evidence-based program, determine whether you have the capacity to support the program over time or to identify what resources you will need to seek out or reallocate to support sustainability. Look beyond startup costs to identify the costs associated with implementing and sustaining the program.

## Structure, culture, and alignment

To implement interventions that are sustainable, you must ensure that the program aligns with the structure of your organization, is consistent with your organizational culture, and aligns with other interventions and programs you have in place. Assess how your school's or district's capacity, culture, and structure will affect your ability to implement, integrate (alignment with coherence), evaluate, and sustain new programming.

## TAKEAWAYS

- Ensure that the interventions you select are developmentally and culturally appropriate, address relevant risk and protective factors, and have worked with similar student and community contexts like your own.
- Examine evidence as a critical consumer.
- Consider your school's or district's needs, assets, and priorities, including its culture and its historical experience with addressing the problems, and adapt the program if necessary while retaining its core components.

- To ensure a good fit, assess how your school's or district's capacity, culture, and structure will affect your ability to implement, integrate (alignment with coherence), evaluate, and sustain new programming.
- Evidence is necessary, but not sufficient, to ensure effective implementation of an intervention or strategy.

# FIVE

# Funding a Comprehensive Community Approach

*Frank Rider, Elizabeth V. Freeman, Aaron R. Butler,*
*Sara Wraight, and David Osher*

SCHOOLS AND THEIR COMMUNITY partners have common interests, but they often don't collaborate sufficiently, if at all. This chapter provides a strategy and rationale for using community resources to support student learning and development. We describe an effective approach for matching interventions and student supports with community systems that aligns resources and funding with identified gaps and challenges.

Health and mental health, economic security, housing, child welfare, court, community policing, disability, and other systems can unify their efforts to generate positive outcomes for students that are cost-effective and provide long-term benefits.[1] To be successful students and individuals, children and youth must experience emotional and physical safety, connectedness and support, academic challenge and engagement, and peer and adult social-emotional competence.[2] Schools provide optimal locations for these kinds of student supports and services: the challenge of access to services is lessened, students' outcomes are more likely to occur naturally in schools, and schools have the capacity to address nonacademic barriers to learning, too.[3] Supporting student success also benefits communities, in the form of significant financial returns on investment: preventing an individual dropout generates $292,000 in productivity benefits and avoided dependency costs for that individual over a lifetime.[4]

To reap the benefits of working toward positive student outcomes, however, schools and communities must overcome challenges—primarily in the area of funding.

## LIMITED AND VOLATILE FUNDING

Schools and communities often struggle with insufficient and volatile funding. State education funding formulas and federal "Title" programs are embedded in larger annual budgeting processes that are influenced by political climates. Local funds in most states depend greatly on property tax rates that reflect inequities and can be changed only with voter approval. Budget cuts have often resulted when economic downturns have yielded lower sales, income, and property tax revenues. Yet there are strategic approaches that can be used to reduce financial vulnerability to budgetary instability. Schools and community partners can combine an array of funding streams to support student success and distribute risk, while sharing responsibility for providing a comprehensive approach to children's wellness.

The Every Student Succeeds Act (ESSA) creates some opportunities for addressing inequities. It includes provisions to improve the equitable distribution and use of resources for school improvement. States must collect and report data on school-level per-pupil spending and periodically review how resources are allocated to support school improvement in districts with struggling schools. The law allows the secretary of education to grant a limited number of districts the ability to use federal funds more flexibly, provided they use a weighted student funding approach when allocating resources. In addition, ESSA authorizes the new Student Support and Academic Enrichment Grant, which provides additional funding to support local school improvement efforts, including initiatives to promote safe and healthy students.

## A SUCCESS STORY

The Hennepin County School Mental Health Initiative, a collaboration involving the Minneapolis Public Schools and seventeen other school districts, illustrates a novel approach to funding school mental health (SMH) programming in which the community takes on a significant role in SMH intervention and treatment. The initiative builds bridges to mental health resources by partnering with families, medical and mental health providers, social services, and other community professionals who work with students with mental health disorders. About ten years ago, Hennepin County implemented SMH initiatives with funding from state grants that covered nonreimbursable services and clinical care for uninsured students. Forming and sustaining this initiative required the county to build a strong foundation of support, beginning with developing a common understanding and shared language around SMH. "The school- and community-based providers worked for a long time just getting to know each other and what everybody is doing in their agencies or schools," according to Mark Sander, director of SMH at Hennepin County and Minneapolis Public Schools. "Four years into the partnership, we wrote a consensus statement about what SMH is in Hennepin County. Everybody had their version of SMH heard and appreciated. Then we really started digging into the schools' roles and responsibilities."

To reach as many students affected by mental health needs as possible, as early as possible, many schools have engaged mental health providers from community agencies to provide services on their campuses. Each provider delivers a broad range of services, from diagnosis through treatment. Providers work as part of student support teams and consult with teachers and other school personnel to provide a full continuum of coordinated care to students and their families, and to build SMH capacity among school staff.

Engaging community mental health partners from local neighborhoods helps address unique needs among the county's diverse schools. For example, much of the SMH work focuses on reaching students and families who have financial, cultural, or transportation issues that would otherwise limit their ability to access community-based mental health services.

SMH is having a positive impact on student outcomes. School data show decreases in school suspensions and office referrals, along with increases in SMH access and engagement.

"Keeping community partners motivated is easy once they see the benefits," says Sander. "Spending money to reach students with mental health problems early results in healthier kids and adolescents. And this ultimately saves the county and health insurance companies money by keeping kids out of costlier intensive services, reducing dropouts and improving graduation rates, and helping state and local agencies achieve their children's mental health system mandates." This is a success story, with many lessons learned.

In the following section, we expand on these lessons by describing common mistakes to avoid in funding for improvement.

## POTENTIAL PITFALLS

School systems commonly make the following mistakes in their well-intentioned attempts to produce school improvement:

- **Separating the planning process and the budgeting process.** Schools and districts often decouple planning from funding. Their budgeting processes fail to analyze the extent to which their spending is yielding desired results. For example, districts and schools may set aside funds for staff positions they end up not filling, then scramble to spend that money on "allowable" but sometimes unnecessary expenditures, just to avoid losing the money the following year.
- **Budgeting year to year.** Districts and schools often limit their resource allocation work to an annual activity. By concentrating only on the immediate needs of the coming year, they miss opportunities to develop long-term, sustainable solutions that have higher returns on investment. Districts and schools might, for example, fund a few new staff positions, hit a funding cliff, and then must lay off personnel or quickly shuffle funds around to save the positions.
- **Taking patchwork approaches.** Approaching school improvement as an add-on to existing school programs, and not taking steps to fully align all supports provided to students, is likely to be more expensive and less effective than using an integrated approach that blends or aligns school programming, whole-child learning, and related resources.
- **Conceding to the status quo.** Schools and agencies may limit themselves by not considering different funding sources or alternative ways to use existing resources.

## A STRATEGIC SIX-STEP APPROACH

Successful schools and districts and their community partners identify, access, and allocate their resources to *fund a plan for school improvement,* rather than simply plan how to use available funds. Encourage your community partners to take a long-term view by redirecting funding from costly backend efforts to manage the results of school failure (e.g., incarceration, drug treatment, hospitalization) to frontend investments in school improvement and students' lifelong success. We suggest a strategic financing process comprising six steps to secure the resources required to sustain your comprehensive improvement plan.

### Step 1: Identify Common Goals and Indicators Across Schools and Community Agencies

Both schools and communities have mandates that affect what they do and can do. Some goals are particular to agencies, and others are long-term outcomes to which multiple systems share a commitment. School attendance and graduation, for example, are of primary importance to many agencies, not only to schools. Work with community agencies to identify common goals and indicators.

### Step 2: Form a District School Improvement Finance Team

Assemble a multifaceted team of school and collaborating partners to develop the funding plan. Include people with technical (financial and regulatory) and programmatic (best practices) expertise, as well as students, families, and school staff who will bring firsthand perspectives about "what works," what does not work for them or schools, and what might be inefficient or wasteful. Secure official endorsements from the directors of the collaborating partner agencies and organizations. Take advantage of a shared commitment to developing policy, budgeting, information-sharing, and accountability mechanisms. The organizational responsibility might be situated within the school board, a board of county commissioners, a human services council, or a similar local structure. With the backing of the official authority for public systems, develop and implement the strategic funding plan. The plan may include interagency structures, agreements, and partnerships for coordination and financing; dissemination of rules, guidelines, standards, and practice protocols; common language and expectations across contracts, job descriptions, requests for proposals, and measurable data indicators for progress monitoring and ongoing refinement; and links with and expansions of other community initiatives.[5]

### Step 3: Determine Your Financing Needs

For each intervention or strategy, the finance team should identify specific quantities and values to determine the level of fiscal resources needed to support it. For example, a selective strategy might call for recruitment, training, and support for a group of adult mentors for a subpopulation of students. But how many mentors will need to be recruited, by when, to support how many students, over what period—and what costs will be associated with their recruitment, screening, background checks, training, ongoing coordination, and so on? Will they be compensated with stipends? Will they be compensated for mileage or incidental expenses?

The finance plan should be designed to cover a specified period of time. You might develop a plan for a single year, but if the improvement strategies call for building capacity from an initially small pilot or limited demonstration to a broader reach, the strategy might need to be phased in over a three-year period. In such a case, at what pace will the new program grow each year? What costs might be unique to each phase of growth, versus common to all three, or proportionate to the pace of growth?

Consider infrastructure components or operational mechanisms on which the school improvement program might depend; for example, whether mentors will be coming through a longstanding interfaith council, through a newly envisioned consortium of local institutions of higher education, or as individual retired volunteers will have potential cost implications. Similarly, if a new computer system must be established or extensive programing is required to exchange data between local health-care entities and school nurses, the related details will need to be identified and assigned appropriate time frames and costs.

For ongoing service arrangements, determine the number of students for whom the service will likely be indicated, estimate the cost of service delivery, and project anticipated incremental changes to the unit cost in the future. If an existing service in one school will now be replicated in a second, the team should anticipate the unique startup costs at the new site, in addition to the ongoing service costs at both sites.

For new programs, the team may consider options that have different implications for both cost and operational success, addressing the cost factors described in chapter 4. We recommend undertaking a thorough cost analysis to compare two or more specific programs or improvement reforms and identify expected costs per expected outcome for each option. Fiona Hollands and Henry Levin summarize four methods of cost analysis available for this purpose and point to a free, online tool, called CostOut, to help estimate and compare the costs of implementing different education programs.[6]

## Step 4: Map Current Spending and Develop Potential Funding Directions

Identify all resources that are currently committed to your school improvement goals. This step will lay the groundwork for the development and selection of funding strategies that will make up your funding plan. There will likely be a gap between the resources currently available and those needed. A comprehensive mapping exercise will make clear where these gaps exist and identify their size.

We recommend the following tools, which are available in the public domain and can be adapted to organize your financial mapping task:

- *Resource Mapping and Management to Address Barriers to Learning: An Intervention for Systemic Change*[7]
- *Resource Mapping in Schools and School Districts: A Resource Guide*[8]
- *Adding It Up: A Guide for Mapping Public Resources for Children, Youth and Families*[9]
- The online "Community Tool Box" from Kansas University

Each partner should bring complete records of potentially relevant expenditures to the mapping process, broken out in amounts per funding source, including specific conditions or requirements of each funding source (e.g., eligibility restrictions, service limitations, matching funds requirements, expiration dates).

### Locating resources: Funding streams and funding ponds

Funds for school improvement come from many sources—public and private; national, state, and local. An effective funding strategy will first capitalize on the narrowly restricted funds (i.e., *funding streams*) to the greatest extent possible, and will then use more flexible funds to fill in gaps, leverage additional investments of resources, and "seed" or stimulate new funding opportunities in the future—resulting in a sufficient local *funding pond*. It is important to know your federal, state, and local funding formulas, and the rules governing the use of funds. You should also be familiar with resources that local philanthropic organizations (e.g., corporate foundations, churches, community-based organizations, and local volunteer organizations) can provide. We have included helpful tables detailing multiple funding streams in appendix A.

Let's take a moment to explain further what we mean by "funding streams" and "funding ponds."

- **Funding streams.** Some resources flow downward. A funding stream can be identified at its national or state source and can then be traced to a local endpoint, where communities, districts, or schools have access. Funding streams are often redirected as they flow downward from their original sources. For example, Medicaid begins at the federal level, but as a federal–state partnership, it takes on a unique identity in every state, and is mainly implemented through state-specific plans, regulations, and procedures that are accepted by the federal Centers for Medicare and Medicaid Services. In nearly all states, Medicaid-funded services have increasingly been shaped into managed care designs that determine delivery of specific services in various categories of health services (e.g., regional care organizations) within a state.
- **Funding ponds.** Funding ponds are where local, federal, and state funds mix with public and often nonpublic local resources. They differ greatly from one community to another, across states, and even within states, and may be affected by the nature of local foundations, corporations, and endowments.

A funding pond may provide flexible resources that can help pay for expenditures such as underwriting professional development, providing universal health screenings, hiring subject matter specialists, implementing drug prevention programs, assigning individual mentors for students, and reducing class sizes.

## Mapping the financial topography

Develop a "map" that accounts for the resources that are in your funding pond. Once current resource commitments are identified, analyzed, and compared against the fiscal resources needed to support the school improvement plan, your team can widen its focus to examine a broader set of *potential* funding streams and resources to complement what is already available. We recommend a systematic approach in which you work through all three tiers of services and supports (see chapters 11, 14–16) and consider local, state, and federal resources in the public sphere, as well as opportunities for private-sector investments.

Trust is important here. Many financial managers have grown accustomed to "defending" their allocated budgets. One defensive tactic is to limit what others know and understand about the resources that make up those budgets. It is important to cultivate a strong sense of common purpose and mutual trust among your team members, because this crucial mapping step depends on the team's openness to providing the details of existing budgets and identifying resources that can be potentially repurposed to achieve greater overall impact.

### Step 5: Select Financing Strategies for School Improvement

Collaborative approaches among public and private partners can include:

- aligning and coordinating the use of categorical funds to enhance efficiency;
- pooling funds across agency or program lines to create a less restrictive source of funding for local programs;
- "braiding" funds so that each agency can track and retain its identity and meet the requirements for funds it manages, while it funds portions of a single activity or program; and
- capturing and reinvesting funds saved through programs that appropriately reduce costs (e.g., when fewer referrals for costly services are made).

The basic financing strategies are outlined next. Your team can mix and match these to create the best recipe for your school improvement funding pond.

*Optimize available funding streams*

It is important to determine the current public funding streams that have the most potential to fund improvement strategies. Medicaid is a particularly valuable funding stream to focus on, as it includes a comprehensive benefit to eligible children in all fifty states that "trumps" otherwise limiting factors in an individual state's plan. The comprehensive Medicaid benefit is called EPSDT, for Early and Periodic Screening, Diagnostic, and Treatment.

Check with your state education, mental health, and Medicaid agencies to determine how your school can use EPSDT in particular, and Medicaid reimbursement more generally (see table A.2 in appendix A). And don't stop there: explore the potential to expand this option in your state through the National Health Law Program scan, which can be found in appendix B.

In all states, children in families with incomes slightly above the Medicaid eligibility standards are similarly covered by the Children's Health Insurance

Program (CHIP), another federal–state partnership funding stream with state-by-state variations. Collectively, Medicaid and CHIP cover 48 percent of American children.[10] The "Medicaid Prevention Pathways" toolkit from Moving Health Care Upstream—a partnership between the Nemours Foundation and the UCLA Center for Healthier Children, Families and Communities—illustrates how state Medicaid agencies can partner with schools and other systems to deliver a range of preventive services and strategies at both the individual and population levels.[11] A complementary resource is Milbank Memorial Fund's *Medicaid Coverage of Social Interventions: A Road Map for States.*[12]

A state-by-state analysis comparing both ESSA and the Individuals with Disabilities Education Act (IDEA) in each state's implementation can reveal strategies to optimize school improvement funding you might adapt to your state. Formula, block, and discretionary grants create federal funding streams that can provide funding for workforce development and tele-medicine infrastructure (Health Resources and Services Administration), staff training (Administration for Children and Families/Title IV-E), information and support for parents of children with special health-care needs (Maternal and Child Health), and even internet connectivity (US Department of Agriculture). Your finance team can use the same type of analysis to discover examples of how funds are being optimized in other communities within your own state.

### Redeploy inefficiently deployed resources

Current spending may not be generating intended results. For example, you may discover that traditional student discipline approaches focusing on in-school detention, out-of-school suspensions, and expulsions are draining administrators' time and generating costly problems for the community while adversely affecting grade completion and graduation rates. Consider how resources currently dedicated to these counterproductive activities could be reinvested in schoolwide positive behavior programs and restorative justice practices that promise more desirable results.

Similarly, you might uncover instances where several well-intentioned service systems are each offering different clinical programs intended to provide treatment for the same group of young victims of community violence or domestic trauma. Are significant resources required to maintain all of these programs? Could the services be rearranged and streamlined?

Look for opportunities to free up existing resources by first downsizing or eliminating ineffective or redundant programs as well as counterproductive or even harmful programs.[13] You can also implement preventive approaches that enable you to shift resources away from intensive (and expensive) treatments to earlier, less costly supports and interventions. Remember that even ineffective programs have supporters, however, and that there may be political or ideological factors that contribute to their ongoing use. This should be addressed with caution, sensitivity, and respect.

### Create new funding structures

Some communities have formed cross-sector partnerships that offer elaborate networks of services and supports for positive student achievement. Typically, such efforts begin with a focus on "troubled or troubling" students with acute and complex needs, and then recognize "upstream" opportunities to join forces to slow down, interrupt, halt, or even reverse acute conditions.[14]

States can and should provide or expand care coordination, case management, and other "wraparound" approaches for children who are at risk. State and local education agencies, state Medicaid agencies, and state departments of health and child welfare services have the option to use Medicaid funding to support district- and school-based wraparound processes. Case managers can refer Medicaid-enrolled students to necessary health and related support services like housing and transportation. Some communities have created pools of flexible funds, time banks for exchange of services, and faith-based models of support and care coordination (e.g., The Open Table, a multinational model in which volunteers make a yearlong commitment to help participants "set goals, foster accountability, and implement a plan to create change"[15]).

Partnering systems can coordinate budgets to multiply their impact. Your mapping process will identify how local and state funds can best be matched by federal Medicaid and CHIP dollars. Child Abuse Prevention and Treatment Act (CAPTA) funds, Medicaid EPSDT benefits, IDEA Part C early intervention funds, and state public health resources can all be braided together to pay for developmental, emotional, and behavioral health screening, assessment, and treatment services for young children. More elaborate case rate and collaborative funding approaches are now numerous.[16]

### Raise new revenues

When your finance team can demonstrate that school improvement is a compelling investment opportunity for your community, you can persuade political leaders and citizens to make direct investments today to generate impressive returns tomorrow. Sometimes these begin as pilot programs or limited demonstrations, often funded by discretionary, time-limited grant opportunities offered both by federal agencies and by foundations and other philanthropies. The Grantsmanship Center offers a "clickable map" that shows the foundations in every state.[17]

Exemplars for this strategy include the 2008 St. Louis County, Missouri, "Putting Kids First" ballot initiative, and targeted tax levies approved by voters in three Ohio counties in 2014 specifically to fund installation in their local schools of an evidence-based curriculum called the Good Behavior Game, which has been demonstrated to reduce behavior problems in first and sixth grade, and many costly negative outcomes when youth were nineteen to twenty-one (smoking, substance abuse, antisocial personality disorder, violence and criminal behavior, and suicidal thoughts). The nation's largest single school district, in New York City, benefits from the mayor's THRIVE NYC initiative, an $850 million overhaul of the city's mental health service system that is capitalizing on school campuses for access not only to students, but their families and neighbors as well. On an even larger scale, California's 2004 Mental Health Services Act, Proposition 63, has generated millions of dollars each year for the state's fifty-four counties to address locally determined mental health priorities.

In some cases, you can also identify strategic funding for longer-term investments through social impact bonds and Pay for Success strategies that leverage private-sector investments in early childhood, delinquency diversion, and other programs, providing local governments with upfront capital for new programs that also help them to manage risks. Goldman Sachs' early-childhood social-impact bond in Salt Lake City is one example of about two dozen such investments. Harvard University provides free technical assistance and resources to support this innovative funding model. Links to both resources can be found in appendix B.

Not-for-profit organizations with the right capacities can serve as intermediaries that help communities link to private-sector investors and manage Pay for Success initiatives.

Your school improvement funding strategies should include resources that can be leveraged by the school's schoolwide teams and student support teams. Specifically, the plan should:

- describe specific strategies to combine and coordinate resources from multiple sources;

- specify formal linkages among child-, family-, and community-serving systems;
- enable proposed funding and collaborative approaches;
- build supportive connections with community and state initiatives;
- focus the majority of effort on securing the school improvement resources;
- determine creative strategies that emerge from your team's discussions; and
- ensure that strategies incorporate supports for developing staff readiness to implement them.

### Step 6: Develop and Execute Your School Improvement Funding Plan

After you have selected financing strategies to address all component costs in your school improvement proposal, it is time to develop a written plan that assigns expectations and responsibilities in an intentional progression. The sequence of planned actions should be thoughtfully mapped out.

#### *Prioritization*

As you develop an actionable plan, how will you know what actions to prioritize? Here are some questions to think about:

- Which strategies will reduce disparities and maximize equity in academic success and social-emotional and physical health and well-being?
- Which strategies will have the greatest impact?
- Which can most easily be achieved?
- Which might take the longest time to achieve?
- Which will best capitalize on current/imminent opportunities?
- Which cost the least to pursue?
- Which are foundational/prerequisite to other strategies in the plan?
- Which are already supported by a broad consensus of involved decision makers and stakeholders?
- Which are most likely to be stable and reliable in the long run?
- Which are the least risky?

#### *Financial action planning*

As with your overall strategic planning, you should develop an action plan for funding. This plan should specify:

- who will do what, by when, and how you will know it is completed;
- any arrangements to be made by whom and with what specific entities to secure funding and resources;
- responsibilities and timelines for initial execution;
- plans for regular review of action plan progress; and
- a process for refining strategies when necessary.

### Accessing support and buy-in

You must still work to generate support for the plan among high-level policy makers and decision makers whose political and administrative support is essential. What will be required to secure their substantial and active commitment to the plan in the long term (e.g., a three-year horizon)?

To secure official buy-in, make sure you are prepared to clearly present evidence that supports the selected school improvement strategies, documentation of the viability of your proposed funding strategies, relevant examples of those strategies in action in other communities, and stakeholder testimonials that put a human face on the economic and best-practice foundations that undergird your plan. Involve students, parents, and community groups whose support can help "make the case." Allocate resources (time, people power, and printing/media) for effective "marketing" for your plan.

Expect to repeat and refine this strategic planning process on an annual basis, now including data from your formative evaluation. Commit to reviewing and revising the funding plan to respond to significant changes: (a) in the administrative environment or in key leadership; (b) because of plan progress and changing student, family, and community needs; and (c) in light of emerging new opportunities and needs.

## TAKEAWAYS

- Schools and community agencies have many common interests, but they often don't collaborate sufficiently or at all.
- Strategic approaches can reduce financial vulnerability to budgetary instability. Schools and community partners can combine an array of funding streams to support student success and distribute risk while sharing responsibility for providing a comprehensive approach to children's wellness.
- Encourage your community partners to take a long-term view by redirecting funding from backend efforts to manage the results of school

failure (e.g., incarceration, drug treatment, hospitalization) to frontend investments in school improvement and students' lifelong success.

- Identify common goals and indicators across schools and community agencies and organizations.
- Implement a financial planning process that optimizes national and state funding streams, leverages flexible local funding ponds, and redeploys inefficiently used resources.

PART TWO

# Engage

# SIX

# The Centrality of Cultural Competence and Responsiveness

*Karen Francis and David Osher*

EACH OF US ENGAGES the world through a lens grounded in our own experience and framed by culture and language. We rely on these lenses to consciously and unconsciously navigate our interactions with and reactions to the world around us and to give us perspective. In this process, our lenses are either sharpened by congruent models, guidance, and reinforcement, or blunted by counteracting information. These lenses provide a semblance of order to our lives, but at the same time create blinders to the vantage points of others, inasmuch as everyone sees and experiences the world differently. These blinders undermine our efforts as leaders, educators, and thinkers. They also compromise our efforts to engage and learn from all members of the community in and beyond the school. Cultural competence and cultural responsiveness, which are described in this chapter, can contribute to equity with excellence by helping you avoid, minimize, or avert these challenges in your school improvement efforts.

It is important to ground your planning and implementation efforts in the theory and practice of cultural and linguistic competence and responsiveness.

For example, when school staff develop policies and implement practices that authentically and respectfully partner with children and their families in decision making, they recognize the importance of their lived experience of engaging with schools and other services and supports. When we have a shared or mutually understood lived experience, we can use our shared knowledge and motivation as a powerful engine for ensuring that change occurs and succeeds.

We see some examples of this happening when:

- the phrase "all are served here" means a welcoming and engaging environment, where there is respect for diverse cultural backgrounds (a step toward cultural competence);
- the perspectives of diverse youth and families are used to inform the development of programs and services (a step toward authentic integration of cultural competence);
- the innate capacity of families and communities to actively support the learning and development of their children is valued (a step toward respect for culture and cultural proficiency);
- multilingual approaches to communication are viewed as the norm, not the exception (a step toward linguistic competence);
- everyone feels welcome at the school; and
- diverse cultural perspectives are authentically included in approaches to learning and development (a step toward cultural and linguistic competence).

Culture is integral to everyday life; it influences the habits, customs, values, and behaviors of individuals and groups of people. Culture is the road map that individuals figuratively and practically rely on to navigate the world and the communities in which they live. It is at the center of how individuals interact and react to living and engagement. How individuals perceive their needs, communicate those needs, access services to address those needs, and respond to services is influenced by culture. Consequently, for engagement, partnering, and service delivery efforts to be effective, they must be culturally competent and responsive.

Culture affects everyone—it provides us with knowledge, scripts, frameworks, and language that affect how we think, feel, and act.[1] Culture has been defined as an "integrated pattern of human behavior that includes thoughts, communication styles, actions, customs, beliefs, values, and institutions of a racial, ethnic, religious or social group."[2] It contributes to shared patterns of thinking, behaving, and meaning making among group members, and, if unacknowledged, creates discordance between groups. Culture can support inclusion, collaboration, engagement, identity safety, equity, and justice. Alternatively, it can reinforce exclusion, prejudice, alienation, identity stress, privilege, and unfairness. Individuals, groups, and institutions embody and reinforce culture, both explicitly and implicitly. While we all have biases and limited perspectives, we can—both individually and in organizations—develop cultural competencies (or proficiencies), including awareness; learn more about ourselves and others; and develop practices and mindsets, including self-reflection, that value and address diversity.

*Cultural competence* refers to the ability of individuals to learn and develop the interpersonal skills and attitudes that enable them to better understand and appreciate the rich, fluid nature of culture and the differences and similarities within, among, and between cultures and individuals. Cultural competence, we now know, must also address the effects of intersectionality. For example, how do race, class, gender, sexual orientation, religious affiliation, ethnicity, age status, and/or disability status affect perceptions and outcomes? How are individuals affected by the fact that they may be treated differently in different settings or when they have different statuses or play different roles? Think, for example, of the different experience a teacher may have when visiting a school as a parent rather than a teacher. Or think about how respected community elders may feel when they perceive a school to be treating them as lacking knowledge.

Cultural competence is not merely a set of tools learned at one point in time and applied repeatedly. Rather, it is a process that educators and other service providers (as well as students and family members) must learn to adapt to each new individual encounter. Culturally competent approaches:

- recognize the cultural grounding of teachers' and service providers' views, behaviors, and methods;
- acknowledge the power of language and the diverse communication styles of students and their families;
- address culturally based definitions of family networks and of showing respect;
- view family and community as critical parts of a student's support system; and

- demonstrate a willingness and ability to draw on community-based values, traditions, customs, and resources.

Cultural competence should ideally contribute to *cultural humility*, which involves self-evaluation and self-critique.[3] It should also contribute to *cultural reciprocity*, which involves learning from people while they learn from you.[4]

*Linguistic competence* should encompass "the capacity of an organization and its personnel to communicate effectively and convey information in a manner that is easily understood by diverse audiences," as well as the ability of the organization and its staff to learn from people who have other types of linguistic and social assets.[5] When combined with cultural competence, linguistic competence can help schools avoid the harms caused by deficit approaches to individuals and "subtractive" approaches to English language learners—such as not viewing speaking another language as a leverageable asset.[6]

Cultural and linguistic competence (CLC) is more than cultural "sensitivity"; it should contribute to cultural humility, reciprocity, and responsiveness. It is demonstrated (both when applied to individuals and groups) by the capacity to: value diversity, self-assess and/or conduct self-assessment, manage the dynamics and politics of difference in privilege, acquire and institutionalize cultural knowledge, adapt to diversity and the cultural contexts of the communities served, be culturally responsive, and demonstrate cultural humility.[7]

These capacity areas span all aspects of policy making, administration, practice, and service delivery, and systematically involve students, families, and communities.[8] Further, schools must emphasize organizational, structural, and staff supports that promote policies, procedures, behaviors, and the acquisition of knowledge that facilitates and integrates CLC. Without these necessary supports, authentic implementation of CLC will not be realized.

## THE CULTURAL AND LINGUISTIC COMPETENCE CONTINUUM

CLC is a "developmental process that evolves over an extended period."[9] Both individuals and organizations possess various degrees of awareness, knowledge, and skills along the CLC continuum. Therefore, CLC needs to develop concurrently in two contexts: individual and organizational. The CLC continuum has six graduated stages:[10]

- **Cultural destructiveness.** Advancing attitudes, policies, practices, and/or structures that are destructive to cultural groups (e.g., "It's our way or the highway").

- **Cultural incapacity.** Lacking capacity to respond to the needs of cultural groups (e.g., inadequate or limited workforce capacity and staff who can address the cultural and linguistic needs of diverse children, youth, and families).
- **Cultural blindness.** Encouraging assimilation and ignoring cultural strengths (e.g., "melting pot" versus "the salad bowl"), manifested by the false expectation that children, youth, and families need to adapt to the dominant culture of the community or organization, instead of the organization or service provider adapting to and integrating the cultural perspectives of the children, youth, and families to be served.
- **Cultural precompetence.** Being aware of strengths and areas for improvement to respond effectively with CLC (e.g., willingness to accept feedback about the quality of services and develop strategies to effectively address needs).
- **Cultural competence.** Demonstrating an acceptance of and respect for cultural difference (e.g., understanding and modeling policies and practices that incorporate the voices of diverse children, youth, and families).
- **Cultural proficiency.** Holding culture in high esteem and using it as a foundational guide for endeavors (e.g., operating under measurable standards that encompass CLC, with policies, practices, and procedure built on cultural inclusion, respect, and an appreciation for diversity).

The CLC continuum is often referred to as "the journey."[11] The journey represents constant learning and development, recognizing that culture and cultural competence are dynamic and evolving concepts. We add one more stage: cultural humility, which, as mentioned earlier, involves the commitment and ability of individuals—alone and together—to understand the cultural boundedness of their own knowledge, to avoid jumping to quick conclusions, and to "engage in self-reflection and self-critique as lifelong learners and reflective practitioners."[12]

## PRACTICAL APPLICATION OF CULTURAL AND LINGUISTIC COMPETENCE

CLC focuses on recognizing the real and perceived barriers that children, youth, and families experience as they engage with schools and other service systems, and then developing policies and practices that reduce these barriers, while authentically and respectfully including children and their families in decision making. You can demonstrate CLC by developing strategies that address the following needs:[13]

- **Availability** asks the question, "Do services and supports exist?"
- **Accessibility** relates to the ease and convenience of obtaining and using services.
- **Affordability** addresses the issue of cost and financial burden to families that may prevent accessibility.
- **Appropriateness** defines the effectiveness and quality of services to meet the specific needs of children and their families.
- **Acceptability** refers to the extent to which engagement activities and service delivery models are congruent with the cultural beliefs, values, and worldviews of children, youth, and their families.
- **Identity safety** counters institutionalized acculturation messages and involves individuals feeling that their identity is safe and respected.

Your strategies to address CLC should be informed by data to drive effective decision making. Consider beginning by determining the root causes of disparities, and do so in a manner that does not merely trigger guilt and defensiveness, but instead identifies gaps and needs. You may benefit from scripts and facilitation guides such as those identified in *Addressing the Root Causes of Disparities in School Discipline: An Educator's Action Planning Guide*.[14] For example, you can pose the following questions to explore the root causes of disparities:

- **Privilege.** In what way do we as individuals benefit from privilege (e.g., in terms of race, gender, sexual orientation), and to what extent do our organizational practices privilege some groups of individuals?
- **Power.** In what ways do policy making, leadership, and management equally empower and include the voices of all members of the school community?

## CREATING CULTURALLY RESPONSIVE LEARNING ENVIRONMENTS

Culturally and linguistically diverse students from nondominant or marginalized groups often experience identity unsafety and disconnects between schools' curricula and pedagogy and their own resources—their experiences, cultural capital, and needs.[15] These disconnects place additional cognitive and emotional demands on them in comparison to other students. They must master new content without the explicit or implicit culturally embedded knowledge that students from dominant groups benefit from and that teachers may take for granted—hence the importance of understanding privilege.[16] These cultural disconnects make it harder for students to perceive themselves as successful learners.

It is imperative that school administrators, teachers, and support services personnel understand the importance of creating and maintaining learning environments that are *culturally responsive* so they can effectively meet the needs of a changing and diverse student population. That is, educators must understand the impact of privilege and use the cultures and experiences of racially and ethnically diverse youth as a scaffold to learning and growth.[17] A culturally responsive learning environment requires a shift in pedagogy to incorporate the cultural experiences and backgrounds of students into all aspects of learning and development.[18] Culturally responsive approaches address the individuality and cultural groundedness of learning and intentionally provide appropriate supports so that failure is not an option for any child.

## PRACTICAL APPROACHES TO DEVELOPING CULTURALLY RESPONSIVE LEARNING ENVIRONMENTS FOR SCHOOLS AND SCHOOL PERSONNEL

Here are some practical suggestions for schools and school personnel who wish to increase their cultural and linguistic competence and be culturally responsive:[19]

- Create a welcoming environment that embraces diversity, is identity safe, and is open to different perspectives.
- Identify strategies that facilitate partnerships, collaboration, and work with youth, families, community members, and community-based organizations.
- Create a professional learning community and discuss the implications of books such as *Culturally Responsive Teaching and The Brain*, *Whistling Vivaldi*, and *Promoting Racial Literacy in Schools*.[20]
- Address microaggressions preventively and in codes of conduct.
- Address status-based bullying and harassment.
- Understand perceptions about and the dynamics of power/authority.
- Understand the roots and dynamics of institutionalized racism and prejudice.

- Avoid victim blaming and approaches that ignore the effects of ecological factors, including institutionalized prejudice and inequality.
- Identify and address the effects of both privilege and discrimination.
- Respect people's ability to use their language of choice when it does not directly interfere with group instruction.
- Harness the positive energy of families as part of the solution instead of seeing their cultural perspectives as part of the "problem."
- Facilitate language access (i.e., translation and interpretation services)— for staff as well as families.
- Reflect upon implicit bias and provide training and support to school personnel to address it.[21]
- Examine how discipline practices and enrichment opportunities disproportionately impact some groups of students.
- Utilize the knowledge and skills of family members as experts.
- Ensure that guidance for parents on addressing challenging behavior is tailored, creating service approaches that will work for an individual family.
- Employ and support *culturally responsive teaching*, which uses culturally mediated and situated pedagogy to address emotional, motivational, interpersonal, and learning needs; build upon strengths; and create learning environments where students feel a sense of belonging, emotional and intellectual safety, and appropriate support and challenge.[22]
- Employ interventions that have been demonstrated as effective and culturally competent.

## TAKEAWAYS
- Cultural and linguistic competence and responsiveness are necessary.
- Cultural competence involves the capacity to: value diversity, self-assess and/or conduct self-assessment, manage the dynamics and politics of difference in privilege, acquire and institutionalize cultural knowledge, adapt to diversity and the cultural contexts of the communities served, be culturally responsive, and demonstrate cultural humility.
- It is important to identify the root causes of disparities, and to do so in a manner that does not merely trigger guilt and defensiveness.
- It is also important to create culturally responsive and identity-safe learning environments.

# SEVEN

# Engaging Students in Creating Safe, Equitable, and Excellent Schools

*Robert V. Mayo and David Osher*

CHILDREN AND YOUTH can help us design and calibrate programming and instruction. Their perceptions of school climate and their knowledge of what their peers are doing can help us monitor and improve conditions for learning and school safety. They can support a culture that promotes academic productivity and collaboration. They can stand up against bullying, disruption, and risky behavior. At the same time, providing young people with opportunities to voice their opinions, to make choices, and to be involved in decision making contributes to both their learning and to their healthy development. This chapter provides strategies to engage and leverage student interest, passion, and knowledge to drive and support school improvement, as well as to promote youth development.

## INCLUSIVE VERSUS EXCLUSIVE APPROACHES TO STUDENT ENGAGEMENT

Involving students in decision making can lead to increased feelings of belonging and purpose in schools; transform the attitudes and systems that underlie the culture of organizations, schools, and communities; and provide contexts within which students can be critical partners who challenge ineffective, antidemocratic, and inequitable practices throughout education.[1] Authentic student engagement and inclusion of student voice can help classroom communities become mutually supportive for teachers and students while contributing to the creation of safe and supportive schools.[2] Addressing personal challenges and organizational barriers to student voice can lead to healthier, more democratic cultures where everyone is engaged as partners. When students are more aware of, *and have authentic input into*, the development and implementation of curricula, instructional activities, and social-behavioral initiatives, it enhances buy-in, peer-to-peer support, and accountability.[3] Schools and other organizations also benefit from engaging students, who can provide practical input on effective strategies to improve programs and services. This includes youth *participatory action research*, where youth identify issues and collect information to address questions, and their findings are used to inform decisions and policy.[4]

On the other side of the coin, traditional approaches that rely on establishing student government associations and student councils as the primary mechanisms for including students risk attracting only high-agency and high-achieving students and potentially excluding students who don't fit that mold. Moreover, there are very real limits to the number of students in traditional student government structures. Traditional student engagement approaches often exclude the voices of many of the students that social-emotional, behavioral, academic, and even equity initiatives seek to support. Other engagement structures that are susceptible to exclusion include school activity planning committees and voluntary school clubs and extracurricular activities, including competitive athletics, which may privilege some students due to timing, style, selective outreach (i.e., who is invited), participation rules, or cost requirements.

Traditional engagement approaches also often neglect the most regular opportunity for voice—the classroom. This missed opportunity is unfortunate, as students can help teachers calibrate their teaching as well as develop additional ways of engaging students. Approaches to engagement that involve students in the creation of class norms build upon students' desire to learn.

Authentic engagement is a two-way street. While educators should actively and intentionally engage with students, students may take the lead and initiate engagement. For example, this can happen when students are elevating issues—whether local, national, or even international—that matter to them.

## HOW TO ENGAGE STUDENTS AS POWERFUL PARTNERS IN BUILDING SCHOOL AND CLASSROOM COMMUNITIES

Opportunities for authentic student engagement in school and classroom community building include collaborating with students in site- and grade-level leadership teams. Authentic student engagement helps initiatives become, from a student perspective, "our initiatives" rather than top-down approaches that adults apply to students without their input, buy-in, or ownership for individual and collective outcomes. The same can be said for authentic student engagement in norm setting and problem solving, particularly when it comes to establishing classroom norms and addressing behavioral issues in a restorative manner.

Through its efforts to incorporate student voice in district, school, and classroom community building and improvement, Cleveland Metropolitan School District (CMSD) provides two examples of authentic student engagement. First, CMSD's Class Meetings initiative focuses on developing ninth-grade students' core social-emotional competencies—self-management, relationship skills, self-awareness, social awareness, and responsible decision making—via proactive, structured and semistructured, twenty-minute, teacher-facilitated (at least initially) classroom community-building, problem-solving, and decision-making activities that focus on process over product. Ideally, Class Meetings take place daily, and they have proven most effective when held in a circle structure.

The district's use of a Student Advisory Committee (SAC) provides a second example of authentic student engagement and inclusion of student voice in both district- and site-level decision making, as detailed in "Cleveland Metropolitan School District: Student Advisory Committee."

## EXPANDING OUR UNDERSTANDING OF YOUTH ENGAGEMENT

When considering the term *youth engagement*, many educators think only of academic engagement, but youth engagement also has other meanings. From a positive youth development perspective, youth engagement refers to sustained connections that young people have with their school, community, and other youth and families, as well as to *youth voice, youth involvement, youth participation*, and *youth governance*.[5] While youth engagement is important for all students, it may be particularly so for middle and high school students, who are more likely to disconnect. As educator, former gang member,

## Cleveland Metropolitan School District: Student Advisory Committee

As part of CMSD's collaboratively developed and binding Cleveland Plan, the district's superintendent established a Student Advisory Committee (SAC) of high school students in 2014. Each high school was required to establish a SAC. SAC members were not to be traditional "student leaders," honor roll students, or the like. The superintendent wanted each SAC to represent a social and academic cross-section of each school community—including students who aren't necessarily doing well in all areas of high school student life. SACs initially meet in their individual school committees to problem-solve about tough topics such as police–youth relationships, chronic absenteeism, equity and inclusion, climate and culture, school discipline, and obstacles to widespread academic achievement. SAC members don't approach this important work by griping or finger-pointing; instead, they emphasize inclusion, ownership, and strategic problem solving.

SAC members are often tasked with taking recommendations back to their respective school-based leadership teams, who consider these recommendations in their school community improvement decision making. For example, SAC members are asked to review their school's Conditions for Learning Survey reports (the survey is described in chapter 3), review the data points and trends to identify strengths and weaknesses, develop actionable recommendations focused on improving identified areas of weakness, and then formally take these recommendations back to their school leadership teams.

and former "student at risk" Paul Hernandez relates, youth often feel like imposters, and their negative experiences push them away from academic learning and school and toward oppositional cultures, both in school and in the streets: "I exercised my only form of power in the classroom as a student: resisting the teacher at the expense of my own success."[6]

Youth engagement provides the opportunity for young people to be actively involved in their communities, build their skills, and network with community leaders and other professionals to create services. Youth engagement is "the result when young people are involved in responsible, challenging actions to create positive social change" across environments such as schools, communities, and systems providing services.[7]

## Why Is Youth Engagement Important?

A resounding phrase synonymous with youth engagement is "nothing about us without us." This sentiment is particularly important to adolescents, who are sensitive to matters of autonomy and who seek opportunities for expressing agency, voicing their opinions, and making decisions in their lives.[8] Acting with autonomy in these ways enables youth to apply what they have learned from their lived experience and to help determine effective approaches that can improve the classroom and school. With effective engagement, youth are also able to gain knowledge and skills by interacting with teachers, other educators, community members, agency representatives, and decision makers—at a particularly important time when they are developing their own identity. These experiences lay the groundwork for developing the next generation of community leaders and advocates. Additionally, young people can serve as youth engagement experts to their school as well as to other organizations, providing guidance and insight about their lived experiences, which should inform decisions being made within their communities.

Several principles are foundational to facilitating positive outcomes for youth and their families across systems and in communities. The principle of youth engagement and youth-guided approaches goes hand in hand with other guiding principles such as family-driven approaches and cultural and linguistic competence. A youth-guided approach "allows young people to participate in the development of their own service and supports . . . giving them a voice in deciding on activities."[9] For example, many communities across the country have established juvenile justice councils or advisory boards to build authentic youth voice into school improvement planning activities. These councils or advisory boards can enhance their effectiveness in serving youth in the community by representing the voices, lived experiences, and ideas of young people when providing guidance to community leadership. The same is true of inclusive school-based councils and advisory boards as they work to address social exclusion, increase awareness of needs, understand service utilization patterns, and increase positive outcomes for children, youth, and their families.

## WHY ESTABLISH YOUTH–ADULT PARTNERSHIPS?

There are several benefits youth derive from partnering with educators and other adults:[10]

- Youth benefit from partnerships with adults when they are seen as individuals who are competent and able to contribute to important decisions that impact their communities. The benefits include leadership skill development, improved self-esteem and agency, and increased ability to interact with adults.
- Youth involvement in positive social relationships and activities with adults is associated with a decrease in risk behaviors, stronger communication skills and leadership experience, increased status and stature in the community, and improved competencies and self-esteem.

There are also benefits to youth partnering with adults specifically in the school setting:

- Connectedness to school has been shown to be a significant predictor of higher academic achievement among youth.[11]
- Students' perceptions of safety, belonging, respect, and feeling cared for at school appear to play a particularly important role in healthy adolescent development, including the reduction of antisocial behavior.[12]
- Supportive, caring relationships between students and teachers, as well as teachers' positive perceptions of students' efforts in the classroom, have been associated with improved achievement.[13]

## WHAT DOES PLACING YOUTH AT THE CENTER LOOK LIKE?

A study of eight organizations identified six practices for promoting youth engagement and voice: (1) provide young people with meaningful and authentic experiences; (2) infuse or involve youth in innumerable aspects of the program and the organization; (3) employ adults with a high level of education or knowledge about young people and a demonstrated willingness to share power with them; (4) secure adequate resources and funding to accomplish the organization's stated goals; (5) provide opportunities to authentically engage the voices, ideas, and opinions of youth; and (6) facilitate youth and adult partnerships in which both parties contribute strengths and resources and learn from each other for mutually beneficial results.[14]

Meaningfully collaborating with youth, and promoting youth engagement, goes beyond representing youth on boards or advisory councils or seeking their input on an ad hoc basis. It encompasses a process for the development of meaningful, mutually beneficial partnerships between youth and adults. A youth–adult partnership is a relationship that "emphasizes mutuality for support in teaching, learning, and interaction between youth and adults."[15] The approaches to cultural and linguistic competence and engaging diverse groups in decision making described in chapter 6 also provide basic tenets for effective youth engagement—they place youth at the center of transformational community and systems change.[16]

Meaningful collaboration and engagement benefit from child-guided and youth-directed approaches. These benefits include:

- youth as strengths and assets to schools and communities;
- youth as experts in their own lives;
- youth as having agency, with a right and capacity to contribute;
- adults as allies and supporters or partners in youth-directed efforts; and
- meaningful and authentic engagement by youth.

Approaches that place youth at the center can range from efforts that are completely youth-led (e.g., action research) to those that are adult-initiated but youth-informed and/or youth-directed (e.g., collaborative participatory research) to those that are intergenerational, involving collaboration between youth and adults (e.g., task forces).[17]

An effective plan for youth engagement can involve the following:

- **Assessing the organization.** Assess the school's and/or organization's readiness to engage students and young people.
- **Providing supports.** Help young people to determine where they can start by allowing them to assess their personal level of readiness.
- **Organizing a forum.** Create a forum to gather youth and adult representatives together to establish relationships and roles and a shared understanding of the initiative.
- **Developing a strategic plan.** Based on the organizational and youth assessments, create a youth engagement plan that includes strategies to build the capacity of decision making and leadership among young people.
- **Implementing and continuously evaluating the plan.** Formalize the action plan into a document that is easy for all current and future youth and adult stakeholders to understand and follow. This includes educating key youth and adult partners on the necessity of evaluating youth engagement, jointly creating the plan, and establishing a process to monitor and evaluate the work plan.

Multiple resources for youth participation and engagement are provided in appendix B. We encourage you to check them out with your youth collaborators.

## TAKEAWAYS

- Youth agency is important.
- Involving students in decision making increases belonging and purpose.
- Addressing personal challenges and organizational barriers to student voice enhances buy-in and peer-to-peer support and accountability.
- Traditional approaches to student government risk attracting high-agency and high-achieving students and potentially excluding other students who don't fit that mold.
- Effective engagement of youth involves meaningful, mutually beneficial partnerships between youth and adults and has youth development benefits.

# EIGHT

# Partnering with Families

*Lacy Wood, Trina Osher, and David Osher*

LIKE THE YOUNG PEOPLE we described in the previous chapter, families are an underused and often alienated education resource. Families and school staff should be partners and should actively collaborate in supporting children's learning and development.[1] This is possible when schools and other community groups are committed to partnering with families in meaningful ways and have the capacity to do so. As students mature, the commitment to family engagement should be continuous, evolving in a developmentally appropriate manner.

In 2011, the National Family, School and Community Engagement Working Group defined family engagement in education as:

> a shared responsibility in which schools and other community agencies and organizations are committed to reaching out to engage families in meaningful ways and in which families are committed to actively supporting their children's learning and development. Family engagement is continuous across a child's life and entails enduring commitment but changing parent roles as children mature into young adulthood. Effective family engagement cuts across and reinforces learning in the multiple settings where children learn—at home,

in prekindergarten programs, in school, in afterschool programs, in faith-based institutions, and in the community.[2]

This chapter builds on this definition, highlighting the importance of collaborating with families and providing approaches that will enable you to engage families in a family-driven, culturally competent manner.

## EFFECTIVE FAMILY ENGAGEMENT IS FAMILY-DRIVEN AND CULTURALLY COMPETENT

### Taking a Family-Driven Perspective

Partnering with families requires a paradigm shift from a professionally driven system to one that is *family-driven*—where families are the active agent of change, rather than the target of change. Family-driven approaches and systems actively ensure that families have a primary decision-making role in determining what their own children experience, as well as in the policies and procedures governing the education, services, and care provided for all children in their community. Family-driven approaches and systems incorporate family voice and choice as key influences when choosing supports, services, and providers; setting goals; designing and implementing programs; monitoring outcomes; funding services, treatments, and supports; and determining the effectiveness of all efforts to promote the learning, mental health, and well-being of children and youth.[3]

Meaningful family engagement and parental leadership in schools occurs when a child's family gains the knowledge and skills to support their child's education, function in meaningful leadership roles, and represent the "parent voice" to help shape the direction of their school's programs and student achievement outcomes. District/school culture, environment, and administrators' leadership styles can influence these partnerships. Leaders should model a collaborative approach that focuses on relationships and encourages staff and family leadership. This work may require differentiated or targeted strategies that address family context and cultural and linguistic competence.

Schools can do a variety of things to engage families in a family-driven way:

• Include a diverse set of families during the school's visioning process.
• Provide families with opportunities to access information on student progress, including providing avenues to coordinate support when students need extra help and explaining (in a manner that families

understand) what kinds of support are available and how families can access them.

- Schedule activities during times that will allow families to participate. Consult with families to determine when and how they can engage with the school and how the school can support and facilitate their engagement.
- If a student is struggling, include the family in the discussion to trouble-shoot issues and engage in identifying solutions and coordinating how all parties can support the plan.

## Addressing Cultural Competence

Your approach to developing family engagement initiatives should reflect the needs of families, address the cultural and linguistic competence of staff, and be intentional and tailored to the context of your school community. Addressing cultural competence is a key factor in enabling educators to be effective with students and families from cultures other than their own. Staff should understand their own cultural identity and worldview about diversity, be culturally humble, and be open to learning about the different cultural backgrounds and norms of the families with whom they work. Helping staff understand differences and use that knowledge to inform and strengthen their interactions with families will improve practice and help build cultural reciprocity and lasting partnerships. Addressing cultural bias and ably promoting family assets will help broker long-term relationships with families and community.

## WHY ENGAGE FAMILIES?

### Better Student Outcomes

There is a positive and convincing relationship between family engagement with schools and benefits for students. This relationship holds for families of all economic, racial/ethnic, and educational backgrounds and for students of all ages.[4] We also know that family engagement has a protective effect. The more families can be involved in their children's education and their progress, the better their children do in school and the longer they stay in school. Districts should develop systemic engagement practices for students at all grade levels, as well as policies that promote family engagement and support education transitions at all grades.[5]

When parents and school staff work together to support learning, students are more likely to improve grades and test scores, enroll in college preparatory programs, progress in the curriculum and be promoted annually, earn more credits, attend school more regularly, adapt to their school environment, develop social skills and prosocial behaviors, and graduate from high school and go on to higher education.[6]

### Benefits for School Improvement and Education Reform Efforts

School improvement efforts also benefit from family engagement. A systematic study of school reform in Chicago identified key strategies that help turn schools around.[7] Anthony Bryk and colleagues cite *parent–community ties* as one of the "five essential supports" for a successful school.[8] This study found that in the elementary schools that used effective family engagement practices, students were ten times more likely to improve their math performance and four times more likely to improve their reading performance than students attending elementary schools that did not implement meaningful family engagement practices.[9]

Federal legislation recognizes family engagement as a key element of education reform—with the goal of increasing student achievement, improving schools, and supporting systems change. The Every Student Succeeds Act (ESSA) calls for increased stakeholder engagement. Specifically, ESSA requires schools identified for Comprehensive Support and Improvement or Targeted Support and Improvement to develop and implement their school-level improvement plans in partnership with stakeholders, including families and community members.

## FRAMEWORKS DRIVING WORK IN THIS FIELD

Currently, there are three primary frameworks or sets of standards that states, districts, and schools use to organize their work around family engagement: the PTA's National Standards for Family–School Partnerships; the National Network of Partnership Schools' (NNPS) Six Types of Parent Involvement; and the Dual Capacity-Building Framework for Family–School Partnerships. PTA's National Standards are similar to the NNPS's Six Types of Parent Involvement. Both are based on research and highlight important components of successful family engagement programs, which include welcoming all families into the school, communicating effectively, sharing power, and collaborating with the community. States and districts that adopt one of these sets of standards can simultaneously use the Dual Capacity-Building Framework to keep the opportunity conditions and program goals front and center as they move toward successful implementation. More information on the Dual Capacity-Building Framework can be found in appendix B.

The Dual Capacity-Building Framework is based on research in effective family engagement, partnerships, adult learning, and leadership development. The framework guides states, districts, and schools to address the goals and conditions necessary to establish family engagement efforts that are linked to student achievement and school improvement.[10] The framework's central premise is that to build effective family-school partnerships you need to focus on building capacity for family engagement not only with the parents but also with the school staff, including the principal, teachers, secretaries, cafeteria workers, administrative staff, custodial workers, bus drivers, and even crossing guards—hence the name *dual* capacity-building.

## INNOVATIVE APPROACHES TO FAMILY ENGAGEMENT

Family engagement requires staff to employ differentiated strategies to foster family–school collaboration and provide opportunities for family members to support their child's learning. This can be done through a three-tiered approach (figure 8.1).[11] *Foundational or universal strategies* (welcoming environment, relational trust, two-way communication) are represented in the first tier. The second tier comprises *selective strategies* for families that need additional support (translation, child care, transportation) to get involved. The third tier consists of *intensive strategies* intended to meet families' individualized needs (e.g., safe transportation or care for a family member with disabilities). In this section we describe three innovative approaches to family engagement, each of which can be implemented in this three-tiered manner: home visits, data-informed decision making toward family engagement, and academic parent–teacher teams.

### Home Visits

Home visiting is a powerful universal strategy. Visiting students' homes not only provides teachers with insight into family culture, context, strengths, and needs but can also transform their perspective and help them develop strong bonds and relationships with families. Home visits are also a way to strengthen the cultural competence of staff while supporting the academic and social-emotional needs of students. The Parent Teacher Home Visits

**Figure 8.1** The three-tiered approach

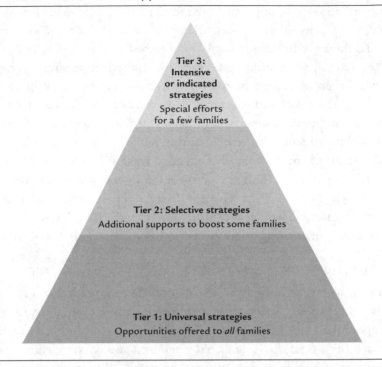

Tier 3:
Intensive
or indicated
strategies
Special efforts
for a few families

**Tier 2: Selective strategies**
Additional supports to boost some families

**Tier 1: Universal strategies**
Opportunities offered to *all* families

*Source:* Trina Osher and Barbara Huff, "Supporting Family Involvement in Correctional Education Programs," July 27, 2006 (webinar for National Technical Assistance Center for the Education of Neglected or Delinquent Children and Youth [NDTAC], Huff Osher Consulting), https://www.neglected-delinquent.org/events/practical -strategies-family-involvement-correctional-education.

project is one example of a home visiting model used across the United States. More information on the Parent Teacher Home Visits project can be found in appendix B.

## Data-Informed Decision Making

Data-informed decision making is an approach that can be used for all students and provides a key opportunity to engage families. Making data accessible and sharing monitoring and evaluation data with families can help family members understand what their schools are doing well and where improvement is needed, as well as involve them in prioritizing actions to improve schools.[12] Understanding school and student data can build family members' self-confidence as decision makers with respect to their child's education, and as advocates for resources and efforts that can support the whole school population.

### Academic Parent–Teacher Teams

Academic Parent–Teacher Teams (APTT) provide an innovative approach that meaningfully engages families using data to help build parents' social capital and relationships with teachers.[13] This process is designed to work in schools that already value family engagement; promote an inclusive, welcoming environment; and respect and honor parents as full partners.

APTT includes scheduling one thirty-minute individual parent–teacher conference, along with three other seventy-five-minute meetings that include all parents in the classroom or grade. The individual thirty-minute conference occurs once per year and is designed to provide personalized support to each student and family. The student, parents, and teacher discuss the child's progress both at home and at school and then collaboratively develop a plan to support student improvement. The seventy-five-minute group meetings are designed to provide parents with information about grade-level expectations and data about student performance. In addition to the individual and group meetings that are core to the APTT process, parents get strategies to support their children's academic success and have opportunities to exchange those strategies with other parents. Parents who participated in APTT reported that the meetings encouraged their involvement in the school and improved their confidence and ability to support their child. Students whose parents participated in APTT performed better compared to students in the same school whose parents did not attend meetings.[14] More information about the APTT model can be found in appendix B.

## FAMILIES AS LEADERS AND DECISION MAKERS

Families and school staff should be equal partners in decisions that affect children and families and jointly inform, influence, and create school policies, practices, and programs. Schools that provide opportunities for shared leadership with families are better able to meet the needs of the school and community.[15] Parent leaders can help schools and districts uncover barriers and issues and acquire valuable insights about family experiences that can guide efforts to meaningfully engage families in school improvement activities. Family perspectives and experience can help contextualize instruction and identify ways to support learning at home, in the community, and at school.

Parent leaders and partners in decision making can participate in advisory committees, parent committees, policy councils, and other governing bodies, as well as community or state coalitions; provide input on academic goals and curricula; and represent children and families in the development of policy and legislation.

Adequate funds, supportive policies, and dedicated staff are key to successfully preparing families and staff for shared decision making. Here are some strategies to leverage funds and resources from multiple programs and funding streams to support family engagement initiatives:

- **Partner with other organizations, funding streams, and departments for staff and resources.** Partner with local community- or faith-based organizations to secure shared space for events, staffing for activities, and resources for family events.
- **Collaborate on funding proposals.** Collaborate with colleagues across agencies—health and human services, juvenile justice—or with community-based organizations to develop funding proposals to local community foundations.
- **Combine federal, state, and private funds.** Match federal funds with state or local funding and those from community- and faith-based sponsorships to fund parent liaisons or other dedicated positions to support this work. (See "Federal Education Funding That Can Support Family Engagement.")

## SUPPORTING STAFF AND FAMILIES

Districts and schools should be intentional about finding concurrent opportunities to build the capacity of staff and families (i.e., dual-capacity preparation) to engage with each other and share responsibility for student and school success. Providing training for staff and families in *collaborative decision making* and facilitation skills (such as brainstorming, role playing, and small-group activities) that encourage everyone to speak openly in a safe environment can be key to sharing power with families, as is training staff in cultural humility. In addition, districts and schools can offer *communication and leadership training* for families and professionals, and design workshops or sessions for families and staff to help them understand *data*

## Federal Education Funding That Can Support Family Engagement

- Title I: Improving the Academic Achievement of the Disadvantaged (http://www.titlei.org/resources)
- Title II: Preparing, Training, and Recruiting High-Quality Teachers, Principals, or Other School Leaders (https://ed.gov/policy/elsec/leg/essa/legislation/title-ii.pdf)
- Title III: Language Instruction for Limited English Proficient and Immigrant Students (https://ncela.ed.gov/files/uploads/5/NCLBTitleIII.pdf)
- Title IV, Part A: Student Support and Academic Enrichment (https://safesupportivelearning.ed.gov/resources/essa-title-iv-part-A-SSAE-non-regulatory-guidance-webinar-series)
- Individuals with Disabilities Education Act (https://sites.ed.gov/idea/?src=policy-page)
- Migrant Education Program (https://www2.ed.gov/programs/mep/index.html)
- Fostering Connections to Success and Increasing Adoptions Act (https://www2.ed.gov/about/inits/ed/foster-care/index.html)
- McKinney-Vento Homeless Education Assistance Improvements Act (https://nche.ed.gov/index.php)
- 21st Century Community Learning Centers Afterschool Grants
- Early childhood programs such as Head Start, Early Head Start, and Even Start

*systems, tools, and school/student data.* Finally, it is also important to encourage and provide *opportunities for parent-to-parent and parent–staff networking.* Consider the following key strategies to support the dual-capacity preparation of staff and families as they begin to implement or refine their practices for shared decision making.

## Collaborative Decision-Making Strategies

Collaborative decision making involves helping participants find mutual ground in their conversations rather than focusing on differences. Ways to encourage collaborative decision making include creating teams that are small yet inclusive of all family and community stakeholder groups, and reassuring families that their voices count, they're being heard, and they will not be punished for speaking up. As a starting point, hold small focus groups with staff and families to elicit ideas and bring concerns to the surface. Staff and families can practice consensus decision-making strategies where:

- all members contribute to the discussion;
- everyone's opinion is encouraged and considered;
- differences in opinion are viewed as helpful insights rather than hindrances;
- members who disagree are willing to try alternate strategies; and
- all members share in the final decision.

## Communication Strategies

Districts and schools should use everyday language to increase communication and sharing among stakeholders, and provide visuals (charts and infographics) to help participants understand, explore, and analyze important issues. Training everyone involved to use communication strategies like the following, which promote shared understanding and encourage everyone to have a voice, lays the groundwork for strong partnerships and collaborative decision making:

- Share information in a family-friendly context.
- Use graphics, videos, and recordings.
- Avoid jargon and pejorative language.
- Focus on big-picture ideas that matter.
- Provide guiding handouts that promote group discussion.
- Use targeted questions, moving from broad topics to more specific details.

## Leadership Strategies

Having parents and teachers attend professional development sessions together to learn about collaborative leadership, consensus decision-making, and communication strategies is a key step in preparing for shared leadership and incorporating family voice. Other strategies for developing parent leaders and building shared leadership include the following:

- Involve families in research projects, such as conducting surveys of other families, to ensure that assessments of assets and problems are informed by the perspective and knowledge of families.

- Take families on trips to visit district offices and meet district administrators.
- Encourage families to attend school board meetings. Offer to accompany them as mentors or coaches until they feel comfortable in this setting.
- Host meetings with local officials, such as school board members and other community leaders, so that families can learn about resources and issues in the community.
- Include parent and community members on staff selection committees.
- Hold a series of parent leadership academies or other parent university classes with a focus on leadership. Develop a curriculum, and start with a small group of parents selected to be representative of the school's population.
- Hire parents to become advocates for other families and students.

## Strategies for Understanding Data Systems, Tools, and School/Student Data

Empowering families to understand the US education system, monitor their student's progress, and review data to support student and school success contributes to strong family–school partnerships and prepares families to engage in shared decision making. Schools and districts should consider designing training for families and staff to help them better understand data systems, tools, and school/student data. As mentioned earlier in the chapter, sharing this data can help parents feel more confident collaborating with staff to address achievement gaps, improve teaching and learning, and motivate students. Specific strategies for doing this include the following:

- Create parent classes and academies to help parents learn about district priorities, learning standards, and key issues in public education, and how to review and understand data to assess where schools are doing well and where improvement is needed.
- Provide training in small-group settings, host training in both school and community venues, and engage parent ambassadors who can recruit and encourage other families to attend and participate.
- Explain standards and milestones, attendance requirements, and graduation and credit requirements.
- Provide families with useful and useable information on evidence-based programs and strategies.

## Networking Strategies

Promoting networking and establishing social networks can support parent empowerment and increase the social capital of both families and staff. Providing opportunities like the following for parent-to-parent and parent–staff networking prepares individuals to engage, collaborate, and participate in shared decision making:

- Provide opportunities for families to share their stories and get to know each other in settings where they feel safe and supported.
- Create opportunities for parent-led meetings and discussions, such as Parent Cafés, both at school and in other settings around the community.
- Encourage staff to engage in conversations with parents in nonacademic contexts, such as during school athletic events, pick-up and drop-off times, and brown bag lunches at the library or community parks.

Involving families in decision making and sharing power with families to drive continuous improvement can be a big culture shift for schools and districts. The key to success is making sure that practitioners get training and ongoing support to embrace family engagement as an overall value, recognize the strengths families bring to their partnership with school personnel, and develop their own skills and capacity to fully participate in this new relationship.

## TAKEAWAYS

- Family engagement can enhance learning and school improvement.
- Family engagement can be realized through a culturally responsive, three-tiered approach.
- Partnering with families requires an attitudinal and behavioral shift from professionally driven approaches to culturally competent, family-driven approaches.
- Family-driven approaches and systems incorporate family voice and choice as key influences in decision making.
- There are several frameworks for effective family engagement, as well as strategies to help build effective partnerships, in the areas of collaborative decision making, communication, leadership, using data and tools, and networking.

# NINE

# Partnering with Communities

*Vanessa Coleman and David Osher*

SCHOOLS EXIST WITHIN the broader neighborhood and community of a village, town, city, or region, made up of a combination of systems, cultures, neighborhoods, and resources. As educators work to make their schools safe, supportive, and equitable with excellence, they need to engage the broader community to ensure that the changes have deep roots and are responsive to and sustainable for the community.[1] This chapter addresses the importance of working with communities, the nature of community, principles for working with communities, and building readiness for and securing community engagement. We go into further detail on how to involve community partners in creating an agenda and vision for change, as previewed in part I of this book, and specifically, how community partners can work with schools to:

- coordinate services to efficiently and effectively provide needed student supports;[2]
- support family engagement;
- improve school climate survey response rates, share results, and get input on what the data mean and what can be done to improve school climate;

- identify and address community-based challenges to learning;
- provide and develop resources; and
- expand learning opportunities.

## DEFINING COMMUNITY

Community is more than colocation. Communities of affiliation involve interdependence and feelings and relationships among people.[3] (See "Community Is More Than Location" for a specific example.) Members of such communities have "a sense of trust, belonging, safety, and caring for each other. They have an individual and collective sense that they can, as part of the community, influence their environments and each other."[4] We start with this definition because it moves us beyond location and acknowledges both the aspirational goals that people bring to a place and the sense of connection that emerges—these aspirational goals are often understated, particularly for communities where individuals struggle with discrimination and disadvantage. Community connections can build social capital and collective resilience, allowing community members to "flock together," nurture each other, and not feel they must (to use Robert Putnam's metaphor) "bowl alone."[5]

Each community has a complex makeup of intricate systems, cultures, informal and formal networks, and resources. Community resources include both community-based organizations and public agencies. Tackling complex problems in communities depends upon change within and across institutions and local systems, and among the individuals working and living within them.

Schools exist within communities, and are community assets. When a community is engaged in schooling, the entire school (including students

---

### Community Is More Than Location

While Southeast Alaska is a region spanning 35,138 square miles, it is also a community that has been tied together for generations through complex family lines, economics, waterways, and ways of life. The Sealaska Heritage Institute (http://www.sealaskaheritage.org/node/781) supports a biennial celebration bringing together families, clans, and the Tlingit, Haida, and Tsimshian tribes from across Southeast Alaska to celebrate song, dance, language survival, and other cultural contributions.

and teachers) has expanded access to the resources offered by the community. The community also has an opportunity to deepen its investment in youth outcomes, facilitated by learning from and leveraging community engagement strategies. Engagement should go beyond tokenism and be community driven, and ideally it should involve a shift from sporadic or selective outreach efforts to shared leadership (as illustrated in figure 9.1).

## PRINCIPLES AND PROCESS FOR COLLABORATING WITH COMMUNITIES

This section describes a six-part process (shown in figure 9.2) for collaboratively working with communities to create safe, supportive, and equitable schools. First, however, here are some guiding principles to keep in mind throughout the community engagement process:

- All perspectives matter.
- Assumptions and values should be explicit.
- Inclusion is complex and not always easy to implement.
- Broadened definitions of knowledge and data are necessary.
- Community is complex and diverse.
- Culture matters.

### Getting Ready for Community Engagement

Broad and inclusive change processes are strengthened when implementers plan and understand the current climate for collaboration and change. We can employ the readiness framework described in chapter 1 to mitigate barriers to community engagement. Common challenges include motivating community stakeholders and groups to collaborate with each other and

**Figure 9.1** Moving toward shared leadership

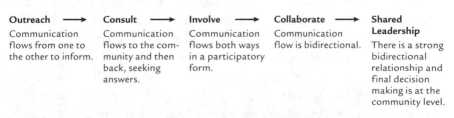

| Outreach → | Consult → | Involve → | Collaborate → | Shared Leadership |
|---|---|---|---|---|
| Communication flows from one to the other to inform. | Communication flows to the community and then back, seeking answers. | Communication flows both ways in a participatory form. | Communication flow is bidirectional. | There is a strong bidirectional relationship and final decision making is at the community level. |

**Figure 9.2**  Working with communities to create safe, supportive, and equitable schools: A six-part process

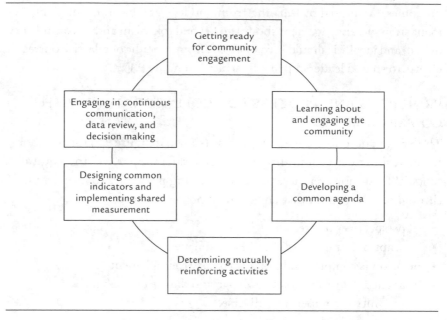

schools (e.g., they might view doing so as "giving up turf"), ensuring the capacity for collaboration (e.g., common indicators, aligned time tables) and school-specific capacities (e.g., understanding schools), and ensuring general organizational capacity.[6] Here are a few key questions to consider before you launch a concerted effort to expand community engagement in your school or district:

- **Is there shared information and concern about the conditions and outcomes that are the target of change?** Launching a communication campaign to present the issues could be the catalyst for creating a level playing field where all stakeholders have the same information and some common understanding of the challenge.
- **What is the local readiness for broad and inclusive collaboration with the community?** Collecting information about perceptions of partners and of past and current change efforts will provide insights that can be used to heighten awareness and empathy for historical experiences.
- **Are there existing broad and inclusive collaborations in place?** Surveying the landscape to determine if there are existing collaborative change

efforts might provide an opportunity to consider potential leverage points.

- **Will we be able to develop shared goals and objectives?** What must be done to create the conditions in which that can occur?
- **Can we support the development of a broad base of local leaders?** Can we support, without controlling or undermining community involvement, ways to continually renew or circulate leadership over time?[7]

## Learning About and Engaging the Community

You may have already been working with the community or you may just be starting. Either way, you should not assume that you sufficiently know the community or what/who makes up that community. You'll need to learn more about the community in a manner that addresses and acknowledges the different types of neighborhoods and circumstances that exist within and across it.

Start with current community partners, but also address who is not at the table, considering both diverse communities and the partners who will have the necessary power, influence, or resources. Schools are often well positioned to convene a broad cross-section of the community. Gather current partners and parallel systems of support (e.g., public health, transportation, families, food sources, neighbors, the public). Although your current partners are leverageable assets, they (like all of us) bring their own tunnel vision and interests. The best time to invite new partners is at the beginning. You may not succeed on your first try, but if you act with interpersonal and cultural competence, you can show respect and learn about a group that is not yet involved.

Once the partners have been identified and convened, launch the partnership with a presentation of how you want to work together. This provides an opportunity to communicate your hopes for their participation, and establish expectations for how you will collaborate. Your first meeting will set the tone for authentic collaboration, where each individual and organization/group understands their responsibility to and respect for unique voices, knowledge, skills, beliefs, and cultures. Consider the following tone-setting tips:

- **Introduce the way you hope to work together.** Outline each component of the work and the anticipated milestone for each component. Indicate partnership roles in realizing the agenda.
- **Share expectations and benefits of collaboration.** Gather, report out, and discuss different perspectives.

- **Collaborate to adopt decision-making protocols early.** Consider various options (e.g., modified consensus, ranking, and charting) to ensure that all perspectives can be considered in the decision-making process.
- **Develop culturally responsive and respectful communication practices.** Create inclusive terminology.
- **Adopt guiding rules of engagement (e.g., listen for understanding; critique ideas, not people; articulate hidden assumptions).** Post rules at every meeting.

With the groundwork laid and a shared understanding about how you will collaborate, work with your community partners to implement participatory *asset-based community development*, a type of asset mapping led by community members as they build upon their knowledge about the community (see "Asset-Based Community Development"). A thoughtful and inclusive asset mapping process can provide insights into a range of "local resources," including people, spaces, and materials. Participatory asset mapping offers many benefits, including: helping partners define the community spatially; reducing gaps in perspective and participation; providing reference information throughout the implementation process; presenting an early opportunity to share influence and engage the broader community in implementation; and providing a shared understanding about the community's capacity for specific changes.[8]

## Developing a Common Agenda for Change

To develop a common agenda, the partners will need to understand the relevant community needs. Doing so requires collaborative data reviews and

---

### Asset-Based Community Development

*Asset-based community development* (ABCD) is a useful tool for identifying the robust resources in communities. Its premise is that the community already possesses what is needed to lead and implement change, and it aims to help you understand and leverage those assets. ABCD offers a practical strategy for getting to know a place from the inside. The Advancement Project provides a toolkit to guide the application of ABCD, which can be found in appendix B.[9]

root-cause analyses of a range of data at multiple levels of the community—individual, organizational, and systemic. The collaborators should:

- collect data from all sources (surveys, focus groups, interviews) to understand community concerns and needs;
- select data and sources to describe relevant situations (consider using storytelling as a way to share data and bring it to life for the community);
- identify findings from each data source (representing broad community perspectives);
- note recurring topics;
- conduct a root-cause analysis for selected topics and themes;
- zero in on the root causes and systemic factors that affect community concerns;[10]
- list themes and prioritize key findings; and
- align findings to individual and organizational behaviors and activities.

Once you've shared data and collected feedback about the root causes of the challenges that children and schools face, you can begin the collective creation of the agenda and vision for change, guided by some version of the question, *How might we create a safe, supportive, and equitable school where children can thrive and excel academically?* Make the "agenda" time-specific and measurable, and define the target populations.

### Setting goals and objectives for collaboration targets at a community level

Now that you've clarified the issues and challenges, the collaboration should answer the following questions to develop targets to realize the agenda:

- What are the goals and objectives of the collaboration?
- What are the strategic targets for collective action?
- What would success look like? How will [community members, students, families, school, local agencies] be changed by this initiative?
- How will the community know if an intervention(s) is successful? (goals)
- What will change, and by how much? (objectives)

Because this effort seeks to create change across a broad set of community-based organizations, each organization should step away from the collaboration to consider the same questions for their specific clients and target audiences.

## Determining Mutually Reinforcing Activities

The process of aligning activities (for each partner) to the goals and objectives is an important phase of community-centered change. During this phase, each partner should respond to the following question: How will you leverage your resources to support the desired change? The collective-impact approach to change encourages each individual and organization in a community to join a change strategy using their unique perspectives and assets. This step in community-centered change rests on buy-in and shared accountability.

Features of mutually reinforcing activities include:

- building upon existing efforts and discouraging duplication;
- supporting and leveraging each other's efforts;
- distributing activities to take advantage of existing skills, passion, and expertise;
- using data as the basis for a learning system focused on the continuous improvement of the participating organizations' practices;
- using data to help determine which innovation should be scaled and which should be stopped;
- developing common indicators; and
- engaging the broader community in supporting activities (which can be tracked over time).

In this phase of the work, reflect on the asset-based mapping activity you completed at the start of the collaboration. Consider ways in which each organization can find opportunities to contribute. These include types of services, capacity to implement particular strategies (e.g., engaging particular groups of family members), skills, and resources. It is also important to assess how feasible the objectives are given the participating partners at the table. Also, consider using an innovation design strategy to help organize stakeholders around the collaboration and leverage their creativity.[11] Facilitated brainstorming sessions might yield new activities that directly address challenges and assets.

## Designing Common Indicators and Implementing Shared Measurement

Once the activities, goals, and objectives have been established, the collaborators can focus on aligning indicators and measurement at the individual and organizational levels. Shared measurement (i.e., a set of agreed-upon metrics to be used to track and focus progress) makes it easy to: improve the richness of the data, track progress toward the agenda targets, support ongoing coordination and collaboration, support accountability for both individual organizations and the collective group, and make course corrections.[12]

To ensure sustainable shared measurement, you should first identify your common goals and the performance indicators related to moving toward or realizing these goals. Identifying common indicators, such as a reduction in chronic absenteeism or an increase in college enrollment, can help ensure collective investment in continuous quality improvement as well as the braiding of funding.[13]

Sometimes community collaboration can be facilitated by third parties, but they should not own the process. Say Yes to Education's work in the Buffalo Public Schools district exemplifies how a third-party facilitator can supportively—not authoritatively—help school systems and communities align around common goals, indicators, and activities to bring about positive, sustainable change for students. (See "Facilitating a Community Partnership in Buffalo.")

Once you have common indicators, develop outputs and outcomes for the collaboration. These should be defined in terms of size, scope, and time. To determine your outputs and outcomes, use a *logic modeling* process, which helps you make your theory of change explicit by specifying the strategies that will help you realize your particular targets, such as the reduction of chronic absenteeism. By developing multiple logic models—one at each level of change and focused on the common challenges and agenda—you create a road map for the change. The outputs will lead to desired outcomes. *Outputs* should be represented in quantifiable and descriptive terms (i.e., numbers and detailed activities). *Outcomes* describe the intended change you seek.

The Logic Model Workbook offers some direction about developing outcomes, namely that they should: "represent the results or impacts that occur because of program activities and services; be within the scope of the program's control or sphere of reasonable influence; be generally accepted as valid by various stakeholders of the program [at each level of change]; be phrased in terms of change; and be measurable."[14]

## Engaging in Continuous Communication, Data Review, and Decision Making

While your change effort begins with broad and targeted communication, you also need to maintain this practice throughout the process. Designing a

## Facilitating a Community Partnership in Buffalo

With support from families, funders, agencies, and the school district, Buffalo city officials reached out to Say Yes to Education, an operating foundation that works with cities and counties to design, implement, and improve efforts to promote the success, growth, and postsecondary attainment of all students. Say Yes works with communities committed to collaborating across sectors, including families and the faith community, with the goals of improving postsecondary readiness for success for all students, increasing resource utilization, and using a data-informed approach to examine student- and school-level outcomes.

"Say Yes doesn't come in and take over," says Say Yes Chief Operating Officer Gene Chasin, who believes that this supportive, rather than authoritative, approach is key to its success. "Typically, new programs or initiatives are dependent on leadership, and those initiatives and programs tend to end when the leadership leaves. Say Yes places great emphasis on sustainability, which is built around community ownership. The programs in Buffalo and Syracuse that we helped build are now completely sustained by community partners."

Say Yes helps community organizations learn how to work together, without competing. Each organization performs asset mapping so that services are not duplicated and unmet needs are identified. The partners also sign memoranda of understanding and data-sharing agreements, as well as completing equity analyses to identify and address institutional racism. The partners explore the ways in which institutionalized racism can be addressed in rolling out services.

Once agreements are in place, the partners analyze data and choose three to four priority focus areas, around which they form task forces. Say Yes helps with root-cause analysis and then customizes a planning system based on community strengths and needs. Only then do partners begin to choose and implement programming and assemble a governance team.

This approach has brought great success. The community raises and endows the funding for scholarships to in-state public colleges and provides postsecondary scholarships to two- and four-year state institutions for every eligible graduating student in the Buffalo Public Schools. Buffalo has seen significant increases in high school graduation and college enrollment rates (with notable increases among African American students), and significant reductions in the utilization of health and human services and the number of students placed in foster care.

process that builds in regular engagement, with a consistent focus on progress toward common indicators and making choices about how to proceed, is key to the success of the collaborators' work. Ongoing engagement should solicit feedback about experience and progress; consider if changes have adverse effects; work to maintain and build the collaborative relationships; and continue to reach out to and engage new segments of the community. (Remember, communities are complex and possess multiple cultures and resources.)

## PUTTING IT ALL TOGETHER: A "PARTNERSHIP MARRIAGE" IN SAGINAW

The Saginaw Public Schools take a strategic approach to engaging with families, students, and staff from over forty-five community organizations in what they call a "partnership marriage," developed by the district's family engagement leader. The district conducted an environmental scan to see what engagement activities were already in place and created a logic model spelling out engagement goals and activities to achieve those goals. Today, every school in the district has a school action team for family engagement, as well as a community engagement and action team that includes parents, community partners, administrators, staff, and students. These stakeholders meet on a regular basis to have an equal voice in districtwide decision-making processes and school policy.

"All administrators and staff in Saginaw are part of the engagement work," explains Tiffany Pruitt, family and community engagement specialist for the Saginaw Public Schools.

> Our biggest focus is positive relationship building and authentic family partnerships. We include everyone and share responsibility so nobody carries the heavy load. The focus is on the whole child and making sure our schools are safe and students are healthy. We make decisions based on data and feedback we get from students and parents on what their needs are. We make it clear that everybody has a role and every role is important. We are trying to be as intentional as possible in including families and making sure they have input on school improvement, academic goals, and climate and culture goals.

The district's approach includes student voices in efforts to improve school climate. For example, student advisory councils at the two high schools' youth health centers promote positive behavior and social-emotional supports. Students in Saginaw also participate in focus groups, forums, and advisory boards to give input on what programming and services they would like to see in their schools.

Pruitt says students are eager to participate because they feel a sense of belonging and ownership in the programming they inform, rather than feeling that initiatives are pushed on them. With grant funding, Saginaw provides small incentives for students who participate in these activities. Pruitt says, "Students and their families may come to events and activities because they hear we give incentives, but they come back because they want to be part of these ongoing activities that have made a connection with them. Integrating youth voices into these typically adult-only activities means that they are now youth-led and youth-guided."

Saginaw recognizes that a true partnership marriage features communication as a two-way street. Pruitt and her staff share data about academics and social-emotional programming with students, families, and community members and collaborate with them to problem-solve.

Partnering with community agencies allows the district to provide resources that reach all members in its partnership marriage. For example, the district works in conjunction with community agencies to provide free training to parents on topics such as trauma, social and emotional learning, and restorative practices. The school system has even leveraged community resources to create a train-the-trainer model in which families train other families in these topics. As a result, the district has parent liaisons in most of its schools. Additionally, the local mental health authority trains school staff and other partners in cultural competency, a key element that guides all the interactions in schools and with partners.

"Anything that happens in our schools, we make sure also happens in the community," Pruitt states. "We are focusing on putting systems in place where everybody is a leader. Family engagement means we are moving toward making sure children are successful, that this is a safe place to live, and that people want to be in our schools and communities. Everyone understands that 'family engagement' is not just educational jargon because we are really invested in our work with families. We are no longer working in silos. We all have one thing in common—children being successful."

TAKEAWAYS
- Community engagement and collaboration with the community is important.
- Each community has a complex makeup of intricate systems, cultures, informal and formal networks, and resources.
- Employ participatory asset-based community development.
- It is important to develop a common agenda for change, build and sustain community engagement, design common indicators, and implement shared measurement.

# TEN

# Out-of-School Time Programs

*Deborah Moroney, Jessica Newman, and David Osher*

LEARNING AND DEVELOPMENT occur 24/7 in the home, in the community, and in schools. While other chapters focus on in-school efforts, this chapter focuses on what happens outside of the school day—specifically, the role of high-quality out-of-school time (OST) programs as a universal intervention to promote children's academic success and social-emotional well-being. We use "OST" throughout the chapter as an umbrella term for programming before and after the school day, and for components of the community school model that also extend into these hours, unless a different term is specified by the research or organization we are discussing. OST programming varies based on *when* the program is offered (before school, after school, during an expanded day, or during the summer); *where* the program is offered (at the school, through a community-based organization, in a camp/residential setting, or through an academic or cultural institution); *what* the program is focused on (e.g., English language arts, or ELA; science, technology, engineering, and math, or STEM disciplines; the arts; health and wellness; youth leadership; community service; tutoring and homework help); and *how* the program designs activities (e.g., youth development, academic enrichment, support services, apprenticeships). The community school model brings in programming from the community and centers it in the school building. Programming can happen before, after, or during school, and it often includes meals, supports for families, and health services.[1] In sum, OST programming can be standalone in the school or community, or it can be coordinated through a community school approach. Regardless of the approach, OST programs are effective when offered in partnership with the local community.

Although there is no "one size fits all" approach to OST programming, there are research- and evidence-based practices that have been field-tested. These practices are more likely to yield positive outcomes for youth, schools, families, and the community (when they align with local contexts) than isolated or "canned" programs. This chapter describes the critical elements of effective OST programs and illustrates the potential benefits that result from effective programming. We highlight recent research on quality practices in OST programming; the critical voices of families, schools, and communities in OST programming; and the importance of adopting a strengths-based approach to programming. A strengths-based approach acknowledges and elevates the assets or resources that participants and their families bring to programs and aims to build upon those strengths, rather than focusing on participants' deficits or challenges. This is an important distinction of promotion- or strengths-based approaches that represents a move away from a risk or prevention mentality.

## THE BENEFITS OF HIGH-QUALITY OST PROGRAMMING

Research demonstrates that high-quality OST programs that engage in strengths-based programming through collaborative partnerships with schools and communities are more likely to benefit children's academic success and social-emotional well-being.[2] A 2007 meta-analysis of seventy-three afterschool programs shows that these programs have positive effects, particularly when they offer high-quality, skill-focused experiences over multiple sessions.[3] This stands in stark contrast to programs with short-term activities (i.e., individual sessions), unstructured programs, and programs that do not have an intentional focus on skill building. The amount of youth participation is also important: higher levels of afterschool program attendance are more likely to result in positive youth outcomes, such as increased prosocial behavior, attendance during the school day, and academic achievement.[4] Community schools also produce promising results: students who attend community schools show gains in math, reading, and graduation rates, as well as improved school-day attendance, compared to their nonattending peers.[5]

## CHARACTERISTICS OF EFFECTIVE AND HIGH-QUALITY OST PROGRAMS

All OST programs should welcome all youth, not just those identified for services or support (i.e., are universal). Decades of research, evaluation, and fieldwork have produced information that outlines seven components of effective and high-quality OST programming—namely, that effective programs:

- build on youth, family, and community assets (i.e., are culturally responsive);
- foster strong partnerships among community organizations, services, and schools;
- focus on youth development and create a warm and welcoming environment;
- support skill building;
- provide authentic opportunities for youth voice, choice, and leadership;
- build staff capacity through ongoing professional development and support; and
- strive for continuous improvement.

The following sections describe each of these components of high-quality practice and highlight strategies and practices for implementation.

### Building on Collective Assets

Strengths-based programs view participants, their families, and their community as a resource, emphasizing what they bring to the table and finding ways to support and build on their assets. This is the opposite of a deficits-based approach, which focuses on problems to be solved or needs to be met. Strengths-based programs focus not only on the strengths that individuals bring to the program, but also on the strengths and resources of the school and community. Community assets include cultural resources, such as local artists, and access to meaningful opportunities for service learning and mentoring.

There are many ways to support a strengths-based and assets-focused approach. One way to identify school or community assets is through asset mapping, which we described in the previous chapter.[6] Youth-driven asset mapping results in a shared (and for adults, deepened) understanding of local resources, including people, spaces, and materials. Another strategy is to identify the strengths and areas of expertise of youth and program staff and engage them as a resource above and beyond their specific program roles. For example, staff can support professional development by lending their expertise on relevant topics. Similarly, older youth can mentor younger youth in areas where the older youth are skilled.

## Fostering Strong Partnerships

OST programs build on local partnerships with schools, community- and faith-based organizations, families, and community members. These partnerships are fostered in a variety of formal and informal ways. Formal partnerships occur through memoranda of understanding between the school, local community-based organizations, and the OST program; through family and community advisory boards; via programming that includes families and communities, such as services or classes geared toward adults hosted in the OST program; and through employment opportunities within the program. Informal mechanisms for partnering with families and communities leverage opportunities such as health fairs and community forums. Informal and formal partnerships support a program's efforts to reflect community assets and contribute meaningfully to the community.

### Partnering with schools

Partnerships between OST programs and schools involve aligned goals, ongoing communication, and shared resources, from physical space to youth-related data. These are mutually beneficial relationships wherein the program and school work together to expand and provide greater continuity of learning opportunities for youth. These benefits are stronger when the school and program align in complementary ways to help youth make a deeper connection to learning. For more on these types of partnerships, see "Establishing School–OST Partnerships."

### Partnering with families

There are multiple avenues for engaging families in OST, including providing opportunities for family members to learn more about what occurs during the school day and OST program; enabling them to contribute to program-

## Establishing School–OST Partnerships

Partnerships should be mutually beneficial. OST programs can enable schools to offer a more diverse set of activities and experiences, a new learning environment, and access to new people. Schools can support programs in accessing resources such as space, materials, and program participants, and they can ensure continuity between what happens during the school day and what happens out of school. You can enable this type of partnership from either side by taking the following steps:

- **Create a line of open communication.** Reach out to the school principal or program director by email, phone, or in person, and ask to set up a time to discuss potential partnership opportunities.
- **Meet to discuss your vision, goals, and current plan.** Find areas that may align or complement each other. How can you work together to support mutual goals?
- **Establish a memorandum of understanding.** This document outlines each partner's expectations, responsibilities, and resource commitments.
- **Establish a communication plan.** Who will communicate with whom, when, and how?
- **Revisit your goals and vision for the partnership regularly.** Review your plan on a regular basis, and modify it as needed.

ming by volunteering, teaching, mentoring, or sharing knowledge; and offering them support services, such as classes, counseling, or recreation activities. It is important to bear in mind that levels of family engagement vary, and that each family has their own reasons for how and why they engage (or do not). To better understand families' needs and the best methods for engaging with them, ask them. Even better, work with families to find out the interests and needs of other families. You can employ a multitiered approach to family-driven practices and employ differentiated strategies that will enable all family members to support their child's learning. You can build a foundation for engagement through respectful, informal communication during program drop-off and pick-up, by distributing a short and easy-to-complete survey (such as the *Beyond the Bell* Family Engagement and Interest Survey), or by hosting family events and soliciting feedback.[7]

## Partnering with the community

When OST programs reflect community assets and resources, they engage in a bidirectional partnership: the community provides resources to the program, and the program provides resources to the community. Authentic partnerships reflect the cultures in the community and draw upon community resources to foster cultural competence and responsiveness. For example, programs may be offered by or in partnership with community-based organizations that bring in professionals from the community for programming or events. Alternatively, programs may offer a neutral and friendly space for community members to engage in activities or receive support services, such as mental health counseling, food assistance, or adult education. OST programs often serve as a hub for family and community involvement in the school.

In the *community school* model, the school offers resources to the community—including students—in the school. Common examples of services and supports include health clinics, dental screenings, and child care. Community schools foster partnerships with local organizations to ensure families have access to essential services and enrichment for both children and families. (See "What Is a Community School?" for more about how this model operates.)

Using public schools as hubs, community schools bring together many partners to offer a range of supports and opportunities to children, youth, families, and communities. Partners work to achieve the following results: children are ready to enter school; students attend school consistently; students are actively involved in learning and their community; families are increasingly involved with their children's education; schools are engaged with families and com-

---

### What Is a Community School?

A community school is both a place and a set of partnerships between the school and other community resources. Its integrated focus on academics, health and social services, youth and community development, and community engagement leads to improved student learning, stronger families, and healthier communities. Community schools offer a personalized approach that emphasizes real-world learning and community problem solving. Schools become centers of the community and are open to everyone—all day, every day, evenings and weekends.

munities; students succeed academically; students are healthy—physically, socially, and emotionally; students live and learn in a safe, supportive, and stable environment; and communities are desirable places to live.[8]

## Focusing On Youth Development and Creating a Warm and Welcoming Environment

Effective programs are often underpinned by positive youth development approaches. These programs are intentionally warm and welcoming, support relationship development, and offer skill-building activities that are hands-on, interactive, and promote youth voice, choice, and leadership. Program staff can use the *Beyond the Bell* Youth Development Checklist to gauge how well their initiative aligns with youth development principles, and to identify areas for improved youth development practices.[9] A quality assessment observation tool may also be useful.[10]

Relationships that youth form in OST programs influence their life trajectory.[11] The Search Institute offers a framework and tools to help programs and initiatives foster strong developmental relationships that express care, challenge growth, provide support, share power, and expand possibilities.[12]

Quality OST programs are *intentionally* warm and welcoming, and this can also be measured.[13] (See "A Note on Intentionality.") Staff members know participants' names and ensure that participants' contribution is evident in the program space, that participants have a sense of ownership and belonging, and that there is sufficient safe space and materials.

Program staff should engage youth in making the space their own by allowing them to decorate, and to help determine where and how activities take place. Formal strategies for relationship building include group tasks, team-building activities, traditional and peer mentoring, and youth-

### A Note on Intentionality

Effective programs are purposeful in the development and implementation of their efforts. They demonstrate intentionality in many ways—through the allocation of resources, the hiring of qualified staff, and the design and implementation of program activities.[14] High-quality programming does not happen by accident; it takes quite a bit of forethought and planning.

led service projects. Programs should also leave time and space for informal interactions that allow relationships to develop for youth and staff. This can be facilitated through open choice time, with access to resources (e.g., games) and events that foster relationship building. Ideally, programs should also offer youth opportunities to lead, engage actively in exploring their interests and learning, and build new skills and competencies.

## Supporting Skill Building and Competency Development

OST programs may focus on building a variety of skills, such as social-emotional, academic-related (e.g., time management), and content-based skills. Programming to promote skill building must be intentional and "SAFE" (sequenced, active, focused, and explicit).[15] Skill-building activities must build on one another, so that learning is scaffolded and supported by prior knowledge. Learning should be active, and the content should be focused (i.e., staff have devoted time to building skills) and explicit (i.e., staff are clear about the skill building and goals they hope to achieve). Examples of effective skill-building programs include WINGS for Kids, which offers a successful curriculum that immerses younger children in skill building, and Say Yes to Education, which employs embedded strategies to help older youth build skills that will support college and career success.[16]

There are tools available to help practitioners and educators improve skill-building practices that support social and emotional learning (SEL). *Beyond the Bell* has released *Social and Emotional Learning Practices: A Self-Reflection Tool for Afterschool Staff*, and the Partnership for Children and Youth offers assessment tools to help practitioners gauge their SEL practice.[17]

## Providing Authentic Opportunities for Youth Voice, Choice, and Leadership

OST programs differ from school-day programs because their goals typically emphasize youth agency and leadership in determining their own interests and trajectory. Programs should allow youth to choose activity topics and materials, have a say in program design and implementation, and lead and participate in activities designed by others.

### Youth voice and choice

There are many methods for engaging young people in activities while ensuring that they have developmentally appropriate and authentic opportunities to share their voice and make decisions, both of which are critical to promoting youth engagement and skill development. Staff can ensure that activities allow youth to engage with each other, through both informal discussion and intentional sharing and reflection. Many programs encourage choice and decision making at different levels—for example, by allowing youth to select the day's activities or ensuring authentic opportunities for decision making within activities. It is important, however, to ensure that choice remains developmentally appropriate.

### Youth leadership

Leadership opportunities provide a space for youth to collaborate, discuss, serve, create cultural products, and address significant issues, such as problems in the community, political issues, or environmental actions.[18] The driving components of youth leadership program models include decision making, reasoning, and critical thinking skills.[19] Research shows that impactful youth leadership opportunities include facilitating youth–adult partnerships; granting young people decision-making power and holding them accountable for consequences; providing a broad context for learning and service; and recognizing young people's experience, knowledge, and skills.[20] For example, the New York City Department of Youth and Community Development (DYCD) created a framework for youth leadership development that is used across their youth-serving systems (see figure 10.1). To support implementation of leadership development practices, DYCD created tools and resources for staff, including a self-reflection tool on youth leadership development practices and an aligned glossary. DYCD's Promote the Positive initiative intentionally emphasizes the connection between youth development, SEL, and youth leadership.

### Supporting Staff Development

A supportive relationship between staff and youth in OST programs is key for youth to experience program benefits.[21] Essential features of these relationships include shared norms, high expectations, stability and continuity, and connectedness to each other's lives.[22] Ample time should be provided for staff to learn from the field and from each other, and to reflect on their own practice, if they are to be successful in implementing a high-quality program. The National AfterSchool Association (NAA) has developed *Core Knowledge and Competencies for Afterschool and Youth Development Professionals* to "describe

**Figure 10.1** DYCD framework for youth leadership development

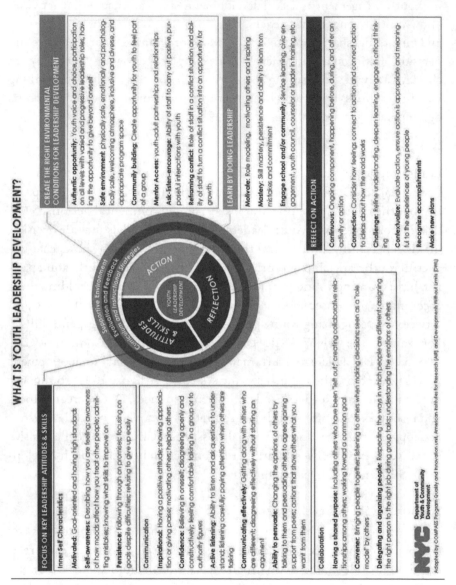

WHAT IS YOUTH LEADERSHIP DEVELOPMENT?

CREATE THE RIGHT ENVIRONMENTAL
CONDITIONS FOR LEADERSHIP DEVELOPMENT

**Authentic opportunity:** Youth voice and choice, participation on all levels with varied and progressive leadership roles, however the opportunity to give beyond oneself

**Safe environment:** physically safe, emotionally and psychologically safe, welcoming atmosphere, inclusive and diverse, and appropriate program space

**Community building:** Create opportunity for youth to feel part of a group

**Mentor Access:** youth-adult partnerships and relationships

**Ask-listen-encourage:** Ability of staff to carry out positive, purposeful interactions with youth

**Reframing conflict:** Role of staff in a conflict situation and ability of staff to turn a conflict situation into an opportunity for growth

LEARN BY DOING LEADERSHIP

**Motivate:** Role modeling, motivating others and inspiring

**Mastery:** Skill mastery, persistence and ability to learn from mistakes and commitment

**Engage school and/or community:** Service learning, civic engagement, youth council, counselor or leader in training, etc.

REFLECT ON ACTION

**Continuous:** Ongoing component, happening before, during, and after an activity or action

**Connection:** Consider how feelings connect to action and connect action to ideas about how the world works

**Challenge:** Refine understanding, deepen learning, engage in critical thinking

**Contextualize:** Evaluate action, ensure action is appropriate and meaningful to the experiences of young people

Recognize accomplishments

Make new plans

FOCUS ON KEY LEADERSHIP ATTITUDES & SKILLS

Inner Self Characteristics

**Motivated:** Goal-oriented and having high standards

**Self-awareness:** Describing how you are feeling; awareness of how moods affect how you treat other people; admitting mistakes; knowing what skills to improve on

**Persistence:** Following through on promises; focusing on goals despite difficulties; refusing to give up easily

Communication

**Inspirational:** Having a positive attitude; showing appreciation or giving praise; motivating others; helping others

**Confidence:** Believing in oneself; disagreeing openly and constructively; feeling comfortable talking in a group or to authority figures

**Active listening:** Ability to listen and ask questions to understand; listening carefully; paying attention when others are talking

**Communicating effectively:** Getting along with others who are different; disagreeing effectively without starting an argument

**Ability to persuade:** Changing the opinions of others by talking to them and persuading others to agree; gaining support from peers; actions that show others what you want from them

Collaboration

**Having a shared purpose:** Including others who have been "left out;" creating collaborative relationships among others; working toward a common goal

**Convener:** Bringing people together; listening to others when making decisions; seen as a "role model" by others

**Delegating and organizing people:** Respecting the ways in which people are different; assigning the right person to the right job during group tasks; understanding the emotions of others

**NYC** Department of Youth & Community Development

Adapted by COMPASS Program Quality and Innovation unit, American Institutes for Research (AIR) and Developments Without Limits (DWL)

*Source:* "Promote the Positive: Lead Efforts to Advance Positive Youth Development, Social and Emotional Learning, and Youth Leadership," New York City Department of Youth and Community Development, November 2016, https://www1.nyc.gov/assets/dycd/downloads/pdf/Youth_Leadership_Development_Framework.pdf.

the knowledge, skills, and dispositions needed by professionals to provide high-quality afterschool and youth development programming and support the learning and development of children and youth."[23]

### Striving for Continuous Improvement

OST programs can leverage continuous improvement strategies to engage youth, adopt a strengths-based approach, remain contextually relevant, and partner effectively with families, schools, and communities. Continuous improvement approaches can also help ensure that programs are warm and welcoming, foster relationships, and allow participants to engage in activities that explore their interests, build skills, and offer opportunities to lead.

While continuous improvement is the focus of chapter 20, tools for self-reflection on OST-specific continuous improvement can be found in appendix B. For example, we provide tools for quality improvement and inventories of youth outcome measures. We also encourage you and your community partners to use asset mapping tools for continuous improvement purposes, to help determine if the program reflects the strengths and assets in a community over time.

Youth understand best what can be done to make a program more engaging, so they should be actively involved in the continuous improvement process. They can work with program staff on reviewing information and making data-informed action plans. Youth leaders can also cofacilitate feedback sessions with their peers and serve on formal program councils and boards to provide ongoing input. Finally, youth can provide feedback on program quality and offerings through questionnaires, conversations, and focus groups.

Ultimately, the most critical component of a continuous improvement process is the act of staff collaboratively reflecting on their own practice and making plans focused on improvement. Data may exist in many forms (e.g., attendance and participation, stakeholder perceptions, youth outcomes, program quality) and data-gathering efforts should be ongoing, reflective of the program's purpose, and actionable. The cycle of program improvement never ends, and programs and staff should constantly strive to understand and improve their practice.

Regardless of the time of day, the setting, or the approach, all strong OST programs are assets-based, inclusive of partners, and reflective of community context. High-quality programs offer a warm and welcoming environment characterized by participants who have a sense of belonging, form positive relationships, and engage in and drive their own learning and skill building. In this chapter we have outlined explicit and embedded strategies to support skill building that include sequenced, intentional, experiential activities. Exemplary programs also provide youth opportunities to share their voice and demonstrate leadership. OST program quality is dependent on staff who are prepared to do their job, are supported in their roles, and have opportunities to plan and reflect on their work. OST programs, participants, staff, and the communities they are embedded in change over time, so continuous improvement practices are essential.

## TAKEAWAYS

- High-quality OST programs can play an integral role in promoting children's development, including social-emotional well-being.
- A strengths-based approach elevates the assets that participants and their families bring to programs and builds upon those strengths, rather than focusing on deficits or challenges.
- OST programs have demonstrated positive effects, particularly when they offer high-quality, skill-focused experiences over multiple sessions.
- Effective OST programs engage in partnerships with schools, families, and the community and ensure that programming is culturally responsive and relevant.
- Effective OST programs create a welcoming space, support relationship development, provide interactive opportunities for skill building, and promote youth voice, choice, and leadership.
- Supportive staff–youth relationships (characterized by shared norms, high expectations, stability and continuity, and connectedness to each other's lives) are key for youth to experience program benefits.
- Staff in high-quality OST programs engage in ongoing reflection and use data to inform improvements to ensure programs are continually elevating the strengths and meetings the needs of young people.

# PART THREE

# Act

# ELEVEN

# Building a Schoolwide Foundation for Social-Emotional and Academic Support

*Sandra Williamson and David Osher*

STUDENTS LEARN BEST when there are strong conditions and opportunities for learning, and when barriers to their learning are addressed. Creating such an environment requires a multitiered approach based on a solid foundation of universal programming or interventions, which is fortified when necessary with additional supports, to address the type or level of need that exists in a school. In other words, the foundation—or tier 1—will look different depending on the risks and protective factors that students experience. This foundation provides a common language for social-emotional and academic learning that can be employed across intervention levels. It also makes it easier to identify and serve students who need additional services, while reducing the costs of removing students from common learning and relationship-building activities. Moreover, since students and teachers are affected by the competencies of everyone with whom they interact, the foundation makes it easier for selective (tier 2, or secondary) and indicated (tier 3, or tertiary) interventions to work.

In addition to outlining this coordinated, multitiered approach, this chapter describes how you can ensure that your schoolwide foundation is strong, meaning it provides the conditions and opportunities necessary for learning while addressing barriers to learning. This chapter is the first of nine that explore in depth how school leaders and others can act upon their goals to create equitable schools with excellence that are safe, engaging, and supportive.

## A RELATIONAL AND SOCIAL-EMOTIONAL APPROACH TO MULTITIERED INTERVENTION

The multitiered intervention approach we introduce here is common in education, public health, mental health, prevention, and juvenile justice. When employed well, it can support coherent, cost-effective, and cost-beneficial collaboration both within schools and between schools and the community. Usually it includes three tiers, as illustrated in figure 11.1. The tiers should align and should build upon strengths while also addressing needs. The approach should support the individuality of learning and development and avoid stigmatization, segregation, tracking, and harmful labeling. It is important that you and your partners from schools, families, and the community all understand that the tiers are about *services*, not students.

This kind of approach provides services that span a wide range of domains involved in a student's cognitive and noncognitive development, and organizes services delivery to address different levels of student development and need. It includes but is not limited to Multitiered Systems of Support (MTSS), a model building upon and aligning Response to Intervention (RTI) and Positive Behavioral Interventions and Supports (PBIS) approaches. A multitiered approach can also be used to address emotional or behavioral needs or levels of student engagement; can be built around the promotion of social and emotional learning (SEL) or aligned with universal SEL and PBIS programming; and can be realized at a community level that includes schools. The multitiered relational model we delineate builds on a strong foundation that includes SEL, promotes relationship building, and fosters safety, connectedness, and a supportive school environment.

### Tier 1: Universal Supports

The foundation (tier 1) provides universal academic and social-emotional supports. These ensure that all students experience academic engagement and success as well as emotional, identity, and physical safety, connectedness,

**Figure 11.1**  A multitiered approach to safe and supportive schools

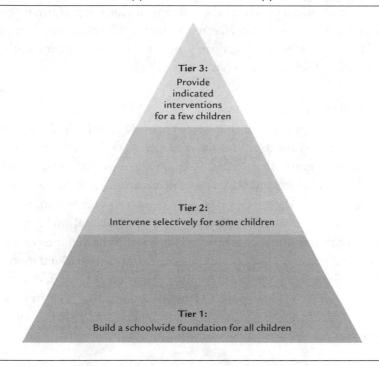

**Tier 3:**
Provide
indicated
interventions
for a few children

**Tier 2:**
Intervene selectively for some children

**Tier 1:**
Build a schoolwide foundation for all children

attachment, support, academic challenge, and integrated SEL and academic learning within the general curriculum. The foundation should include pedagogy and robust curricula that are culturally responsive and accessible to all students; include well-scaffolded, active, personalized, and collaborative learning; and are responsive to students' prior knowledge and experiences. It should also provide a systemic SEL approach to foster self-regulation, executive function, intrapersonal awareness, interpersonal skills, a growth mindset, and a sense of agency. The foundation should facilitate the strategies for family engagement described in chapter 8 and provide educators with the support they need to engage all learners, personalize learning, and form developmentally positive relationships with their students.

## Tier 2: Selective Interventions

Selective interventions (see chapter 15) should eliminate or mitigate risk factors and build or strengthen protective factors for students at risk for academic or behavioral difficulties. They are designed to address student needs when information about the student (including performance data) suggests that he or she is at an elevated level of risk for academic, behavioral, mental health, or school engagement problems. Tutoring and mentoring are two examples of selective interventions.

### Tier 3: Indicated Interventions

Indicated interventions (see chapter 16) provide coordinated, comprehensive, intensive, sustained, culturally appropriate, child- and family-focused services and supports that scaffold SEL and academic learning. They are designed to address student needs when information (including performance data) suggests that the student has, or is at high risk for, serious academic, behavioral, mental health, or engagement problems. School- and community-based wraparound supports are two examples of indicated interventions.

A safe and successful school should ensure that a solid foundation exists to support the effective and cost-efficient provision of tier 2 and 3 services. The remainder of this chapter details the conditions that constitute a strong foundation of universal programming and supports, and points to some tools that you can use to assess these conditions in your context.

## THE SAFE AND SUPPORTIVE SCHOOLS MODEL: CONDITIONS FOR A SOLID FOUNDATION

A solid foundation depends on the presence of positive relationships between and among students and adults that are characterized by support, reciprocity, respect, trust, and cultural responsiveness.[1] Such relationships are important for healthy development and school success, can buffer the effects of stress and trauma, and promote resilience.[2] Positive relationships also help build young people's capacity to regulate their emotions, behavior, and thoughts, and to feel connected with other people.[3]

Efforts to support safety, engagement, and positive physical and instructional environments contribute to positive relationships, healthy physical and emotional development, and effective learning, and are the foundation for SEL and academic support as well as the basis of the Safe and Supportive Schools Model illustrated in figure 11.2.[4] (See "A Free, Valid, and Reliable Suite of School Climate Surveys That Provide Actionable Data in Real Time" to learn about tools based on this model.)

**Figure 11.2** Safe and Supportive Schools Model

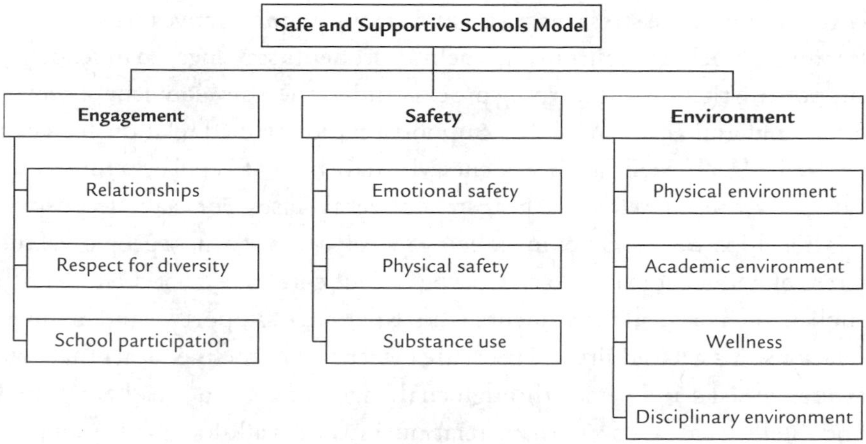

Source: https://safesupportivelearning.ed.gov/safe-and-healthy-students/school-climate

---

### A Free, Valid, and Reliable Suite of School Climate Surveys That Provide Actionable Data in Real Time

The US Department of Education provides a suite of four surveys—based on the Safe and Supportive Schools Model—for students, teachers, other school staff, and families that is freely available to schools, districts, and states. The surveys are on an online platform, provide results in real time, and are backed by a help desk and web-based tool. The Department of Education's free school climate surveys (EDSCLS) can also be accessed through a link in appendix B.

---

## Engagement

Engagement in the Safe and Supportive Schools Model refers to the quality of relationships between and among students, staff, and families; respect for the diversity of subgroups in the school and community; and the level of participation, involvement, and inclusion of staff, students, families, and the larger community in school activities and governance.[5]

Building supportive, attuned, and trusting relationships between students and adults is at the core of student engagement and positive school climates.

These relationships can buffer and avert the negative effects of stressful experiences inside and outside of school for students (such as bullying), helping children modulate stress reactivity and engage in productive tasks (such as learning).[6] Such relationships also help all students stay engaged in school by supporting them in the learning process and in their development of social-emotional and academic skills.[7] Supportive and attuned relationships can be particularly beneficial for students who have been affected by trauma, and can help reduce the effects of persistent societal biases. For example, positive relationships are one factor in reducing *stereotype threat*, where people feel the stress of being compared to stereotypes about core aspects of their identity such as race or gender.[8] Students who experience supportive and attuned relationships with adults and peers are better able to focus on learning, take academic risks and persist through challenges, and build social-emotional and intellectual skills.[9] Trusting relationships with adults can also support positive self-concepts, as well as a growth mindset and motivation to learn.[10]

Cultural and linguistic competence and responsiveness are essential to building positive relationships between students, staff, families, and the larger community, and fostering engagement. Cultural and linguistic competence and responsiveness can address the social-emotional and learning needs of culturally and linguistically diverse students by creating learning environments where students feel emotionally and intellectually safe, supported, and challenged.[11] Culturally and linguistically competent schools continuously assess how their policies, attitudes, practices, and procedures may or may not privilege some students, and make adjustments accordingly.[12] Schools that lack cultural competence and responsiveness disadvantage and disengage many students by increasing cognitive and emotional demands on them. This drives negative outcomes including low attendance, poor grades, lack of motivation, discipline problems, and, eventually, dropout or school failure.[13]

Practices that foster engagement across the school community build quality relationships between students, staff, families, and the larger community; model practices, behaviors, and attitudes that show respect for diversity; and encourage participation among all members of the school community.[14]

Instructional practices that keep students motivated foster engagement and learning. Motivation depends on many factors, including a sense of efficacy and control in one's learning, a belief that one can improve through effort, and the perceived value of learning tasks. Motivation also depends on contexts that are adaptable to students and congruent with their identities and a sense of purpose.[15] Instructional practices that are student-centered and engaging, adapt to students' varied ways of learning, allow for reflection, and connect to students' prior knowledge and experiences help students stay motivated to learn.

## Safety

Safety includes emotional, identity, and physical safety as perceived, experienced, and created by students, staff, families, and the community. In emotionally and identity-safe schools, students and adults feel secure, safe to express emotions, confident in taking risks, and intellectually and emotionally challenged. Physically safe schools have secure learning environments that protect students and adults from violence, theft, and exposure to weapons and threats.[16] A sense of safety in school among students and adults supports the development of students' social-emotional competencies, as well as trusting relationships between students and teachers. Building these relationships gives students the space to respond positively to their teachers as well as to exchange feedback with them.[17]

Many students do not feel physically, emotionally, intellectually, or identity safe in their schools.[18] This can be stressful and taxing, limit attention and creativity, impair working memory, and distract from learning.[19] A lack of safety reflects and contributes to the quality of relationships in school, as do students' experiences with harsh, punitive, inconsistent, and palpably biased discipline. Students who have trusting relationships with adults and peers are less likely to feel unsafe in school. A school climate in which most students experience positive relationships will feel safer.[20]

### Bullying and cyberbullying

Many students experience or participate in bullying and cyberbullying, which undermine all students' and adults' sense of physical and emotional safety. Bullying involves a real or perceived imbalance of power. It can be physical, when it involves injuring someone or damaging property; verbal, when it involves saying or writing offensive or hurtful things; or social, when it involves intentionally damaging someone's reputation or relationships. Cyberbullying involves the use of electronic devices to harm someone.[21] Bullying can have serious short- and long-term consequences for students' psychosocial development, mental health, school engagement, and learning.[22] It is not just the victim who suffers from bullying behaviors—perpetrators and witnesses of bullying also exhibit psychosocial problems.[23]

Bullying can be both a cause and a consequence of a negative school climate. High levels of bullying can contribute to a sense of insecurity among students and adults, disengagement from school, and disconnection from other members of the school community. It can also be made worse by other aspects of school climate, including how adults structure the school day or group students. Alternatively, educators can foster a sense of belonging, safety, and resilience through positive student-teacher interactions, antiharassment policies, developmentally appropriate disciplinary approaches, and consistent and fair rule enforcement.[24]

Universal violence prevention programs that address all students, as well as families and communities, rather than targeting individual students who exhibit antisocial behaviors, can reduce the prevalence and effects of bullying.[25] Everyday practices that can reduce bullying include acknowledging how painful it can be, modeling positive behaviors when bullying situations arise (e.g., clearly stating school rules and taking time to listen), and helping students become allies by allowing them to learn and talk about effective strategies for resolving conflict and understanding each other's differences.[26] Adults can also foster a stronger sense of connection among each other; positive adult relationships are an important factor in supporting a positive school climate.

### Substance abuse and trade

Substance abuse and trade in the school community also influences school safety.[27] Substance abuse can undermine academic achievement and prompt harmful behaviors, which can disrupt students' and adults' sense of respect, safety, and trust. Positive relationships with adults and school connectedness can prevent students from engaging in health risk behaviors such as substance abuse.[28]

### Emergency preparation

Another contributor to school safety is how schools plan to ensure that members of the school community are safe in the event of an emergency, including violence, crime, natural disasters, epidemics, and accidents. Schools and communities can play a key role in preventing or protecting students and staff from emergency situations.[29] They can preventively identify and address warning signs of school violence through the three-tiered approach, supplemented by well-implemented threat assessment and the judicious use of trained school resource officers (who should be trained to eliminate the effects of bias on their actions and never be used to enforce school discipline or attendance).[30] Aspects of a positive school climate, including trusting relationships and connectedness among members of the school community, are key to a school's readiness to face emergencies, as well as how individuals and the school community are able to overcome challenges.[31]

## Environment

The environment in the Safe and Supportive Schools Model includes the instructional, behavioral, and personal aspects of the learning experience. In a positive instructional environment, instruction engages students and supports developmentally appropriate skill building. A positive environment depends on the quality of student–teacher relationships, teacher expectations, academic supports for struggling students, and teacher satisfaction, as well as the peer environment and the degree to which teachers have sufficient resources.[32] Positive instructional environments support student motivation, engagement, social-emotional competency development, learning, and achievement.[33] They are characterized by a high level of support, trust, and nurturing among students and teachers; an explicit expression of high expectations and belief in students' capabilities; culturally responsive instruction; and well-managed classrooms.[34] Classroom management depends on teachers' ability to maintain students' cooperation, which includes engulfing students in learning and positively supporting behavior—factors that, along with their social-emotional skills, affect student engagement, motivation, and cooperation in learning activities.[35] Positive instructional environments also depend on teacher well-being, which is affected by factors such as principal support, job stress, and students' feelings and behavior.[36]

The physical condition of the school building, as well as noise, lighting, air quality, and location, can affect attendance, concentration, academic performance, and physical health.[37] Children are highly sensitive (and more exposed than adults) to toxic substances in the environment.[38] Schools' air quality can be improved through implementation of best practices including air quality programs and healthy energy efficiency policies.[39] Physical disorder in a school building, such as graffiti and litter, is also associated with increased bullying in high school.[40] The school's physical environment, including dilapidated buildings and overcrowded classrooms, can also contribute to teacher frustration and burnout.[41]

Students cannot learn if they are suffering physically or mentally, and the promotion of physical and mental wellness contributes to learning and a positive school environment. Students have better academic and health outcomes in schools when their physical and mental health is better.[42] Physical health can be supported through schoolwide efforts such as exercise programs and recess, as well as the school nurse's work to promote students' health and well-being.

School mental health services that take a whole-child approach can contribute to a positive school environment by providing resources for all students, but especially for those who face mental health disorders associated with persistent stressors, including students with chronic physical conditions; students who are of sexual, racial, or ethnic minorities; and students who are immigrants or refugees. School-based mental health services can help equalize the utilization of mental health services for students of racial and ethnic minorities who may face barriers to service access not faced by other students.[43] A comprehensive whole-child and whole-community approach to mental health services integrates SEL with other school practices, stakeholder engagement and support, collaboration across systems within and outside of schools, family involvement, and the implementation of universal and targeted services, and also links different school teams through an integrated data system.[44]

The disciplinary environment includes the communication of discipline and behavior policies to the school community and the adequacy and fairness of policy enforcement.[45] A key concern is whether students experience the school's rules and norms as fair and consistently and effectively enforced. Students experience harsh (e.g., corporal punishment) and exclusionary discipline as unfair, and are sensitive to who does and does not get suspended. This includes feeling watched as well as the overuse or inconsistent use of suspensions and other disciplinary measures.[46]

## TAKEAWAYS

- Students learn best when there are strong conditions and opportunities for learning, and when barriers to their learning are addressed.
- This can be supported by a multitiered approach based on a solid foundation (which is fortified when necessary) to address the type or level of need that exists in a school.

- The foundation provides universal academic and social-emotional supports that ensure that all students experience strong conditions for learning, engagement, and academic success.
- The foundation should include robust academic and social-emotional pedagogy and curricula that are culturally responsive and accessible to all students; include well-scaffolded, active, personalized, and collaborative learning; and are responsive to students' prior knowledge and experiences.

# TWELVE

# Building and Restoring School Communities

*Greta Colombi, Robert V. Mayo, Manolya Tanyu,*
*David Osher, and Amy Mart*

**People connect with people before
they connect with institutions.**[1]

ALL MEMBERS OF A SCHOOL COMMUNITY need positive social interactions that contribute to a climate of trust and a feeling of belonging, safety, and support, as caring, developmental relationships and connectedness drive learning and development.[2] This does not occur automatically; leadership must work to create and sustain a strong school community, where staff are willing and able to attune to students, and both students and staff experience care, support, and connectedness.

Since positive relationships play a central role in building the foundation for equity with excellence, we devote this entire chapter to fostering these relationships. A cornerstone of cultivating positive relationships is building a school community where *all* members feel welcome and respect each other.[3] Nurturing these relationships involves building strong communities within schools, where individual members of the school community can choose to affiliate with others who share their role or interests, and creating structures to sustain those communities.[4] There are two big questions surrounding school community building:

- How can schools build stronger communities that cultivate positive school relationships?
- What can schools do when their goals, values, policies, and practices run counter to cultivating positive school relationships?

This chapter addresses these questions. We first walk through how to build school communities—an overall school community, a community of educators, and a community of students—and we then explore how to restore community when policies and practices have negatively affected school relationships.

The school community and its members are connected by their shared experiences at school.[5] Some connections are relational: teachers and students as they interact in classes and public spaces, students while walking the halls and participating in class and other school activities, school leaders and teachers as they prepare for their educational roles, families and students as they live with and love each other, students and bus drivers while they travel together. Other connections are instrumental and can be overlooked in the hustle and bustle of schools: teachers and bus drivers coordinating information when supporting students, school nurses and cafeteria workers communicating about allergies and nutrition, and custodians and students communicating informally on school grounds.

Research demonstrates the importance of relationships to learning and development, and the importance of positive relationships in creating safe, supportive, and equitable schools with excellence.[6] Developmental relationships (see the Search Institute's Developmental Relationships Framework at https://www.search-institute.org/developmental-relationships/developmental-relationships-framework/) and positive relationships at school underpin social-emotional and academic learning and contribute to greater attachment to school, diminished behavioral incidents, lower dropout rates, and improved teacher satisfaction.[7] Conversely, poor relationships contribute to (and reflect) bullying, peer victimization, punitive disciplinary actions, absenteeism, and reduced academic achievement.[8]

When school community members have a clear vision and goals for building an inclusive school community where caring, respectful, and supportive relationships are the norm, the community can thrive. Members of the entire school community can develop shared norms and values, and, over time, relational trust. In this process, staff and students co-construct their vision for an ideal school, what they need to feel safe and respected, and how they wish to be treated. This dialogue allows students and adults to share their perceptions and experiences, and creates a basis for upstanding and shared accountability when someone (student or adult) behaves in a way that violates their shared agreements. These conversations can then be synthesized and distilled into agreements that describe expectations of roles and responsibilities for the whole community and sets of members.

## BUILDING RELATIONSHIPS WITH STUDENTS
### In the Classroom
Student participation in classroom community building contributes to, as well as extends, school community building. Engaging and inclusive classroom communities rarely form organically. Educators must be open to student agency and be authentic, thoughtful, and intentional about the ways in which they engage students academically and socially to cultivate positive relationships and inclusivity. Here are some practical tips we have learned from young people through thousands of interviews, focus groups, and listening sessions—both where things were working and where they were not:[9]

- Connect with your students and understand them in their uniqueness.
  - *Listen.*
  - *Find out what we know and build on it.*
  - *Know me—don't prejudge me or assume I am just like you were when you were my age.*
  - *Care about us, what is going on with us, and our progress.*
  - *Understand that we will make mistakes.*
  - *Don't write me off because of one thing that I do.*
  - *Know what embarrasses me and don't do it.*
  - *Don't betray my confidence.*
- Be both a teacher and a human being.
  - *Prepare for class, know your content, be passionate about it.*
  - *Grade fairly.*
  - *Be a role model.*
  - *Be authentic.*
  - *Be more than your job (and don't say this is only my job).*
- Demonstrate respect.
  - *Respect me, don't denigrate me.*
  - *Respect my family's language and spiritual choices.*
  - *Treat all students fairly—there should not be a halo effect for "good kids."*

- Support your students.
  - *Help me and other students understand concepts and standards—keep trying, but don't just say the same thing over and over again.*
  - *Provide helpful and timely feedback that can contribute to revision.*
  - *Mentor me.*
  - *Provide opportunities.*
- Challenge and engage your students.
  - *Challenge us.*
  - *Push us to do our best, and work hard and support us in doing so.*
  - *Ask questions to make us think.*
  - *Employ active learning and group projects.*
  - *Connect to things we care about.*
  - *Don't just focus on the textbook and test preparation.*

### Through School Practices and Routines

Educators can systematically create opportunities for students to form deep relationships with peers and adults. Create time and space within the school day for people to get to know each other, as well as structured opportunities for interactions beyond the usual school routines that deepen relationships. The small schools approach exemplifies a structural change that has successfully strengthened community.[10] Large schools can also be broken up to create smaller learning communities where students and teachers interact on a deeper level with a smaller number of peers and adults. *Looping*, which allows students to remain with the same peers and teacher for multiple years, can serve the same purpose in elementary schools. Restructuring the school schedule to create longer class periods and regular community-building sessions can also maximize opportunities for relationship building.[11] Additional community-building activities include the following:

- Ensuring school leadership and staff are visible and engaged in welcoming students each morning and interacting with them personally, whether it be in the hall or cafeteria. Staff can also look out for students whom they know are struggling and positively engage them at the start of the day, as well as identify others who may be having a particularly hard day or are starting to exhibit warning signs.
- Confirming all students have a close relationship with at least one staff person in the school building or campus. Some schools list all students

on posters and ask staff to indicate the students with whom they have good relationships. For any students who seemingly do not have a good relationship with a staff person, staff plan how they will work on building a relationship with those students.

### In Schoolwide Activities and Rituals

Schools can also provide regular, schoolwide, community-building activities and rituals, which engage all students and adults in the school in a set of shared experiences that break away from the normal routines of teaching and learning. Such activities not only create space for relationship building, but also provide opportunities for students to assume more ownership and agency. Examples of such activities include the following:

- Facilitating youth-led forums where all adults and students come together to discuss issues facing their school community and/or neighborhood. When working on school climate improvements, students can join staff in reviewing and analyzing data to determine what is working well and what needs improvement, and to brainstorm about how all students and staff can be part of a solution. (We provide a link to a video of the Cleveland Metropolitan School District's Student Advisory Committee in appendix B that provides an inside look at a youth-led forum, which was also described in chapter 7.)
- Including advisories during the school day where students and educators engage in meaningful youth-driven discussions and activities to build stronger relationships.

## BUILDING COMMUNITIES OF EDUCATORS

Teachers' work can be isolating and stressful. Although teachers may have informal relationships with other educators whom they can turn to for information or advice, they may not have professional and social relationships with a larger community of educators.[12] Stronger communities of educators within a school can be built through professional organizations or faculty meetings that serve as a bridge between "islands" of teachers. Recognizing that teaching is a team effort, and having a supportive network to lean on, frees teachers from the misconception that they must be all things to all students. (See "Beyond the Notion of the Lone Teacher 'Superhero'" for more on this false narrative.)

## Beyond the Notion of the Lone Teacher "Superhero"

The mythical narrative of the solo super-teacher working in isolation, against all odds, to improve the outcomes of his or her students is, perhaps, one of the most destructive myths about teaching that is allowed to proliferate. No successful teacher is equipped with the expertise to be a teacher, nurse, counselor, social worker, and world language interpreter. Instead, the best teachers readily and frequently acknowledge the team effort it takes to meet an individual student's needs and to support a classroom full of students. The best teachers are cognizant of the individual contributions made by each staff member to the collective effort to successfully meet the needs of a school community full of students and families.

Educators must be part of a learning community that honors the expertise we bring as individuals and creates an environment for sharing that doesn't just allow us to learn from each other, but also compels us to do so (in the most constructive sense). Rather than a sign of weakness, it is a sign of profound responsibility to work in concert with colleagues, as fellow professionals, to complement each other in providing safety, support, and engagement to our students.

*Mary Cathryn Ricker*
*Senior Vice President, American Federation of Teachers*

In this section, we describe vehicles for cultivating positive relationships and building or strengthening communities among educators. These supports are also summarized in table 12.1.

### Targeted Learning Opportunities

Targeted learning opportunities range from facilitated and collaborative professional development workshops to professional learning communities (PLCs).[13] For example, schools or teacher leaders can organize PLCs focused on cultural responsiveness and the individualized nature of learning, where they view TED talks and discuss books on these topics by such authors as Zaretta Hammond and Todd Rose. Similarly, if educators want to improve their social-emotional competencies, they could meet as a work group on a regular basis to plan and then implement peer observation and coaching for all educators; or they could create a community of practice that regularly

**Table 12.1** Web of supports that build educator communities

| | LEADERS | TEACHERS | INSTRUCTIONAL SUPPORT PERSONNEL (SOCIAL WORKERS, COUNSELORS, NURSES, PSYCHOLOGISTS) | PARA-EDUCATORS |
|---|---|---|---|---|
| Targeted learning opportunities | X | X | X | X |
| Grade-level and departmental planning meetings | X | X | | X |
| Teams and task forces | X | X | X | X |
| Wellness and self-care | X | X | X | X |

discusses what is working and what is not, adjusting strategies based on evolving needs and others' experiences.[14] We also recommend Jobs for the Future's sample professional development toolkit on motivation, engagement, and student voice for educators to gather around and share learning.[15]

## Grade-Level and Department Planning Meetings

Many schools organize educators into groups by grade level or department, and these groups may meet regularly to develop lesson plans and coordinate instruction. A portion of this time can be dedicated to community building as well. For example, as educators discuss how to differentiate instruction, they can also discuss what they know about the interests that spark student motivation, students' strengths and needs, and connections with students, and plan relevant follow-up activities. While these are job-related discussions, positive peer support from colleagues builds relationships. In addition, from a positive school culture perspective, this type of teacher–teacher support is more productive—both in terms of community building and fostering wellness—than deficit-oriented lunchroom venting about students or families.

## Teams and Task Forces

Creating teams, task forces, and work groups of educators provides opportunities for teachers to collaborate and build community among their ranks. Teams could analyze data (e.g., academic, school climate, behavioral) to identify needs and interventions that can support positive and productive relationships and strengthen school culture. Together, group members can plan data efforts and collect, review, and report data, while working with students, families, staff, and community partners to identify and implement interventions that align with the school community's vision and goals. If the groups' processes are collaborative and respectful, they play an important role in building relationships, relational trust, and social capital among team members. Productive and collaborative teams can symbolize collaboration and distributive leadership, which can contribute to transforming top-down, solitary school cultures into collaborative and participatory school cultures.

## Wellness and Self-Care

It is important to provide and support opportunities for educators to come together as a community to focus on their wellness. In addition, creating opportunities to improve wellness as a community is useful—for example, teachers or schools may organize yoga and running clubs. When educators engage in these informal activities together, they have other opportunities to deepen relationships while improving their wellness, which in turn helps them attune to students.

When conducting these activities, educators can:

- focus on a vision of equity with excellence;
- give themselves space to have strengths-based conversations rather than focusing on deficits when discussing students, families, and the community;
- support the development of relational trust by providing meaningful opportunities for educators to demonstrate and experience it;
- foster problem solving as opposed to blame-oriented conversations and balance it with individual and collective responsibility;
- support culturally competent, responsive, and respectful conversation and create safe spaces to address sensitive issues pertaining to race and culture; and
- honor individual voice and nurture engagement.

This work can foster individual and collective efficacy and accountability, which in turn supports teachers' ability to have positive relationships with students, families, and community partners. However, for this to happen, educators need time—and, in some cases, permission from administrative leadership, their peers, and/or their professional association/union—for wellness and self-care. Although these activities might be verbally encouraged by principals and unions, they may need to be facilitated by staffing patterns and budgeting decisions, and, where necessary, by provisions in teacher contracts that support teachers' participation in these activities. While these decisions might appear mundane, they are necessary to enhance educators' cognitive and emotional readiness to benefit from strengths-based, student-centered discussions.

## RESTORING COMMUNITY WHEN POLICIES AND PRACTICES HAVE HAD A NEGATIVE IMPACT

Cultivating positive relationships and building community can be challenging for schools when some students are experienced as troubling and when educators feel unable to handle their behavior. Thus, it's also important for educators to be able to build community when policies and practices have negatively affected school relationships.

Punitive, harsh, and exclusionary discipline policies and practices like suspending students don't work. Although they may aim to deter misbehavior or violence, there is little evidence that these practices are effective in achieving this goal.[16] In fact, research suggests these practices have harmful effects, both on the students who are suspended and on their peers. Take vandalism, for example. An experimental study of a vandalism intervention that involved punishment found that it led to increases, not decreases, in the behavior.[17] Moreover, research suggests that when students are suspended or expelled, *all students* tend to feel less safe, are less likely to bond with teachers and other staff, and are less likely to get along with one another.[18]

Some states, districts, and schools—along with teacher and administrators' professional organizations—have been working to change disciplinary practices. This includes implementing restorative approaches that help cultivate relationships and restore community while reducing the harmful consequences of suspension (which, in addition to alienation, include grade repetition, dropout, arrest, and diminished likelihood of attending college).

### Restorative Practices

Restorative practices engage students and adults in building positive relationships and a sense of community to address individual behaviors and improve school culture. These practices include restorative circles, family group conferencing, and the use of affective questioning.[19] Restorative practices enable students to take full responsibility for their behavior by understanding how it affected others, recognizing that it was harmful, repairing the harm, and working on avoiding that behavior in the future. Particular practices have roots in a variety of ethnic cultural traditions as well as other service domains. The circle process, for example, builds upon the tradition of indigenous Native American talking circles, and group conferencing is consistent with both youth work approaches and therapeutic group techniques. These practices are also consistent with social science research on how to develop social capital and achieve social discipline through participatory learning and decision making.[20]

Although the empirical research base on restorative practices is just beginning to be assembled, several exploratory studies and many qualitative studies report positive effects on school climate, student behavior, and relationships between students and with staff, among other outcomes. Many rigorous evaluations are currently being conducted.[21]

Restorative practices cultivate a culture in which the whole school can be connected through common expectations. These practices empower educators and students to engage each other in dialogue, develop a shared understanding, and enhance positive interactions.[22] Whole-school implementation builds a sense of community, in which students, staff, and stakeholders have input, are heard, and are respected.[23] Restorative practices, when relationally grounded, consistent, and well implemented, can transform the school environment, enhance learning, and encourage students and staff to become more responsible and empathetic.[24]

Restorative practices in schools can build classroom communities that are based on collective agreements, authentic communication, and reflective dialogue that frames conflict in a proactive manner.[25] For example, the Four Ps is a framework that helps educators promote restorative practices in these areas:[26]

- **Person:** How each individual interacts with others in the school community, and how that interaction has an impact on relationships
- **Place:** The environmental conditions and factors that affect how individuals interact with one another
- **Practice:** Opportunities for educators to prevent conflict, resolve challenges, and create chances for relationship growth
- **Plan:** A school community's plan for making restorative practices a regular part of school culture

*What is the relationship between restorative practices and restorative justice?*
While they are more than an alternative to traditional punishments, restorative practices are often associated with the broader concept of restorative justice—that is, repairing harm by engaging the victim and offender in dialogue, rather than simply punishing and removing the offender from school through exclusionary discipline techniques (suspension and expulsion).[27] Restorative justice in the school setting views misconduct not as school rule breaking (and therefore a violation of the institution), but rather as a violation against people and the relationships in the school and wider community.[28] Its emphasis on repairing these relationships provides an opportunity to engage the offender in competency and skill development.

*How are schools implementing restorative practices?*
Some schools and districts employ a multitiered approach to restorative justice that builds on universal practices, including training staff and students in the principles of restorative practices, to reinforce a positive school environment. The multitiered approach can be used to coordinate restorative supports.[29] For example, a variety of restorative practices can be implemented at the universal, schoolwide (tier 1) level to build relationships and prevent problematic behavior. Some teachers use classroom circles or have peace circles to respond to student conflict as well as build community. Others use an incident or ongoing conflict to engage groups of students and other stakeholders (e.g., witnesses, friends, family) in a group conference to resolve the conflict. Together, the group conference participants aim to determine a reasonable way for the offender to make amends, rather than employing traditional punishments like suspension. These sanctions are restorative in nature and could include community service, restitution, apologies, or specific behavioral change agreements, such as the offender agreeing to comply with certain conditions.[30] Some schools also use restorative practices (e.g., planning centers) or restorative justice to address higher levels of misbehavior (tiers 2 and 3).

Restorative practices in schools are not limited to formal processes. Informal practices include making affective statements that communicate people's feelings, as well as asking questions that cause people to reflect on how their behavior has affected others. Impromptu restorative conferences, groups, and circles may be structured, but do not require the elaborate preparation needed for formal conferences.

A critical step in restorative practices aimed at redirecting student behavior is providing agency and voice to students who would traditionally be punished for misbehavior based on rules created by adults. This creates a sense of fairness and reestablishes relationships between adults and students. A restorative approach to school discipline operates on the premise that when students do harm, they are responsible for repairing that harm and restoring a sense of emotional and physical safety within the school community. Although it still holds students accountable for their behavior, the restorative approach focuses on addressing the root causes of the behavior and repairing relationships between members of the school community.

### How can restorative practices be integrated with other interventions?

Restorative practices work better when they are scaffolded by relational, trauma-sensitive, multitiered interventions and include social and emotional learning (SEL), mental health, and positive behavioral supports. Restorative circles require time and emotional readiness, neither of which will be available if there are too many infractions. Restoration after harm often requires time for people to share, listen, reflect, and problem-solve. Because restorative practices leverage and build upon students' sense of connection to and responsibility for others—and upon student and adult social-emotional capacity—they are likely to work best in schools that:

- support SEL;
- are culturally responsive;
- employ positive approaches to reduce the number of behavioral incidents; and
- use a trauma-sensitive and -informed multitiered approach that pairs universal training for teachers about the effects of trauma with appropriate supports for small groups or individuals experiencing difficulties as a result of trauma or grief.

Many schools are already implementing multitiered interventions—Positive Behavioral Interventions and Supports (PBIS) and SEL in particular—to prevent and address problematic student behavior and build social competence.

The Oakland Unified School District (OUSD) provides an example of how a district aligns restorative practices with other schoolwide interventions, supports for students engaged in conflict, and targeted services for students who display disruptive behaviors. The district aligns restorative practices with Multitiered Systems of Support (MTSS), and uses PBIS and SEL practices to support relationships and trauma-informed education. It has developed modules of restorative justice trainings at all three tiers of prevention, implementing alternatives to suspension and helping students reenter after suspension. The district has trained over one thousand staff members in restorative practices, including law enforcement. Research conducted in 2014 in Oakland schools found that the multitiered approach helped the district decrease suspensions by half from 2011 to 2014; and in a 2014 evaluation of SEL in Oakland, educators reported that student and teacher SEL was contributing to an improved disciplinary climate.[31] Read more about the district's successful implementation of restorative practices in "Oakland Unified School District: A Three-Tiered Approach to Restorative Justice."

### Oakland Unified School District: A Three-Tiered Approach to Restorative Justice

OUSD's tiered approach to restorative justice includes these levels of interventions:

- **Tier 1:** Educators promote social-emotional skills and practice (classroom circles) to build relationships, create shared values and guidelines, and encourage restorative conversations following behavioral disruption. The goal is to build a caring, intentional, and equitable community with conditions conducive to learning.
- **Tier 2:** Educators employ nonpunitive responses to harm/conflict, such as harm circles, mediation, or family-group conferencing, to respond to disciplinary issues in a restorative manner. This process addresses the root causes of the harm, supports accountability for the offender, and promotes healing for the victim(s), the offender, and the school community.
- **Tier 3:** Educators provide one-on-one support and plan for the successful reentry of youth following suspension, truancy, expulsion, or incarceration. The goal is to welcome youth to the school community in a manner that provides wraparound support and promotes student accountability and achievement.

## How are restorative practices reinforced in a school?

The key to the successful adoption of restorative practices is a school vision that focuses on inclusion, community building, problem solving, and learning from experience. Even if the vision is there, discipline is one of the places where the rubber hits the road; hence, it may be necessary to change mindsets. You can foster a restorative perspective through: (1) awareness-building events, discussions, and workshops to change the attitudes of educators, parents, and other school community members (such as law enforcement) and help them understand the benefits of restorative practices; (2) ongoing skill-building training for staff; and (3) providing supports to achieve sustainable change.

Adopting a restorative approach begins with individuals reflecting on their own interactions with other adults and students. It encourages adults to share their decision-making roles with students, instead of making top-down decisions that may have harmful consequences for individual students. Taking a few minutes at each staff meeting to describe and exercise restorative approaches can help staff deepen their relationships as they understand how restorative practices are similar to or different than other approaches. Knowledge gain can be facilitated by consistent expectations for practice in multiple settings within the school, as well as through additional supports for making the practices part of adult interactions with students. Many schools allocate staff for training and to support the implementation of restorative practices, while other districts leverage community partnerships to support educator training. (See appendix B for resources to build staff capacity in restorative practices integrated with SEL, informed by student voice, and in support of youth/adult partnerships.)

Families play a significant role in supporting the development and implementation of restorative practices that are culturally relevant and contextually appropriate for a school community. Engaging family members in understanding the conflict and solution is key to creating a set of restorative practices. For example, involving parents in a small-group conference to address fighting among students may encourage parents to address fighting at school with their children at home. Families may also be able to provide information about the underlying causes of the fight that would not be known to school educators otherwise.

Restorative practices can provide a viable avenue for schools to reestablish a sense of community in the wake of problematic policies and practices, support an inclusive school community, and empower both educators and students to build smaller communities that deepen relationships and connections. However, this work is not easy, and it requires changes in punitive mindsets, the development of educator skills, and the provision of organizational supports—in other words, readiness. In embarking on this work, it is important to focus on your goals for equity with excellence and to address the fact that restorative approaches require a major shift for many educators and families in both perspective and skill sets.

Exclusionary discipline is institutionalized in educational systems, and punitive approaches have deep roots in many cultures. Educators and families may view suspension as normal, when that is not the case in some countries or schools. They may also believe that punishment works or is the only response available. And even if adults are motivated, they may lack the capacity or the organizational backup to implement restorative practices. You can address these challenges by focusing on readiness and employing the Concerns-Based Adoption Model (CBAM) described in chapter 20. In addition, staff SEL and training on trauma sensitivity, child and youth development, and cultural competence can support staff capacity to handle stress and implement restorative practices.

## TAKEAWAYS

- Student participation in classroom community building contributes to, as well as extends, school community building.
- Create time and space within the school day for people to get to know each other, as well as structured opportunities beyond the usual school routines for interactions that deepen relationships.
- Provide regular community-building activities and rituals.
- Support the development of teacher communities.
- Employ restorative practices to build community.
- Align restorative practices with relational, multitiered approaches.
- Build readiness to implement restorative practices.

**THIRTEEN**

# Creating Respectful
# and Inclusive Schools

*Jeffrey M. Poirier, Ilene Berman, Kathleen Guarino,*
*Fausto Alejandro López, and David Osher*

WHEN STUDENTS AND STAFF feel safe, respected, welcome, and included, they are better able to take on academic challenges and learn from their peers and each other; more likely to develop social-emotional, cognitive, and academic skills that will help them succeed in school and life; and less likely to engage in problematic behavior.[1] When teachers experience the school as safe, supportive, and collaborative, they are better able to attune to students' needs, less likely to experience stress and burnout, and less likely to employ punitive and exclusionary discipline.[2]

While many students bring their fears to school, unsupportive school environments drive negative academic outcomes, emotional challenges, self-harm, and suicidal thinking.[3] Some students experience disrespect, mistreatment, and exclusion because of their life experiences, family background, identity, faith, gender expression, native language and accent, or other characteristics that make them "different." Valuing and addressing diversity provides a range of educational benefits—cognitive, social, and emotional.[4] However, student diversity is ignored in many schools across the country, and many students are disadvantaged by a lack of support or become targets for bias, rejection, or violence due to their differences.

Some school practices—such as one-size-fits-all approaches, or harsh and exclusionary discipline—are school-created adversities that limit opportunities to learn and can make students feel less safe and more disconnected from the school community. Instead, by fostering a sense of emotional safety and engaging all students in an inclusive and academically productive community, schools can increase inclusion and reduce inequities. In this chapter, we discuss the effects of trauma, adversity, and marginalization and provide examples of promising approaches that can contribute to a safe and respectful environment.

## UNDERSTANDING AND ADDRESSING THE EFFECTS OF STRESS AND TRAUMA

Schools should consider how stressful or traumatic experiences can affect how students, families, and staff act. An understanding of the effects of trauma can help schools adopt practices and protocols that minimize the likelihood that they will create additional trauma or adversity.

Despite their assets, many students confront institutional and individual adversities. For example, epidemiological data suggest that about 46 percent of young people in the United States are exposed to a potentially traumatic event that can affect health and well-being.[5] About one in six students experiences chronic physical health conditions.[6] Many more students face harassment, microaggressions, and negative stereotyping. Students of immigrant origin and students who are refugees, as well as students who are LGBTQ, face overlapping and distinct adversities, including social exclusion and challenges related to prejudice, acculturation, and fears (such as fear of deportation of themselves, family members, or friends).[7] Other students face adversities as well; for example, divorce, military deployment, and excessive demands and expectations can contribute to toxic stress and poor mental health.[8] Some students are fearful of violence at school. Students are not alone here; educators may also experience adversity and stress in both their nonschool and school lives.[9]

### Definition and Types of Trauma

The term *trauma* refers to an event or set of circumstances that is experienced as physically or emotionally harmful or life-threatening, overwhelms the body's ability to cope, and adversely affects a person's mental, physical, social-emotional, or spiritual well-being.[10] Experiencing a traumatic event can alter how people view themselves and others by challenging their beliefs that the world is a safe place, that other people can be trusted, and that they are worthy of care and protection. Potentially traumatic experiences for students, families, and school staff come in many forms (see "Types of Traumatic Experiences"), and range from one-time events to chronic or even generational experiences.

## Types of Traumatic Experiences

**Acute trauma:** Traumatic events that occur at a time and place and are usually short-lived, such as witnessing or experiencing a single act of violence, the sudden loss of a loved one, a serious accident, or a natural disaster.[11]

**Chronic trauma:** Traumatic experiences that occur repeatedly over long periods of time.[12] Examples include chronic abuse or neglect; ongoing domestic or community violence; chronic bullying; long-term illness; forced displacement; chronic exposure to poverty and related stressors; and ongoing experiences of oppression, discrimination, and isolation.

**Historical trauma:** The collective and cumulative trauma experienced by a group across generations.[13] Examples include violent colonization and assimilation policies, slavery, segregation, racism, heterosexism, discrimination, and oppression. Groups that continue to be impacted by historical trauma include communities of color, American Indian and Alaska Native communities, members of LGBTQ communities, and immigrant populations.

**Racial trauma:** Potentially traumatic experiences related to race that may include direct experiences of racial harassment, including threats of harm or injury and being humiliated; witnessing racial violence toward others; and/or experiencing discrimination and structural and institutional racism, including daily microaggressions such as verbal slurs and rude behaviors that convey bias and demean a person based on racial identity.[14] For groups such as LGBTQ youth of color, trauma may be related to racial, cultural, and gender identity/expression.

**Complex trauma:** Exposure to multiple traumatic events from an early age *and* the immediate and long-term effects of these experiences over the course of development.[15] Examples include chronic abuse, neglect, or exposure to family and community violence. This type of trauma is particularly devastating because it occurs in early childhood during critical periods of brain development, before a child develops strong, positive ways to cope with stress.

## Prevalence of Trauma

The majority of students will be exposed to a potentially traumatic event before they graduate from high school.[16] Exposure to violent events that are potentially traumatic for children and youth is particularly common, especially so in neighborhoods where violence and homicide are present.[17] Adult reports of multiple adverse childhood experiences are also common, and include experiences of abuse or neglect, witnessing family violence, exposure to household substance abuse or mental illness, and incarceration of a family member, and these stressors are particularly prevalent among youth who are homeless, in child welfare, and in the juvenile justice system.[18] It is important to consider the ways in which a history of trauma exposure impacts school staff and parents, along with students.

## Impact of Trauma on Students, Staff, and Schools

Exposure to excessive and repeated stress and trauma can affect students, caregivers, and school staff in ways that compromise safety and security in the school environment. Many factors influence how youth and adults respond to potentially traumatic events, including their internal coping resources; external supports; and broader community, cultural, and societal factors that shape how they understand and respond to their experiences.[19] Most youth exposed to trauma do not develop more significant challenges.[20] However, for too many students, traumatic experiences are frequent and prolonged (exacerbated by their experiences at school), and the effects are profound.[21]

## Effects of Trauma on Students and Caregivers

Students exposed to trauma may exhibit a range of reactions that could interfere with school success. Students may experience physical symptoms, such as headaches, stomachaches, poor appetite, and a decline in self-care (e.g., poor hygiene). Intense feelings of fear, anxiety, and concern for safety are also common. Students may have intense responses to trauma reminders (i.e., triggers) and may struggle to calm themselves down and identify and express their emotions safely. Difficulties regulating emotions can lead to behavior problems, such as angry or aggressive outbursts; over- or under-reacting to situations; withdrawing from peers and adults; and engaging in risky behaviors such as alcohol or drug use, fights, or self-harm to manage feelings related to the trauma. Students may also develop more significant, long-term mental health issues related to traumatic experiences, such as post-traumatic stress disorder, anxiety, or depression.[22]

Exposure to trauma can lead to difficulties with concentration, learning, and memory that directly impact academic performance. Emotional and behavioral issues and trouble trusting adults and building relationships exacerbate these challenges, leading to more time out of class, increased absences, and more frequent suspensions and expulsions, further disconnecting students from their school community. Compared to their peers, students affected by trauma have more learning difficulties, are referred more often to special education, score lower on standardized tests, and are more likely to fail a grade.[23]

Parents or caregivers with their own histories of trauma, particularly chronic trauma, may have their own difficulties managing emotions, controlling behaviors, forming relationships, and managing stress related to their child's difficult behaviors. In addition, parents with negative or traumatic experiences related to school may be distrustful of educators and the education system and may have trouble forming relationships with school staff.

### Effects of Trauma on School Staff and the Learning Environment

School staff may bring their own histories of trauma to work or may experience trauma on the job—for example, being threatened or assaulted, or witnessing violence. In addition to direct experiences of trauma, teachers who work with highly traumatized students are at risk of being indirectly traumatized because of exposure to their students' trauma.

Reducing stress, and providing a supportive environment for teaching and improving teachers' social-emotional skills, can also help teachers handle the demands required to engage diverse students and personalize learning.

High rates of trauma among students and staff, when not addressed, can negatively affect school culture and conditions for learning. Students struggling with trauma responses are more likely to escalate and act out in ways that compromise their safety and the safety of other students and staff. In response, adults may become increasingly rigid and reactive. For example, adults may be quick to threaten students with negative consequences, escalate with students, and use punitive discipline strategies. Without recognizing the connection between trauma and current behaviors, school staff may misunderstand, mislabel, or even misdiagnose trauma-related responses.

Under these circumstances, schools risk retraumatizing students by creating environments that mirror or replicate previous trauma. Retraumatizing practices could include employing harsh or shaming discipline practices that mimic abuse experiences for youth; allowing environments to become chaotic, disorganized, unpredictable, or unsafe; treating students or caregivers disrespectfully and minimizing their voice; and using practices like seclusion or restraint. When many members of the school community are affected by traumatic events—whether within or outside of school—student perceptions of unpredictable and unsupportive environments can compromise their engagement and sense of safety and community. For more on the dangers of retraumatization, see "Effects of Retraumatizing Practices on LGBTQ Youth."

## Trauma-Sensitive Approaches

In a trauma-sensitive school, all aspects of the educational environment—from workforce training to engagement with students and families to procedures and policies—are grounded in an understanding of trauma and its impact, and are designed to promote resilience for all. Trauma sensitivity is embedded in the schoolwide foundation, or tier 1, of our multitiered model for safe and supportive schools (see figure 13.1). Schoolwide trauma sensitivity maximizes support for all students, some of whom will not be identified by screening, and helps staff members recognize those who need more intensive services. This fosters an environment in which selective and indicated interventions for trauma (tiers 2 and 3) are more likely to be successful. A trauma-sensitive approach also addresses negative effects of trauma on families and school staff. Schools with an awareness and understanding of trauma and its impact can create environments where all students feel safe,

### Effects of Retraumatizing Practices on LGBTQ Youth

Students who are further traumatized within schools that do not recognize, understand, or address their needs face increasingly negative outcomes. For example, LGBTQ youth who experience unsupportive conditions in schools are more likely to have higher rates of absenteeism, be disciplined at school, have lower grade point averages, drop out of school, have higher rates of depression and anxiety, and have lower self-esteem.[24]

**Figure 13.1** Trauma sensitivity and multitiered systems of support

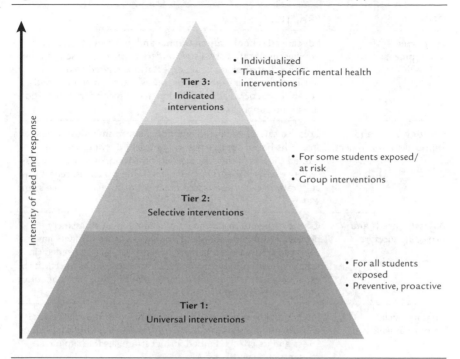

connected, and supported, and the skills critical to building resilience are modeled and taught.

Adopting a universal approach to addressing trauma requires modifications to school practices, policies, and culture. In table 13.1 we offer a framework for adopting trauma-sensitive practices that covers six core domains: (1) supporting staff development, (2) creating a safe and supportive environment, (3) assessing needs and providing support, (4) building social-emotional skills, (5) collaborating with students and families, and (6) adapting policies and procedures. Practices in each domain reflect common elements of a trauma-sensitive approach.[25] These practices can be adapted to address the unique needs of groups with high rates of exposure to trauma. For example, this could include training all staff on the specific experiences of LGBTQ youth, considering exposure to racial trauma when conducting assessments with students of color, and ensuring that trauma-related interventions are culturally relevant.

**Table 13.1** Trauma-sensitive practices across core domains

| DOMAIN | PRACTICES |
| --- | --- |
| Supporting staff development | Educate all school staff on trauma and its effects on students, families, and staff; assess staff understanding and use of trauma-sensitive strategies; integrate expectations related to trauma sensitivity into job expectations, reviews, team meetings, and new-hire practices; address the impact of secondary traumatic stress and support staff resilience. |
| Creating a safe and supportive environment | Create a safe physical and emotional environment using positive, strengths-based approaches; recognize and reduce trauma-related triggers in the school environment; incorporate trauma-sensitive crisis prevention and intervention practices; reflect the culturally relevant norms and practices of students, families, and staff. |
| Assessing needs and providing support | Consider the potential impact of trauma in all assessment protocols and behavior plan templates. Ensure students have access to trauma-specific mental health services as needed (in school or community settings). Tailor interventions to reflect the experiences and needs of particular groups (e.g., youth of color, immigrant populations, and LGBTQ youth). |
| Building social-emotional skills | Integrate universal strategies for teaching and modeling social-emotional skills. Educate students and families about traumatic stress and its effects. Embed formal strategies for helping students cope with adversity. |
| Collaborating with students and families | Provide opportunities for students and families to share input on programming and voice concerns. Treat students and families as partners. Include students and families in schoolwide efforts (e.g., work groups, training activities, action planning) to adopt a trauma-sensitive approach. |
| Adapting policies and procedures | Include a commitment to trauma sensitivity in the school mission; adopt positive and restorative approaches to discipline; ensure communication practices are trauma-sensitive; review policies and procedures to ensure continued alignment with a trauma-sensitive approach. |

## Aligning Trauma Sensitivity with Restorative Practices

A school's disciplinary environment and culture affects students' sense of safety and connectedness, and can traumatize or retraumatize students. Problematic disciplinary practices include harsh exclusionary policies and inconsistently enforced disciplinary policies, including suspensions and expulsions (and how they are employed), corporal punishment, restraint, and

> ## Massachusetts Safe and Supportive Schools and Trauma Sensitivity
>
> A collaboration between Massachusetts Advocates for Children and Harvard Law School, the Trauma and Learning Policy Initiative (TLPI) is a leader in promoting trauma-sensitive policy and practice. It offers educators tools for adopting a whole-school, trauma-sensitive approach. A trauma-sensitive school reform model is currently being implemented in Massachusetts. We provide links to two TLPI resources on trauma sensitivity and approaches in appendix B.

exclusion. These practices disproportionately affect students of color, students who are economically disadvantaged, LGBTQ students, and students with high-incidence disabilities.[26] They also contribute to a more negative school climate, undermine academic achievement, and traumatize or retraumatize some students.[27]

Schools and districts have developed strategies to align trauma sensitivity with restorative practices because both are grounded in common guiding principles, and both offer complementary ways of promoting safe and supportive environments for all students. Trauma sensitivity and restorative practices also require similar shifts in school culture and procedure, and the use of strengths-based, relationship-focused, culturally appropriate practices to increase student safety, choice, control, empowerment, and skill building.

Each approach offers something uniquely important for schools, and when combined, trauma-sensitive and restorative-practice approaches are strengthened by each other (see table 13.2). For example, educators adopting restorative practices are often aware that understanding trauma and its impact can inform practice and interventions; and trauma-sensitive approaches to identifying and reducing trauma-related triggers and traumatizing practices can also be part of a proactive effort to understand and prevent particular behaviors. Schools implementing strategies that align trauma sensitivity and restorative practices recognize that both are necessary for creating consistency across practice and interventions.

Given the connection between trauma sensitivity and restorative practices, aligning implementation efforts avoids duplication and minimizes burden, and promotes a collective understanding of the commonalities and

**Table 13.2** Aligning restorative practices and trauma sensitivity

| RESTORATIVE PRACTICES | TRAUMA SENSITIVITY |
| --- | --- |
| • Provides an empathic and compassionate space for understanding behavior, including trauma-related responses.<br>• Fosters relationships and connections that are often compromised for students exposed to trauma.<br>• Reduces likelihood of retraumatizing students.<br>• Creates an environment where trauma-sensitive practices are more likely to be adopted and sustained. | • Seeks to identify and reduce trauma-related triggers that can result in negative behaviors and harm to others.<br>• Provides another lens through which to view underlying reasons for problem behaviors.<br>• Encourages use of a restorative-practices approach to discipline.<br>• Fosters an environment where restorative practices are more likely to be adopted and sustained. |

*Sources:* Dan W. Butin, "Justice-Learning: Service-Learning as Justice-Oriented Education," *Equity & Excellence in Education* 40, no. 2 (2007): 177–83; Kay Pranis, *The Little Book of Circle Processes* (Intercourse, PA: Good Books, 2005).

relationships between the two approaches. Here are some alignment strategies schools can apply:

- **Align work groups and teams.** It is helpful for staff to view trauma sensitivity and restorative practices as part of a larger effort to support a safe, respectful, and inclusive environment.
- **Develop a shared vision.** Integrated teams can develop a shared, holistic vision for implementing trauma sensitivity and restorative practices.
- **Integrate professional development activities.** The core principles of trauma sensitivity and restorative practices are similar and require similar cultural shifts, and joint training sessions may help staff to see the commonalities. Similar skill building may be necessary to support staff in making the cultural and behavioral shifts needed to adopt trauma-sensitive practices and restorative practices.

Once aligned, trauma-sensitive and restorative approaches can also be integrated with other school efforts, such as social and emotional learning (SEL) and interventions such as Positive Behavioral Interventions and Supports (PBIS), within a multitiered system of support.

## PROMISING PROGRAMS AND STRATEGIES FOR SUPPORTING RESPECT AND INCLUSION

Students may encounter significant life stressors, the effects of which compromise their sense of safety and disconnect and isolate them from the broader school community. Adopting strategies that promote respect and inclusion for all students helps to foster student resilience and reduce the risk of causing additional stress or trauma in the educational environment. In a safe, supportive school culture, students and staff treat each other with respect, regardless of their backgrounds and characteristics. Everyone feels included and experiences emotional, physical, and intellectual safety, and students' and staff members' identities and authentic selves are accepted and supported. In addition, educators' own experiences of inclusion and respect from administrators and peers affect school climate, and how they treat one another can offer a positive and supportive—or negative and unsupportive—model.

There are many "doable" and inexpensive improvements that schools can make to promote safety, support, engagement, and inclusivity. Schools can collaborate with students from diverse backgrounds to identify areas of need regarding respect and inclusion, to recommend practices that would address their needs, and to help monitor implementation of respect and inclusion strategies. Staff can welcome and support new arrivals to the school, neighborhood, and country.[28] Staff can foster a welcoming culture of inclusion and respect by establishing clear norms and expectations—ideally with students—and by acting as role models who exemplify inclusive and respectful behavior and attitudes. Staff can also reinforce norms and expectations through posters and other materials in the classroom and throughout the school building, by establishing or supporting ground rules that exclude disrespect and named microaggressions, and by holding group discussions or whole-class meetings about issues that undermine inclusivity (e.g., bullying). Modeling the desired behavior can expand students' knowledge and understanding of diversity, encourage connections and respect between students (as well as dialogue around diversity), and introduce inclusive language to students and families.[29]

Teachers play a pivotal role in creating classrooms that foster equity, respect, and inclusion. For example, teachers can employ universal design principles to support diverse learners, provide opportunities for group decision making, offer different ways for students to participate beyond writing or speaking in front of an entire class, and embrace cultural responsiveness.[30] They can also ensure that students from different backgrounds experience identity safety and are represented in class assignments and activities—for example, by making certain that supplementary reading materials include diverse and nonstereotypic characters. Even in the early grades, schools can source age-appropriate books that incorporate and address diversity, featuring students with same-gender parents, for example, or students from families who are recent immigrants. Incorporating such practices in the early grades can help to set norms and expectations for how students from diverse backgrounds are treated both in school and beyond.

While it is important that schools address harmful behaviors (e.g., harassment, bullying), visible issues, and microaggressions (such as a student calling another student a name, or using a slur to describe another student's background, sexual orientation, or visible disability), they should also examine teacher and school practices such as signage that signal what is valued or marginalized, and avoid what Ralph Ellison characterized as being "invisible" and Adrienne Rich described as "psychic disequilibrium"—like looking in a mirror and seeing nothing.[31] Do teachers pronounce students' names correctly and demonstrate respect for each student's culture and spiritual values? Or, do students and families from different backgrounds see themselves represented in posters around the school? In school events and extracurricular activities? What recommendations do students have regarding classroom materials, activities, and even rules and expectations for students?

Culturally responsive education happens both through the stated curriculum (such as what authors students read) and the "hidden curriculum" of classroom management, which includes teachers' communication style and the pictures and materials posted on classroom walls.[32] While a single teacher can create a welcoming environment, the effects are greater when everyone within a school setting is oriented toward improving students' and educators' sense of belonging, and when everyone models and practices SEL skills and other behaviors promoting positive school climate.[33]

School and district leaders play important roles too. They can generate data by surveying everyone about whether they feel respected, safe, and included, and ensure that these data are acted upon.[34] The use of reliable and valid school climate measures—disaggregated by subgroup—helps identify areas for focus, enabling schools to recognize problems and select appropriate interventions. For example, the free ED School Climate Surveys include a subscale on stakeholder perceptions of cultural competence in a school, and its data can be analyzed by subgroup to help schools address *intersectionality*, or impacts to an individual arising from belonging to multiple subgroups (e.g., black youth who are also English language learners).[35]

Leaders can also establish policies that foster the desired environment, such as alternatives to suspension that treat discipline as nonpunitive and teach students how to interact with each other in positive ways.

## ADDRESSING DIVERSITY

A recent analysis by the Annie E. Casey Foundation examined the likelihood that children from various racial groups would grow up to become middle class by the time they reached middle age. The study found that African American, American Indian, and Latino children face some of the biggest obstacles on the pathway to opportunity, and research suggests that unsupportive schools play a key role in this.[36] Youth from immigrant backgrounds, the majority of whom are children of color, often face additional barriers, including language barriers or hardships stemming from discrimination.[37] In addition to adjusting to new communities, students from immigrant backgrounds may struggle with navigating language barriers and social isolation in their school.[38] They may experience challenges not only in understanding content but also in adjusting to new teaching styles and academic expectations.[39] Schools can address these challenges by supporting teachers' cultural responsiveness, and through newcomer programs that facilitate transition and adjustment for students from immigrant backgrounds.

Negative experiences of LGBTQ youth in schools and other venues impair their learning, sense of agency and belonging, and well-being.[40] Affirming policies, programs, and practices that also address intersectionality not only promote safety and inclusion in school, but also support student well-being and resilience. These include school nondiscrimination and antibullying policies in school handbooks and materials that list specific actual and perceived sexual orientations and ways to self-identify and express gender, educator training on how to intervene when students are harassed, LGBTQ-affirming information and resources, and an LGBTQ-inclusive curriculum.[41] School-based support groups or extracurricular groups are also essential in creating safe, supportive middle and high schools. For example, a gay–straight alliance (GSA) is a student-led club that includes all students, regardless of sexual orientation or gender identity/expression, and provides a safe place for them to access resources and information, connect with supportive peers and a caring adult, develop a positive sense of self, and address heterosexism and trans bias. GSAs can make schools and communities safer by building awareness of LGBTQ-related concerns. Their group-specific and schoolwide activities can develop leadership and community-building skills that not only support restorative practices and cultivate more welcoming schools for LGBTQ students and their families, but also promote respectful, inclusive schools for all students.[42]

## TAKEAWAYS

- Unsupportive school environments drive negative academic outcomes, emotional challenges, self-harm, and suicidal thinking.
- Many students are vulnerable and can benefit from universal trauma-sensitive approaches.
- Trauma-sensitive and restorative-practice approaches support positive relationships schoolwide, and work best when aligned with each other and integrated with other supportive school efforts and interventions.
- There are many practices that schools and educators can employ to prevent and address students experiencing disrespect, mistreatment, and exclusion because of their life experiences, family background, identity, faith, gender expression, native language and accent, or other characteristics that make them "different."

# FOURTEEN

# Multitiered Systems of Support

*Stephanie Jackson, Juliette Berg,
Sandra Williamson, and David Osher*

MANY SCHOOLS EMPLOY Response to Intervention (RTI) and Positive Behavioral Interventions and Supports (PBIS), which address academic and behavioral needs within a coordinated and organized system.[1] Researchers and practitioners have found that implementing RTI and PBIS (as well as other multitiered approaches) with fidelity can improve school climate, learning, and achievement.[2] As originally conceptualized, RTI addressed academics, while PBIS focused on behavior. Schools focusing on RTI and PBIS realize better results when they integrate RTI and PBIS into a comprehensive and cohesive Multitiered System of Support (MTSS), rather than tackling these issues separately. MTSS is a well-used version of the more generalized multitiered approach described in this book that can be valuable for turning around schools, using data to make decisions, and improving student outcomes.[3] This chapter delineates the essential components of MTSS.

## SCHOOLWIDE, MULTILEVEL INSTRUCTIONAL/BEHAVIORAL SYSTEM FOR PREVENTING SCHOOL FAILURE

What we have defined elsewhere in this book as the universal foundation (i.e., tier 1) of a multitiered approach to safe and successful schools is called the *primary prevention level* in MTSS; it includes high-quality core instruction for academics and clear guidelines for behavior for all students. The school implements a district curriculum and establishes schoolwide expectations for behavior. Instruction is delivered within the general education classroom, is aligned with state or district standards, and incorporates differentiation and interventions for students who are having trouble meeting expectations for academics or behavior.

What we call selective intervention (tier 2) is called the *secondary level* in MTSS; it includes evidence-based intervention(s) of moderate intensity. In the academic realm, students who need additional support receive evidence-based interventions that are supplemental to primary instruction and closely aligned with the core curriculum. Instruction is typically delivered within the general education classroom or another general education location within the school to small groups of students; group size is based on students' ages and needs. Procedures are in place to monitor the fidelity of implementation of secondary-level interventions.

What we call indicated intervention (tier 3) in our generalized multi-tiered approach is called *tertiary prevention* in MTSS; it includes individualized intervention(s) of increased intensity for students who show minimal response to secondary interventions. The intensity and nature of the interventions are adjusted based on a student's responsiveness or progress. If fewer than 80 percent of students are benefiting from the primary prevention system, schools can focus on improving student support in the secondary and tertiary levels. If the percentage of students in the secondary or tertiary level is too large, consider implementing large-group instructional activities, additional supports, and system changes at the primary level to reduce the number of students requiring additional support.

Table 14.1 provides a snapshot of how instruction differs at each level of prevention. It shows the instructional approach, group size, assessments used to monitor progress, and population served. It is important to note that students can move between intervention levels in one area independent of the level of intervention they are receiving in another area.[4]

**Table 14.1**  Intervention levels and tiers of MTSS

|  | TIER 1 | TIER 2 | TIER 3 |
|---|---|---|---|
| Instruction or intervention approach | Comprehensive, research-based curriculum | Standardized, targeted small-group instruction | Individualized, based on student data |
| Group size | Classwide or small-group instruction | Three to seven students | No more than three students |
| Assessment | Screening, three times yearly | At least biweekly or monthly | Weekly |
| Population served | All students | Students identified as being at risk (~15%–20%) | Students with significant and persistent learning needs; nonresponders (~3%–5%) |

## ESSENTIAL COMPONENTS OF A MULTITIERED SYSTEM OF SUPPORT

MTSS integrates assessment and intervention within a schoolwide, multi-level *prevention system* to maximize student achievement and reduce behavior problems (see figure 14.1).[5] MTSS uses a collaborative, iterative, and data-based decision-making model that creates a structure for the delivery of high-quality instruction and increasingly intensive intervention and supports based on students' needs. In this section we describe the essential components of MTSS.

### Screening

Screening is conducted to identify students who may be at risk for poor academic, social-emotional, and behavioral learning outcomes. Universal screening assessments are typically brief and are conducted with all students at a grade level at the beginning of the school year and ideally at regular intervals throughout the school year, followed by additional testing or short-term progress monitoring to confirm students' risk status. At a minimum, screening should be administered more than once per year, such as at the beginning of the school year and the middle of the school year. Screening can answer these questions: Is our core curriculum and instruction effective? Which students need additional assessment and instruction? For example,

**Figure 14.1** The MTSS multilevel prevention system

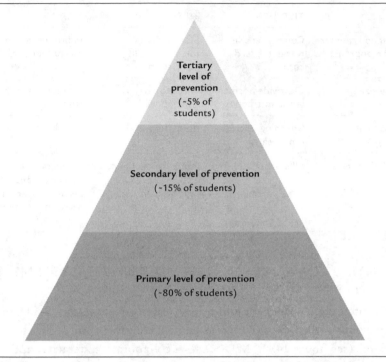

*Source:* National Center on Response to Intervention, *RTI Implementer Series: Module 3: Multi-level Prevention System Training Manual* (Washington, DC: US Department of Education, Office of Special Education Programs, National Center on Response to Intervention, 2012), https://rti4success.org/sites/default/files/ImplementerSeries_MultiLevelManual.pdf.

if the desired outcome is graduation, a quick screen of attendance and credits—predictors of graduation—can reveal which students are likely to need additional support. If the desired outcome is mastery on end-of-year tests, student performance measures like curriculum-based measurements can reveal which students need additional support.[6]

## Progress Monitoring

Progress monitoring is used to assess a student's academic performance; quantify a student's rate of improvement or responsiveness to primary, secondary, or tertiary instruction; and evaluate the effectiveness of instruction. Progress monitoring data can be used to estimate rates of improvement, which allows for comparison to peers; identify students who are not demonstrating adequate progress so that instructional changes can be made; and compare the efficacy of different forms of instruction. Progress monitoring can also help to identify the instructional approach or intervention that has led to the greatest growth among students. It is intended not just for students identified for supplemental instruction—teachers should be assessing *all* students regularly to determine whether instruction is meeting their needs. Progress monitoring tools should be brief, valid, reliable, and evidence based, and students should be assessed at regular intervals (e.g., weekly, biweekly, or monthly) to produce accurate and meaningful results that teachers can use to quantify short- and long-term student gains toward end-of-year goals. At a minimum, progress monitoring tools should be administered at least monthly. Teachers typically establish end-of-year goals that indicate the level of proficiency students should demonstrate by the end of the school year.[7]

## Data-Based Decision Making

Data analysis and data-based decision making are critical to the success of a schoolwide MTSS. Schools should collect, analyze, and report data at all levels of implementation and all levels of instruction to answer questions about students' needs and match students with appropriate instruction. Data analysis and decision making occur in all tiers of the support system.

Schools should establish routines and procedures for making decisions to increase the fidelity of the data-based decision-making process. Schools should also follow explicit decision rules for assessing student progress, including adhering to goal-setting procedures, changing instruction/interventions, referring students to special programs, and moving students to more or less intensive levels. These are the more common types of decisions that schools make:[8]

- **Instruction:** How effective is the instruction? What instructional changes need to be made?
- **Effectiveness:** Is the core curriculum effective for most students? Is one intervention more effective than another?
- **Movement within the multilevel prevention system:** How do we know when a student no longer needs secondary prevention or should move from secondary prevention to tertiary?[9]

## ENSURING EFFECTIVE MTSS IMPLEMENTATION IN SCHOOLS

There are certain ingredients that ensure MTSS is effective in schools. In this section, we describe the role of leadership, the importance of engaging families, the function of professional development and coaching, and culturally and linguistically responsive practices that are key to the success of a multitiered system.

## Leadership

Leaders establish the purpose of MTSS, build a shared vision for MTSS among their staff and community, and help shape the culture and expectations for sustained MTSS implementation. Leaders who involve the entire school community in the decision-making process related to MTSS will more likely get buy-in, which will increase the likelihood of MTSS being effective and moving forward. Without commitment from staff to "make it work," it is unlikely that MTSS will take hold. We have learned that, most often, effective and sustained MTSS approaches begin with a leader's vision and commitment to providing the necessary funding, staffing, professional development, and resources to support a schoolwide effort.

## Family Engagement

Creating an environment where families work as partners helps to build a sense of community that supports successful MTSS implementation. Families should receive information about plans to initiate an MTSS framework prior to implementation. This gives them time to ask questions and get a clear understanding of their role in the process. When MTSS is successfully implemented, families (1) understand the essential components, (2) get regular updates on the progress of their child receiving interventions, (3) are informed about decision making related to MTSS implementation, and (4) have voice, while professionals (1) learn from families about their and their child's cultural resources and (2) develop respectful relationships with families that are marked by cultural reciprocity.[10]

## Professional Development and Coaching

Without the necessary knowledge and understanding of MTSS, teachers cannot successfully implement all of the system's components. Therefore, it is imperative that schools increase staff knowledge by providing job-embedded training, access to needed resources, and ongoing practice with coaching support. Training itself is not enough to ensure that staff will change their behavior and integrate new practices into their daily instruction, however; successful schools must also ensure that teachers apply the new practices over time so that they become routine. Coaching enables staff to build on content learned from training to apply the newly acquired knowledge and skills to their classrooms.[11]

### Fidelity Checks

Schools that implement MTSS with fidelity adhere to the curriculum and instructional and assessment practices throughout the day, and across lessons, with consistency and accuracy. Implementing MTSS with fidelity will help schools evaluate the MTSS framework to better understand whether all essential components are being used, and the degree to which they are effective for increasing student performance.[12] Several tools and measures are available online to help you assess fidelity in your context.[13]

### Culturally and Linguistically Responsive Practices

Instruction and interventions must consider and address students' cultural backgrounds, experiences, and linguistic proficiency in English and their native language, as well as socioeconomic factors that may affect their school performance.[14] By requiring the use of research-based practices that reflect individual children's specific needs, MTSS has the potential to effect change for English learners, as long as those practices have demonstrated robust short- and long-term outcomes for learners in similar settings.

Ideally, MTSS is coordinated with other efforts to bolster safe, supportive, and equitable schools. In the following section, we share how the Rhode Island Department of Education integrates its school climate and MTSS initiatives.

## PUTTING MTSS TO WORK IN RHODE ISLAND TO IMPROVE SCHOOL CLIMATE

Rhode Island (RI) MTSS helps schools across the state operationalize school climate practices and strategies in alignment with state-level initiatives, regulations, and policies defined by the Rhode Island Department of Education. The staff from RI MTSS work to build the capacity of school administrators and staff to use data-based decision making to monitor progress in improving school climate.

As a first step in helping schools select appropriate leading indicator data, RI MTSS staff coach school teams through the process of choosing an area of focus that is aligned with their school improvement plan. Because there are vastly different needs and foci across schools, school teams first define the benchmark for key indicators—such as literacy, suspension, or attendance rates—for each grade across schools.

"In the beginning stages of working with schools, we help them create the structural pieces for measurement, and then look discretely at indicators," explains Michele Walden-Doppke, technical assistance provider and school psychologist at RI MTSS. "It is too hard to measure everything at once, so we break indicators into four parts: math, reading literacy, behavior, and social and emotional learning, which includes school climate."

Changing adult behavior around progress monitoring can be difficult, but it is key to the success and sustainability of school climate work. "Folks were initially afraid of data. Now people are recognizing the value of data—how important data are to identify the students in need and what kind of intervention they need. They are asking better questions, and thinking in more systematic ways. Our work is not changing student performance as much as adult behavior at this point," says Ellen Reinhardt, technical assistance provider with RI MTSS.

One story of success resulting from RI MTSS's work with schools is the creation of a measurement tool called the "Connections Survey."[15] This instrument was developed by school psychologists Kim Pristawa and Alyson Doumato in a school district at a time when staff morale was low—which, in turn, was negatively impacting students. The tool collects data to measure students' feelings of connectedness with teachers and other students, and includes a process for administering and analyzing the results. The instrument also assesses how these connections change over time in relation to improvements in school climate, which has helped teachers think about what "connection" really means, beyond being in the same classroom. The process of reviewing data on student connections has helped to transform school climate in the district for which it was created. Additionally, Pristawa and RI MTSS's Walden-Doppke present nationally about the survey, and other schools in Rhode Island and additional states are piloting the survey.

## TAKEAWAYS

- MTSS combines RTI and PBIS to address academic and behavioral needs within a coordinated and organized system.

- MTSS can be a valuable approach for turning around schools, using data to make decisions, and improving student outcomes.
- MTSS involves a multilevel system for preventing school failure, screening, progress monitoring, and data-based decision making for instruction.
- Effective MTSS implementation requires leadership, professional development, fidelity checks, cultural responsiveness, and family involvement, and necessitates empowering educators to use data.

# FIFTEEN

# Selective Strategies

*Allison Dymnicki, Kimberly Kendziora,*
*Sandra Williamson, and David Osher*

WHILE THE PREVIOUS four chapters focused largely or in part on how schools can build a solid foundation to meet the needs of all students through universal (tier 1) interventions, we now turn to implementing *selective* (tier 2) strategies—those that focus on groups of students who need additional supports.

When you are implementing school-based selective strategies, examining local data is essential to selecting, adapting, and delivering the right interventions. So is addressing the individuality of learning, the specificity of effects, the ecology of intervention, and the strengths and needs of students.

Hillsborough County, Florida, provides an example of how to implement these practices. The district has many Title I schools and a population of students who, in spite of their strengths and promise, have multiple risk factors and high-level needs. Although the district delivers universal programming, many students require more personalized interventions. To identify students with high levels of need, the district uses a database that allows administrators and teachers to access information about student risk factors, such as poor attendance, low grades, or frequent disciplinary actions, and see what services students are receiving.

"Many of the students in our district need tier 2 and 3 interventions," explains Kristine Hensley, Supervisor of Student Services. "Often, students' needs don't surface as being academic or disciplinary, so we work on relationship building with students in addition to looking at their indicator data. Then, leadership teams collaborate to see what social-emotional and mental health supports we can provide to meet their needs."

Once teams pinpoint students' service needs, such as homework help, a friendship group, or more time with an adult mentor in the building, they continue to use data to determine how best to deliver selective interventions that address these needs at individual schools and for individual students.

## WHAT ARE SELECTIVE INTERVENTIONS AND SUPPORTS, AND WHO ARE THEY FOR?

Although universal interventions are designed for all students in a school or grade, selective interventions provide specific strategies and supports for students who have experiences associated with heightened risk (e.g., grief or trauma) or whose behavior suggests that they are at an elevated level of risk (e.g., frequent interpersonal conflict and attendance problems). Indicated, or tier 3, interventions (described in chapter 16) are intended for that small number of students who appear to have more serious behavioral or academic problems and need even more intensive supports. Selective interventions are more likely to be effective if the universal interventions deliver appropriate levels of support to students who are part of the child's ecology, and who can contribute both to problems and to solutions—for example, by reinforcing negative or positive behavior. In addition, selective interventions should be consistent in overall approach and tone and should employ the foundational language provided by universal programming (e.g., social and emotional learning).

More specifically, selective interventions provide additional supports for students who are showing signs of academic, social-emotional, or behavioral problems but have not received a formal diagnosis.[1] For example, selective interventions have been developed for children who are demonstrating early signs of depression, aggression, or social isolation, or who are experiencing academic challenges.[2] Selective interventions are typically implemented in a regular education classroom.[3] The US Office of Special Education Programs (OSEP) Technical Assistance Center on Positive Behavioral Interventions and Supports describes selective interventions as being designed "for students who are not responsive to primary intervention practice . . . to provide more focused, intensive, and frequent small group–oriented response in situations where problem behavior is likely."[4] The Center suggests that selective interventions apply to students who visit the office between two and five times per year. Similar criteria could be developed for students who do not attend school routinely or experience ongoing academic problems.

Selective interventions vary in how groups of students are identified for interventions, the services and supports delivered, and the goals for those services and supports. For example, the Primary Mental Health Program (PMHP) provides supports for students affected by poverty by strengthening positive relationships among members of the community, family, and school.[5] The PMHP restructures the role of school mental health professionals and uses a team of paraprofessional child associates to work more intensively with a larger population of students in a structured playroom environment. Based on an initial screening of all students, the team identifies children who seem most appropriate for PMHP services. The team then gathers more extensive information about these children and develops and implements an intervention plan, which may include teaching students life skills such as taking turns, following rules, and persisting on a task. PMHP shares several key features with other selective strategies described later in this chapter: universal screening and identification, supplemental supports, alignment with core academic and social and emotional learning (SEL) curricula, small-group delivery of evidence-based interventions, and progress monitoring and diagnostic assessments.

## IDENTIFYING STUDENTS WHO ARE AT RISK

There are several ways to identify students who may be at risk. We will discuss three: referral, analyses of administrative data and monitoring systems, and universal screening.

### Referral

Teachers, other students, or families can refer students for assessment or treatment. When educators and parents build close, caring, and supportive relationships with children and youth, they increase the likelihood that a child or youth who is in trouble will reach out to them. When schools establish trusting relationships with families, families are more likely to reach out. Teachers, due to their experience with many same-age children, are uniquely positioned to identify students who are at greater levels of need. They have frequent interactions with students, and already monitor student academic performance and behavior. When students trust adults and processes, they are more likely to disclose feelings of isolation, observations of bullying behavior, situations of abuse or neglect, suicidal ideation, or threats that peers are making toward others or the school. Similarly, close and caring relationships between teachers and students can increase the chances that a student holding critical knowledge about another child or a potentially violent situation will disclose that information sooner rather than later. By getting to know children and youth, teachers and support staff are more likely to recognize a pattern or a change in behavior that may be an early warning sign, allowing them to seek assistance for the child from appropriate school or community services.

## Analysis of Administrative Data and Monitoring Systems

Reviewing both academic and behavioral data can help ensure that the range of selective strategies in a school meets the needs of diverse learners. For example, if data show that increasing numbers of female students are leaving school to raise children, then strategies such as providing information about both sex education and alternative education programs for parenting students may help address dropout. Similarly, data showing slow credit accrual in high school can identify students in need of academic interventions to prevent dropout.

## Universal Screening

### Identifying mental health concerns

Not everyone can or will refer, or do so accurately. In addition, there are always false positives (identifying someone who does not need the intervention) and false negatives (missing a student who needs the intervention). Within a three-tiered model, universal screening can be a critical first step in identifying students who may benefit from selective interventions, although it, too, has false positives and negatives.[6] Because as many as 20 percent of students experience an emotional or behavioral disorder but less than 1 percent receive special education services for these issues, most students with these concerns will be served in regular education classrooms.[7] Students benefit from early intervention for emotional and behavioral challenges, so thorough screening can identify students who may experience long-term benefits from intervention.[8] Screening typically includes all students in a grade and proceeds in a two-stage process: (1) universal screening with a validated tool and (2) more in-depth testing or progress monitoring for students who scored at or below the cut score to verify whether they are truly at risk.

### Predicting educationally valid outcomes

Universal screening measures usually consist of brief assessments focused on target skills (e.g., phonological awareness, numeracy, attention, behavior) that predict future outcomes.[9] Universal screening instruments should be developmentally and culturally appropriate, as well as technically valid.[10] Be aware that the use of screening tools does carry some risks, as detailed in "Challenges in the Use of Screening Tools."

Table 15.1 provides a sample of commonly used universal screening instruments for student behavior.

Researchers recommend that to be technically valid, effective universal screening tools include four markers of quality: sensitivity, specificity, practicality, and consequential validity.[11] *Sensitivity* refers to the degree to which a screening measure reliably identifies the students that need supports ("true positives"), which helps to reduce the number of students incorrectly

### Challenges in the Use of Screening Tools

Although we encourage the use of existing screening tools, there are several concerns about screening. First, some tools have been developed using convenience samples, and therefore may not be culturally and linguistically appropriate for all groups of students.[12] Second, some tools will produce inaccurate results when insufficient data are used to interpret an individual student's trajectory. Third, the context of the assessment may affect student performance on self-report assessments, creating measurement error. To address this, the Center on Response to Intervention recommends looking at five weeks of progress monitoring data to improve classification accuracy, and recommends using multiple screening measures.[13] Experts on the individuality of learning suggest multiple measurements within relatively short periods of time. Finally, screening does not focus on student strengths in other areas, and can potentially label a child and create expectations of problematic behavior, which may cause school staff to respond to the child more negatively or contribute to learned helplessness.[14]

**Table 15.1** Commonly used screening tools

| SCREENER | APPLICABLE GRADES | CONTENT | NUMBER OF ITEMS | NOTES |
|---|---|---|---|---|
| Behavioral and Emotional Screening System (BASC-2/BESS) | Prekindergarten through grade 12 | • Internalizing problems <br>• Externalizing problems <br>• School problems <br>• Adaptive skills | Twenty-five items, five minutes per student | Web-based screening capacity available via AIMSweb <br><br>Three versions: <br><br>• Teacher: Grades preK-12 <br>• Student self-report: Grades 3-12 <br>• Parent: Grades preK-12 |
| Social Skills Improvement System (SSIS) Performance Screening | Ages three through eighteen | • Prosocial behaviors <br>• Motivation to learn <br>• Reading skills <br>• Math skills | Five-point rubric per student; thirty minutes/class of twenty-five | Computer and web-based (AIMSweb) administration and scoring available |
| Strengths and Difficulties Questionnaire (SDQ) | Elementary (ages three through ten); secondary (ages eleven through seventeen) | • Emotional symptoms <br>• Conduct problems <br>• Hyperactivity/inattention <br>• Peer relationship problems <br>• Prosocial behavior | Twenty-five items per student; sixty to seventy-five minutes for a classroom of twenty-five | Pencil/paper and online versions available; can be scored online |
| Student Risk Screening Scale (SRSS) | K-6; some evidence it may be used in grades 7-12 | Externalizing and internalizing behaviors | Twelve items per student: seven externalizing items and five internalizing items | Conducted three times per year—fall, winter, and spring—at no cost |
| Systematic Screening for Behavior Disorders (SSBD) | Grades 1-6 | Internalizing and externalizing behaviors | Forty-five minutes for a classroom of twenty-five | A multigated system that relies on teacher nominations |

*Sources:* Randy W. Kamphaus and Cecil R. Reynolds, *Behavior Assessment System for Children,* 2nd ed. (*BASC-2*): *Behavioral and Emotional Screening System (BESS)* (Bloomington, MN: Pearson, 2007); Stephen N. Elliott et al., "Development and Initial Validation of a Social Emotional Learning Assessment for Universal Screening," *Journal of Applied Developmental Psychology* 55 (March–April 2018), http://dx.doi.org/10.1016/j.appdev.2017.06.002; Robert Goodman, "The Strengths and Difficulties Questionnaire: A Research Note," *Journal of Child Psychology and Psychiatry* 38, no. 5 (1997): 581–6; Kathleen Lynne Lane et al., "Student Risk Screening Scale for Internalizing and Externalizing Behaviors: Preliminary Cut Scores to Support Data-Informed Decision Making," *Behavioral Disorders* 40, no. 3 (2015): 159–70, https://doi.org/10.17988/BD-16-115.1; Hill M. Walker, Herbert H. Severson, and Edward G. Feil, *Systematic Screening for Behavior Disorders (SSBD) Technical Manual: Universal Screening for Pre-K–9,* 2nd ed. (Eugene, OR: Pacific Northwest Publishing, 2014).

identified as needing additional supports. Culture, language, and implicit bias can affect sensitivity. *Specificity* refers to the degree to which the screening measure accurately identifies the students who do not need additional supports or students who are truly not at risk for future academic or behavioral difficulties ("true negatives"). *Practicality* refers to the simplicity and brevity of the screening measure. Having *consequential validity* means that the screening measure will not harm the student and is linked to effective interventions.[15] Different measures are needed to identify different early warning signs, so multiple screening measures should be used. Since each measure has its own criteria (e.g., cut scores or percentile ranks), staff should be trained on the criteria for each screening measure. In addition, once a school or district identifies a set of screening measures, they should use the same set of measures consistently—changing measures makes it impossible to compare results over time.

## SELECTION OF EVIDENCE-BASED INTERVENTIONS

Once universal screening has identified a group of students that would benefit from additional supports, the next step is to choose the interventions that would be most appropriate.[16] Because learning and development are individual, and interventions address an issue and must build upon a specific set of student strengths, no one intervention is right for every student. To ensure a good match between the student and the intervention, collect accurate information about:[17]

- student strengths, needs, and desires (from screening measures, teacher reports, and conversations with student and family); and
- the intervention (what problems or early warning signs it is designed to address, and what the research says about its effectiveness for students like the ones you are focusing on, in contexts like yours).

The selection process should not be rushed; resources are wasted if a student receives additional supports in a topic area or format that does not address his or her needs and strengths. In addition, the selection process should not be a one-time event; engage the student, teacher, and family about desirability, whether it appears to be working, and any unanticipated consequences. Staff and the student support team (SST) should continuously revisit student data to ensure that the program still meets students' needs.

## ENSURING ACCESS TO AND AVAILABILITY OF A RANGE OF SUPPORTS

Schools should offer a range of selective strategies that are designed to meet the diverse needs of their students. These could include different types of specialized strategies for students who have trouble reading, show early signs of anxiety or depression, or are not consistently showing up to school or doing their schoolwork. Notably, one specialized strategy might not work for all students experiencing the same type of problem, so offering a range of supports increases the likelihood of improving outcomes for all students. Although schools routinely implement many interventions and supports simultaneously, school staff do not always have a shared understanding about how these programs align with each other or meet different student needs. It might become evident to the SST, after reviewing the data from universal screening measures, that the school has a need that none of the existing interventions address. In this case, a new strategy should be introduced. Conducting a thorough resource mapping to identify gaps in programming, duplication of services, and interventions that are not producing desired outcomes is an important first step. (See appendix B for more information and resources.) Staff can use tools to assess whether each selective strategy is evidence based, has outcome data available, includes data collection about the program activities, and is effective. Then, SST members can determine whether they should eliminate, modify, integrate, or sustain the selective strategy.[18]

## ALIGNMENT WITH CORE ACADEMIC AND SEL CURRICULA

Selective strategies should align with core curricula and incorporate the foundational skills that support core instructional learning. This could mean using companion evidence-based materials (if these are available) or an evidence-based intervention program that addresses the same subject (e.g., math) but at a different pace or through different methods. Teachers should provide explicit preteaching of core content as a supplement to core instruction, explicit instruction, and practice in the underlying skills, as well as use culturally responsive strategies whenever possible.[19]

The take-home message regarding core curriculum alignment is that a selective strategy should reinforce the concepts taught in the classroom and help students develop desired social-emotional skills, including the metacognitive skills that can help learners manage their learning. This is true even if different methods are used to engage students and to allow them to demonstrate their mastery and understanding. Implementation of this idea is more critical when the selective strategy focuses on teaching academic content versus teaching life skills, such as ways to attend to tasks or persist in learning after facing a challenge. However, even when selective strategies are focused on helping students with concerns such as anxiety, depression, or disruptive behavior, staff should consider the alignment between the selective strategy and what is taught in the general education classroom, and focus on building assets, not just remediating problems. For example, if students are experiencing anxiety about completing an upcoming project that factors heavily into their grade, the topic for the selective strategy could be managing anxiety about homework assignments by conceptualizing smaller, less intimidating steps to complete the project.

## SMALL-GROUP DELIVERY OF SELECTIVE INTERVENTIONS

Selective strategies are often administered by well-trained staff in a group size that is optimal for students. Staff training is critical to an intervention's success, and "is most effective when delivered in multiple stages, including initial learning sessions followed by observation and feedback by experts, with subsequent ongoing in-service training and coaching once the program is up and running."[20] The recommended group size for selective strategies is usually five to eight students, whereas for indicated strategies, group size is usually three to five students or one-on-one instruction.[21] The small-group format for selective strategies has many benefits, such as allowing staff to provide more corrective feedback and allowing students to use multiple response formats that meet their needs for engagement and motivation.[22] There are also, however, some potential downsides that you should be careful to avoid in your group intervention efforts; see "Harmful Effects of Group Interventions" for details.

## PROGRESS MONITORING AND DIAGNOSTIC ASSESSMENTS

Once students have been screened and those in need have entered appropriate interventions, it is important to monitor student progress toward goals, so that they spend enough time in interventions to receive a benefit but not so much that they miss out on instruction. The additional data collection is called *progress monitoring*.

There are several benefits to progress monitoring. When teachers use progress monitoring to make decisions about curriculum and supports, students

## Harmful Effects of Group Interventions

Well-intentioned adults and programs may exacerbate tendencies toward antisocial behavior by placing youth with problematic behavior into programs and settings that are populated with similarly troubled youth. In fact, the most common practice is to segregate these youth from the mainstream peer group and to place them in groups composed entirely or mostly of peers who have broken rules or struggle to meet expectations. New studies indicate that sometimes this practice results in harmful effects; that is, the children whom we are attempting to help may in fact be made worse by our efforts. Placing an adolescent with challenging behavior with like-minded peers can reduce the intended benefits of interventions and lead to less positive, sometimes even negative, outcomes, especially under conditions of poor supervision and lack of structure.[23]

learn more, teachers' decision making improves, and students become more aware of their performance.[24] Progress monitoring tools should be brief; reliable, valid, and evidence based; inclusive of measures repeated over time that capture student learning and performance; and age appropriate.

It is important to collect data over a sufficient period so that an intervention's effects can be demonstrated (researchers recommend at least eight data points). For example, you would not expect improvements in reading after the student participates in a reading program for only a few weeks.[25] It is also important to collect data frequently enough to show a stable trend in student performance. Some recommend the Four-Point Method, in which the trend for a student's four most recent data points is compared to the goal line and performance is rated as *below, on track*, or *above goal*. If a student's scores are above the goal, the goal can be increased; below-goal performance may indicate the need for a more modest goal.[26]

There are many different monitoring and assessment tools. The National Center on Response to Intervention provides a tools chart to review academic progress monitoring tools and determine which ones are right for your students and school.[27] We recommend monitoring progress for the entire period that students receive selective strategies, and then for at least six months after they stop receiving services. Monitoring students during the follow-up period is important given the possibility of students' performance declining after the program ends.

## Approaches to Changing the Intensity or Type of Intervention

When reviewing information about the effectiveness of a selective strategy for a student, you might find that the current selective strategy is not producing the desired outcomes. In this case, you could make changes to the amount, type, or format of supports. Decision-making rules should be applied accurately and consistently to ensure fairness.[28]

Based on what the data suggest, you can modify the selective strategies being offered to students in a number of ways, including changing the intervention itself; how long the selective strategy lasts (e.g., forty-five versus thirty minutes of instruction); how often students receive a selective strategy (e.g., weekly versus biweekly support); who delivers the intervention (e.g., a teacher versus a paraprofessional); and the size of the group (e.g., two versus five students in a group).[29] The "data" that are used should include student input. There is no simple guidance to offer schools about how to decide which changes to make for whom. Group conversations with key stakeholders (including the students who are receiving the selective strategies) should weigh the advantages and disadvantages of each type of change (e.g., the effect of increasing the amount of time or number of meetings on staff caseload and burden) given what is known about the students receiving the strategy and their strengths and needs. Students might reveal other factors of which school staff are unaware that could be influencing the success of these programs.

## SCHOOL-BASED TEAMS AND COMMUNITY AGENCIES

Although many schools can provide selective services and supports to students using their own staff (including counselors, social workers, and school psychologists), schools can expand their capacity by establishing partnerships with community mental/behavioral health agencies.[30] These partners can provide students and families with an extended network of services that may be delivered either in the school building or in the community. A variety of mechanisms may be used in conjunction with multitiered systems of support to enrich resources for students who require selective interventions. One approach particularly relevant to selective interventions is called *integrated student supports* (ISS).[31]

ISS represent a broad set of supports for students' academic and social development that are generally offered for students who experience some risk factors, such as poverty. Resources range from traditional tutoring and mentoring to linking students to physical and mental health care and connecting families to parent education, family counseling, food banks, or employment assistance. Although each provider's approach varies, essential ISS components include needs assessments, community resource mapping, and coordination of supports. ISS staff are generally based in the school or district, and use data to monitor student needs and outcomes over time.

ISS approaches have an emerging body of evidence on their effectiveness in improving outcomes, including attendance, grade retention, dropout prevention, GPA, and math achievement (reading achievement results have been mixed).[32] In addition, return-on-investment analyses have been positive, with studies showing a range of $4 to $11 returned for each dollar invested in ISS programming.

## Communities In Schools

The national nonprofit organization Communities In Schools (CIS) is an example of an ISS organization. Respect, inclusion, and community are the guiding principles behind the holistic services CIS provides to students.

CIS partners with schools to address the social-emotional and physical needs of students in twenty-three hundred schools in twenty-five states and Washington, DC, collaborating with school districts and community partners to empower students to stay in school and succeed in life.

In Chicago, CIS provides direct services and supports to 147 schools and individual students, and connects essential programs and services with schools in the city. Jessica Juarez, one of several CIS of Chicago student support managers who are embedded in a local school, adopts universal SEL strategies like trauma sensitivity and restorative practices and integrates them into the school culture.

From art-based SEL groups that focus on teaching self-management skills to a boys' council and a girls' circle, CIS of Chicago student support managers promote schoolwide and student-specific practices that emphasize inclusion and respect. Practices include restorative chats and peace circles to address behavior problems and connect students with other school-based supports and community partners.

"It's important to consider the various social, cultural, emotional, and environmental factors to meet students' and families' needs," Juarez emphasizes. "We try to provide a holistic approach to each student. As much as we would like to meet all their needs, CIS can't be everything to everyone, but with multitiered supports provided in partnership with community agencies, we can do a lot."

Juarez strives to engage all school staff in initiatives and services, working closely with her school's principal, teachers, counselors, maintenance staff, and lunchroom workers. She also strongly believes that to work with students, she must work in partnership with families, so she meets with parents and guardians regularly to set and monitor goals, as well as connect them with community resources that might be helpful for them.

Last year, CIS of Chicago connected more than seventeen hundred services and programs to sixty-eight thousand Chicago Public Schools (CPS) students. According to Juarez, this has had a major impact. Of the approximately three hundred CPS students who received support from CIS in Juarez's school last year, 100 percent stayed in school, and 99 percent of those who were seniors graduated.

## BUILDING A COORDINATED SCHOOL AND COMMUNITY INTERVENTION TEAM

Key components of developing integrated services include coordinating student support/intervention teams (SITs), which should align with the school's student support team to collaborate and share information with school and community partners, and develop sustainability strategies. Parents and students who have personal experience with supports and have successfully reached their goals can offer a wealth of information and a perspective that professional service providers do not have. SITs can then develop integrated programs to address student mental health or behavioral health needs that incorporate early intervention, as well as interventions for students in need of more structured or therapeutic services, perhaps in accord with students' individualized education programs, if applicable. Each agency, organization, and school takes responsibility to develop and create funding strategies to support interventions such as care management, social work services, and early intervention groups.

Another purpose of the SIT is to develop protocols to share information and protect student confidentiality. Schools often develop SITs to address various issues that a student may be experiencing (e.g., academic, behavioral, and/or emotional challenges). SITs provide identification, screening, and assessment of individual-, school-, and family-related problems; develop a student intervention plan, which may include participation in an intervention group, counseling, or behavior intervention plan; and make referrals to a community provider for treatment, if needed. The SIT leader provides oversight to ensure that the intervention plan is implemented; consults with teachers, school staff, and community providers; and follows up on student progress with the team. The SIT provides continued support to ensure that appropriate and accessible services and resources are offered to meet the diverse needs of individual students.

To develop and provide a comprehensive intervention plan, it is important to include all individuals who work with the students, such as school staff, community professionals, parents, and family advocates. The school becomes the central place for the intervention team to meet and brings the community partners together to provide comprehensive interventions and a coordinated student care plan.

## TAKEAWAYS

- Selective strategies provide additional supports for students who are showing signs of academic, social-emotional, or behavioral problems but have not received a formal diagnosis.
- They incorporate universal screening; the selection of interventions that meet the needs of the students being served; alignment with the core curriculum; routine data collection, review, and progress monitoring; and appropriate referral to school-based teams and additional supports from community agencies.
- When implemented with quality, and in a way that is culturally and linguistically responsive, selective strategies can lead to improved outcomes for students with signs of academic and problem behaviors, and ensure that schools meet the needs of all learners.

# SIXTEEN

# Indicated Strategies

*Allison Gruner Gandhi, Kimberly Kendziora,*
*and David Osher*

WHEN THE UNIVERSAL FOUNDATION (tier 1) and selective (tier 2) strategies within a multitiered system of support are sufficiently robust and implemented with fidelity, we expect that most students will benefit. However, research indicates that 3–5 percent of all students do not respond to the current array of validated, evidence-based strategies.[1] These students need more intensive and individualized intervention, which we refer to as *indicated* strategies. These are also sometimes referred to in the field as *intensive* or *tertiary* interventions. This chapter provides information on how to select, implement, and assess indicated interventions.

In theory, only a very small percentage of students in a school should need indicated strategies. However, this assumes that there is a robust foundation and strong early interventions in place; sometimes students whom teachers identify as needing indicated strategies in fact may need only better universal conditions for learning or universal prevention, or selected strategies that more appropriately target their needs and are implemented with fidelity. If the foundational tiers within a multitiered system of support are implemented appropriately, the students in need of indicated intervention strategies include only those:

- who have not responded to appropriate evidence-based strategies or other appropriate interventions;
- with very low academic achievement or severe behavior problems who are not making adequate progress in their current intervention program; and
- with disabilities who are consistently not making adequate progress in meeting their individualized education program (IEP) goals.

Although indicated strategies are intended to be provided to any student in the school who needs them, students who have disabilities are those who most often receive services in this category. Because student needs are greater and the interventions are more intense, intrusive, and costly, it is important that these strategies are consumer-driven and culturally competent, build on student strengths and assets, and avoid harmful effects.[2]

## THE CHARACTERISTICS OF INDICATED STRATEGIES

Although indicated strategies can take different forms, in general they should include individualization and assessment of academic instruction or behavior support, as well as increasing intensity (e.g., smaller group, expanded time). In this section we describe these characteristics in detail.

### Individualization and Assessment

From a multitiered system of support (MTSS) perspective, the hallmark of indicated strategies is the integration of assessment into the interventions to achieve appropriate individualization that meets a student's unique needs. Reliable and valid assessment is required to ensure that the intervention is tailored to students. Appropriate assessment techniques (which should include multiple sources of data) are strengths-based, culturally competent and responsive, and attentive to the student's and family's perceptions, desires, and unique needs. Without this holistic assessment process, teachers cannot accurately identify students who need indicated strategies, diagnose specific needs, or make appropriate, timely instructional changes. *Wraparound* is an example of consumer-driven individualized planning that is dynamic, ecological strengths-based, responsive, and richly informed by students' and families' knowledge, goals, and needs (see "Wraparound Strategies" for more information).

## Wraparound Strategies

Wraparound strategies are a collaborative, child- and family-driven, culturally competent, relationship-based, and multisystemic approach to providing services and supports to children with intensive needs. Although wraparound plans include formal and informal therapies or programs, wraparound is not itself a therapy or a program. It has been successfully used to address attendance, mental health, and other academic and behavioral problems, both in and out of school. Research suggests that effective wraparound reduces out-of-home placements, behavioral health functioning, and youth participation in the community.[3]

Wraparound uses an individualized planning process involving the child and family, community agencies, and school staff that results in a unique set of school and community services and supports tailored to meet the needs of the child and family. A care coordinator develops a relationship with the youth and family and works with them to outline their vision and identify their needs and goals. In addition to the youth, family, and care coordinator, the wraparound team includes professional service providers and natural supports (e.g., friends, clergy). The team integrates the identified vision, needs, and goals into a single plan, regardless of how many service systems are involved, developing the individualized set of services and supports necessary to achieve those goals. The wraparound plan employs a strengths-based assessment, is coordinated by the care coordinator, specifies a crisis/safety plan, and identifies measurable targets that can be monitored regularly. School-based wraparound planning provides additional supports for the child that are implemented during the school day to aid teachers and other school staff. For a visualization of wraparound, see *Wraparound: Stories from the Field.*[4]

## Increasing Intensity

Indicated strategies should also be ecological, and viewed as a process of increasing intensity rather than as a single program. While there may be intervention programs with evidence demonstrating their effectiveness for students with intensive needs—such as cognitive behavioral therapy, mentoring, or multisystemic family therapy—these may not necessarily be the right choice for every student in need of indicated intervention support. Although these strategies may be an appropriate starting point, the student's unique needs will likely require some specific modifications to individualize the intervention. Indicated strategies are typically implemented in a sustained, progressive way over time; they are not a quick fix. Students needing indicated strategies generally have severe and persistent learning or behavioral needs and therefore require ongoing support to make progress toward their goals. Often, indicated strategies involve an intentional connection to systems outside the school setting that are serving the student and his or her family.

## DATA-BASED INDIVIDUALIZATION: A FRAMEWORK FOR INDICATED STRATEGIES

Recent research points to *data-based individualization* (DBI) as a promising approach for providing indicated strategies to students with the most intensive needs. DBI, which was initially employed only as an academic intervention, is a systematic method for using data to determine when and how to intensify intervention in reading, math, and behavior. Whether a student's needs are academic, behavioral, or both, DBI relies on systematic and frequent collection and analysis of student-level data, modification of intervention components when those data indicate inadequate response, and use of teachers' clinical experience and judgment to individualize intervention. Benefits of DBI include the ability to use the framework to plan intervention that addresses both academic and behavioral needs simultaneously.[5] Figure 16.1 depicts the DBI process.

DBI requires access to valid and reliable data. It is impossible to underestimate the importance of data when you are implementing indicated strategies. Progress monitoring tools are critical. These assessments must be sensitive to small changes in student achievement or behavior, and they should be able to graph or display data in a way that allows visual inspection and analysis. They should also have clear decision rules for when an intervention change should be made. The National Center on Intensive Intervention offers a tools chart that lists (and reviews the technical rigor of) commonly used academic and behavioral progress monitoring tools, which can be accessed through the link in appendix B. For an example illustrating the successful implementation of DBI, see "A DBI Case Study: Swartz Creek Community Schools."

**Figure 16.1**  Data-based individualization process

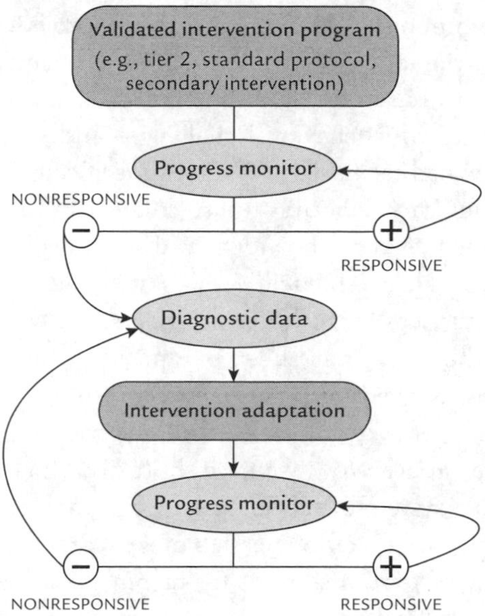

*Source:* National Center on Intensive Intervention, www.intensiveintervention.org.

## THE INTERCONNECTED SYSTEMS FRAMEWORK: AN EXTENDED REFERRAL PROCESS FOR INTERAGENCY COLLABORATION AND SUPPORT

Most schools do not have the resources in-house to address the complex needs of students identified for indicated interventions. Students with more intensive needs, particularly those involving other child- and family-serving systems, may require a more comprehensive organizing framework than the integrated student supports (ISS) framework described in the prior chapter. The *interconnected systems framework* (ISF) was developed to facilitate the links between education and other systems, particularly mental health.[6] The ISF works across all tiers of support in a school, employs cross-system problem-solving teams, uses data to decide which evidence-based practices to implement, uses progress monitoring for both fidelity and impact, and actively engages youth, families, and other school and community stakeholders.[7] Learn more about its engagement benefits in "Moving Toward Family- and Youth-Driven Services."

## A DBI Case Study: Swartz Creek Community Schools

Swartz Creek Community Schools, in Michigan, provides an example of how to maximize the efficiency and effectiveness of indicated programs by making decisions based on data. Students who receive indicated services include those with behavioral challenges and students with IEPs. The school district has earmarked resources specifically for indicated programming, allowing each school's staff to create a system that focuses on selecting programs based on individual and schoolwide data and implementing those programs with fidelity. This system ensures an uninterrupted continuum of services for high-need students.

"In the past, there may have been one person who kept track of the services a student received," explains Derrick Bushon, Executive Director of Student Services for Swartz Creek Community Schools. "If that person left, everything fell apart. Now, we have shifted our focus from centering on one person to a system of support where everyone—from the superintendent to school staff—takes ownership of kids' progress and success."

To support the system of services for high-need students, the district emphasizes an overall culture of learning, placing heavy emphasis on hiring staff who are dedicated to improving school climate and who will focus on setting expectations for positive behaviors.

"Ten years ago, special education was focused on compliance," Bushon recalls. "In our schools now, we focus less on compliance, and more on giving kids what they need. That compliance piece will happen when culture is in place." Swartz Creek's systems-based approach has reduced siloes and removed barriers to service delivery, all while increasing the number of students who are educated in mainstream classrooms. Bushon says, "We are student-focused in Swartz Creek. We constantly strive to improve the culture of the district, and improving our culture helped us create districtwide initiatives for students needing indicated services. We've seen our special [education] numbers and service time decrease because we provide interventions to kids. We no longer wait for kids to fail—we provide supports so they don't fail. We are expecting more from our kids and they are stepping up to the plate."

## Moving Toward Family- and Youth-Driven Services

Although engaging families in educational and support services for their children is associated with better outcomes, families of children with emotional disorders are the least engaged compared to families of students with other disabilities or students without identified needs.[8] The ISF framework does not solve this problem, but it facilitates the introduction of more advanced family engagement practices from the worlds of community mental health and systems of care. Family-driven care means families have a primary decision-making role in the care of their own children, as well as in the policies and procedures governing care for all children in their community, state, tribe, territory, or nation. This includes choosing supports, services, and providers; setting goals; designing and implementing programs; monitoring outcomes; participating in funding decisions; and assessing the effectiveness of all efforts to promote the mental health and well-being of children and youth.[9]

Table 16.1 shows how the ISF reframes traditional practices so that mental health and other professional services can be coordinated with and integrated into a school system at all levels of intervention. The ISF centralizes and streamlines management and combines school and community-based staff to provide services and supports collaboratively. The ISF employs blended teams to organize supports around the specific needs of a student and family—not around the service units of different disciplines.[10]

The ISF requires changes in how typical educational and community mental health services are delivered, and in how educational and mental health systems work together. Like any change, it requires school readiness; strong leadership from a superintendent, school board, or leadership team; and provider readiness to work with schools. Schools that have successfully implemented the ISF have noted that their success was guided by district-level and mental health leaders who made student and family outcomes the foundation from which all efforts were assessed, and who clarified and validated the effort through formal policies and systems.[11]

### Systems of Care

The ISF integrates similar elements to those of *systems of care*, which are integrated networks of services for children with serious emotional and mental

**Table 16.1**  Interconnected Systems Framework

| TRADITIONAL PRACTICE | ISF PRACTICE |
| --- | --- |
| Each school works out its own plan with a mental health or other service agency | The district has a plan for integrating mental health and other services at all buildings based on both school and community data |
| A counselor is housed in a school building one day a week to see students | A mental health professional participates in teams at all three tiers |
| No data to decide on or monitor interventions | A professional service provider leads group or individual interventions based on data |
| School personnel are alone in attempting to "do mental health" | A blended team of school and community providers "divide and conquer" based on strengths of the team |

*Source:* Adapted from Lucille Eber, "Integrating Mental Health & Other Community Partners into the PBIS Framework" (paper presented at the 10th Annual New England Positive Behavior Support Forum, "PBIS: Research to Practice," Norwood, MA, November 2014), https://www.mayinstitute.org/presentation/A%20 PBIS%202014%20-%20Eber%20Mulit-Tiered%20Behaviroal%20Systems.pdf.

health needs. ISF approaches involve comprehensive, interagency collaboration to provide individual children and their families the services they need through partnerships among key stakeholders. At their best, these elements represent a paradigm shift focused on creating cross-agency collaboratives that operationalize family-driven and youth-guided practice, cultural and linguistic competency, and community-based supports and services.[12] The services coordinated through a system of care can include wraparound, care coordination, counseling, crisis outreach, education and special education, health care, legal services, protection and advocacy, psychiatric consultation, and therapeutic foster care. The system-of-care approach emphasizes evidence-based models; its overarching goal is to facilitate a family- and youth-driven process that results in culturally competent services.

Effective systems of care yield improved outcomes for academic achievement, behavioral problems, and school and community engagement for children and families. National evaluation data show that system-of-care programs increase the number of youth who receive treatment, and produce positive, lasting outcomes (e.g., fewer behavioral and emotional problems and fewer contacts with law enforcement). Research has found improved school attendance (more than 80 percent of children attend school regularly twelve months after entering services), reduced disciplinary actions in school, and improved school performance. In addition, nearly 90 percent of youth showed a significant reduction in or stabilization of emotional and behavioral problems, including fewer arrests and suicide-related behaviors. Systems of care also reduce in-patient and juvenile justice costs to communities. See "Lessons from Youth from the Foster Care System" for firsthand accounts from youth who have benefited from these supports.

Many state and local educational initiatives successfully employ MTSS as a framework for their coordinated systems of care.[13] Because of the com-

---

### Lessons from Youth from the Foster Care System

Although interventions are important, relationships and support are particularly vital. Youth in foster care often have complex needs that challenge their educational success. We conducted a focus group with outliers—youth who made successful transitions. Here are their responses to the question, "What is the single most important thing that youth need to be successful?"

- Caring, motivated **mentors**
- **Role models**
- **Adults who listen** to them
- Encouragement and **high expectations** from others
- **Boundaries and structure** from adults
- To have their **basic needs met** (e.g., housing, nutrition, clothing)
- A stable living situation
- **Supportive friends** who are a positive influence; avoidance of peers who are a negative influence
- Support to develop **good mental and emotional health**
- Adequate **educational support** (e.g., financial aid for higher education, assistance transitioning to college, help learning how higher education systems work)
- Hope, self-confidence, and a sense of responsibility and personal goals
- Faith—a belief in something
- Opportunities to develop and model **healthy relationships** (e.g., with younger siblings)
- Opportunities to develop talents and participate in **enrichment activities** (e.g., sports)
- Opportunities to develop **skills for leadership** and professionalism (e.g., presenting self well, being articulate)

plexity of the service delivery system and the need to individualize services for each child, a care coordinator is usually assigned to help a family access services and to assist service providers, and this person ideally develops a supportive relationship with families and youth. All agencies involved, as well as the child and family, actively participate in decision making regarding the student's care. The team develops an individualized service plan based on a wraparound approach, as described earlier. As an individualized approach, this process can be an important aspect of selected and indicated strategies, and is an extension of interventions provided in community and school applications of MTSS.[14]

The student support team can also implement this level of coordination. Continued professional development of teams that review individual data is essential to improve their ability to review behavioral and academic data, make recommendations for interventions, monitor intervention implementation, and then modify services and approaches as needed. For example, a school might include a community-based clinician as a member of the SST on a rotating basis; this person could be scheduled to participate on the team for approximately an hour (per week, biweekly, or monthly, depending on resources available for support), during which the team would review and discuss any students experiencing social-emotional or behavioral issues during that time.

If a school does not have an existing relationship with a community-based clinician or agency, a relationship can be developed, often with little or no additional cost to the school or district. Identify partnerships and collaborations with other agencies that could provide community-based clinicians as a resource to the school, often funded by other agency or federal funding streams. The clinician is typically an employee of a community-based agency, and the clinician's time is often covered by the agency, through a negotiated fee structure between the school district and the agency, or via Medicaid funds (in some states). Districts and agencies usually develop a memorandum of agreement/understanding addressing the clinician's role and the legal issues involved in sharing student information.

To start such a relationship, designate a member of the SST to contact the partner agency and discuss the potential role for a clinician. The ideal clinician partner is one who has experience working with schools and with children and youth within the targeted age range. The clinician becomes an ongoing consultant to the team, and can provide guidance; suggest resources, strategies, or programs within and outside of the school; and report back to the partner agency about the types of needs being seen in the community.

## TAKEAWAYS

- Indicated strategies support students in a school who do not (or are unlikely to) respond to universal or selected strategies implemented within an MTSS.
- Because student needs are greater and interventions are more intense, intrusive, and costly, it is important that they be consumer-driven and culturally competent.
- Wraparound strategies are student- and family-driven ecological approaches.
- DBI offers a structured process for using data to guide decisions about when and how to intensify an intervention to meet a student's individual needs.
- Supports for providing indicated interventions can come from outside of the school system itself, but best practice integrates these interventions with educational goals through the ISF.

# SEVENTEEN

# Social and Emotional Learning Matters

*Jessica Newman, Allison Dymnicki, Edward Fergus,*
*Roger P. Weissberg, and David Osher*

SOCIAL-EMOTIONAL COMPETENCIES can be learned and developed by all students and adults. Social and emotional learning (SEL) happens in a variety of settings, with a variety of people, and at a variety of levels. There is no "one size fits all" approach, although research demonstrates what has worked best in previous studies with specific groups of schools and out-of-school time initiatives. This chapter describes a universal SEL approach that meets the needs of all students in a school, whereas other chapters provide tools for addressing selective and indicated SEL needs such as anger management. We emphasize a sociocultural perspective to acknowledge that social-emotional competencies may be expressed and valued differently by diverse individuals, and that interventions to build these competencies should be culturally competent and responsive, and should counter marginalization.

Effective SEL can take place during the school day, or in out-of-school time, such as during afterschool programs and at home with family members. In addition, new legislative policies support social-emotional development at the broader federal, state, and district levels, such as state learning standards and the Every Student Succeeds Act (ESSA). We highlight the ways in which school leaders, teachers, staff, families, and community members can support student social-emotional growth. We begin by defining SEL before describing the characteristics and benefits of quality implementation. Finally, we discuss best practices to produce positive outcomes for students and adults in the school community.

## SOCIAL AND EMOTIONAL LEARNING, DEFINED

The Collaborative for Academic, Social, and Emotional Learning (CASEL) defines SEL as "the process through which children and adults acquire and effectively apply the knowledge, attitudes, and skills necessary to understand and manage emotions, set and achieve positive goals, feel and show empathy for others, establish and maintain positive relationships, and make responsible decisions."[1] In any discussion of SEL, it is important to distinguish among (1) the *process* of social and emotional learning, (2) the *approaches and practices* that support effective SEL, and (3) the knowledge, attitudes, and skills (what we call *competencies*) that students and adults will develop and apply as a result.

CASEL has identified five competency domains of SEL: self-awareness, self-management, social awareness, relationship skills, and responsible decision making.[2] Other frameworks emphasize different, but related and often overlapping, competencies.[3] The CASEL Guide, which describes these competencies and quality SEL programs in depth, can be accessed through the link in appendix B.

CASEL's framework extends beyond most classroom-based SEL curricula. Instead, it focuses on implementing SEL school- and districtwide. The goal of implementing SEL systemwide is to maximize the potential benefits of SEL for all students.

## BENEFITS OF QUALITY SEL

Extensive research demonstrates the impact of quality SEL (discussed in depth later in this chapter) for students and adults on a variety of outcomes. Students who engage in quality SEL are more likely to demonstrate better social-emotional competencies, improved classroom behavior and interpersonal relationships, reduced conduct problems and emotional distress, and improved academic performance.[4] Long-term benefits also have been documented; for example, adults who engaged in SEL practices and programs as children are more likely to engage in healthy adult relationships, demonstrate less criminal behavior, and have higher levels of engaged citizenship.[5] Moreover, there is evidence to suggest long-term benefits for youth who experienced practices and programs that promoted SEL in preschool or elementary school.[6] This research suggests that the benefits of SEL extend beyond influencing short-term outcomes to putting youth on a long-term trajectory that positively impacts families, communities, and our global society.

Research has shown that engaging in SEL as an adult also promotes positive outcomes.[7] For example, two studies of elementary and secondary school teachers found that teachers who completed a mindfulness training (focused on improving teachers' ability to direct and sustain attention intentionally and nonjudgmentally) demonstrated more focused attention and lower levels of stress and burnout immediately after the program and three months later.[8] Providing SEL to teachers can influence their students as well; in one example, a teacher mindfulness intervention reduced cortisol levels—a stress marker—in students.

## SEL AND INCLUSIVE PRACTICES

Another potential benefit of SEL is its contribution to the creation of inclusive educational settings. Massachusetts provides an example. According to Matthew Holloway, Coordinator for Educator Development in the Center for Instructional Support at the Massachusetts Department of Elementary and Secondary Education (ESE), a fundamental strategy for improving schools' inclusive practices is to give educators the professional development and classroom support they need to integrate students of all abilities into their classes. ESE defines *inclusive practices* as strategies that improve outcomes for all students, with and without disabilities, both academically and in the area of social and emotional learning (SEL).

Holloway explains, "We seek to support better collaboration between the systems and, in fact, to encourage a single system. ESE teams function on the principle that improving social-emotional learning and school climate improves inclusive practice."

ESE strives to create a high-quality educator workforce to increase educational equity practice. The department began working with stakeholders on an initiative called the Leading Educational Access Project (LEAP) and created a series of resources promoting inclusive practice. One such resource was the *Educator Effectiveness Guidebook for Inclusive Practice*. The Guidebook has tools that support professional development around inclusive practice, lesson planning resources for SEL, feedback on inclusive practice, and ideas for job-embedded professional development.

ESE has included supporting SEL, health, and safety in its statewide strategic plan. Often called "the heart strategy," this plan establishes SEL alongside curriculum, accountability, and educator development as one of ESE's key levers in improving outcomes for all students in Massachusetts.

ESE supports educators in their wider SEL initiatives in its ESSA implementation plan as well. Additionally, Massachusetts includes guiding principles for SEL in the state's new curriculum framework for math and English language arts.

## ELEMENTS OF QUALITY SEL

Meta-analytic research on SEL has identified several key elements that contribute to *quality* SEL:

- **Systemic, coordinated, and contextually relevant implementation.**[9] Quality SEL builds from and is aligned with federal, state, and/or districtwide policies and supports, and is facilitated through a schoolwide approach that often starts in the classroom. There are policy and implementation supports for SEL at all levels of the school system, both during the school day and during out-of-school time programming, to ensure that SEL is comprehensive and aligned. High-quality SEL practices are relevant for the specific schools, programs, students, and adults, taking into account sociocultural dimensions such as race/ethnicity and income.[10]
- **A safe and supportive environment.** Quality SEL creates strong, supportive conditions for learning and collaboration at the classroom level, schoolwide, and among all members of the school community.[11]
- **Competence building, prosocial attitudes, and growth mindsets.** Extending beyond simply hanging up signs in a school instructing students to be respectful to each other, quality SEL requires interactive activities focused on a clearly defined set of competencies and practices that promote competency development.[12]
- **Engagement of all youth.** Quality SEL engages all youth through interactive, youth-driven opportunities for competence building. Youth share their voice, describe their own experiences, and make connections with others. Engaging in high-quality SEL has the potential to increase

student motivation to come to school, show up to class on time, and participate in class work and discussions with peers.[13]

- **Formative evaluation.** In quality SEL, practices are reflected on and evaluated in an ongoing way that promotes continuous improvement.[14] The school community collects information about how SEL is being implemented, by whom, and how well it is working.

In the following sections, we describe each component of quality SEL in greater detail.

## Systemic, Coordinated, and Contextually Relevant Implementation

Quality SEL involves a system of supports and buy-in from multiple stakeholder groups who all endeavor to support the social-emotional and academic development of children.[15] SEL is most effective when it is part of teacher pedagogy and integrated seamlessly into all academic and school activities, when teachers are given the time and resources required to implement it with quality, and when it accounts for the unique context and sociocultural dimensions from which youth and adults draw. Six critical steps promote systemic, coordinated, and contextually relevant SEL: (1) identify and engage stakeholders; (2) understand assets, needs, and readiness to implement SEL; (3) identify, agree to, and clearly articulate a vision for SEL; (4) focus on aligning the SEL initiative and existing efforts; (5) develop and apply a sociocultural lens; and (6) identify necessary supports for adults in the school.

## A Safe and Supportive Environment

A safe and supportive environment starts with the adults. When teachers—and, by extension, all adults, including paraprofessional staff and administrative staff—engage with students in a way that is warm, is sensitive, and promotes a sense of connection, youth feel safe and supported, which gives them the space and freedom to develop new competencies. An environment that fosters attachment and a sense of belonging is foundational to effective SEL. Likewise, youth are more motivated to engage in SEL when adults, especially primary teachers or staff they interact with frequently, meet their innate needs for autonomy, belonging, and competence.[16] Finally, adults in the school influence and demonstrate critical social-emotional competence, from the tone of their voice to their body language to the ways in which they engage with each other and with young people.[17]

## Classroom-level practices

Effective classroom-level SEL always incorporates the teaching and modeling of social-emotional competencies, along with opportunities for students to practice those competencies in real-world situations to receive constructive feedback.[18] Classroom structures and practices that promote relationship building, conflict resolution, positive approaches to behavior, restorative practice, and student engagement are critical to effective SEL. Classrooms can include peace corners, for example, that provide a safe and constructive space for young people to resolve conflicts that may arise. Or classrooms may have a quiet table that is removed from the main area of the room for times when students need to take a break, to calm down, or to regulate any intense emotions they may be feeling.[19] Teachers might begin the day's class with a short classroom meeting that involves an icebreaker activity or pair sharing to enable students to get to know each other.[20] Small- and large-group discussion and collaborative work is another effective strategy that engages youth and promotes the development of key relationship skills, such as communicating effectively, listening actively, negotiating, and making responsible decisions. Students, with guidance from the teacher, might develop and agree to adhere to norms and behavior guidelines, often associated with logical consequences. This not only promotes equitable behavior management practices but also facilitates students' understanding of cause and effect and responsible decision making.

## Schoolwide practices

Effective schoolwide SEL includes all adults—not just the teachers—in supporting students' social-emotional development.[21] This category encompasses school leaders, administrative staff, paraprofessionals, custodians, cafeteria workers, bus drivers, sports coaches, security guards, and others that interact with youth during the day and the policies, processes, or structures in place to ensure that their interactions support student social-emotional growth. What training and professional development can be offered to ensure that everyone understands how to co-create a caring school climate that promotes student social-emotional development?

## Family and community practices

Partnering with families and community members to enhance SEL will also promote social-emotional development of students, as well as engage some of the most critical stakeholders for your school community.[22] Employ respect-ful cultural reciprocity to ensure that the views and values of families and community members around SEL are incorporated, and understand the role that families play in their child's socialization.[23] When family and commu-nity members understand what SEL is, why the school is engaging in it, the competencies their children are developing, and how they can continue and extend competency development practices to promote SEL at home, young people begin to meaningfully connect what happens during the school day with their out-of-school experiences. Connecting with families around their students' social-emotional development might be a welcome change from the typical interactions—about attendance, behavioral, and academic issues—that families have with schools. Community-based organizations can also support SEL by offering SEL opportunities during out-of-school time. SEL works best when the foundational SEL language is employed at home, in school, and in the community, and across all three tiers of the multitiered system of support.

## Competence Building, Prosocial Attitudes, and Growth Mindsets

Developing competence, prosocial attitudes, and growth mindsets is facili-tated by a culturally responsive, emotionally safe, and identity-safe environ-ment where students and adults feel connected and where adults and peers embody and model these skills. Competence building, prosocial attitudes, and growth mindsets are also facilitated by four key components, represented by the acronym SAFE:

- **S**equenced approaches are connected and coordinated to promote com-petency development.
- **A**ctive learning and engagement supports students as they develop and master new competencies.
- **F**ocused approaches emphasize and make time for competency development.
- **E**xplicit approaches target specific social-emotional competencies in an intentional way.[24]

The following approaches also support competence building, prosocial attitudes, and growth mindsets:

- standalone lessons that are sequenced appropriately and focus explicitly on developing students' social-emotional competencies, often through an evidence-based SEL program;

- teaching practices and pedagogy (e.g., project-based learning) that promote the application of social-emotional competencies in real-world situations; and
- integration with an academic content area.[25]

Teaching social-emotional competencies is a critical component of development but is not sufficient to promote transfer and application of these skills. For young people to effectively develop these competencies, they have to use them and receive feedback. In figure 17.1 we present a *modeling–practicing–feedback loop* built upon the idea that quality SEL may be both explicitly emphasized *and* embedded in the day-to-day. In this loop, adults model social-emotional competencies and provide opportunities for students to practice using them (either by explicitly naming them, demonstrating them, and role-playing their use, or by creating embedded opportunities for real-life modeling and practice, such as through community service). Adults (and peers, if developmentally appropriate) can then give feedback and engage in coaching as students work to develop and master the competency.

The characteristics of the classroom and school community are important here.

## Engagement of All Youth

If young people are to develop social-emotional competencies, they must show up and engage in the process of SEL. *What makes SEL engaging to young people?* It is critical to remember the *A* in *SAFE*—active. When students are active participants in their learning, reflect on and develop intrapersonal awareness, practice competencies, and build successful interpersonal relationships with others, SEL happens. Developmentally appropriate activities are a key consideration here, as older youth will need more and deeper active learning than younger youth. Offering students authentic choices, opportunities to share their voice, and innovative approaches to leadership are all methods of youth engagement that also promote competency development.[26]

Second, research suggests that personal connection to learning supports motivation and engagement to learn.[27] Make the SEL content relevant and meaningful to the students and ensure that SEL materials show examples of students similar to them. Relevance includes enabling students to consider how they can apply these competencies in the diverse contexts they encounter. For example, an elementary school teacher can ask students to

**Figure 17.1**  A modeling–practicing–feedback loop for competency development

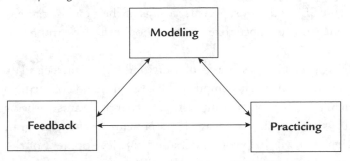

Adults **model** social and emotional competency at all times:
- **Be explicit.** "Today we are going to focus on active listening. One strategy for active listening is repeating what you've heard back to the person who is speaking."

- **Embed it.** When speaking one-on-one with students, engage in the competency in real time. "You just described your experience during recess and shared with me that you needed more time to finish your game before getting in line. Is that correct?"

Students receive **feedback** during and after competency practice:
- **Be explicit:** After each practice opportunity, discuss areas of strength and improvement for next time.
- **Embed it.** Notice when students use (or could have used) new competencies during the day and highlight what students did well and where they could improve.

Students have opportunities to actively **practice** competencies:
- **Be explicit.** Give young people opportunities to role-play and practice the competency in a safe setting.
- **Embed it.** Create opportunities to practice competencies in real time. Group discussions and pair sharing promote active listening, for example.

develop a project where they create a shoebox diorama or other model of a place they consider safe and happy and describe it to their classmates (note that this might bring up complex emotions for students, especially if they can no longer go to that place, so be prepared for this). This will help students learn how to communicate clearly to their peers, use their creativity in the presentation, and develop persistence (since it will probably take several days or weeks to create). Because learning is an inherently social process, these connections and relationship development are essential to effective SEL. The University of Minnesota Extension provides a toolkit with practical strategies to accomplish this.[28]

## Formative Evaluation

Your school or program should routinely reflect on and evaluate its SEL practices to ensure that you are meeting identified goals and intended outcomes
for your setting.[29] For example, a team of school staff could meet to discuss
ways to use universal SEL programs to meet the needs of all students, SEL
practices for groups of people engaged in similar efforts, and how all staff
meetings could better incorporate SEL. Similarly, youth could also reflect
on their experiences with SEL, suggest ways to improve the content or delivery of specific SEL programs, provide ratings of their own social-emotional
development, and conceptualize overall school practices and principles to
support SEL.

There are different types of information (or data) to collect and use based
on what you are trying to accomplish.[30] We recommend collecting both information related to implementing SEL (e.g., what programs are being implemented, by whom, and how engaged students are in those programs) and
information that will help you understand the development of the social-
emotional and cognitive competence that SEL aims promote. You may also
want to assess the outcomes that you hope SEL will help you realize.[31]

## TAKEAWAYS

- Quality SEL is systemic, coordinated, and contextually relevant.
- Practices that promote SEL underpin a safe and supportive environment—in the classroom, throughout the school, at home, and in the
  community—where young people can develop core competencies.
- The most effective approaches to skill building are sequenced, active,
  focused, and explicit.
- SEL should be engaging to all youth, who develop social-emotional
  skills when they have voice, choice, and the freedom and power to lead,
  and when SEL is culturally competent and responsive.
- SEL works best when adults model social-emotional competence and
  strive for continuous improvement based on continual assessment,
  reflection, and informed decision making.

# EIGHTEEN

# Educators Matter

*Nick Yoder, Lynn Holdheide, and David Osher*

EARLIER CHAPTERS HAVE addressed how effective teachers create individualized learning and classroom learning communities where students feel safe; are engulfed in learning; experience or are prepared to participate in deeper learning; and experience the relational and academic support they need to succeed.[1] Teacher effectiveness, which is a product of teacher attributes and school conditions that support good teaching, not only correlates with student achievement and student engagement, but also contributes to students' ability to self-regulate (through coregulation), develop positive student identities and attitudes, exhibit prosocial behaviors, and support the development of social-emotional competencies.[2]

Understanding why educators matter and the impact of educator quality and support on student outcomes—beyond academic achievement alone—is even more imperative considering what we know from the science of learning and development, and what we know about the competencies students need to develop if they are to be successful after they leave school. Educators who can establish positive relationships with students are well positioned to create authentic learning experiences that support integration and the use of skills in real-world scenarios.[3]

This chapter describes the ways in which educators influence student development, their role in creating positive conditions for learning, and the importance of conditions for teaching, which equip teachers with the content knowledge, knowledge of child and youth development, pedagogical skills, cultural competence, social-emotional skills, and organizational support they need to be able to address (ideally in a personalized way) the needs of a diverse student population.[4] Throughout the chapter, we provide several recommendations and practices for educators and administrators to support teacher quality and effectiveness. As with previous chapters, for help implementing these recommendations and practices in your own context, please see the tools and other resources listed in appendix B.

## EDUCATORS' ROLE IN SUPPORTING STUDENT DEVELOPMENT

Students need more than academic skills and content knowledge; they need to develop positive identities as learners, individuals, and community members. They also need to develop the ability to apply knowledge, strategically solve problems, think analytically, make decisions, regulate their behavior, manage their learning, and collaborate effectively—skills enumerated in the college- and career-ready standards and needed to engage in learning.[5] This work starts early and continues as children (with support) acquire the building blocks for learning illustrated in figure 18.1.[6] While these skills are important for student success in school and beyond, educators often do not feel they have the time or support to help students gain these skills and successfully transition to life after high school.[7] However, individuals carry their social-emotional competencies with them throughout their day, in the multiple contexts in which they interact. Thus, social-emotional competencies are already a part of a good education and good teaching, and can be more strategically and systematically emphasized in schools and classrooms.[8]

Attempts at improving teaching often focus on an educator's contribution to students' academic achievement, carried out through the revision of educator evaluation systems with a considerable focus on high-stakes testing. These ideas are inconsistent with what we know about the science of learning and development. Learning and attainment is enhanced when teachers can address a student's individuality by personalizing learning and teaching the *whole child*, as well as by supporting classroom communities

**Figure 18.1** Building blocks for learning

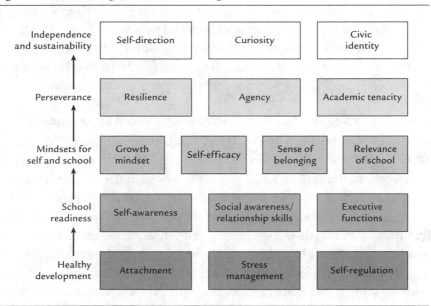

*Source:* K. Brooke Stafford-Brizard, *Building Blocks for Learning: A Framework for Comprehensive Student Development* (New York: Turnaround for Children, 2016), https://www.turnaroundusa.org/wp-content/uploads/2016/03 /Turnaround-for-Children-Building-Blocks-for-Learningx-2.pdf.

of learners, thereby creating safe, collaborative spaces where students feel comfortable taking intellectual risks.[9] Ideally, teachers are prepared to provide challenge, engagement, and support within a student's *zone of proximal development* (the difference between what students can do on their own and with help) and to respond to changes in that zone. Teachers should be able to provide immersive, well-scaffolded, culturally responsive instruction that builds metacognitive skills; accounts for students' prior knowledge and experiences; and creates a social-emotional environment that fosters safety, engagement, learning, deeper learning, and creativity.[10]

Examples of the types of learning experiences students benefit from include the following:

• Classroom discourse that allows students to learn how to communicate effectively with their peers, persuade others using facts, defend an argument, and solve problems collectively

- Instruction that involves rigorous and challenging academic content, helping students learn to both recognize and regulate their own frustration, and to leverage their resources and persevere
- Collaborative learning that includes opportunities for direct instruction and feedback, so students can learn to take responsibility for their own learning and how to work with their peers toward a common goal

## Practices to Support Student Academic and Social Development

A recent review by the Center on Great Teachers and Leaders (GTL Center) identified ten general pedagogical practices that are theorized to support the development and application of social-emotional and academic competencies. The practices include student-centered discipline; teacher language; responsibility and choice; warmth and support; cooperative learning; classroom discussions; self-assessment and self-reflection; balanced instruction; academic press and expectations; and competence building through modeling, practicing, feedback, and coaching.[11] This list can be used in the classroom to support caring learning environments, social-emotional competency development, and academic learning.

## TEACHERS' ROLE IN CREATING POSITIVE CONDITIONS FOR LEARNING

### Supporting a Positive and Inclusive School Climate

Teachers who create positive conditions for learning, where students are fully engaged and feel a sense of agency, support both student learning and development.[12] Conditions for learning affect student emotions, which in turn affect attention, concentration, and memory. Safe and supportive learning environments facilitate and support skill acquisition, which in turn enables students to establish and maintain a positive learning environment. In positive classroom environments, students learn and master academic and social skills by collaborating with their peers and engaging in reflection through perspective taking, obtaining and receiving feedback, and appreciating and respecting differences. In classroom environments where students feel emotionally and physically safe, students are more inclined to try new skills—even at the risk of being wrong or doing something incorrectly in front of their peers. In environments with consistent expectations, chaos is reduced and there are more opportunities for students to develop self-awareness, self-regulation, and other prosocial behaviors.

## Supporting Student Social-Emotional and Academic Development

Teachers are on the front lines, working day in and day out supporting students' development. This consistent interaction provides opportunities to greatly influence students' acquisition and mastery of academic and social-emotional skills through modeling, direct and explicit instruction, and collaborative projects. Here are some specific approaches teachers can take to support students' social-emotional and academic development:

- **Focus on their own social-emotional competencies.** Programs for mentoring, workplace wellness, social and emotional learning (SEL), and mindfulness improve teacher well-being and student outcomes.[13] An understanding and appreciation of their own social-emotional competencies equips teachers to establish positive relationships with their students and colleagues, make sound instructional decisions, improve conditions for student engagement, reduce disciplinary infractions, and support students' academic achievement.[14] Developing and maintaining their own social-emotional competencies also enables them to manage the multiple life stressors—teaching-related and otherwise—that can impinge on teaching directly (e.g., by drawing on their emotional reserves) or indirectly (e.g., illness).[15]
- **Integrate social-emotional and academic competencies.** Teachers can ensure that their lessons support the academic and social-emotional components of the classroom both by (1) creating a scope and sequence for the social-emotional competencies they want their students to experience, being focused in the skills they teach, and being explicit about expectations for students; and (2) integrating SEL into their pedagogy.[16] Note, however, that this does not mean backing away from academics. Rather, it means that academic content and pedagogy should be richer, particularly as social-emotional competencies connect with metacognition and the ability to participate in deeper learning.[17]
- **Provide regular opportunities for student voice.** Teachers should provide opportunities for student voice and choice in their educational experience, allowing students to experience agency and take responsibility for their learning.
- **Collaborate with colleagues.** To support professional growth, teachers should collaborate with their colleagues to develop a sense of collective responsibility about the development of the whole child. When teachers

collectively feel responsible, engage in peer learning, and discuss the needs of all their students, they are more likely to create relational trust while creating a better teaching and learning environment. Teacher collaboration also provides an antidote to teacher isolation and feelings of hopelessness or inadequacy (i.e., feeling that they cannot succeed with many students).

## IMPORTANCE OF CONDITIONS FOR TEACHING

Teachers are affected by school climate, which has been conceptualized as "the quality and character of school . . . based on patterns of school life experiences, [that] reflects norms, goals, values, interpersonal relationships, teaching, learning and leadership practices, and organizational structures."[18] Like students, teachers are affected by their subjective experience, which in turn creates social-emotional conditions for teaching—safety, connectedness, and support; challenge and engagement; the cultural responsiveness of the environment; and peer, leader, and student social-emotional competency.

Teachers' working conditions affect teacher retention, student achievement, and teacher effectiveness.[19] For example, Matthew Kraft and John Papay found that positive working conditions partly contributed to teacher improvement over a three-year period compared with other teachers who did not improve.[20] So, while we must examine school climate in relation to the student's experiences with the school, we must also address how educators experience school climate and the conditions for teaching. We can do this through confidential surveys, such as the teacher version of the US Department of Education's School Climate Surveys.[21]

Next we describe one of many symptoms of poor working conditions: teacher stress.

### Teacher Stress

Like students, teachers can face adversity and stress in both their school and nonschool lives.[22] In a 2014 Gallup Poll, 46 percent of teachers reported great daily stress, with compromised health, sleep, quality of life, and teaching performance. This figure is the same as that reported by nurses (also 46 percent) and higher than that for other occupational groups.[23] These findings are consistent with those from a 2013 MetLife survey, in which 59 percent of teachers reported being under great stress in 2013, compared with 35 percent of teachers in 1985.[24] The findings are also consistent with those of a rigorous qualitative study that the American Institutes for Research conducted in collaboration with the American Federation of Teachers, National Association for the Advancement of Colored People, and League of United Latin American Citizens.[25]

Teacher stress also affects student learning and development and school performance. Teachers who exhibit greater stress and show greater signs of depression contribute to poor conditions for learning, more behavioral problems, poorer social adjustment, and lower academic performance.[26] To prevent or address teacher stress, it is important to first identify the causes. Next we discuss how to mitigate three main organizational sources of teacher stress: problematic school organization and culture, job press, and lack of teacher voice.

### Problematic school organization and climate

Interventions on the organizational or individual level can reduce teacher stress by improving climate and culture. A cohesive school culture that values teachers and builds relational trust with colleagues, leadership, students, and families can increase teacher job satisfaction and retention. Promoting a participatory environment, open communication, principal/peer support, and job redesign can improve morale.[27] A collegial work environment and strong and supportive principal leadership also improve morale. Effective leaders take an authoritative, not authoritarian, approach; "walk the talk"; support a problem-solving (as opposed to blaming) environment; and promote continuous improvement.

### Job press

Teachers work in "busy kitchens." If they are to teach within students' zones of proximal development, they need to be able to balance multiple factors. This challenge is great under strong conditions for learning and teaching. It is even greater, however, under poor conditions for learning (which teachers also contribute to), or when teachers have too many students or face high-stakes-testing-related pressure, multiple assessments, and curriculum scope and sequence demands. Leadership can eliminate, moderate, or buffer the impact of these pressures by providing staffing support (e.g., assistant teachers), adjusting teacher workloads (e.g., through planning time), employing performance measures that go beyond mandated high-stakes tests, and changing curriculum coverage mandates.

Teachers also experience stresses due to a lack of capacity to personalize instruction, establish relationships with some students and families, and manage troubling behavior. These stresses can be addressed through tailored and sustained professional development and support, and through programmatic decisions such as morning meetings with students and home visits.

### Lack of teacher voice

Teachers often complain about the lack of voice and autonomy. This feeling of disempowerment undermines morale and limits their ability to affect other stress-provoking working conditions. Greater job control reduces the impact of stress on teacher health. Teachers feel empowered, report higher satisfaction, and are less likely to change professions when they can collaborate with their peers and engage in decision making.

## Teacher Effectiveness

Local teacher evaluation systems can support a whole-child pedagogy. States and districts have designed more rigorous evaluation systems to identify, support, and develop effective teachers.[28] (See "Measures of Teacher Effectiveness" for commonly used methods of evaluation.) Most definitions for effective teachers now include teaching practices that support whole-child development. For example, Laura Goe and colleagues' five-point definition of teacher effectiveness states that "effective teachers contribute to positive academic, attitudinal, and social outcomes."[29] This concept is reflected in the Every Student Succeeds Act (ESSA), which provides more flexibility in the definition of student academic growth and includes an optional fifth ("nonacademic") indicator to help define school success.

Most commonly used frameworks within educator evaluation models assess teaching practices based on classroom interactions between teachers, students, and content.[30] Many of these professional teaching frameworks—for example, the Classroom Assessment Scoring System (CLASS), the Framework for Teaching (FFT), and the Protocol for Language Arts Teaching Observations (PLATO)—are grounded in practices correlated with student achievement and other important student outcomes (e.g., student engagement, enjoyment), and provide a foundation to advance the teaching practices that are most meaningful for students.[31]

As states and districts continue to refine and implement evaluation systems, there is an opportunity to align these systems with professional

## Measures of Teacher Effectiveness

Educator evaluation systems typically call upon many methods for measuring teacher effectiveness, including the following:

- **Teacher inputs**, or those personal aspects a teacher brings to the classroom—for example, teacher qualities (e.g., personality characteristics), beliefs (e.g., expectations), and knowledge (e.g., content knowledge, knowledge of human development)
- **Teaching processes**, or the ways in which the teacher interacts with students in the classroom—for example, instructional practices (e.g., cooperative learning) and other teacher behaviors (e.g., warmth and support)
- **Teacher outputs**, or the effect that a teacher has on student outcomes, which has almost exclusively focused on student achievement[32]

learning and support.[33] For example, talent management systems can promote and reinforce the evidence-based practices that support academic and social-emotional development and success. The way forward, therefore, is to pull from existing research to identify evidence-based practices and leverage points across the educator career continuum (e.g., preparation, licensure, induction, mentoring) to reinforce and support skill acquisition.

## Effective Educator Talent Management

The following is a set of recommendations—targeted to district leaders, but also relevant to state education agency (SEA) officials and policy makers—for establishing the foundation for a talent management system that values and supports educators in their quest to support the whole child:

- **Incorporate social-emotional and academic skills within education visions.** Emphasize supporting the whole child through educator evaluation and learning systems.
- **Prioritize the integration of social-emotional and academic development in school policies and practices.** Emphasize that students' social-emotional development is as important as—and is a means to support—their academic achievement. Doing so will encourage teachers to reinforce these practices in their classrooms.

- **Embed the science of learning and development in talent management systems.** Leaders should recognize and reward teachers (through incentives, teacher leadership positions, etc.) who implement teaching and instructional practices that support the whole child in a culturally responsive and developmentally appropriate manner.
- **Focus on excellence with equity.** Leaders should ensure that all teachers implement effective and individualized instructional practices by allocating resources to support all teacher development, including mastery of relevant content knowledge, cultural responsiveness, and integration of social-emotional and academic development. In addition, leaders can monitor teacher practices through induction and mentoring, educator evaluation systems, and professional learning activities.
- **Attend to the conditions that contribute to teacher capacity.** For example, according to Matthew Holloway of the Massachusetts Department of Education, "'educators matter' means using teaching strategies that are effective for students of all abilities and giving educators the supports they need to help all students succeed."

## Principals and Teacher Leaders

Principals and teacher leaders create the tone within schools, signaling what is valued. Principals set the tone through their language and the questions they regularly ask teachers and students, and reinforce it in how they allocate resources, create schedules, provide professional development and support, and act with cultural humility and emotional intelligence. Teacher leaders can do the same through their language, organization of teacher meetings, and participation on schoolwide teams. When leaders believe that education matters for the whole child—and enact procedures that align with this belief— teachers and students are more likely to behave in ways that are congruent with those beliefs. Here are several example strategies administrators can use to set a supportive and positive tone in their schools:

- **Create positive conditions for teaching and for learning.** Leaders can allocate resources to support teachers, model expectations of behavior, and reward teaching and instructional practices that support the whole child. In addition, administrators can ensure that the school's disciplinary policies are restorative, equitable, and focused on inclusionary practices.

- **Model social-emotional competencies as a means of supporting teacher social-emotional capacity.** Leaders can support teacher social-emotional competencies by modeling them in their interactions with teachers, students, and families, and by embedding SEL practices within professional development meetings, which provides opportunities for educators to discuss their and their students' social-emotional well-being, and to connect the social-emotional and academic components of classroom instruction.[34]
- **Create a professional culture focused on student development.** Leaders can support a culture that ensures that educators work together and share responsibility in the development of student social-emotional and academic skills.[35]
- **Embed cultural responsiveness throughout the school.** Leaders should be knowledgeable about and support the integration of a culturally responsive curriculum within schools.[36]

## TAKEAWAYS

- Educators matter, but they cannot work in isolation. They benefit from a professional community.
- Teachers play a key role in SEL and student engagement.
- Teachers can enhance their social-emotional competencies, but they should and can be supported in doing so.
- School climate and conditions for teaching matter for enhancing educator quality.
- Leadership and talent management systems can and should support teachers' whole-child pedagogy and the organizational practices that foster conditions for teaching the whole child.

# NINETEEN

# Academic Interventions— Use with Care

*Terry Salinger and David Osher*

THE INTERVENTIONS in this volume are central to school improvement and have tremendous power to help students learn and develop, especially when implemented as part of a multitiered system of support. But, even when used in the early grades, they also carry risks to students' long-term chances for success. This chapter discusses what can happen when school-based interventions for students who struggle academically, especially in reading, emphasize students' academic needs without acknowledging the risks of inappropriate screening and intervention. It focuses in particular on students who have promise but are identified as "at risk" for failure, and then subsequently fall, often permanently, into the "struggling student" category. This can happen in all core content areas, but in this chapter, we use reading as an example.

Far too many students encounter reading difficulties, sometimes beginning from school entry, and their difficulties intensify as they progress in school. In many instances, students come to identify themselves as somehow deficient in this core subject, which is measured by formative and summative assessments throughout their school careers.[1] For many of these students, their initial challenges in school expand as low reading skills lead to difficulty in other content areas. Even supposed mastery of the so-called reading "fundamentals" of letter-sound correspondence is not enough as students encounter increasingly difficult texts and are asked to read deeply and critically.[2]

## REALLY MEETING THE NEEDS OF STRUGGLING READERS

Schools that strive to meet the needs of all students are not structured as education factories, with different "production lines" for kids who struggle and for those progressing along a more normal developmental trajectory. The schools' standards for excellence accommodate the individuality of learning and celebrate student differences, and teachers and administrators do not conflate risks, academic difficulties, and behavior problems. Administrators and teachers understand that schools are layered, dynamic contexts, where instruction and discipline, expectations and rigor, and teacher and student needs should all be acknowledged and accommodated. Students must learn to exist within these contexts, but they bring their own characteristics—including their strengths and needs—to their learning.[3] For example, staff understand that learning is less accessible to a child who is stressed or hungry than to one who is at ease and well fed.[4] Further, children who have seen their peers and parents reading and writing for various purposes are primed to make these behaviors part of their own communication skills.

A primary goal for teachers at all schools should be to create what Steele and Cohn-Vargas have termed *identity-safe classrooms*. These are spaces in which teachers help "students to navigate the complexities of the 21st century . . . places that foster creativity, critical thinking, a sense of responsibility toward others, and a strong foundation in literacy and numeracy."[5]

Teachers "are aware that their students need social-emotional learning, prosocial skills, and tools for cooperating, communicating, and fostering empathy."[6] This description rightly connotes a warm, caring community, but Steele and Cohn-Vargas caution that "it is crucial that [the teacher–student] relationship extends *beyond* warmth and kindness." In these classrooms, teachers safeguard the identities of all students as learners by scaffolding their instruction to ensure that all students have authentic opportunities to achieve competence by "engaging with new ideas and developing skills to analyze and interpret information."[7]

Such scaffolding for deep learning and engagement is not easy, as it involves a delicate balancing act, especially in mixed-ability classes. When students struggle academically, those struggles may become the primary characteristic that defines them. Students who struggle with reading often go on to struggle in all content areas. Collectively, they become their own subgroup, one as distinct as those defined by race, ethnicity, gender, or family income. Teachers make choices about how to group students, but in identify-safe classrooms, teachers know that grouping only by ability is likely to reinforce the negative self-perceptions of lower performing students and do nothing to counter the weakened sense of competence these students have developed from immersion in remedial classes.[8] Their task is to challenge all students by teaching rigorous academic content and maintaining high expectations for all while providing the social-emotional-academic supports that enable students to benefit from a robust education.

Teachers who are able to challenge all their students have high levels of professional knowledge: they know their content well, including the background skills and knowledge that students must master if they are to be truly competent. They also understand child development—the cognitive and affective stages students move through as they mature—and consider these developmental levels in planning instruction.[9] The most knowledgeable teachers understand where each literacy concept and skill fits in the structure of the subject (e.g., the relationship of phonemic awareness to decoding to spelling); they know the declarative and procedural knowledge prerequisite for students' learning and can envision how future learning will build on current instructional content. These teachers' instruction allows students to make connections to and build on previous understanding; these teachers also are adept at providing in-the-moment explanations, examples, and metaphors to help students compensate for insufficient background knowledge, misconceptions, or poorly learned skills. Knowing that teacher knowledge is malleable, they are always expanding their own knowledge of content and of pedagogical approaches to teaching it.[10]

Knowledgeable teachers also know the misconceptions students may form and the common errors students make on their way to expertise, and can articulate to students how to avoid them. For example, weak comprehension strategies, rather than a lack of basic skills, stymie most upper elementary, middle, and high school students as they try to progress in content area coursework.[11] Teachers who ask thoughtful questions that motivate critical thinking can help all their students improve in reading—especially if they then "think aloud" to explain how they, as expert readers, have derived their answers. Unfortunately, too many teachers may ask struggling readers only low-level questions or provide inadequate feedback on partially correct answers because of their misplaced assumption that these students can't interact with texts at a higher level.

## CONDITIONS FOR LEARNING: A PROPOSED FRAMEWORK

In schools that protect students' identities irrespective of their academic achievement, students are truly engaged in the learning process, regardless of their background, their home language, and, for young learners, their level of readiness for school. To engage students fully, schools must reject the cycle of automatic pull-out/remediation, which communicates to students that they are "outside" the general flow of their classrooms. Teachers must find ways to provide students with support on specific skills but, to every extent possible, not deprive them of the classroom instruction that fosters skills practice, builds background knowledge, and engenders academic and social bonding.

Steele and Cohn-Vargas provide a four-part framework for creating such classrooms for all students, regardless of how diverse the student population may be:[12]

- Create an air of intellectual excitement.
- Provide an appropriate level of challenge and encourage students to ask for help.
- Make classrooms safe places for thinking.
- Differentiate instruction to encourage higher levels of thinking for all students.

The first two components are complementary and require teachers to believe in the ability of all their students to learn as well as in their own ability to teach all students. Only teachers with a positive mindset toward all their students can interrupt inequitable practices, such as focusing instruction for lower achieving students on mastery of low-level skills and content rather than on meaning making. In order "to help all students learn deeply, schools will need to provide them with regular opportunities to practice high-level skills such as solving complex problems, conducting research, and communicating in multiple forms and using new technologies to find, analyze, and evaluate information."[13]

The necessary backdrop for implementing the first two components of the framework—intellectual excitement and challenge accompanied by help and support—includes in equal measure providing rich, diverse materials to engage a wide range of students and establishing an environment where asking questions, seeking help, and sharing information are natural parts of the learning process. Print and online dictionaries, encyclopedias, and other references play an important part in normalizing help-seeking behaviors—but only when teachers provide direct instruction to ensure that all students know how to take advantage of these resources. Telling students who have never used a print or online dictionary to "go look it up!" reinforces their sense of deficiency, but modeling how mature readers use such resources and make decisions about correct meanings not only teaches a valuable skill but also demonstrates that "being intelligent doesn't mean you know everything."[14]

Teachers' words also encourage students to seek help, to view mistakes as learning experiences, and to believe in themselves—but only if the words are delivered with warmth, authenticity, and awareness of students as individuals. Even young students can tell when a teacher is condescending to them in their answers or explanations. Research shows that students' belief that their intelligence is malleable strongly contributes to positive academic outcomes over time, and teachers' verbal interactions with students directly impact these beliefs.[15] Supportive comments, reminders to "keep going" or "try again," and feedback on efforts need to be personalized and situation-specific. Maintaining this level of support can be especially difficult with some students, especially those who have started to doubt themselves and seem to resist teachers' help.

Steele and Cohn-Vargas acknowledge that some students continually disrupt the class or retreat into their own private world, making it difficult "to be warm when a student is hard to love."[16] Teachers' genuine effort to be encouraging pays off, however, as all students—but especially those who have experienced repeated failures—learn to counter and challenge their own internal and external negative self-talk and develop "learned optimism."[17] Thus, instead of saying, "This book is too hard for me!" students automatically run through a battery of dependable strategies or recognize that there is no disgrace in finding different material on the same topic.

The final two components of the framework—making classrooms safe places for thinking and differentiating instruction to encourage higher levels of thinking for all students—also work together. It is perhaps easier to think about these components than it is to put them into practice. The obvious questions are, "Well, isn't RTI [Response to Intervention] a form of differentiated reading instruction? And don't students need to master certain reading skills before they can really 'think' at higher levels?" The answers to these questions may be "yes," but it is a qualified "yes," because even though many students do need additional support and instruction to become proficient readers, the emphasis here is *thinking*—ensuring that all students have opportunities to think deeply about what they are learning and to engage in a productive give and take of ideas and perspectives, which is necessary for equity with excellence. One key to implementing these two components is sensitive, flexible grouping within the regular self-contained elementary or content area classroom. A second, equally important key is having materials at multiple difficulty levels. The third key is teacher professional knowledge: when teachers are fully knowledgeable about their content, not just about the current grade's scope and sequence, they can fill in gaps in students' background knowledge or repertoire of skills and fully ensure that lower performing students are not left out of the flow of instruction.

Many students experience stress, disengagement, and a lack of academic challenge and support. Engaging all students in a classroom that is culturally responsive and a safe place for thinking acknowledges that learning has cognitive, affective, and social dimensions. While this environment benefits all students, it can be particularly helpful for struggling students who may form assumptions about their academic helplessness. Research suggests that they can escape this pattern of pessimistic thinking, especially if classrooms offer situations where they can experience success.[18] To learn more about aspects of the school context that create safe, supportive conditions for thinking and learning, see "Features of Learning Environments That Buffer Student Stress, Foster Engagement, and Support Learning."

## CONDITIONS FOR LEARNING: EFFECTIVE PRACTICES FOR TEACHERS AND STUDENTS

Steele and Cohn-Vargas provide many persuasive descriptions of classrooms that safeguard students' identities and detail several approaches for creating such spaces.[19] The following sections build on Steele and Cohn-Vargas's ideas and draw on research about and best practices for creating schools that fully support all students' learning and development.

### Teacher Practices That Support Learning

Schools that strive to keep their students' identities safe, to meet their social needs, and to optimize their learning are ones where teachers are also nur-

## Features of Learning Environments That Buffer Student Stress, Foster Engagement, and Support Learning[20]

- A caring, culturally responsive community, where students are well known and appreciated and can learn in physical and emotional safety
- Relational trust and respect between and among staff, students, and parents
- Continuity in relationships, consistency in practices, and predictability in routines that reduce cognitive load and anxiety and support engaged learning
- Meaningful and challenging work for students that engages them in active learning experiences that are both individualized and social, as needed
- Opportunities to exercise choice and develop intrinsic motivation for learning
- Clear expectations for achievement for students and teachers that convey ideas of worth and potential, as well as information about how to meet standards
- Instruction that intentionally uses a range of teaching strategies, tools, and technologies to engage students and meet their individual needs
- Schoolwide practices and instruction that systematically develop students' social-emotional and academic skills, habits, and mindsets
- Inquiry and discovery as major learning strategies, thoughtfully interwoven with explicit instruction and opportunities to practice and apply learning
- Opportunities to receive timely and helpful feedback, develop and exhibit competence, and revise work to improve
- Ongoing diagnostic assessments that are developmentally guided and informed
- A capable and stable staff, connected to parents and community resources, who work together to support children's healthy development and learning

tured and supported, where expectations for teachers are high, and where teachers and administrators share a schoolwide vision for teaching and learning.[21] Schools need to be committed to helping all teachers, even novices, understand the shared vision and master pedagogical skills.

### Embrace deeper teaching

Magdalene Lampert, writing about teaching to develop deeper learning in mathematics, lays out specific teacher behaviors and methods, which do not necessarily come naturally to all teachers.[22] The first tenet of a "different way of teaching" is to build on what students know and not fault them for what they don't. This can be tricky for teachers who tend to privilege right answers and dismiss those that are only "in the ballpark." Lampert recommends that teachers learn to use the pronoun *we*, which "communicates that engaging with the content is a group effort, and that this content is not something 'out there' and impersonal, but something 'we' in this room are working on together."[23] Thus, students come to see their teachers as trusted adults who will work with them to co-construct understandings of new content and skills, and who "can be trusted not to belittle or embarrass them, and [teach them] that learning is a process of connecting what you know to what you need to know."[24]

Lampert refers to this as *deeper teaching*, and its success depends on teachers striving to identify students' relevant knowledge and experiences to form the foundation for new learning. Lampert would add that teachers need to know what is going on in students' lives outside of school, especially the stressors that can make it more difficult for students to participate in instruction.[25] Teachers must also demonstrate that they will help students integrate new facts or skills into what the learners already know and thereby help students become aware of, think about, and evaluate their own learning.[26] A great example of this kind of teaching is the Reading Apprenticeship model, which builds its professional development for teachers around a "metacognitive conversation."[27] Teachers verbalize their thinking as they present new printed material, modeling how they bring in background knowledge, figure out unfamiliar vocabulary, note technical terminology, and build new understandings. Although Reading Apprenticeship is designed for content area classes in high school and community colleges, teachers of the youngest learners can easily apply this approach, especially with students who seem to be struggling in the earliest stages of literacy.

*Demonstrate the value and relevance of learning*

Students need to see that what their teachers are asking them to learn will both be immediately relevant and have long-term value. Some students recognize the intrinsic value of their school subjects—or perhaps of one favorite subject—early on. But students who struggle with reading are far less likely to experience these early intellectual attractions, and as reading becomes more and more difficult, they may see less value in all their subjects. Personalizing learning for students can help even struggling elementary school students see the relevance in their school work, as can judicious use of grouping. Forming dyads or small groups encourages students to share their interests and enthusiasm, to support and to help each other. Rich and diverse classroom print, video, and digital libraries; trips to the school and public libraries; and availability of magazines designed for students offer a range of opportunities for engaging even reluctant learners and showing them the value of the hard work and persistence their teacher encourages them to adopt.

Exposing older students both to career and technical education (CTE) opportunities and challenging college preparatory courses can alter student beliefs, goals, and identities. CTE demonstrates relevancy and supports students for whom college holds no immediate attraction as they work toward graduation.[28] Embedding reading and math instruction within the content of CTE courses is a proven technique for "remediating" skills deficits while also demonstrating the applicability of these subjects. At the same time, access to appropriately scaffolded Advanced Placement (AP) and International Baccalaureate (IB) classes can create opportunities that change the mindsets of both students and educators. Equal Opportunity Schools, a not-for-profit organization that works with over three hundred schools, provides an example of this deep relational scaffolding, as we discuss next.

*Provide equitable opportunities for students to excel*

A large part of creating a positive learning environment is providing all students with opportunities not just to succeed, but to excel. Equal Opportunity Schools (EOS) is an organization that partners with school and district leaders across the nation to close race and income education gaps and increase equitable enrollment in AP and IB classes.

"Opportunity precedes achievement," says Sasha Rabkin, EdD, chief program officer at EOS. "We work to help schools understand how the ability to provide equitable opportunities is one of the prerequisites for sustaining academic success for all students."

Using a strengths-based approach that builds upon the assets of each school, EOS promotes mindsets and classroom environments that support learning and challenge students—especially those whose potential is not being recognized—with rigorous classes and curricula. After working with EOS, schools adopt new ways of viewing student capabilities and change adult thinking and practice.

"These schools have advanced courses, and students from historically underrepresented groups are right across the hall from the education they deserve," says Rabkin. "That's our entry point. We share data about students enrolled in advanced classes, and offer trainings on changing teacher and staff mindsets. We are building relationships and helping students of color enter advanced classes and feel like they belong there."

With EOS coaching, school staff strive to boost student achievement by creating rich learning experiences all along the academic journey. For example, EOS works with schools to find "missing students"—that is, students who are likely to succeed in advanced classes if given the opportunity—using Student Insight Cards. The cards contain survey and academic data, teacher recommendations, test scores, and learning mindset assets and skills that are indicators of AP/IB readiness.

Once these missing students are identified, EOS helps schools prepare the students to enroll and excel in advanced courses. The students participate in activities, online courses, and assemblies; meet with other students who are enrolled in advanced courses; and have one-on-one meetings with trusted adults whom students have identified as mentors in their schools. Additionally, each school has an EOS partnership director who visits once a month to strategize with school staff about best practices for student achievement, which are contextual and differentiated for each individual school community.

Rabkin explains, "We help to create an understanding of the equity ecosystem of each school. We want adults in the building to see their own roles are important and have their own sense of belonging so their students can do the same. We work on policy, practices, and attitudes. Working on those things allows us to look at specifically the who, what, why of each school as a 'living ecosystem,' and craft strategies in different ways, based on real-time data."

Fostering environments that support academic success continues when students enroll in advanced courses. EOS works with schools to implement sustainable support strategies and plans for the student and teacher, again tailored specifically to each school. Challenging students who perhaps never thought that advanced courses were available to them has had a profound positive effect in schools across the country.

"Through our advocacy and outreach approach, adults are creating experiences for students that challenge and change expectations that they have heard before, like that they do not belong in AP classes. We want students to know that they belong and see that the community has high expectations for them," Rabkin states.

## Intentional Classroom Environments

Increasingly, classes in America's schools are not just mixed academically; they are also ethnically and racially diverse. The concept of *multicultural education* was introduced in the 1960s in response to educators' awareness that all students need to develop a more sophisticated understanding of the increasingly pluralistic population in the United States.[29] The approach, as implemented, often focused only on superficial cultural objects and processes (e.g., food, holidays, dress, or literature). While affirmation of the diverse cultural backgrounds of students in many of today's classes is important, multicultural education won't help students process information or learn more deeply.

Instead, teachers should strive to provide intentional, culturally responsive instruction that creates the type of emotional safety that is both a relational and neurobiological basis for academic risk taking and deeper engagement, while providing students with the cultural grounding necessary to engage with content and with each other. Cultural responsiveness as experienced by students engenders the feeling, even in the youngest, that "I *belong* in school; I'm comfortable here." Teachers who strive to create this feeling seek to discover how each student engages with content as a learner. Most important, they identify and challenge their own stereotypes about "different" groups, especially when their students are from different racial, ethnic, or economic backgrounds.[30]

Cultural competence and humility are also important here. Teachers may not recognize the stereotypes they hold and how their stereotypes often influence their expectations for students and shape their teaching. In a study about the balanced literacy approach to reading instruction and accompanying professional development (PD), teachers from around the country gave in-depth cognitive interviews.[31] The teachers almost universally said they saw the value of their PD sessions, and of an approach that encourages students to read widely from books they self-selected. But many teachers also emphasized that teaching this way was challenging for them *in their particular classroom setting.* When asked why, they said that the PD they received had not prepared them to teach what they considered to be "atypical" students. They wanted PD that was customized to "their kind of classrooms"—that is, ones with students reading below level, learning English, or perhaps merely coming from a different economic background than the teacher.

The teachers' concerns about not being able to accommodate their "atypical" students forced them to adopt a more traditional approach—often one that relied on the sort of whole-class approach that ignores the individuality of learning and makes it more difficult for struggling readers to get the attention they need. It was indeed a vicious cycle—teachers' frustration with their lack of ability to meet the needs of "atypical" students forcing the teachers away from the kinds of grouping strategies that could best meet these students' needs.

## Supports for Students

It can be helpful to think of two forms of supports for students: institutional or programmatic supports, and ad hoc supports. The former are woven into the fabric of a school or district, and the latter are designed to meet specific purposes and offered for specific students. Both are designed to improve students' school experiences and outcomes, but they go about meeting this goal in different ways.

### *Institutional or programmatic supports*

Perhaps the most obvious institutional or programmatic support for students is access to preschool programs and all-day kindergarten. High-quality programs can help equalize school readiness for students from low-income and minority backgrounds, before—as Gutiérrez and colleagues have suggested—socialization takes place through experiences in remedial classes.[32]

Other examples include community schools that provide wraparound social, legal, and emotional support to students and their families, as well as physical support such as eye exams, medical and dental care, and sometimes food banks.[33] Centralizing these services at school can be the deciding factor in whether students receive health care or an unemployed single mother with limited English learns about housing or food subsidies to which she is entitled. Community schools often encourage cross-age tutoring or buddy systems, both excellent opportunities for older students to use their skills effectively by helping younger learners. Along the same line, summer and afterschool programs, especially for students who need additional help or opportunities for engagement, are often part of the whole-child approach that schools can take (chapter 9 covers how this is being successfully done by Say Yes to Education in Buffalo).[34]

Advising is another example of supports for students—albeit one that is often provided in such a cursory way that students who are marginalized either are not given adequate attention or consider their advisor just one more adult reminding them of their inadequacies. Strong advisory programs support developmental relationship building between students and advisors. They work in tandem with the curriculum in a school to ensure all students can succeed, with advisors "reach[ing] out to [students'] teachers to develop strategies to turn things around."[35] Just as multiple forms of evidence make the best classroom assessment approach, advisors can be effective only if they depend on more than standardized test scores to get to know their advisees and provide appropriate guidance.

### Ad hoc supports

Ad hoc supports include interventions designed to supplement classroom instruction in elementary schools and to bolster the skills of middle and high school students so that they can achieve in their content coursework. As discussed previously, assigning students to even the most carefully developed and well-implemented intervention program can have negative social-emotional consequences, without necessarily increasing students' skills. An experimental study that compared the reading achievement of two groups of struggling ninth-grade readers—one that received no extra help and the other enrolled in one of two research-based interventions—found no statistically significant difference in reading achievement after a full year of daily reading instruction.[36] In fact, across all three conditions, most students in the experimental and comparison conditions were as far below grade level when they exited grade 9 as they had been when they exited grade 8. This means that they had made a one-year gain as measured by a standardized reading test, but that gain was far from enough to ensure them success in their academic courses. The takeaway from results such as these is the importance of developing more effective and personalized ways to provide struggling students with the support they need, and approaches that will motivate them to engage more actively in learning in all their classes.

Additionally, the students in the two experimental groups just discussed missed out on two electives. Electives are often considered dispensable for struggling students, but they can maintain student engagement in school. They give students some say in what they study, opportunities to explore different ways of learning, and even different kinds of reading materials. The College Board suggests that college-bound students select electives that let them explore their interests, lighten demanding course loads, and have fun studying something they love.[37] Struggling students deserve these opportunities, too. In fact, giving students opportunities to practice skills in personally meaningful situations and to achieve immediate goals can instill a sense of belonging—something required classes may never be able to do.

Another support for students, especially those who struggle with reading, is access to high-quality reading material on engaging, relevant topics, written at accessible reading levels. Grade 7 struggling readers participating in focus groups about their reading habits and their intervention program said they wished the program had more real-life stories with characters who were more like them—stories that offered drama and romance; graphic novels; mysteries; and books about sports, history, and famous people like Nelson Mandela. Even the most inveterate nonreader often becomes engaged with books, articles, or online material about topics of personal interest. From the earliest grades, classroom and school libraries should be full of a wide variety of books, other printed materials, and audiobooks that are easily accessible to students in open bins or on convenient shelves. The popularity of materials as varied as children's magazines such as the iconic *Weekly Reader* (for elementary grades), graphic novels, and the books in the *Bluford* series (for adolescents) are evidence that if the topics are engaging, students will still gravitate to print and its spoken equivalents.[38]

A second key is finding the medium by which students want to read. Many of the same grade 7 focus-group participants said they preferred a tablet to the print version of what they read, but others said they liked to be able to hold a book and gauge their progress as they turned the pages. Some of the students valued the oral supports in tablet formats as well as the embedded dictionaries.

## QUESTIONS STILL TO BE ANSWERED

Despite decades of research on reading development, countless evaluations of reading interventions, and intense efforts to provide professional development on reading for teachers, students continue to struggle to master the literacy skills they need for success in school and beyond. Many of these students learn English as a second or third language, come from low-income homes, and are members of minority communities. They may quickly find themselves consigned to pull-out or other programs designed to identify and remediate their reading difficulties. Even if they are separated from their classmates for only a brief amount of time each day, these students get the subtle message that they don't fit into their school's expectations for performance. Over the years, this sense of separation can grow to real alienation, even as schools provide more and more intense interventions.

The reasons why many interventions continue to be ineffective may lie as much in the school environment as in the programs. The concept of an "identity-safe classroom" must extend to all students who struggle academically. For reading instruction, this means that students who are not reading at grade level still participate as full members of classroom discussions and of the learning communities their teachers seek to establish. This participation builds their sense of belonging in school and allows them to gain content knowledge and skills along with their peers. Scaffolded lessons, reading materials at various difficulty levels, inclusion in elective classes that require reading and writing—these are other artifacts of schools that include and do not stigmatize struggling students.

## TAKEAWAYS

- All students need to feel that school is a safe place—one where they belong and are part of a community of learners.
- Efforts to address the needs of students who struggle academically often make students feel as though they don't fully belong in the school environment.
- When teachers identify the stereotypes they may have about "atypical" students, such as those not reading at grade level or those learning English, they have taken a first step toward making their classrooms identity-safe.

- Teachers can always do more to support students who struggle academically, such as providing scaffolded lessons, building background and vocabulary knowledge, providing reading materials at varying levels, using technology and culturally responsive pedagogy, and differentiating instruction.
- The best interventions for students who struggle academically are targeted to students' identified needs, minimize the amount of time students are pulled out of the general flow of their school day, and are intellectually appropriate for the age of the students involved.
- Programs must recognize the individuality and social-emotional lives of students who participate in them and demonstrate the value of mastering the skills being taught. For example, a reading intervention for middle school students that includes independent reading in self-selected, high-interest books will likely be more effective than one that depends primarily on work sheets and drills.

# PART FOUR

# Improve

# TWENTY

# Continuous Improvement

*Aaron R. Butler, Jason Katz, Jessica Johnson,*
*David Osher, Jill Pentimonti, and Sam Neiman*

CONTINUOUS IMPROVEMENT, which includes both progress monitoring and evaluation, is central to implementing any intervention or initiative well and realizing all the benefits we have discussed in this volume. Because it is so important, in this chapter, we do a deep dive into continuous improvement, defining it and going into detail about progress monitoring and the role of formative and summative evaluation.

## DEFINING CONTINUOUS IMPROVEMENT

Continuous improvement for schools and districts embodies an improvement life cycle in which district staff, school staff, other members of the school community, agencies that work with the school, and community stakeholders (1) collect and analyze data; (2) set measurable and achievable short-, medium-, and long-term goals; (3) plan for improvement using various strategies, resources, and actions that address implementation quality and readiness; (4) implement short-, medium-, and long-term benchmarks and outputs; and (5) evaluate progress and modify practice if necessary. Although continuous improvement models typically follow this sequential approach over the course of a school year (and over multiple years), it is important to realize that improvement is a dynamic—rather than linear—process in which student and school development are influenced by activities and factors that often happen in parallel. It is carried out at multiple levels—district, schools, classrooms, and students—and involves the coinfluence and connectedness of social-emotional and cognitive factors, along with the ecological factors that affect performance, growth, and development. Further, the process includes assigning and engaging staff and stakeholders to accomplish specific tasks, establishing timelines, and allocating necessary resources. The process should be owned by everyone in the district, schools, and community.

As we envision it, the fluid and flexible process of continuous improvement:

- includes some indicators that are likely to lead change, and others that are more likely to follow improvements on these leading indicators;
- engages and supports a broad, diverse group of stakeholders in developing and monitoring district and school plans;
- addresses the resources required for effective implementation, including readiness, the implementation team, timelines, and proposed measures and benchmarks;
- focuses on quality measures for ongoing performance excellence; and
- includes a "reality check," where stakeholders come together twice annually to look closely at the data, assess progress, and recommend midcourse corrections as needed.

The approach outlined in this chapter focuses on quality measures for ongoing performance excellence. Often districts and schools fall into the trap of implementing reforms at a low to moderate level of quality, which is insufficient to change outcomes significantly. For example, professional learning communities may be in place, but the conversations within them are not rich, and teacher growth is not taking place at the expected levels. Quality measures—which include observations, surveys, and other specific data about what is happening in the school—dig deep into implementation and monitor progress.

## PROGRESS MONITORING

Successful districts and schools utilize progress monitoring to regularly analyze data to learn what is working well and what may need adjustment. Their reason for progress monitoring includes a commitment to ensuring that all students succeed, not just a select few. These organizations are proactive, making sure they are on track to reach their annual or long-term goals for all students, instead of waiting until it is too late to make improvements.

Progress monitoring includes using relevant, current data from various sources to inform timely decisions that lead to changes in ineffective practices to improve outcomes.[1] Progress monitoring is highly iterative and can include daily feedback loops at the classroom and student levels, as well as rapid feedback at the school level. Because what happens in the classroom has the greatest effect on student achievement, understanding data and modifying classroom approaches accordingly (instructional and otherwise) are critical to prevent students from experiencing unnecessarily high levels of frustration, and to accelerate deeper learning. Timely access to schoolwide data is essential, because schools and districts cannot afford to wait until the end of the school year to make changes if the data warrant them.

Progress monitoring in schools involves examining both implementation and outcomes. Monitoring implementation means verifying that the operational work of active projects or initiatives is occurring as planned, and that any related staff concerns and other challenges are being addressed. (For an example approach, see "CBAM: A Framework for Monitoring Implementation.") Monitoring outcomes involves analyzing data to identify the gap between where you are now and where you want to be, according to your measurable goals. Effective progress monitoring includes regularly looking

---

### CBAM: A Framework for Monitoring Implementation

The Concerns-Based Adoption Model (CBAM) is an example of a research-based framework that can be used to support and monitor implementation.[2] CBAM is based on the premise that successful implementation requires educators to do more than follow a set of steps after reading a manual or receiving training; it requires the people who are involved in the school's daily activities to bring the new program or strategies to life, which in turn depends on both their feelings about changing practices and their ability to master and practice new skills. The three dimensions of the CBAM framework—an Innovation Configuration Map, Stages of Concern, and Levels of Use—can provide progress monitoring teams with important data to diagnose implementation issues and determine appropriate course corrections to keep implementation on track.

at outcomes to verify that the organization's efforts are not in vain, but are leading toward long-term goals.

Effective progress monitoring at the district and school level should be a team effort. It should be embedded within a problem-solving culture of a district or school that is committed to continuous improvement and does not hide, avoid, or explain away negative data, but rather reacts to such data constructively.

## Progress Monitoring in Cleveland

The Cleveland Metropolitan School District (CMSD) rollout of the Promoting Alternative Thinking Strategies (PATHS) program, which we described in chapter 1, provides a good example of how one district used progress monitoring to develop readiness for implementing an evidence-based intervention. Once implementation got started, CMSD school psychologist Bill Stencil found that providing feedback to school and district administrators was imperative to building momentum and gaining support. During implementation year one, the PATHS team regularly communicated outcome data to show administrators the program's effects. Stencil and his team also provided reports to principals on a routine basis about implementation progress at their schools, and offered guidance about implementation levels (low, medium, and high) for the schools to use as a model. Stencil explains this process as follows:

> We connected the implementation process to student outcomes. When you regularly monitor outcome data and connect it to implementation quality, you have very good points to discuss when a school is having trouble, and you likewise have good points to sell when a school is successful. We regularly met to review data with principals because they are the ones who promoted PATHS, communicated the need for PATHS, and helped us find ways to continue to integrate PATHS into academics.

> Throughout early implementation, data showed that PATHS was having its intended positive effect across the district, due in no small part to the leadership's commitment and engagement before and during early implementation. "We got feedback from students that they were becoming more effective social learners in school," says Kevin Dwyer.

> CMSD data showed that schools with high implementation standards had positive results with grades, attendance, and discipline referrals. The turnaround of what discipline looks like in schools was evident.

One evaluation showed that about thirty schools reported reduced discipline referrals, and reported that kids were referring themselves to the planning center to calm down and then were reentering the classroom, rather than being out for the day. And the teachers were trained to reaccept those youth ready to learn.

Eight years later, Stencil states that "PATHS is now part of the fabric of our district and what we want to promote in our district to move our staff, scholars, and parents in a direction where SEL [social and emotional learning] becomes an everyday occurrence."

A culture of continuous improvement must include buy-in from the top—with the principal or superintendent—and must have all staff taking ownership of the culture.[3] The schoolwide team can lead or authorize a progress monitoring team, using the team-building and community engagement strategies described earlier in this book.

## Selecting Appropriate Leading Indicator Data

Once school leaders have built a team (either the schoolwide team or an aligned group composed of district staff, school staff, and other members of the school community) to lead progress monitoring, they will need to determine what *leading indicators* to monitor. Leading indicators should predict the success of both shorter-term goals (e.g., one year) and long-term goals (e.g., three year).[4] Districts and schools should identify a variety of quick-win and leading indicators to ensure that there is a dual focus on timely improvement as well as longer-term sustained change that deepens learning and supports the healthy development of all students. These leading indicators should address academic, social-emotional, and behavioral goals, as well as equity and conditions for learning, to ensure that all students are both set up for success *and* succeeding. Some examples of short-term indicators are weekly and monthly attendance rates, survey data on student perceptions of peer social-emotional competence, and suspension rates. Identifying leading indicators is one of the earliest and most important tasks for the progress monitoring team to complete. Questions to address include the following:

- What data are currently available to us? If something is not available but we must have it, how do we get it, or what is an appropriate proxy?
- Are any of these data aligned with or related to our annual goals? Three-year goals? Five-year goals?

- If we show consistent progress on these data, will we meet our annual goals? Three-year goals? Five-year goals?
- How often are these data updated? Is this often enough to make them a leading indicator?
- What are the data collection methods for key data? Who is responsible for maintaining key data?
- Are there any leading indicators that we overlooked if we want to ensure safety, engagement, equity, achievement, learning, and support for healthy development?

The leading indicators should match the level of the district, school, or class for which they will be monitored so that progress monitoring conversations and efforts are focused on the right "grain size" for the team. For example, a district-level progress monitoring team will benefit from analyzing and discussing leading indicators that include school-by-school comparisons or districtwide data. A school-level progress monitoring team will benefit most from analyzing and discussing leading indicators that focus on grade-level, classroom, or even male versus female comparisons. Classroom-level leading indicators should focus on the individuality of students—their personal academic and social-emotional growth—rather than aggregating their data or comparing them to an average.[5] Once leading indicators are identified, you can use a graphic such as figure 20.1 to help you assess alignment with annual goals.

Effective progress monitoring has a clear purpose and user-friendly tools, and is embedded within a rapid-cadence continuous improvement process that employs planning an intervention, doing or trying the intervention, monitoring the results, and acting on what is learned. For examples and tools, see appendix B.

## Monitoring Implementation

There is often a difference between what action steps or strategies are written in a plan and what happens daily. Known as *implementation drift*, this discrepancy is often the product of small compromises or changes made along the way that ultimately lead to a strategy that is sometimes unrecognizable compared to what is written in the plan. Monitoring implementation is straightforward and addresses implementation drift with the following questions:

**Figure 20.1**  Relationship between long-term goal and leading indicators

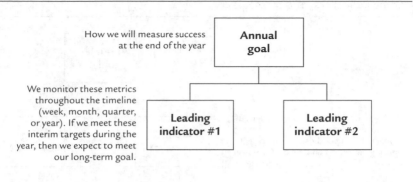

- Did we do what we said we would do? Why or why not?
- Did we do it when we said we would? Why or why not?
- Did we do it how we said we would? Why or why not?
- How does our staff feel about implementing these strategies?
- What, if any, implementation challenges need to be addressed rapidly, and how can the district or school support staff in addressing these challenges?

You can use the Progress Monitoring Tree shown in figure 20.2, which adds another layer to the outline in figure 20.1, to see how your implementation and results align to your annual goals in order to monitor improvement work in your context.

## Monitoring Results

"Check the temperature" along the way by analyzing leading indicator data. You do not have to monitor every leading indicator at every meeting, especially ones that have not changed or been due for an update since the last meeting. Create a schedule for when each leading indicator will be updated so that your team has a regular cadence for reviewing the leading indicators.

Once your team has your on-cycle leading indicator data at the meeting, you should discuss a few simple questions:

- Are these the most accurate and up-to-date data for this leading indicator?

**Figure 20.2** The Progress Monitoring Tree: the relationship between goals, leading indicators, and strategies

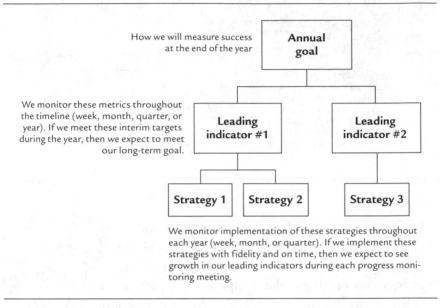

How we will measure success at the end of the year

**Annual goal**

We monitor these metrics throughout the timeline (week, month, quarter, or year). If we meet these interim targets during the year, then we expect to meet our long-term goal.

**Leading indicator #1**

**Leading indicator #2**

**Strategy 1**   **Strategy 2**   **Strategy 3**

We monitor implementation of these strategies throughout each year (week, month, or quarter). If we implement these strategies with fidelity and on time, then we expect to see growth in our leading indicators during each progress monitoring meeting.

- How do these results compare to what we expected (for each leading indicator)?
- What is the gap between where we are and where we wanted to be at this point?

Depending on the answers to these questions, your team may begin working to develop course corrections or next steps in response to insufficient progress toward an annual goal by any subset of students. To keep your team focused on the purpose of progress monitoring, and to maintain a clear relationship between implementation of strategies and leading indicators, we recommend starting with the following questions as guides for this process:

1. If we are not meeting the targets, are we implementing our strategies with fidelity?
   - If not, why not? Do we need to make sure we implement with fidelity and then check again for progress in two weeks? One month?
   - If so, do we need more time to let these strategies work? How much time should we give them before considering modifications? Do we need different leading indicators?

2. Even if we are meeting the goal we have set for the leading indicator—for all students—are we implementing our strategies with fidelity?
   - If not, why not? What are we doing that is leading to these positive results?
   - If so, what do we need to do to ensure that we remain on track in implementing these strategies?

These questions may not be the only questions you ask during a progress monitoring meeting, but they provide a good starting point. Remember, effective progress monitoring is not about an overwhelming collection of data, complex tools and processes, or multihour meetings full of difficult questions. Effective progress monitoring starts with a clear purpose and requires a consistent, disciplined approach that engages a team in the process of monitoring a few leading indicators that are aligned with your goal of success for all students.

## EVALUATION

Evaluation can contribute to continuous improvement when designed well, executed with integrity, and communicated in a manner that is consistent with the recommendations we made in chapter 3. Since your team may do formative evaluation yourselves, we provide guidance on doing the work. However, in the case of summative evaluation—which requires independence and, often, a different level of rigor—we provide guidance on selecting an evaluator.

Formative evaluation occurs at a slower cadence than progress monitoring. Usually, annual progress monitoring can identify challenges that should be addressed to maximize the likelihood of your plan succeeding. Summative evaluation occurs when you have had sufficient time to implement a sizeable intervention, and can help you determine whether the intervention worked, whom it worked for, to what extent, and under what conditions. While these two approaches are often viewed as disconnected, when first conceptualized and when most effectively used, they are parts of an evaluation package.[6]

### Formative Evaluation

Formative evaluation is low stakes—it identifies challenges to improve practices and processes and, if necessary, modify strategies and approaches. The lower stakes allow transparency and collaboration; all parties can work together toward meeting the common goal. Formative evaluation should be done with objectivity, intentionality, and quality. It should provide answers in a time frame that can help improvement; it should not be an autopsy.

The more diverse the stakeholders who have a voice and role in the formative evaluation, the more meaningful the evaluation and its resulting findings (and, ideally, improvements). There are multiple ways to list and categorize your stakeholders, and there are some useful templates online. The Systems Evaluation Protocol offers a low-cost way to map evaluation stakeholders and provides some examples.[7]

### Focusing Your Formative Evaluation

To map your options for evaluation, create a fishbone diagram like the one shown in figure 20.3, ensuring that it provides a full picture of potential improvement targets and anticipated drivers of improvement. Figure 20.3 shows an example mapping for conditions for learning.[8] The diagram has a broad outcome area (outcomes for all students) at the head of the fish (righthand side). The boxes to the left are contributing factors—in this case, sorted by each condition for learning. You can also use simple linear models to identify opportunities for improvement and related activities. Logic models are a common framework for mapping the inputs (what goes into an activity), the activities, the outputs (measurable information that is not an outcome), and the outcomes. We suggest starting with a goal that is shared by stakeholders and mapping from there. A related resource is the National Center on Safe and Supportive Learning Environments' root-cause diagnostic tree template, which can be found in appendix B.

If you need to build stakeholder consensus on what to evaluate, you can use team exercises or activities to prioritize one or more of the options identified through the fishbone diagram activity or other consensus-building processes.[9] For example, each stakeholder receives five "dot" stickers and places them next to his or her preferred candidates for evaluation. The options with the highest number of dots are then selected for evaluation.

### Methods and Data

Employ both qualitative and quantitative data, employ culturally competent and responsive approaches, and dig deep—don't just rely on data that are easy to quantify.[10] Your design should be intentional and representative of what you are trying to study. It should also avoid *selection bias*, which occurs

**Figure 20.3** Sample fishbone diagram

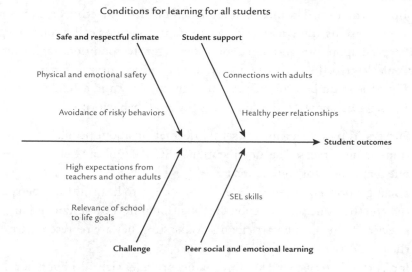

when a subgroup of people is systematically excluded or overrepresented due to your approach—for example, hearing only from parents who can come to school during school hours.

When possible, leverage existing data to reduce the burden of data collection and capture a trend line, which is necessary for your evaluation. The data should be current, reflect the school's diversity, and have a clear, logical connection to the evaluation focus. Conducting a data inventory helps identify existing data. For example, a school may have student surveys, though you should check survey quality and response rates.[11] The interactive School Climate Improvement Resource Package (SCIRP) can support your quality review.[12] School records are useful because they already exist. These records can provide administrative data on attendance, disciplinary incidents, academic achievement, graduation rates, and perhaps cumulative progress monitoring data. Examining school records can also help you identify trends. Disaggregate data to identify similarities and differences between subgroups, paying attention to intersectionality.

Also, consider whether new data are necessary. For example, you might have disciplinary data about minor infractions, but without student subgroup information. The most common methods for collecting data are surveys, observations, interviews, and focus groups. Your data collection strategy will depend upon your questions. For instance, for the conditions for learning example described earlier, you may want to conduct surveys, focus groups, and interviews on perceptions; examine disciplinary and attendance data; and observe behaviors and interactions (e.g., hall behavior):

- **Surveys.** You can get a lot of useful information about people's perceptions using surveys. The aforementioned SCIRP tool can help you select one that is best for your context.
- **Focus groups.** Focus groups are a low-cost way to hear multiple perspectives on the same phenomenon. Be intentional in your design and in selecting focus-group participants. Make sure they are representative of the perspectives you need to learn from.
- **Interviews.** Interviewing key informants provides rich, although not representative, information. Interview questions can be like focus-group and survey questions, or can go deeper and be more specific (because you may spend up to an hour speaking to one person, as opposed to ten to twelve people).
- **Disciplinary and attendance data.** These data should be collected on a daily basis in each school. It is important for school and district leaders to ensure that these data are consistently and accurately reported, at minimum, on a weekly basis.
- **Observations.** Observe behaviors as they dynamically occur. For example, you could employ instruments like the Classroom Assessment Scoring System (CLASS) to observe teacher–student interactions or, with guidance, you could create your own tools or collaborate with others to do so.[13] It is best to have more than one observer, train them, and make multiple observations.

### What to do with the data

One of the perennial challenges in evaluation is that well-meaning leaders collect a lot of data but often do not know what to do with it. Data reduction is important, and you should avoid a vacuum cleaner approach by knowing what data are most important to answer your questions. If you can't do that in advance, then analyze and summarize the information you have by evaluation question. Convene a core group from your original stakeholder group to review and interpret the data by evaluation question to determine next steps. The organization Public Profit offers an online guide to making meaning out of your data as a team.[14] Qualitative evaluation and texts (e.g., Matthew Miles et al.'s book *Qualitative Data Analysis*) provide useful information about what to do to address challenges such as data reduction and drawing and verifying conclusions.[15]

## Summative Evaluation

Summative evaluation has higher stakes, is less time-sensitive, and, with the correct design and methodology, can address matters of causality, coinfluence, and cost benefit. It should not be viewed as a "gotcha," a ritual ("we spent money and we have to evaluate it"), or a matter of compliance ("the board mandated it"). Rather, summative evaluation should be seen as contributing to your ongoing planning and continuous improvement efforts. To do so, it should:

- address implementation quality as well as impact;
- employ a design and methodology that can validly determine impact;
- provide information on both implementation variability and impact variability;
- include and align qualitative and quantitative data, with attention to selection bias in both cases;
- be sensitive to the effects of context and influential factors;
- address the specificity of effects—specific experiences and interventions affect the development of specific characteristics in specific individuals at specific times in specific ways in particular contexts; and
- utilize an independent evaluator if possible to maximize the reliability of data collected and the credibility of outcomes realized.[16]

If you are interested in additional examples for conducting formative evaluation, consider using the techniques described in "Rapid-Cycle Evaluation Methods."

## Rapid-Cycle Evaluation Methods

When evaluating or developing interventions that are intended to promote safe and supportive schools, you may wish to evaluate those interventions using rapid-cycle evaluation methods (e.g., rapid-cycle experimental trials). Traditional evaluation approaches that rely on large, multiyear studies may not be as helpful to practitioners who need to respond to diverse student and school needs throughout an academic year. Rapid-cycle evaluations provide opportunities to observe changes in safety and other school climate measures over shorter durations, with the chance to improve and strengthen those interventions along the way. Emerging research indicates that measures of safety and climate can be used to reliably detect changes in response to intervention over short time periods.[17] To learn more about American Institutes for Research's Improvement Lab, check out appendix B.

## TAKEAWAYS

- Continuous improvement in schools and districts embodies an improvement life cycle in which implementers (1) collect and analyze data and information; (2) set measurable and achievable short-, medium-, and long-term goals; (3) plan for improvement using various strategies, resources, and actions that address implementation quality and readiness; (4) implement short-, medium-, and long-term benchmarks and outputs; and (5) evaluate progress and modify practice if necessary.
- Progress monitoring and evaluation both contribute to continuous improvement.
- Progress monitoring is highly iterative and provides very high-cadence feedback loops at the classroom and student levels, as well as rapid feedback at the school level.
- Formative evaluation occurs at a slower cadence than progress monitoring. It identifies challenges to improve practices and processes and, if necessary, modify strategies and approaches.
- Summative evaluation occurs when you have had sufficient time to implement a sizeable intervention, and can help you determine whether the intervention worked, whom it worked for, to what extent, and under what conditions.

# Funding a Comprehensive Community Approach to Equity with Excellence

**Table A.1** Primary and predominant funding streams for school improvement: Education

| FUNDING SOURCE | CRITERIA/PURPOSE | LEGISLATIVE/REGULATORY REQUIREMENTS | FOR MORE INFORMATION |
|---|---|---|---|
| Individuals with Disabilities Education Act (IDEA) | Individuals ages three to twenty-one within one of thirteen specific categories of disability who need special education and related services. | Development of an individualized education program (IEP); comprehensive evaluation every three years. | http://idea.ed.gov/ |
| Every Student Succeeds Act (ESSA) combined with Title IV Part A: Student Support and Academic Enhancement (SSAE) Grants | ESSA provides funding to local educational agencies with high numbers or percentages of children from low-income families to help ensure all children meet challenging state academic standards. ESSA affirms a direct link between students' mental/behavioral wellness and overall positive student achievement, school climate, discipline, and high school graduation rates. | ESSA can be used to support mental/behavioral health through multitiered supports to address academic, social-emotional, behavioral, and mental health needs of all students; early intervening services; efforts to improve school climate and safety; efforts to increase access to services; adoption of trauma-informed practices; provision of mental health first aid; efforts to improve school–community partnerships; and professional development. | https://www.ed.gov/essa?src=rn  http://www2.ed.gov/programs/titleiparta/index.html |

| FUNDING SOURCE | CRITERIA/PURPOSE | LEGISLATIVE/REGULATORY REQUIREMENTS | FOR MORE INFORMATION |
|---|---|---|---|
| US Department of Education discretionary grants | Various grants:<br>• Integration of Schools and Mental Health Systems<br>• Project Prevent<br>• Promoting Student Resilience<br>• Building State Capacity for Preventing Youth Substance Use and Violence Prevention<br>• School Dropout Prevention Program<br>• Project SERV (School Emergency Response to Violence) | Funding for local education agencies (LEAs) to increase capacity to build and address the comprehensive behavioral and mental health needs of students; to identify, screen, assess, and serve students exposed to pervasive violence (experienced significant civil unrest); to provide mental health services for trauma or anxiety; and to support conflict resolution programs, school-based violence prevention strategies that can reduce the likelihood that these students will later commit violent acts. | Information about all US Department of Education grants:<br>http://www2.ed.gov/programs/find/title/index.html<br>Discretionary grants:<br>https://www2.ed.gov/programs/find/title/index.html?queries%5Bsearch%5D=mental+health<br>How the US Department of Education grant process works:<br>http://www2.ed.gov/fund/grant/about/grantmaking/index.html |
| Twenty-First Century Community Learning Centers | Eligibility is limited to rural or inner-city public elementary or secondary schools, consortia of such schools, and LEAs that apply on behalf of the schools. | Funding may be used for early childhood education, adult literacy/basic education, and parenting education. Grants may be used to recruit and screen children/parents, design programs, train staff, and coordinate with other programs. | https://www2.ed.gov/programs/21stcclc/index.html |
| Safe and Drug-Free Schools and Communities Act, Title IV of IASA, 1994 | Provides funding to state education agencies (SEAs) for grants to local education agencies and funds for community-based organizations. | Funds for school drug and violence prevention, early intervention, rehabilitation, and preventative education. | https://www2.ed.gov/programs/dvpformula/index.html |

| FUNDING SOURCE | CRITERIA/PURPOSE | LEGISLATIVE/REGULATORY REQUIREMENTS | FOR MORE INFORMATION |
|---|---|---|---|
| Institute of Education Sciences' Funding Opportunities Overview | Prioritizes research that contributes to improved academic achievement for all students, and particularly for those whose education prospects are hindered by inadequate education services and conditions associated with poverty, race/ethnicity, limited English proficiency, disability, or family circumstance. | Across its education and special education research programs, the institute has established programs of research that focus on outcomes including: readiness for school; academic outcomes of reading and writing, mathematics, and science; behaviors and social skills; and successful transitions to employment, independent living, and postsecondary education. | http://ies.ed.gov/funding /overview.asp |
| Parental Information and Resource Center (PIRC) | ED discretionary grant to help regional and statewide programs implement effective parental involvement activities, strengthen parent and school personnel partnerships, and implement policies and programs that lead to student academic improvement. | Recipients are required to serve both rural and urban areas, use at least half their funds to serve areas with high concentrations of low-income children, and use at least 30 percent of the funds for an early childhood parent program. | https://www2.ed.gov/programs /pirc/index.html |
| Gaining Early Awareness and Readiness for Undergraduate Programs (GEAR UP) | ED discretionary grant program designed to increase the number of low-income students who are prepared to enter and succeed in postsecondary education; six-year grants to states and partnerships to provide services at high-poverty middle and high schools. | Provides state and partnership grants (six-year matching funds) that must include an early intervention component to increase college attendance and success; raise the expectations of low-income students and a scholarship component; and support an early intervention component. | https://www2.ed.gov/programs /gearup/index.html |

| FUNDING SOURCE | CRITERIA/PURPOSE | LEGISLATIVE/REGULATORY REQUIREMENTS | FOR MORE INFORMATION |
|---|---|---|---|
| Carol M. White Physical Education Program | Grants to LEAs and community-based organizations to initiate, expand, or enhance physical education programs (before-school, afterschool, and summer programs) for K–12 students. | Projects must be designed to help students meet the state's physical education standards, provide instruction in healthy eating habits and good nutrition, and include at least one of the authorized physical fitness activities. | https://ed.gov/programs/white physed/index.html |
| Small, Rural School Achievement (SRSA) Rural and Low-Income School Program (RLIS) | Provides rural districts with financial assistance for initiatives to improve student achievement; is noncompetitive; and determines eligibility by statute. Awards are issued annually to SEAs, which make subgrants to LEAs. | Grantees may use SRSA funds to carry out activities authorized under the following federal programs: Titles 1-A, II-A, III, IV-A, IV-B. LEAs that receive RLIS grants may use the funds to carry out the following types of activities: parental involvement, teacher recruitment and retention, and professional development. | https://www2.ed.gov/programs/reapsrsa/index.html https://www2.ed.gov/programs/reaprlisp/index.html_ Award formula: https://www2.ed.gov/programs/reapsrsa/awards.html |
| Education for Homeless Children and Youth | Homeless children and youth in elementary and secondary schools, preschool children, and parents. | Funds may be used for a variety of activities to ensure educational success for homeless children. | https://www2.ed.gov/programs/homeless/index.html |
| Promise Neighborhoods | Aims to improve the development and education outcomes of children and youth in the most distressed communities. Supports nonprofit organizations (including faith-based), higher education, and Indian tribes. | Competitive implementation and planning grants; applicants must have effectively carried out planning activities described in the Notice Inviting Applications. | https://www2.ed.gov/programs/promiseneighborhoods/index.html |

| FUNDING SOURCE | CRITERIA/PURPOSE | LEGISLATIVE/REGULATORY REQUIREMENTS | FOR MORE INFORMATION |
|---|---|---|---|
| Migrant Education—Basic State Grant Program | Grant to state education agencies to support services to children (birth to age twenty-one) whose parents are migratory agricultural workers or fishers who have moved across school district lines (in previous thirty-six months) to obtain seasonal employment in various food-processing activities. | Funds may address the needs of migrant children by supporting high-quality and comprehensive education programs. Programs are intended to ensure that migrant children receive educational services to compete with peers in stable settings. | https://www2.ed.gov/programs/mep/index.html |

**Table A.2** Primary and predominant funding streams for school improvement: Health, mental health, and behavioral health

| FUNDING SOURCE | CRITERIA/PURPOSE | LEGISLATIVE/REGULATORY REQUIREMENTS | FOR MORE INFORMATION |
|---|---|---|---|
| Title V: Maternal and Child Health (MCH) Services block grant and discretionary grants | Children, adolescents, pregnant women. Grants to ensure quality health care for women, infants, children, youth, and families with special health-care needs. | At least 30 percent for preventative and primary care for children. At least 30 percent for community-based care for children with special needs. | https://mchb.hrsa.gov /maternal-child-health -initiatives/title-v-maternal -and-child-health-services -block-grant-program https://mchdata.hrsa.gov /dgisreports/ |
| HRSA Bureau of Primary Health Care Grants—School-Based Health Center Capital (SBHCC) Program Technical Assistance | Public and private nonprofit community-based health-care entities are eligible to apply for funding. Beneficiaries are students and families attending the schools where a health center is established. | Funds must be used to establish school-based health centers that provide comprehensive primary and preventative health-care services. A 2 percent set-aside is required for technical assistance and to improve collaborative performance. | http://www.federalgrantswire .com/healthy-schools-healthy -communities.html#.WTm –gOvyt0w https://www.hrsa.gov/grants /index.html https://bphc.hrsa.gov/program opportunities/funding opportunities/sbhcc/index.html |
| Health Resources Services Administration (HRSA) | Mental/behavioral health workforce education and training | Funding opportunities and training resources for (new) mental health providers to increase access to mental health services and make schools safer. | http://www.hrsa.gov/grants /mentalbehavioral/index.html http://www.hrsa.gov/grants /index.html. http://www.hrsa.gov/grants /apply/buckets/hrsaprograms overview.pdf |

| FUNDING SOURCE | CRITERIA/PURPOSE | LEGISLATIVE/REGULATORY REQUIREMENTS | FOR MORE INFORMATION |
|---|---|---|---|
| Tele-Health, Telemedicine | Supports providers in rural and isolated areas to improve patient care with the use of tele-health, tele-medicine, and health IT | Improve perinatal health outcomes and reduce racial and ethnic dispari-ties by using community-based service delivery through Healthy Start. | https://forecast.grantsolutions .gov/index.cfm?switch=grant .view&gff_grants_forecastInfoID =74198 |
| Community Services Block Grant | Low-income individuals and families living at 125 percent or less of the national poverty level. | Funds must be subgranted to "eligible entities" to provide services that ad-dress the causes of poverty. | https://www.acf.hhs.gov/ocs /programs/csbg/about |
| Community Mental Health Services (CMHS) Block Grant | Covers all ages and is designed for children/youth with serious emotional disturbance (defined by regulations). | A mental health service plan that is integrated across systems to provide services that include education, sub-stance abuse, health, social services, juvenile, and mental health care. | https://www.benefits.gov /benefits/benefit-details/765 |
| Comprehensive Com-munity Mental Health Services for Children with Serious Emotional Disturbances | Children and youth with serious emo-tional disturbances and their families. | Funding can be used to support a public community-based system of care for children and youth suffering from serious emotional disturbances and their families. | https://business.usa.gov/ program/comprehensive-com-munity-mental-health-services-children-serious-emotional-disturbances-sed |
| Medicaid (Title XIX) Grants to states for medi-cal assistance programs | Low-income members of families with dependent children; low-income children and pregnant women; blind; disabled. Clinical services provided in the school can be reimbursed. | Required services include in-patient and outpatient hospitals; rural health clinics; federally qualified health centers; physicians (pediatric or fam-ily) and nurse practitioners; early and periodic screening, diagnosis, and treatment. | https://www.ssa.gov/OP_ Home/ssact/title19/1900.htm CMCS Bulletin: Prevention and Early Identification of Mental Health and Substance Use https://www.medicaid.gov /federal-policy-guidance /downloads/cib-03-27-2013.pdf |

| FUNDING SOURCE | CRITERIA/PURPOSE | LEGISLATIVE/REGULATORY REQUIREMENTS | FOR MORE INFORMATION |
| --- | --- | --- | --- |
| Early and Periodic Screening, Diagnosis, and Treatment (EPSDT) | Medicaid-eligible individuals under the age of twenty-one. Schools can be reimbursed for EPSDT services. | Some types of services specifically prohibited under federal Medicaid rules include: education, vocational services (including job training), social services, and recreational services with no therapeutic value. | https://www.medicaid.gov /medicaid-chip-program -information/by-topics/benefits /early-and-periodic-screening -diagnostic-and-treatment .html<br><br>*EPSDT: A Guide for States*: https:// www.medicaid.gov/medicaid -chip-program-information /by-topics/ benefits/downloads /epsdt_coverage_guide.pdf |
| State Children's Health Insurance Program (SCHIP) | CHIP provides federal funds to ensure health-care coverage for uninsured children (up to 200 percent of federal poverty level).<br><br>States have flexibility to design their own program. Benefits vary by state and by type of CHIP program. | Funds must be used to initiate and expand child health coverage to uninsured, low-income children. Up to 10 percent of funds may be spent on nonbenefit activities that include outreach, administration, health services initiatives, and other child health assistance. | https://www.medicaid.gov/chip /state-program-information /chip-state-program-information .html<br><br>https://www.medicaid.gov/chip /benefits/chip-benefits.html<br><br>https://www.medicaid.gov/chip /chip-program-information.html |
| CMCS, SAMHSA Info Bulletin: Coverage of BH Services for Youth with Substance Use Disorders | Assists states to design a benefit to meet the needs of youth with substance use disorders, and comply with obligations under Early and Periodic Screening, Diagnostic and Treatment (EPSDT) treatment requirements. | The services are designed to enable youth to receive treatment and continuing care and to participate in recovery services and supports. | https://www.medicaid.gov /federal-policy-guidance /downloads/cib-01-26-2015 .pdf |

| FUNDING SOURCE | CRITERIA/PURPOSE | LEGISLATIVE/REGULATORY REQUIREMENTS | FOR MORE INFORMATION |
| --- | --- | --- | --- |
| Substance Abuse Mental Health Services Administration (SAMHSA); Center for Mental Health Services (CMS) | Provides funding opportunities to support programs for substance use disorder and mental illness.<br><br>2018–2019 Block Grants: Community Mental Health Services; Substance Abuse Prevention and Treatment | Grants that focus on the following: expansion and sustainability of community mental health services for children with serious emotional disturbances; suicide prevention and zero suicide in health systems; integration of primary and behavioral health; trauma; drug-free communities; adolescent and transition-age youth treatment implementation; tribal health and American Indian and Alaska Native Communities Circles of Care VII; opioid crisis. | https://www.samhsa.gov/grants<br>https://www.samhsa.gov/grants/grant-announcements-2017<br>https://www.samhsa.gov/grants/block-grants |

**Table A.3** Primary and predominant funding streams for school improvement: Child welfare

| FUNDING SOURCE | CRITERIA/PURPOSE | LEGISLATIVE/REGULATORY REQUIREMENTS | FOR MORE INFORMATION |
|---|---|---|---|
| Title IV-B, IV-E Other federal funding grants | The child welfare system is a group of public and private services focused on ensuring that all children live in safe, permanent, and stable environments that support their well-being. | Services funded vary by state. Service examples include family support and preservation; assistance to families of needy children; child abuse and neglect prevention; health, behavioral health, and wellness; support for at-risk children and youth; victims of maltreatment; screening and training for kinship, foster care, and adoptive families. | State statutes information: https://www.childwelfare.gov/topics/systemwide/laws-policies/state/ State guides and manuals search https://www.childwelfare.gov/topics/systemwide/sgm/ State 4E waiver profiles http://www.casey.org/communities/ |
| Temporary Assistance to Needy Families (TANF) | Needy families with children as determined eligible by the applicant state, territory, or tribe in the plan. | Funds may be used for cash grants and work opportunities and in any other way to meet the purpose of the program. | https://www.benefits.gov/benefit-details/613 |

**Table A.4** Primary and predominant funding streams for school improvement: Juvenile justice, courts, and labor

| FUNDING SOURCE | CRITERIA/PURPOSE | LEGISLATIVE/REGULATORY REQUIREMENTS | FOR MORE INFORMATION |
|---|---|---|---|
| Courts, Juvenile Justice, and Law Enforcement Office of Juvenile Justice and Delinquency (OJJDP) Prevention Grants | Children and youth under eighteen years of age who have, or are at risk of, involvement in the court, justice, and/or law enforcement systems. | National Institutes of Justice—Comprehensive School Safety Initiative OJJDP Discretionary Grants OJJDP Title II Formula Grants to states that support states and localities to plan, establish, and implement policies and projects to develop more effective education, training, research, prevention, diversion, treatment, and rehabilitation. | http://www.nij.gov/topics/crime/school-crime/pages/school-safety-initiative.aspx http://www.ojjdp.gov/funding/FundingList.asp http://www.ojjdp.gov/programs/ProgSummary.asp?pi=16 |
| Workforce development resources Workforce Innovation and Opportunity Act | Provides funding for employment training and service programs; work-based learning strategies (e.g., registered apprenticeships); sector strategies that address the needs of multiple employers within an industry. Rehabilitation Services Administration (RSA) | Fosters coordinated planning within economic regions. Addresses the needs of veterans and of other populations facing unique economic challenges, including out-of-school youth, people with disabilities, and the long-term unemployed. RSA serves youth and adults with disabilities who need rehabilitative services for job training and employment support. | https://www.doleta.gov/wioa/ https://rsa.ed.gov/programs.cfm Access state portal at https://rsa.ed.gov/request-access.cfm?usp=Y |

| FUNDING SOURCE | CRITERIA/PURPOSE | LEGISLATIVE/REGULATORY REQUIREMENTS | FOR MORE INFORMATION |
| --- | --- | --- | --- |
| US Department of Agriculture (USDA) Positive Youth Development Programs | Engage youth within their communities, schools, organizations, peer groups, and families by providing opportunities, fostering positive relationships, and furnishing the support needed to build on their leadership strengths. | Positive youth development resources are available in research and evaluation, professional development, and learning and engagement. Tools are available for various subjects, audiences, and delivery methods—including school-based, afterschool, clubs, camps. | https://nifa.usda.gov/program/positive-youth-development |
| John D. and Catherine T. MacArthur Foundation | Funding based on three related criteria: juvenile justice to address overincarceration and use of jails; geographic area; and type of funding (i.e., general operating support, research, program support). | Grants must address juvenile justice diversionary practices, overincarceration and use of jails, creative strategies to reduce jail growth, rural incarceration rates, crowded jails. | https://www.macfound.org/info-grantseekers/ https://www.macfound.org/info-grantseekers/grantmaking-guidelines/juvenile_justice-grant-guideline |

**Table A.5** Primary and predominant funding streams for school improvement: Philanthropic sources

| FUNDING SOURCE | CRITERIA | LEGISLATIVE/REGULATORY REQUIREMENTS | FOR MORE INFORMATION |
|---|---|---|---|
| Communities in Schools | Provides a school-based coordinator to connect schools with community resources that empower students to be successful and remove barriers for vulnerable students at risk of dropping out. | Supported through community partners (e.g., foundations, corporations, schools, individuals). | https://www.communitiesinschools.org/ |
| Private-sector initiatives for mental health services | Social Impact Bonds (Pay for Success) | Examples:<br>Early Childhood Program—Salt Lake City<br><br>Delinquency Diversion Program—New York City<br><br>Technical Assistance Lab, Resources | http://www.goldmansachs.com/what-we-do/investing-and-lending/impact-investing/case-studies/salt-lake-social-impact-bond.html<br><br>http://www.nytimes.com/2015/11/14/business/dealbook/why-social-impact-bonds-still-have-promise.html?_r=0<br><br>http://govlab.hks.harvard.edu/social-impact-bond-lab |
| Top-giving philanthropies, community foundations | A listing of funding sources for the United States by state. | Click on your state to find details about foundation, community, and philanthropic organizations. | https://www.tgci.com/funding-sources_ |

# APPENDIX B

# Tools and Resources to Support School Improvement Efforts

For direct access to the tools and resources referenced throughout this volume, please visit www.air.org/SafeEquitableEngaging.

---

### PART I. BUILD CAPACITY

| | |
|---|---|
| **Chapter 1: Building Readiness and Capacity** | |
| — | — |

| | |
|---|---|
| **Chapter 2: Leading, Coordinating, and Managing for Equity with Excellence** | |
| *Safe, Supportive, and Successful Schools: Step by Step* <br><br> https://www.prevention.org/Resources/46797 fad-f5a7-4eac-9b7a-cc1eda920797/AIR_Safe SupportiveSuccessfulSchoolsStepbyStep.pdf | This toolkit helps schools design, coordinate, and evaluate efforts to improve schools. |

| | |
|---|---|
| **Chapter 3: Guiding and Planning Improvement for Equity with Excellence** | |
| *Addressing the Root Causes of Disparities in School Discipline: An Educator's Action Planning Guide* <br><br> https://safesupportivelearning.ed.gov/sites /default/files/ActionPlanningGuide508.pdf | This action guide is for school administrators to address school climate issues and persistent challenges related to school discipline. |

| | |
|---|---|
| Communities That Care<br>https://www.communitiesthatcare.org.au<br>/how-it-works/risk-and-protective-factors | This website provides tools for identifying risk and protective factors. |
| Youth.gov<br>https://youth.gov/map-my-community | This website can be used to map federally funded assets in your community. |
| Community Tool Box<br>https://ctb.ku.edu/en | This website provides tools to help identify community resources. |

### Chapter 4: Selecting the Right Programs, Strategies, and Approaches

| | |
|---|---|
| The What Works Clearinghouse<br>https://ies.ed.gov/ncee/wwc | The website provides reviews on programs, products, practices, and policies in education. |
| Blueprints for Healthy Youth Development<br>http://www.blueprintsprograms.com/ | This website provides information to help easily identify evidence-based programs for youth. |
| CASEL (Collaborative for Academic, Social, and Emotional Learning) Program Guides: Effective Social and Emotional Learning Programs<br>https://casel.org/guide | This guide provides a framework for evaluating the quality of social and emotional learning (SEL) programs and identifies high-quality, evidence-based SEL programs. |
| *The Hexagon Tool: Exploring Context*<br>http://implementation.fpg.unc.edu/sites<br>/implementation.fpg.unc.edu/files/resources<br>/NIRN-Education-TheHexagonTool.pdf | This tool helps states, districts, and schools evaluate new and existing interventions. |
| AERA's Standards for Research Conduct<br>http://www.aera.net/Publications/Standards<br>-for-Research-Conduct | This reference offers quality criteria for types of evidence in research. |

### Chapter 5: Funding a Comprehensive Community Approach

| | |
|---|---|
| CostOut—The CBSCE Cost Tool Kit 2015<br>https://www.cbcsecosttoolkit.org/ | This tool is used to help understand the cost-effectiveness of education and social programs. It is generally used by analysts, researchers, educational administrators, and policy makers but is free to anyone. |
| Goldman Sachs' Early Childhood Social Impact Bond in Salt Lake City<br>http://www.goldmansachs.com/our-thinking<br>/pages/social-impact-bonds.html | This reference provides an overview of the "social impact bond." |

| | |
|---|---|
| Harvard University's "Pay for Success"— Social Impact Bonds<br><br>http://govlab.hks.harvard.edu/social-impact-bond-lab | This reference provides an overview of "Pay for Success" contracts using social impact bonds. |
| *Resource Mapping and Management to Address Barriers to Learning: An Intervention for Systemic Change*<br><br>http://smhp.psych.ucla.edu/pdfdocs/resource mapping/resourcemappingand management.pdf | This guide provides detailed information on resource mapping and management, and assets mapping. |
| *Resource Mapping in Schools and School Districts: A Resource Guide*<br><br>http://csmh.umaryland.edu/media/SOM/Microsites/CSMH/docs/Resources/Briefs/Resource-Mapping-in-Schools-and-School-Districts10.14.14_2.pdf | This guide provides detailed information on resource mapping for schools and school districts. |
| *Adding It Up: A Guide for Mapping Public Resources for Children, Youth and Families*<br><br>http://forumfyi.org/files/Adding_It_Up_Guide_0.pdf | This guide provides information on how to map public resources for children, youth, and families. |
| Community Tool Box<br><br>http://ctb.ku.edu/en/table-of-contents/assessment/assessing-community-needs-and-resources/identify-community-assets/main | This website provides detailed information on how to identify community assets and resources. |
| The Grantsmanship Center: State Grant Resources<br><br>https://www.tgci.com/funding-sources | This web page offers a clickable map where you can see the different sources of grant funding for each state. |
| Healthy Schools Campaign Resource Center<br><br>https://healthyschoolscampaign.org/resource-center/ | This website provides tools to help make healthy changes at school. |
| Robert Wood Johnson Foundation/Nemours Roadmap of Medicaid Prevention Pathways<br><br>https://movinghealthcareupstream.org/innovations/pathways-through-medicaid-to-prevention/roadmap-planning-tools | This road map demonstrates how Medicaid agencies can partner with schools to deliver prevention services. |
| *Toolkit for Expanding the System of Care Approach*<br><br>https://gucchd.georgetown.edu/products/Toolkit_SOC.pdf | This guide provides information to support the development and implementation of strategies for expanding and sustaining the system of care. |

## PART II. ENGAGE

### Chapter 6: The Centrality of Cultural Competence and Responsiveness

| | |
|---|---|
| *Cultural and Linguistic Competence Policy Assessment*<br><br>https://nccc.georgetown.edu/documents/CLCPA.pdf | This assessment can be used to support organizations in their efforts to improve cultural and linguistic competence. It provides a summary of strengths and areas of growth for strategic planning and quality improvement. |
| *Addressing the Root Causes of Disparities in School Discipline: An Educator's Action Planning Guide*<br><br>https://safesupportivelearning.ed.gov/sites/default/files/ActionPlanningGuide508.pdf | This action guide is for school administrators to address school climate issues and persistent challenges related to school discipline. |

### Chapter 7: Engaging Students in Creating Safe, Equitable, and Excellent Schools

| | |
|---|---|
| *Strengthening Communities Through Youth Participation*<br><br>https://ecommons.cornell.edu/bitstream/handle/1813/19326/Strengthen.pdf;jsessionid=7058227D828304BDA5410AFE55CEDF26?sequence=2 | This describes the findings from the Assets Coming Together (ACT) for Youth program. ACT for Youth is a positive youth development initiative that focuses on helping change community structure (polices, roles, resources) and culture (attitudes, norms, values) to provide youth with the support they need to thrive. It includes findings about ACT for Youth, case studies, and recommendations. |
| Youth Participatory Evaluation<br><br>http://www.actforyouth.net/youth_development/evaluation/ype.cfm | This website provides information about Youth Participatory Evaluation, an approach that promotes youth evaluation of programs, organizations, and the systems that serve them. |
| "Community Programs to Promote Youth Development"<br><br>http://journals.lww.com/jrnldbp/Fulltext/2005/10000/Community_Programs_to_Promote_Youth_Development.9.aspx | This journal article is a review of a book by the National Research Council and Institute of Medicine; see Jacquelynne S. Eccles and Jennifer Appleton Gootman, eds., *Community Programs to Promote Youth Development* (Landover, MD: National Academies Press, 2002). |
| *A Short Introduction to Youth Engagement*<br><br>https://adamfletcher.net/wp-content/uploads/2014/09/ASIYE.pdf | This document describes youth engagement and defines different aspects of engagement, such as "How does youth engagement happen?" and "What supports youth engagement?" |

### Chapter 8: Partnering with Families

| | |
|---|---|
| *What Is APTT?*<br><br>https://www.wested.org/wp-content/uploads/2017/03/services-appt-brochure.pdf | This guide explains Academic Parent-Teacher Teams (APTT) and includes links to more information about APTT at the end of the document. |
| *Partners in Education: A Dual Capacity-Building Framework for Family–School Partnerships*<br><br>http://www.sedl.org/pubs/framework/FE-Cap-Building.pdf | This guide helps schools and districts improve family engagement and cultivate and sustain positive relationships with families. |
| Parent Teacher Home Visits: Toolbox of Best Practices<br><br>http://www.pthvp.org/toolbox/toolbox-of-best-practices | This website provides resources for educators, families, and communities to support the implementation of home-visit programs. |

### Chapter 9: Partnering with Communities

| | |
|---|---|
| *Participatory Asset Mapping: A Community Research Lab Toolkit*<br><br>http://www.communityscience.com/knowledge4equity/AssetMappingToolkit.pdf | This toolkit can be used to apply participatory asset mapping to improve organizational knowledge (about community assets, status, condition, etc.) to help efforts in strategic planning. |
| Asset-Based Community Development Institute<br><br>https://resources.depaul.edu/abcd-institute/resources/Pages/tool-kit.aspx | This website provides a number of tools that can be used to assist with community development. |
| *Logic Model Workbook*<br><br>https://www.innonet.org/media/logic_model_workbook_0.pdf | This workbook serves as a guide to creating a logic model for your program. |

### Chapter 10: Out-of-School-Time Programs

| | |
|---|---|
| National AfterSchool Association, Core Knowledge and Competencies for Afterschool and Youth Development Professionals<br><br>https://naaweb.org/resources/core-competencies | This resource describes the "knowledge, skills, and dispositions needed by professionals to provide high-quality afterschool and youth development programming and support the learning and development of children and youth." |
| Beyond the Bell, *Social and Emotional Learning Practices: A Self-Reflection Tool for Afterschool Staff*<br><br>https://www.air.org/sites/default/files/downloads/report/Social-Emotional-Learning-Afterschool-Toolkit-Sept-2015.pdf | This toolkit provides afterschool program staff with the information they need to reflect upon their own SEL competencies and their ability to support youth's SEL through program practices. |

| | |
|---|---|
| *Measuring Quality: Assessment Tools to Evaluate Your Social-Emotional Learning Practices*<br><br>https://www.partnerforchildren.org/resources/2017/11/1/measuring-quality-assessment-tools-to-evaluate-your-social-emotional-learning-practices | This website helps school districts identify tools to assess SEL practices. |
| *Measuring Youth Program Quality: A Guide to Assessment Tools*, 2nd Edition<br><br>http://forumfyi.org/content/measuring-youth-program-quality-guide-assessment-tools-2nd-edition | This guide was designed to help assesses the purpose, structure, content, and technical properties of youth program assessment tools. |
| Coalition for Community Schools<br><br>http://www.communityschools.org/about schools/what_is_a_community_school.aspx | This website provides resources for building community schools. |
| Beyond the Bell<br><br>https://beyondthebell.org/tools-4th-edition<br>• Tool 55: Family Engagement and Interest Survey<br>• Tool 63: Youth Development Checklist | Beyond the Bell is a suite of professional development services and practical tools designed to help afterschool program leaders and staff members create and sustain high-quality, effective, afterschool and expanded learning programs. |
| *NYC Department of Youth and Community Development Youth Leadership Development Practices: Program Staff Self-Reflection Tool*<br><br>https://www1.nyc.gov/assets/dycd/downloads/pdf/15-4105_v12Leadership_Practices_SR_Tool%2003739.001.01_FNL.pdf | This tool provides a framework to guide training and professional learning opportunities for program leaders and staff. |

## PART III. ACT

### Chapter 11: Building a Schoolwide Foundation for Social-Emotional and Academic Support

| | |
|---|---|
| Department of Education (ED) School Climate Surveys<br><br>https://safesupportivelearning.ed.gov/edscls | The ED School Climate Surveys are publicly available to schools for measuring school climate. |

**Chapter 12: Building and Restoring School Communities**

| | |
|---|---|
| Center for Restorative Practice, *Teaching Restorative Practices with Classroom Circles*<br><br>https://www.ocde.us/HealthyMinds/Documents/RP%20Resources/Teaching%20Restorative%20Practices%20with%20Classroom %20Cirlces.pdf | This classroom- and student-centered resource is organized in three parts: Part 1, Restorative Practices and the Skills of Circle Keeping; Part 2, Varieties of Circle Formats and Circles for Building Community; and Part 3, Restorative Circles in the Classroom: Teaching Skills and Setting Things Right. Lesson plans, activities, guidance, strategies, and tips and tricks of the trade are provided for educators seeking to authentically integrate classroom circles into their classroom communities. |
| SoundOut Skill Building Lesson Plans<br><br>https://soundout.org/soundout-workshop-guide-for-studentadult-partnerships/ | SoundOut Skill Building lesson plans include more than twenty workshop outlines designed to help learning groups explore different aspects of meaningful student involvement and student/adult partnerships. All exercises are hands-on, interactive, and focused on taking action. The workshops are designed for learners of all ages, including student-only and adult-only groups. |
| Motivation, Engagement, and Student Voice: Professional Development Series<br><br>https://studentsatthecenterhub.org/wp-content/uploads/2015/10/I.c-Student-Voice-Professional-Development-Module.pdf | This professional development module was created as part of a partnership between Students at the Center, a Jobs for the Future initiative, and the Connecticut Association of Public School Superintendents. The full professional development series includes modules on motivation, engagement, self-regulation, and student voice. The completed professional development series consists of four modules of three to four lesson hours each, totaling around two full days of professional development. |
| Cleveland Metropolitan School District, Class Meetings<br><br>http://www.clevelandmetroschools.org/Page/403 | This robust web page provides an overview of the Cleveland Metropolitan School District's Class Meetings initiative, including its purpose and focus and its flexibility. This site also includes a robust array of Class Meetings resources, including a scope and sequence, guidance on key stakeholder roles and responsibilities, elementary/middle/high school lesson-planning tools, sample SEL-grounded activities, and assessments. |

| | |
|---|---|
| *Restorative Practices: Fostering Healthy Relationships & Promoting Positive Discipline in Schools: A Guide for Educators* http://schottfoundation.org/sites/default /files/restorative-practices-guide.pdf | This toolkit for educators describes restorative practices and how they can be implemented in schools. Additionally, it includes case studies about school districts that are using restorative practices. |
| *Safeguarding our Children: An Action Guide,* Revised and Expanded https://www2.ed.gov/admins/lead/safety /actguide/action_guide.pdf | This guide helps schools develop and implement school violence prevention policies and practices. |

## Chapter 13: Creating Respectful and Inclusive Schools

| | |
|---|---|
| *Creating and Advocating for Trauma-Sensitive Schools* https://traumasensitiveschools.org/tlpi -publications/download-a-free-copy-of-a -guide-to-creating-trauma-sensitive-schools/ | This guide helps schools create a trauma-sensitive environment for their students and develop a policy agenda that supports those goals. |
| *Helping Traumatized Children Learn* https://traumasensitiveschools.org/tlpi -publications/download-a-free-copy-of -helping-traumatized-children-learn/ | This report summarizes the research on trauma's potential impact on children's learning, behavior, and relationships in school. In addition, it includes a tool outlining practices that schools can use to help create a trauma-sensitive environment for children. |
| *A Guide for Understanding, Supporting, and Affirming LGBTQI2-S Children, Youth, and Families* https://www.air.org/sites/default/files/A _Guide_for_Understanding_Supporting_and _Affirming_LGBTQI2-S_Children_Youth_and _Families.pdf | This resource provides information for educators, allies, and community members who would like to support the health and well-being of LGBTQI2-S students and their families. |
| ED School Climate Surveys https://safesupportivelearning.ed.gov/edscls | ED School Climate Surveys are publicly available to schools for measuring school climate. |

## Chapter 14: Multitiered Systems of Support

Center on Response to Intervention

- *Essential Components of RTI—A Closer Look at Response to Intervention*:
  https://rti4success.org/sites/default/files/rtiessentialcomponents_042710.pdf
- Implementer Series Training Modules:
  https://www.rti4success.org/resources/rti-implementer-series/rti-implementer-series-training-modules
- RTI Fidelity of Implementation Rubric:
  https://rti4success.org/sites/default/files/RTI_Fidelity_Rubric.pdf
- RTI Essential Components Worksheet:
  https://rti4success.org/sites/default/files/RTI_Fidelity_Rubric_Worksheet.pdf

The Center on Response to Intervention offers many resources, including an overview of the Response to Intervention (RTI) model with implementation guidance, training modules to guide implementation of RTI or multitiered systems of support, support for monitoring school-level fidelity of RTI, and a tool for collecting information and recording school ratings related to RTI implementation.

## Chapter 15: Selective Strategies

Progress Monitoring Tools Chart

https://rti4success.org/resource/progress-monitoring-tools-chart

This chart helps educators and families select progress monitoring tools to track student progress.

Resource Mapping Tool:

http://3boldsteps.promoteprevent.org/partner/build-your-team

This website offers a resource mapping tool that helps identify gaps in programming and duplication of services and interventions.

The National Resource Center for Mental Health Promotion & Youth Violence Prevention

https://healthysafechildren.org/resources?f[0]=field_type%3A122

This website provides access to several resources that can assist schools in developing strategies for meeting the needs of their students.

PBIS (Positive Behavioral Interventions & Supports) Process Evaluation Tools

http://www.pbis.org/evaluation/evaluation-tools?text-only

The PBIS Office of Special Education and Programs Technical Assistance Center provide tools that schools can use to evaluate the implementation of PBIS.

The National Center on Response to Intervention, Screening Tools Chart

https://rti4success.org/resources/tools-charts/screening-tools-chart

This website provides information on screening tools that schools can use.

## Chapter 16: Indicated Strategies

*Data-Based Individualization: A Framework for Intensive Intervention*

https://intensiveintervention.org/sites/default/files/DBI_Framework.pdf

This report gives detailed information about data-based individualization, which is used to build an intervention based on data.

| | |
|---|---|
| Academic Progress Monitoring<br>https://www.intensiveintervention.org/chart/progress-monitoring | This chart provides information about academic progress-monitoring tools. |
| Behavioral Progress Monitoring<br>http://www.intensiveintervention.org/chart/behavioral-progress-monitoring-tools | This chart provides information about behavioral progress-monitoring tools. |
| *Advancing Education Effectiveness: Interconnecting School Mental Health and School-Wide Positive Behavior Support*<br>http://www.pbis.org/common/cms/files/Current%20Topics/Final-Monograph.pdf | This guide was developed to facilitate the links between education systems and mental health systems. |
| *Shifting Gears to Family-Driven Care: Ambassador's Guide*<br>http://huffosherconsulting.com/wp-content/uploads/2014/08/Ambassadors-Guide-introduction.pdf | This toolkit was developed to promote family-driven care and encourage family involvement. |

### Chapter 17: Social and Emotional Learning Matters

| | |
|---|---|
| SEL in Practice: A Toolkit of Practical Strategies and Resources<br>https://www.extension.umn.edu/youth/training-events/sel-toolkit/index.html | This toolkit provides information about SEL programs, including how to enhance SEL knowledge, establish expectations, infuse SEL into program activities, and collect SEL data for improvement. |
| *The 2015 CASEL Guide: Effective Social and Emotional Learning Programs—Middle and High School Edition*<br>http://secondaryguide.casel.org/casel-secondary-guide.pdf | This guide provides tips on implementing effective SEL programs for middle and high school students. |

### Chapter 18: Educators Matter

| | |
|---|---|
| SEL Online Education Module: Social and Emotional Learning in Washington State Schools: Building Foundations and Strategies<br>http://www.k12.wa.us/StudentSupport/SEL/OnlineModule.aspx?_sm_au_=iVV1R8JV4JjH116r | This online learning module from Washington State is designed to help educators, administrators, school staff and other professionals, and parents build and improve their understanding of SEL skills. |
| CASEL District Resource Center<br>https://drc.casel.org/ | This website provides detailed information on SEL for districts and gives practical advice on how to implement SEL programs. |

| | |
|---|---|
| Center on Great Teachers and Leaders<br>• The SEL School: Connecting Social and Emotional Learning to Effective Teaching: https://www.gtlcenter.org/sel-school<br>• Innovation Station: https://gtlcenter.org/learning-hub/innovation-station<br>• Understanding Teaching Conditions: https://gtlcenter.org/technical-assistance/professional-learning-modules/understanding-teaching-conditions | The Center on Great Teachers and Leaders provides tools for educators to help them understand more about SEL development, including an overview of the SEL school, an educator talent management framework, and a professional learning module on teaching conditions. |
| New Teacher Center's Teaching Conditions Resource Library<br>http://teachingconditions.org/ | This website includes tools and resources to help teachers improve the teaching and learning conditions at their school. |
| *Practical Guide to Designing Comprehensive Teacher Evaluation Systems*<br>https://www.gtlcenter.org/sites/default/files/docs/practicalGuideEvalSystems.pdf | This tool helps school administrators and educators develop teacher evaluation systems. |
| *Self-Assessing Social and Emotional Instruction and Competencies: A Tool for Teachers*<br>https://www.gtlcenter.org/sites/default/files/SelfAssessmentSEL.pdf | This self-assessment tool from the Center on Great Teachers and Leaders helps teachers reflect and improve upon their teaching practices. |
| Identity Safe Classrooms: Places to Belong and Learn<br>http://identitysafeclassrooms.org/resources/ | This website provides resources for educators on how to ensure that students' identities are acknowledged and cultivated. It includes resources on stereotype threat and identity safety, classroom relationships, cultivating diversity, child-centered teaching, and caring classroom environments. |

### Chapter 19: Academic Interventions—Use with Care

| | |
|---|---|
| Concerns-Based Adoption Model (CBAM)<br>http://www.sedl.org/cbam/ | The Concerns-Based Adoption Model is used to assess, build, and monitor readiness. It assists with the effective implementation of new programs by providing dimensions for assessing and guiding the implementation process. |

### PART IV. IMPROVE

### Chapter 20: Continuous Improvement

| | |
|---|---|
| Data Wise<br>https://datawise.gse.harvard.edu/ | This website provides resources to support educators in using data inquiry for the continuous improvement of teaching and learning for students. |

| | |
|---|---|
| Implementation Playbook<br>https://www.gtlcenter.org/learning-hub<br>/equitable-access-supports/implementation<br>-playbook | This resource from the Center on Great Teachers and Leaders provides resources for implementation planning. |
| Academic Progress Monitoring<br>https://intensiveintervention.org/chart<br>/progress-monitoring | This chart provides information about academic progress monitoring tools. |
| Indistar<br>http://www.indistar.org/ | This organization guides leadership teams through effective school or district practices. |
| RespondAbility<br>https://www.respond-ability.org/landing | This organization supports schools and districts in addressing challenges. |
| Resource 7: Root Cause Diagnostic Tree<br>https://safesupportivelearning.ed.gov<br>/addressing-root-causes-disparities-school<br>-discipline | This resource from the National Center on Safe Supportive Learning Environments provides a template for educators to fill in with issues, causes, root causes, and corrective actions. |
| School Climate Improvement Resource Package<br>https://safesupportivelearning.ed.gov/scirp<br>/about | This website provides resources that schools can use to help improve school climate. |
| Classroom Assessment Scoring System (CLASS)<br>http://teachstone.com/class/ | The CLASS tools assess teacher and student interactions in the classroom. |
| Public Profit<br>http://www.publicprofit.net/Dabbling-In<br>-The-Data | This organization provides assistance to support understanding data and improving quality. |
| The Improvement Lab at American Institutes for Research (AIR)<br>http://improvementlab.air.org/ | This website helps you navigate through AIR's approach to collaborative research and development activities toward efficacy and impact, including rapid-cycle evaluation approaches. |

# Notes

## INTRODUCTION

1. US Department of Education Office for Civil Rights, "2013–2014 Civil Rights Data Collection: A First Look," https://www2.ed.gov/about/offices/list/ocr/docs/2013-14-first-look.pdf; "CRDC Data Summaries," https://ocrdata.ed.gov/Data Summary.

2. David Osher, Kevin Dwyer, and Stephanie Jackson, *Safe, Supportive, and Successful Schools Step by Step* (Longmont, CO: Sopris West, 2004).

3. David Osher et al. "Drivers of Human Development: How Relationships and Context Shape Learning and Development," *Applied Developmental Science* (2018), doi:10.1080/10888691.2017.1398650; Pamela Cantor et al., "Malleability, Plasticity, and Individuality: How Children Learn and Develop in Context," *Applied Developmental Science* (2018), doi: 10.1080/10888691.2017.1398649; David Osher et al., *Science of Learning and Development: A Synthesis* (Washington, DC: American Institutes for Research, 2017); Alliance for Excellent Education, *Synapses, Students, and Synergies: Applying the Science of Adolescent Learning to Policy and Practice* (Washington, DC: Alliance for Excellent Education, 2018).

4. Lisa Hunter et al., *Working Together to Promote Academic Performance, Social and Emotional Learning, and Mental Health for All Children* (New York: Center for the Advancement of Children's Mental Health, Columbia University, 2005); David Osher et al., "Warning Signs of Problems in Schools: Ecological Perspectives and Effective Practices for Combating School Aggression and Violence," in *Issues in School Violence Research*, ed. Michael J. Furlong et al. (Binghamton, NY: Haworth Press, 2004), 13–38; Nancy Rappaport et al., "Enhancing Collaborations Within and Across Disciplines to Advance Mental Health Programs in Schools," in *School Mental Health Handbook*, ed. Mark D. Weist, Steven W. Evans, and Nancy A. Lever (New York: Kluwer Academic, 2002), 107–18; Mary Magee Quinn et al., *Teaching and Working with Children Who Have Emotional and Behavioral Challenges* (Longmont, CO: Sopris West, 2000); Darren W. Woodruff et al., *The Role of Education in a System of Care: Effectively Serving Children with Emotional or Behavioral Disorders* (Washington, DC: American Institutes for Research, Center for Effective Collaboration and Practice, 1999); Kevin Dwyer, David Osher, and Cynthia Warger, *Early Warning, Timely Response: A Guide to Safe Schools* (Washington, DC: US Department of Education, 1998); Mary Magee Quinn et al., *Safe, Drug-Free, and Effective Schools for ALL Students: What Works!* (Washington, DC: American Institutes for Research,

Center for Effective Collaboration and Practice, 1998); David M. Osher and Tom V. Hanley, "Building on an Emergent Social Service Delivery Paradigm," in *Making Collaboration Work for Children, Youth, Families, Schools, and Communities*, ed. Lyndal M. Bullock and Robert A. Gable (Reston, VA: Council for Exceptional Children, 1997), 10–15; Kevin P. Dwyer et al., "Team Crisis: School Psychologists and Nurses Working Together," *Psychology in the Schools* 52, no. 7 (2015): 702–13; Trina W. Osher and David M. Osher, "The Paradigm Shift to True Collaboration with Families," *Journal of Child and Family Studies* 11, no. 1 (2002): 47–60; David M. Osher, Mary Magee Quinn, and Tom V. Hanley, "Children and Youth with Serious Emotional Disturbance: A National Agenda for Success," *Journal of Child and Family Studies* 11, no. 1 (2002): 1–11; David M. Osher, Susan Sandler, and Cameron Lynn Nelson, "The Best Approach to Safety Is to Fix Schools and Support Children and Staff," *New Directions in Youth Development* 2001, no. 92 (2001): 127–54.

## CHAPTER 1

1. Allison Dymnicki et al., *Willing, Able, Ready: Basics and Policy Implications of Readiness as a Key Component for Implementation of Evidence-Based Practices* (Washington, DC: Office of the Assistant Secretary for Planning and Evaluation, Office of Human Services Policy, 2014); Abraham Wandersman and Jonathan P. Scaccia, *Organizational Readiness: Measurement & Predictor of Progress, $R = MC^2$* (Princeton, NJ: Robert Wood Johnson Foundation, 2017).
2. Dymnicki et al., *Willing, Able, Ready*.
3. Richard E. Clark, Keith E. Howard, and Sean Early, "Motivational Challenges Experienced in Highly Complex Learning Environments," in *Handling Complexity in Learning Environments: Research and Theory*, ed. Jan Elen and Richard E. Clark (Oxford, UK: Elsevier Science Ltd., 2006).
4. Daphna Oyserman and Mesmin Destin, "Identity-Based Motivation: Implications for Intervention," *Journal of Counseling Psychology* 38, no. 7 (2010), 1001–43.
5. Helen Patrick, Julianne Turner, and Anna D. Strati, "Classroom and School-Level Influences on Student Motivation," in *Handbook of Social Influences in School Contexts: Social-Emotional, Motivation, and Cognitive Outcomes*, ed. Kathryn R. Wentzel and Geetha B. Ramani (New York: Routledge, 2016), 241–57.
6. Sendhil Mullainathan and Eldar Sharif, *Scarcity: Why Having Too Little Means So Much* (London: Allen Lane, 2013).
7. Michael Lipsky, *Street-Level Bureaucracy: Dilemmas of the Individual in Public Services* (New York: Russell Sage Foundation, 2010), xi–xx.
8. Anthony Bryk and Barbara Schneider, *Trust in Schools: A Core Resource for Improvement* (New York: Russell Sage Foundation, 2002), 144.
9. Ibid., 5.
10. "How to Teach Math as a Social Activity," Edutopia, February 25, 2008, https://www.edutopia.org/video/how-teach-math-social-activity.
11. For more information about the PATHS program, see https://www.channing-bete.com/prevention-programs/paths/at-a-glance.html.
12. David Osher et al., *Cleveland Metropolitan School District Human Ware Audit: Findings and Recommendations* (Washington, DC: American Institutes for Research, 2008).
13. David Osher, Lawrence B. Friedman, and Kimberly T. Kendziora, *Cross-District Outcome Evaluation Report: Social and Emotional Learning in Eight School Districts* (Washing-

ton, DC: American Institutes for Research, 2014); David Osher et al., "Avoid Quick Fixes: Lessons Learned from a Comprehensive Districtwide Approach to Improve Conditions for Learning," in *Closing the School Discipline Gap: Equitable Remedies for Excessive Exclusion*, ed. Daniel J. Losen (New York: Teachers College Press, 2015), 192–206.

CHAPTER 2

1. David Osher et al., *Science of Learning and Development: A Synthesis* (Washington, DC: American Institutes for Research, 2017); Anthony S. Bryk et al., *Organizing Schools for Improvement: Lessons from Chicago* (Chicago: University of Chicago Press, 2017); Jason Grissom and Susanna Loeb, "Triangulating Principal Effectiveness: How Perspectives of Parents, Teachers, and Assistant Principals Identify the Central Importance of Managerial Skills," *American Educational Research Journal* 48, no. 5 (2011): 1091–1123; Kerstin Carlson Le Floch et al., *Case Studies of Schools Receiving School Improvement Grants: Findings After the First Year of Implementation*, NCEE 2014–2015 (Washington, DC: US Department of Education, Institute of Education Sciences, National Center for Education Evaluation and Regional Assistance, 2014); Karen Seashore Louis et al., *Investigating the Links to Improved Student Learning: Final Report of Research Findings* (St. Paul, MN: University of Minnesota, 2010).

2. Larry Cuban and Michael Usdan, *Powerful Reforms with Shallow Roots: Improving America's Urban Schools* (New York: Teachers College Press, 2003); Bryk et al., *Organizing Schools for Improvement*.

3. Shirley M. Hord et al., *Taking Charge of Change* (Austin, TX: Southwest Educational Development Lab, 1987), 6.

4. Kimberly Kendziora and David Osher, "Promoting Children's and Adolescents' Social and Emotional Development: District Adaptations of a Theory of Action," *Journal of Clinical Child and Adolescent Psychology* 45, no. 6 (1987): 797–811, doi:10 .1080/15374416.2016.1197834; David Osher, Lawrence Friedman, and Kimberly Kendziora, *Cross-District Implementation Summary: Social and Emotional Learning in Eight School Districts* (Washington, DC: American Institutes for Research, 2014).

5. David Osher, Kevin Dwyer, and Stephanie Jackson, *Safe, Supportive, and Successful Schools Step by Step* (Longmont, CO: Sopris West, 2004).

CHAPTER 3

1. Michael G. Fullan and Matthew B. Miles, "Getting Reform Right: What Works and What Doesn't," *Phi Delta Kappan* 73, no. 10 (1992): 745–52.

2. M. S. Rao, "Spot Your Leadership Style—Build Your Leadership Brand," *Journal of Values-Based Leadership* 8, no. 1 (2015): 11.

3. David Tyak and Larry Cuban, *Tinkering Toward Utopia: A Century of Public School Reform* (Cambridge, MA: Harvard University Press, 1995).

4. "Our Strategy," Say Yes to Education, http://sayyestoeducation.org/strategy/; David Osher and Eugene Chasin, "Bringing Together Schools and the Community: The Case of Say Yes to Education," in *Comprehensive Community Initiatives for Positive Youth Development*, ed. Jonathan F. Zaff et al. (New York: Psychology Press, 2016), 72–104; Kimberly Kendziora, David Osher, and Mary Anne Schmitt-Carey, *Say Yes to Education Student Monitoring System: Research Report* (New York: Say Yes to Education Foundation, 2007); Kimberly Kendziora, David Osher, and Mary Anne

Schmitt-Carey, *Say Yes to Education Student Monitoring System: Updated Literature Review* (Washington, DC: American Institutes for Research, 2014).

5. Nancy Lever and Elizabeth Freeman, "School-Based Mental Health Services" (PowerPoint presentation), https://safesupportivelearning.ed.gov/sites/default /files/School-based%20MH%20Services_final.pdf.

6. Nancy Lever, *Resource Mapping in Schools and School Districts: A Resource Guide* (Baltimore: Center for School Mental Health, 2014).

7. For detailed examples of root-cause analyses (and what to do with them), see David Osher et al., *Addressing the Root Causes of Disparities in School Discipline: An Educator's Action Planning Guide* (Washington, DC: National Center on Safe Supportive Learning Environments, 2015).

8. Fullan and Miles, "Getting Reform Right."

9. David Osher, Kevin Dwyer, and Stephanie Jackson, *Safe, Supportive and Successful Schools Step by Step* (Washington, DC: American Institutes for Research, 2004).

10. Rachel E. Blaine et al., "Using School Staff Members to Implement a Childhood Obesity Prevention Intervention in Low-Income School Districts: The Massachusetts Childhood Obesity Research Demonstration (MA-CORD Project), 2012–2014," *Preventing Chronic Disease* 14 (2017), http://dx.doi.org/10.5888/pcd14 .160381.

11. Jonathan P. Scaccia et al., "A Practical Implementation Science Heuristic for Organizational Readiness: $R = MC^2$," *Journal of Community Psychology* 43, no. 4 (2015): 484–501.

12. Mary Magee Quinn et al., *Safe, Drug-Free, and Effective Schools for ALL Students: What Works!* (Washington, DC: American Institutes for Research, Center for Effective Collaboration and Practice, 1998).

13. Rebecca Herman et al., *Turning Around Chronically Low-Performing Schools: A Practice Guide*, NCEE #2008-4020 (Washington, DC: National Center for Education Evaluation and Regional Assistance, Institute of Education Sciences, US Department of Education, 2008).

14. Ellen Foley et al., *Beyond Test Scores: Leading Indicators for Education* (Providence, RI: Annenberg Institute for School Reform at Brown University, 2008), 2.

15. "My Teaching Partner," Curry School of Education, University of Virginia, https:// curry.virginia.edu/myteachingpartner.

16. Amy Bernstein Colton and Georgea M. Sparks-Langer, "A Conceptual Framework to Guide the Development of Teacher Reflection and Decision Making," *Journal of Teacher Education* 44, no. 1 (1993): 45–54.

17. Monica Janas, "Shhhhh, the Dragon Is Asleep and Its Name Is Resistance," *Journal of Staff Development* 19, no. 3 (1998): 13 16.

## CHAPTER 4

1. Bruce F. Chorpita, Eric L. Daleiden, and John R. Weisz, "Identifying and Selecting the Common Elements of Evidence-Based Interventions: A Distillation and Matching Model," *Mental Health Services Research* 7, no. 1 (2005), 5–20; Bruce F. Chorpita and Eric L. Daleiden, "Structuring the Collaboration of Science and Service in Pursuit of a Shared Vision," *Journal of Clinical Child & Adolescent Psychology* 43, no. 2 (2014), 323–38; Mark W. Lipsey, "The Primary Factors That Characterize

Effective Interventions with Juvenile Offenders: A Meta-Analytic Overview," *Victims and Offenders* 4, no. 2 (2009): 124–47.

2. Stephanie Jones et al., *Kernels of Practice for SEL: Low-Cost, Low-Burden Strategies* (Cambridge, MA: Harvard Graduate School of Education, 2017), http://www.wallacefoundation.org/knowledge-center/Documents/Kernels-of-Practice-for-SEL.pdf.

3. Sheppard G. Kellam et al., "The Good Behavior Game and the Future of Prevention and Treatment," *Addiction Science & Clinical Practice* 6, no. 1 (2011), 73–84.

4. Stephanie M. Jones and Suzanne M. Bouffard, "Social and Emotional Learning in Schools: From Programs to Strategies," *Sharing Child and Youth Development Knowledge, Social Policy Report* 26, no. 4 (2012), 1–33.

5. Centers for Disease Control and Prevention, *Preventing Multiple Forms of Violence: A Strategic Vision for Connecting the Dots* (Atlanta, GA: Division of Violence Prevention, National Center for Injury Prevention and Control, Centers for Disease Control and Prevention, 2016), https://www.cdc.gov/violenceprevention/pdf/strategic_vision.pdf.

6. "Practice Guides," What Works Clearinghouse, https://ies.ed.gov/ncee/wwc/PracticeGuides; Michael Epstein et al., *Reducing Behavior Problems in the Elementary School Classroom: A Practice Guide (NCEE #2008-012)* (Washington, DC: National Center for Education Evaluation and Regional Assistance, Institute of Education Sciences, US Department of Education, 2008), https://ies.ed.gov/ncee/wwc/PracticeGuide/4.

7. "Safe Supportive Learning," National Center on Safe Supportive Learning Environments, https://safesupportivelearning.ed.gov/; "Safe Place to Learn: Prevent, Intercede, Respond to Sexual Harassment of K–12 Students | Safe Supportive Learning," National Center on Safe Supportive Learning Environments, https://safesupportivelearning.ed.gov/safe-place-to-learn-k12.

8. Anthony Biglan et al., "The Critical Role of Nurturing Environments for Promoting Human Well-Being," *American Psychologist* 67, no. 4 (2012): 257–71, doi:10.1037/a0026796.

9. Anthony Biglan et al., *Helping Adolescents at Risk: Prevention of Multiple Problem Behaviors* (New York: Guilford Press, 2004); Brian R. Flay, Frank J. Snyder, and John Petraitis, "The Theory of Triadic Influence," in *Emerging Theories in Health Promotion Practice and Research, 2nd ed.*, ed. Ralph J. DiClemente, Richard A. Crosby, and Michelle C. Kegler (San Francisco: Jossey-Bass, 2009), 451–510.

10. "National-Academies.org. Where the Nation Turns for Independent, Expert Advice," National Academies of Sciences, Engineering, Medicine, http://www.nationalacademies.org/nasem/; Pamela Cantor et al., "Malleability, Plasticity, and Individuality: How Children Learn and Develop in Context," *Journal of Applied Developmental Science*, January 2018, doi:10.1080/10888691.2017.1398649; David Osher et al., "Drivers of Human Development: How Relationships and Context Shape Learning and Development," *Journal of Applied Developmental Science*, January 2018, https://doi.org/10.1080/10888691.2017.1398650; "Bullying Prevention," American Educational Research Association, http://www.aera.net/Education-Research/Issues-and-Initiatives/Bullying-Prevention-and-School-Safety/Bullying-Prevention.

11. John R. Weisz et al., "Bridging the Gap Between Laboratory and Clinic in Child and Adolescent Psychotherapy," *Journal of Consulting and Clinical Psychology* 63, no. 5 (1995): 688–701; Rob Horner, Caryn Blitz, and Scott W. Ross, *The Importance of Contextual Fit When Implementing Evidence-Based Interventions*, ASPE Issue Brief (Washington, DC: Office of the Assistant Secretary for Planning and Evaluation, Office of Human Services Policy, US Department of Health and Human Services, 2014), https://aspe.hhs.gov/system/files/pdf/77066/ib_Contextual.pdf; David Osher and Michael Kane, *Describing and Studying Innovations in the Education of Children with Attention Deficit Disorder* (Washington, DC: Directed Research Branch, Division of Innovation and Development, Office of Special Education Programs, US Department of Education, 1993).

12. "Standards for Research Conduct," American Educational Research Association, http://www.aera.net/Publications/Standards-for-Research-Conduct.

13. Chris Bonell et al., "Realist Randomised Controlled Trials: A New Approach to Evaluating Complex Public Health Interventions," *Social Science & Medicine* 75, no. 12 (2012), 2299–2306; Vivian Louie, "Identifying Responses to Inequality: The Potential of Qualitative and Mixed-Methods Research," *William T. Grant Foundation Digest* 1 (June 2016): 1–10, http://wtgrantfoundation.org/library/uploads/2016/06/The-Value-of-Qualitative-and-Mixed-Methods-Research.pdf.

14. Horner, Blitz, and Ross, *The Importance of Contextual Fit*.

15. Karen Blase, Laurel Kiser, and Melissa Van Dyke, *The Hexagon Tool: Exploring Context* (Chapel Hill: National Implementation Research Network, FPG Child Development Institute, University of North Carolina, 2013).

16. Karen Blase and Dean Fixsen, *Core Intervention Components: Identifying and Operationalizing What Makes Programs Work*, ASPE Research Brief (Washington, DC: US Department of Health and Human Services, 2013).

## CHAPTER 5

1. David Osher, "Creating Comprehensive and Collaborative Systems," *Journal of Child and Family Studies* 11, no. 1 (2002): 91–9.

2. David Osher et al., "School Influences on Child and Youth Development," in *Advances in Prevention Science, Vol. 1: Defining Prevention Science*, ed. Zili Sloboda and Honno Petras (New York: Springer, 2014), 151–70.

3. Courtney Kase et al., "Educational Outcomes Associated with School Behavioral Health Interventions: A Review of the Literature," *Journal of School Health* 87, no. 7 (2017): 554–62; Timothy J. Runge et al., "A Practical Protocol for Situating Evidence-Based Mental Health Programs and Practices Within School-Wide Positive Behavioral Interventions and Supports," *Advances in School Mental Health Promotion* 10, no. 2 (2017): 101–12, doi: 10.1080/1754730X.2017.1285708.

4. Matthew Lynch, "High School Dropout Rate: Causes and Costs," *Education Week*, http://blogs.edweek.org/edweek/education_futures/2013/11/high_school_dropout_rate_causes_and_costs.html.

5. Beth A. Stroul et al., *Toolkit for Expanding the System of Care Approach* (Washington, DC: Georgetown University Center for Child and Human Development, National Technical Assistance Center for Children's Mental Health, 2015), 10, https://gucchd.georgetown.edu/products/Toolkit_SOC.pdf.

6.  Fiona M. Hollands and Henry M. Levin, *The Critical Importance of Costs for Education Decisions* (REL 2017–274) (Washington, DC: US Department of Education, Institute of Education Sciences, National Center for Education Evaluation and Regional Assistance, Analytic Technical Assistance and Development, 2017).

7.  Howard Adelman and Linda Taylor, *Resource Mapping and Management to Address Barriers to Learning: An Intervention for Systemic Change* (Los Angeles: Center for Mental Health in Schools, Department of Psychology, University of California at Los Angeles, 2015), http://smhp.psych.ucla.edu/pdfdocs/resourcemapping/resource mappingandmanagement.pdf.

8.  N. Lever et al., *Resource Mapping in Schools and School Districts: A Resource Guide* (Baltimore: Center for School Mental Health, 2014), https://www.pbis.org/resource/102 /resource-mapping-in-schools-and-school-districts-a-resource-guide.

9.  Margaret Flynn-Khan et al., *Adding It Up: A Guide for Mapping Public Resources for Children, Youth and Families* (Washington, DC: Forum for Youth Investment, 2006), http://forumfyi.org/files/Adding_It_Up_Guide_0.pdf.

10.  Jennifer M. Haley et al., "Together, Medicaid and CHIP Cover More Than 4 in 10 Young Children in Most Metropolitan Areas," *Say Ahhh* blog, Georgetown University Health Policy Institute, Center for Children and Families, January 30, 2018, https://ccf.georgetown.edu/2018/01/30/together-medicaid-and-chip-cover-more -than-4-in-10-young-children-in-most-metropolitan-areas/.

11.  "Pathways Through Medicaid to Prevention," Moving Health Care Upstream, http://movinghealthcareupstream.org/innovations/pathways-through-medicaid -to-prevention.

12.  Deborah Bachrach, Jocelyn Guyer, and Ariel Levin, *Medicaid Coverage of Social Interventions: A Road Map for States* (New York: Milbank Memorial Fund, 2016), https:// www.milbank.org/wp-content/uploads/2016/09/MMF-NYS-Health-Issue-Brief -FINAL.pdf.

13.  See, for example, David Osher et al., "Deconstructing the Pipeline: Using Efficacy, Effectiveness, and Cost-Benefit Data to Reduce Minority Youth Incarceration," *New Directions in Youth Development* 2003, no. 99 (2003): 91–120.

14.  Nicholas Hobbs, *The Troubled and Troubling Child* (San Francisco: Jossey-Bass, 1982).

15.  The Open Table is a faith-based support and care coordination model with which the American Institutes for Research has worked closely in recent years; see http:// www.theopentable.org/.

16.  Beth A. Stroul et al., *Effective Financing Strategies for Systems of Care: Examples From the Field—A Resource Compendium for Financing Systems of Care: Second Edition* (RTC Study 3: Financing Structures and Strategies to Support Effective Systems of Care, FMHI pub. #235-03) (Tampa: University of South Florida, Louis de la Parte Florida Mental Health Institute, Research and Training Center for Children's Mental Health, 2009), http://rtckids.fmhi.usf.edu/rtcpubs/hctrking/pubs/Study3 secondedition.pdf.

17.  See https://www.tgci.com/funding-sources.

CHAPTER 6

1.  Jacqueline J. Goodnow and Jeanette A. Lawrence, "Children and Cultural Context," in *Handbook of Child Psychology and Developmental Science, Volume 4: Ecological*

*Settings and Processes*, 7th ed., ed. Marc H. Bornstein and Tama Leventhal (Hoboken, NJ: John Wiley & Sons, Inc., 2015), 746–86, doi:10.1002/9781118963418.childpsy 419.

2. Terry L. Cross et al., *Towards a Culturally Competent System of Care, Volume 1: A Monograph on Effective Services for Minority Children Who Are Severely Emotionally Disturbed* (Washington, DC: Georgetown University, Child Development Center, 1989).

3. Melanie Tervalon and J. Murray Garcia, "Cultural Humility Versus Cultural Competence: A Critical Distinction in Defining Physician Training Outcomes in Multicultural Education," *Journal of Health Care for the Poor and Underserved* 9, no. 2 (1998): 117–25, 123.

4. Beth Harry, Maya Kalyanpur, and Monimalika Day, *Building Cultural Reciprocity with Families: Case Studies in Special Education* (Baltimore: Brookes, 1999).

5. Tawara D. Goode and Wendy Jones, *Definition of Linguistic Competence* (Washington, DC: National Center for Cultural Competence, Georgetown University, Center for Child and Human Development, 2006), https://gucchd.georgetown.edu/products/DefinitionLinguisticCompetence.pdf.

6. Angela Valenzuela, *Subtractive Schooling* (Albany: State University of New York, 1999); David Osher and Lenore Webb, *Adult Literacy, Learning Disabilities, and Social Context: Conceptual Foundations for a Learner-Centered Approach* (Washington, DC: US Department of Education, 1994).

7. Adapted from Mark A. King, Anthony Sims, and David Osher, *How Is Cultural Competence Integrated into Education?* (Washington, DC: Center or Effective Collaboration and Practice, American Institutes for Research, 2007); Tawara D. Goode et al., "Family-Centered, Culturally and Linguistically Competent Care: Essential Components of the Medical Home," *Pediatric Annals* 38, no. 9 (2009): 505–12.

8. Goode et al., "Family-Centered, Culturally and Linguistically Competent Care."

9. Cross et al., *Towards a Culturally Competent System of Care*; Goode et al., "Family-Centered, Culturally and Linguistically Competent Care."

10. Cross et al., *Towards a Culturally Competent System of Care*.

11. National Center for Cultural Competence, *And the Journey Continues . . . Achieving Cultural and Linguistic Competence in Systems Serving Children and Youth with Special Health Care Needs and Their Families* (Washington, DC: National Center for Cultural Competence [NCCC], Georgetown University Center for Child and Human Development, 2007), https://nccc.georgetown.edu/documents/journey.pdf; National Center for Cultural Competence, *Cultural and Linguistic Competence Policy Assessment* (Washington, DC: National Center for Cultural Competence, Georgetown University, Center for Child and Human Development, 2006), https://nccc.georgetown.edu/documents/CLCPA.pdf.

12. Melanie Tervalon and Murray Garcia, "Cultural Humility Versus Cultural Competence," *Journal of Health Care for the Poor and Underserved* 9, no. 2 (1998): 117–25, 123.

13. Janis Prince Inniss et al., *Serving Everyone at the Table: Strategies for Enhancing the Availability of Culturally Competent Mental Health Service—Making Children's Mental Health Services Successful Series* (Tampa: University of South Florida, College of Behavioral & Community Sciences, Louis de la Parte Florida Mental Health Institute, Department of Child and Family Studies, Research and Training Center for Children's Mental Health, 2009).

14. David Osher et al., *Addressing the Root Causes of Disparities in School Discipline: An Educator's Action Planning Guide* (Washington, DC: National Center on Safe Supportive Learning Environments, 2015).

15. Geneva Gay, *Culturally Responsive Teaching: Theory, Research, and Research*, 2nd ed. (New York: Teachers College Press, 2010).

16. Richard E. Clark et al., "Cognitive Task Analysis," in *Handbook of Research on Educational Communications and Technology*, 3rd ed., ed. J. Michael Spector et al. (New York: Taylor & Francis, 2008).

17. Gay, *Culturally Responsive Teaching*.

18. Gloria Ladson-Billings, "Toward a Theory of Culturally Relevant Pedagogy," *American Educational Research Journal* 32, no. 3 (1995): 465–91.

19. Trina Osher, "What Families Think of the Juvenile Justice System: Findings from the OJJDP Multi-State Study," *Focal Point* 20, no. 2 (2006): 20–23.

20. Zaretta Hammond, *Culturally Responsive Teaching and The Brain: Promoting Authentic Engagement and Rigor Among Culturally and Linguistically Diverse Students* (Thousand Oaks, CA: Sage, 2014); Claude M. Steele, *Whistling Vivaldi: How Stereotypes Affect Us and What We Can Do* (New York: W. W. Norton & Co., 2010); Howard Stevenson, *Promoting Racial Literacy in Schools: Differences That Make a Difference* (New York: Teachers College Press, 2014).

21. Implicit bias is a positive or negative mental attitude toward a person, thing, or groups that a person holds at an unconscious level (https://www.edi.nih.gov/blog /opinion/unconscious-bias-and-public-servant-1-3-what-unconscious-bias). For more information about implicit bias, see https://implicit.harvard.edu/implicit / or Cheryl Staats, *State of the Science: Implicit Bias Review 2014* (Columbus: Kirwan Institute for the Study of Race and Ethnicity, Ohio State University, 2014), http:// kirwaninstitute.osu.edu/wp-content/uploads/2014/03/2014-implicit-bias.pdf; Jeffrey S. Passel and D'Vera Cohn, *U.S. Population Projections 2005–2050* (Washington, DC: Pew Research Center, 2008), http://www.pewhispanic.org/2008/02/11 /us-population-projections-2005-2050/; and Mitchell F. Rice, "Promoting Cultural Competency in Public Administration and Public Service Delivery: Utilizing Self-Assessment Tools and Performance Measures," *Journal of Public Affairs Education* 13, no. 1 (2007): 41–57.

22. For example, see Gay, *Culturally Responsive Teaching*.

## CHAPTER 7

1. Nelson Beaudoin, *Elevating Student Voice: How to Enhance Student Participation, Citizenship, and Leadership* (Larchmont, NY: Eye On Education, 2005); Kathleen Cushman, *Fires in the Bathroom: Advice for Teachers from High School Students* (New York: The New Press, 2003); Michael Apple and James Beane, *Democratic Schools* (Arlington, VA: ASCD, 1995); Jean Rudduck, Helen Demetriou, and David Pedder, "Student Perspectives and Teacher Practices: The Transformative Potential," *McGill Journal of Education* 38, no. 2 (2003): 274–88, http://mje.mcgill.ca/article /view/8685; Karen Young and Jenny Sazama, *15 Points: Successfully Involving Youth in Decision Making* (Somerville, MA: Youth on Board, 2006); Julia Flutter and Jean Rudduck, *Student Voice and the Architecture of Change: Mapping the Territory* (Cambridge, UK: Faculty of Education, University of Cambridge, 2006), http://www .educ.cam.ac.uk/research/projects/researchdevelopment/0706rudduck1.doc;

Julia Flutter and Jean Rudduck, *Consulting Pupils: What's in It for Schools?* (London: Routledge Falmer, 2004); Stuart Critchley, "The Nature and Extent of Student Involvement in Educational Policy-Making in Canadian School Systems," *Educational Management & Administration* 31, no. 1 (2003): 97–106, doi:10.1177/0263211X030311007; Alison Cook-Sather, "Authorizing Students' Perspectives: Toward Trust, Dialogue, and Change in Education," *Educational Researcher* 31, no. 4 (2002): 3–14; Shepherd Zeldin et al., *Youth in Decision-Making: A Study on the Impacts of Youth on Adults and Organizations* (Madison, WI: University of Wisconsin, National 4-H Council, University of Wisconsin Extension, 2000), http://www.theinnovationcenter.org/files/Youth_in_Decision_Making_Brochure.pdf; Jean Rudduck and Julia Flutter, "Pupil Participation and Pupil Perspective: Carving a New Order of Experience," *Cambridge Journal of Education* 30, no. 1 (2000): 75–89; Henry Giroux and Susan Searls Giroux, *Take Back Higher Education: Race, Youth, and the Crisis of Democracy in the Post Civil-Rights Era* (New York: Palgrave MacMillan, 2004); Ira Shor, *When Students Have Power: Negotiating Authority in a Critical Pedagogy* (Chicago: University of Chicago Press, 1996); Henry Giroux and Peter McLaren, eds., *Critical Pedagogy, the State, and the Struggle for Culture* (Albany, NY: State University of New York Press, 1989).

2. Barbara Cervone and Kathleen Cushman, "Moving Youth Participation into the Classroom: Students as Allies," *New Directions for Youth Development* 2002, no. 96 (2002): 83–100; Patricia Houghton, "Finding Allies: Sustaining Teachers' Health and Well-Being," *Phi Delta Kappan* 82, no. 9 (May 2001): 706–12; N. Amanda Branscombe, Dixie Goswami, and Jeffrey Schwartz, eds., *Students Teaching, Teachers Learning* (Portsmouth, NH: Boynton/Cook, 1992).

3. Cushman, *Fires in the Bathroom*; Michael Fielding and Jean Rudduck, "The Transformative Potential of Student Voice: Confronting the Power Issue" (paper presented at the British Educational Research Association [BERA] Annual Conference, University of Exeter, September 12–14, 2002), http://www.leeds.ac.uk/educol/documents/00002544.htm; Alfie Kohn, "Choices for Children: Why and How to Let Students Decide," *Phi Delta Kappan* 75, no. 1 (1993): 18–21, http://www.alfiekohn.org/article/choices-children/.

4. Emily Ozer, Miranda L. Ritterman, and Maggie G. "Participatory Action Research (PAR) in Middle Schools: Opportunities, Constraints and Key Processes," *American Journal of Community Psychology* 46, no. 1–2 (2010): 152–66; Emily Ozer et al., "'Bounded' Empowerment: Analyzing Tensions in the Practice of Youth-Led Participatory Research in Urban Public Schools," *American Journal of Community Psychology* 52, no. 1–2 (2013): 13–26.

5. "What Is Youth Engagement, Really?" Act for Youth Center of Excellence, http://www.actforyouth.net/youth_development/engagement/.

6. David Osher, "The Pedagogy of Real Talk and the Promotion of Student Well-Being and Success," in *The Pedagogy of Real Talk: Engaging, Teaching, and Connecting with Students At Risk*, ed. Paul Hernandez (New York: Corwin, 2015); Cushman, *Fires in the Bathroom*.

7. "What Is Youth Engagement, Really?"

8. Jacquelynne S. Eccles and Robert W. Roeser, "Schools as Developmental Contexts During Adolescence," *Journal of Research on Adolescence* 21, no. 1 (2011): 225–41.

9. Beth Stroul and Gary M. Blau, *The System of Care Handbook: Transforming Mental Health Services for Children, Youth, and Families* (Baltimore: Paul H. Brookes Publishing Co., 2008).

10. Lawrence Winn and Katie Richards-Schuster, "The Importance of Child-Guided and Youth-Directed Approaches: Engaging Youth Participatory Actions Research Practices," in *Keeping Students Safe and Helping Them Thrive: A Collaborative Handbook on School Safety, Mental Health, and Wellness*, ed. David Osher et al. (Santa Barbara, CA: Praeger/ABC-CLIO, forthcoming); "Components of School Climate," Youth. gov, http://youth.gov/youth-topics/school-climate/components-of-positive -school-climate.

11. Jennifer A. Fredricks and Jacquelynne S. Eccles, "Is Extracurricular Participation Associated with Beneficial Outcomes? Concurrent and Longitudinal Relations," *Developmental Psychology* 42, no. 4 (2006): 698–713.

12. "Components (of School Climate)."

13. Chandra Muller, "The Role of Caring in the Teacher Student Relationship for At Risk Students," *Sociological Inquiry* 71, no. 2 (April 2001): 241–55.

14. Shelley Murdock, Carole Paterson, and Mary Claire L. Gatmaitan, "Youth in Community Decision-Making: A Study of Youth-Adult Partnerships," *Journal of Youth Development* 2, no. 3 (Spring 2008).

15. S. Zeldin et al., "Bringing Young People to the Table: Effects on Adults and Youth Organizations," *Community Youth Development Journal* 2, no. 2 (2001): 20–27.

16. Murdock, Paterson, and Gatmaitan, "Youth in Community Decision-Making."

17. Winn and Richard-Schuster, "Importance of Child-Guided and Youth-Directed Approaches."

CHAPTER 8

1. Susan Auerbach, "Beyond Coffee with the Principal: Toward Leadership for Authentic School-Family Partnerships," *Journal of School Leadership* 20, no. 6 (2010): 728–57.

2. "NAFSCE Policy Work," National Association for Family, School and Community Engagement, http://www.nafsce.org/page/PolicyWork.

3. Adapted from Gary Blau, Trina W. Osher, and David M. Osher, "Need for a Definition of Family Driven Care" (January 2005), http://huffosherconsulting.com /wp-content/uploads/2014/08/Need-for-a-Definition.pdf.

4. Anne T. Henderson and Karen L. Mapp, *A New Wave of Evidence: The Impact of School, Family, and Community Connections on Student Achievement* (Austin, TX: Southwest Educational Development Laboratory, 2002), http://www.sedl.org/connections /resources/evidence.pdf.

5. Ibid.

6. Ibid.

7. Anthony S. Bryk et al., *Organizing Schools for Improvement: Lessons from Chicago* (Chicago: University of Chicago Press, 2010).

8. Ibid.

9. Ibid.

10. Karen L. Mapp and Paul J. Kuttner, *Partners in Education: A Dual Capacity-Building Framework for Family–School Partnerships* (Austin, TX: Southwest Educational Development Laboratory, 2013), http://www.sedl.org/pubs/framework/.

11. Trina Osher and Barbara Huff, "Supporting Family Involvement in Correctional Education Programs," July 27, 2006 (webinar for National Technical Assistance Center for the Education of Neglected or Delinquent Children and Youth [NDTAC], Huff Osher Consulting), https://www.neglected-delinquent.org/events/practical-strategies-family-involvement-correctional-education.

12. Marion Baldwin and Sally M. Wade, "Improving Family and Community Engagement Through Sharing Data" (briefing paper, Southeast Comprehensive Center, Metairie, LA, 2012).

13. "What Is APTT?" WestEd, https://www.wested.org/wp-content/uploads/2017/03/services-appt-brochure.pdf.

14. Aysha L. Foster, "Academic Parent Teacher Teams (APTT): How Did the New Parent-Involvement Model Impact Student Achievement in HISD?" *HISD Evaluation Report* 9, no. 2 (2015), http://www.houstonisd.org/cms/lib2/TX01001591/Centricity/domain/8269/pe_districtprograms/2015_APTT_%20Report.pdf.

15. Auerbach, "Beyond Coffee with the Principal."

CHAPTER 9

1. Larry Cuban and Michael Usdan, eds., *Powerful Reforms with Shallow Roots: Improving America's Urban Schools* (New York: Teachers College Press, 2002), 192; Mark Warren and Karen Mapp, *A Match on Dry Grass: Community Organizing as a Catalyst for School Reform* (Oxford, UK: Oxford University Press, 2011).

2. Darren Woodruff et al., "The Role of Education in a System of Care: Effectively Serving Children with Emotional or Behavioral Disorders," in *Systems of Care: Promising Practices in Children's Mental Health, 1998 Series*, vol. III (Washington, DC: Center for Effective Collaboration and Practice, American Institutes for Research, 1999).

3. David M. Chavis and Kien Lee, "What Is Community Anyway?" *Stanford Social Innovation Review: Informing and Inspiring Leaders of Social Change*, May 12, 2015, https://ssir.org/articles/entry/what_is_community_anyway.

4. Ibid.

5. Robert D. Putnam, *Bowling Alone: The Collapse and Revival of American Community*, 1st ed. (New York: Touchstone Books, 2000).

6. David Osher et al., "Interdisciplinary and Cross-Stakeholder Collaboration for Better Outcomes," in *Keeping Students Safe and Helping Them Thrive: A Collaborative Handbook on School Safety, Mental Health, and Wellness*, ed. David Osher et al. (Santa Barbara, CA: Praeger/ABC-CLIO, forthcoming).

7. Elwood M. Hopkins and James M. Ferris, eds., *Place-Based Initiatives in the Context of Public Policy and Markets: Moving to Higher Ground* (Los Angeles: Center on Philanthropy and Public Policy, 2015), 19.

8. Elizabeth Lightfoot, Jennifer Simmelink McCleary, and Terry Lum, "Asset Mapping as a Research Tool for Community-Based Participatory Research in Social Work," *Social Work Research* 38, no. 1 (2014): 59–64.

9. Advancement Project, *Participatory Asset Mapping: A Community Research Lab Toolkit* (Washington, DC: Advancement Project—Healthy City Community Research Lab, 2011), http://www.communityscience.com/knowledge4equity/AssetMapping-Toolkit.pdf; Asset-Based Community Development Institute (ABCD), https://resources.depaul.edu/abcd-institute/Pages/default.aspx.

10. Hopkins and Ferris, *Place-Based Initiatives*, 19.

11. Luisella Borra and John Boult, "Design Innovation in Nonprofits: A Need for New Design Strategies," *Design Management Review* 28 (2017): 8–13, doi:10.1111/drev.12095.
12. Osher et al., "Interdisciplinary and Cross-Stakeholder Collaboration."
13. For a range of examples that address indicators across a broad range of segments of a community, see "Section 10. Community-Level Indicators: Some Examples," Community Toolbox, https://ctb.ku.edu/en/table-of-contents/evaluate/evaluate-community-initiatives/examples-of-community-level-indicators/main.
14. Innovation Network, Logic Model Workbook, https://www.innonet.org/news-insights/resources/logic-model-workbook/.

CHAPTER 10
1. Joy G. Dryfoos and Sue Maguire, *Inside Full-Service Community Schools* (Thousand Oaks, CA: Corwin Press, 2002).
2. Deborah Lowe Vandell, Elizabeth R. Reisner, and Kim M. Pierce, *Outcomes Linked to High-Quality Afterschool Programs: Longitudinal Findings from the Study of Promising Afterschool Programs* (Irvine, CA, Madison, WI, and Washington, DC: University of California–Irvine, University of Wisconsin–Madison, and Policy Studies Associates, Inc., 2007); Joseph A. Durlak and Roger P. Weissberg, *The Impact of After-School Programs That Promote Personal and Social Skills* (Chicago: Collaborative for Academic, Social, and Emotional Learning, 2007); Richard F. Catalano et al., "Positive Youth Development in the United States: Research Findings on Evaluations of Positive Youth Development Programs," *Annals of the American Academy of Political and Social Science* 591, no. 1 (2004): 98–124; Joseph A. Durlak, Roger P. Weissberg, and Molly Pachan, "A Meta-Analysis of After-School Programs That Seek to Promote Personal and Social Skills in Children and Adolescents," *American Journal of Community Psychology* 45, no. 3–4 (2010): 294–309; Robert C. Granger, "After-School Programs and Academics: Implications for Policy, Practice and Research," *Social Policy Report* 22, no. 2 (2008): 3–19; Patricia A. Lauer et al., "Out-of-School-Time Programs: A Meta-Analysis of Effects for At-Risk Students," *Review of Educational Research* 76, no. 2 (2006): 275–313.
3. Durlak and Weissberg, *Impact of After-School Programs*; Durlak, Weissberg, and Pachan, "Meta-Analysis of After-School Programs," 294–309. In 2011, Durlak and colleagues released a meta-analysis of 213 school-based, universal social and emotional learning (SEL) programs involving 270,034 students from kindergarten through high school. Findings from this historic study revealed that SEL participants demonstrated significantly improved social-emotional skills, attitudes, behavior, and academic performance, compared to controls.
4. Tina J. Kauh, *AfterZone: Outcomes for Youth Participating in Providence's Citywide After-School System* (Philadelphia: Public/Private Ventures, 2011); Neil Naftzger, Matthew Vinson, and Feng Liu, *New Jersey 21st Century Community Learning Centers Year 4 Evaluation Report* (Washington, DC: American Institutes for Research, 2013).
5. Martin Blank and Sarah Pearson, *Community Schools Research Brief* (Washington DC: Coalition for Community Schools, 2009), http://www.communityschools.org/assets/1/AssetManager/CCS%20Research%20Report2009.pdf.
6. Janice C. Burns, Dagmar Pudrzynska Paul, and Silvia R. Paz, *Participatory Asset Mapping: A Community Research Lab Toolkit* (Washington, DC: Advancement Project–Healthy City Community Research Lab, 2011), http://www.community

science.com/knowledge4equity/AssetMappingToolkit.pdf; Asset-Based Community Development Institute (ABCD), https://resources.depaul.edu/abcd-institute/Pages/default.aspx.

7. Carol McElvain et al., "Tool 55—Family Engagement and Interest Survey," in *Beyond the Bell: A Toolkit for Creating Effective Afterschool and Expanded Learning Programs* (Washington, DC: American Institutes for Research, 2014).

8. Excerpted from "What Is a Community School?" Coalition for Community Schools, http://www.communityschools.org/aboutschools/what_is_a_community_school.aspx.

9. McElvain et al., "Tool 63—Youth Development Checklist," in *Beyond the Bell*; Stephen F. Hamilton and Mary Agnes Hamilton, *The Youth Development Handbook: Coming of Age in American Communities* (Thousand Oaks, CA: Sage Publications, 2004), 3–22.

10. As our understanding of what effective practice looks like has matured, thanks to new research and fieldwork, so too has our need to be able to assess, reflect on, and improve practice. There are multiple measures of quality at the point of service (i.e., where adults and youth interact) and organization-level processes that support program quality. *Measuring Program Quality* is a practical guide that analyzes multiple program quality assessment tools and compares their purpose, structure, content, and technical properties. See Nicole Yohalem et al., *Measuring Youth Program Quality: A Guide to Assessment Tools*, 2nd ed. (Washington, DC: Forum for Youth Investment, 2009), http://forumfyi.org/content/measuring-youth-program-quality-guide-assessment-tools-2nd-edition.

11. Robert C. Pianta and Bridget K. Hamre, "Conceptualization, Measurement, and Improvement of Classroom Processes: Standardized Observation Can Leverage Capacity," *Educational Researcher* 38, no. 2 (2009): 109–19; Lev Semenovich Vygotsky, *Mind in Society: The Development of Higher Psychological Processes* (Cambridge, MA: Harvard University Press, 1980).

12. "Developmental Relationships," Search Institute, http://www.search-institute.org/what-we-study/developmental-relationships.

13. "21st Century Community Learning Centers (CCLC) Grant Program," Massachusetts Department of Elementary and Secondary Education, http://www.doe.mass.edu/21cclc/ta/sayo.html; "Youth and School-Age Program Quality Assessment (PQA)," David P. Weikart Center for Youth Program Quality, http://www.cypq.org/downloadpqa.

14. McElvain et al., *Beyond the Bell*.

15. Durlak, Weissberg, and Pachan, "Meta-Analysis of After-School Programs," 294–309.

16. "Vision & Mission," WINGS for Kids, Inc., http://www.wingsforkids.org/.

17. Nicholas Yoder and Elizabeth Devaney, *Social and Emotional Learning Practices: A Self-Reflection Tool for Afterschool Staff* (Washington, DC: American Institutes for Research, 2015), http://www.air.org/resource/social-and-emotional-learning-practices-self-reflection-tool-afterschool-staff; Partnership for Children & Youth, *Measuring Quality: Assessment Tools to Evaluate Your Social-Emotional Learning Practices* (Oakland, CA: Public Profit, 2016), http://partnerforchildren.org/measuring-quality/.

18. Richard M. Lerner, *Liberty: Thriving and Civic Engagement Among America's Youth* (Thousand Oaks, CA: SAGE Publications, 2004).

19. John C. Ricketts and Rick D. Rudd, "A Comprehensive Leadership Education Model to Train, Teach, and Develop Leadership in Youth," *Journal of Career and Technical Education* 19, no. 1 (2002): 7–17.

20. Joy Des Marais, Youa Yang, and Farid Farzanehkia, "Service-Learning Leadership Development for Youths," *Phi Delta Kappan* 81, no. 9 (2000): 678–80.

21. Nicole Yohalem, Karen Pittman, and Sharon Lovick Edwards, *Strengthening the Youth Development/After-School Workforce: Lessons Learned and Implications for Funders* (Washington, DC: Forum for Youth Investment, 2010), http://forumfyi.org/files /Strengthening_the_YD-AS_Workforce.pdf; Kim M. Pierce, Daniel M. Bolt, and Deborah Lowe Vandell, "Specific Features of After-School Program Quality: Associations with Children's Functioning in Middle Childhood," *American Journal of Community Psychology* 45, no. 3–4 (2010): 381–93.

22. Deborah A. Moroney, *The Readiness of the Out-of-School Time Workforce to Intentionally Support Participants' Social and Emotional Development: A Review of the Literature and Future Directions* (Washington, DC: National Academies of Sciences, Engineering, and Medicine, 2016).

23. Elizabeth Starr, Ellen Gannett, and Judy Nee, *Core Knowledge and Competencies for Afterschool and Youth Development Professionals* (Oakton, VA: National Afterschool Association, 2011), https://naaweb.org/images/Core-Knowledge-and-Competencies -web.pdf.

CHAPTER 11

1. Ruth Berkowitz et al., "A Research Synthesis of the Associations Between Socioeconomic Background, Inequality, School Climate, and Academic Achievement," *Review of Educational Research* 87, no. 2 (2016): 425–69.

2. Pamela Cantor et al., "Malleability, Plasticity, and Individuality: How Children Learn and Develop in Context," *Applied Developmental Science* (2018), forthcoming.

3. Desiree W. Murray et al., *Self-Regulation and Toxic Stress: Foundations for Understanding Self-Regulation From an Applied Developmental Perspective*, OPRE Report #2015-21 (Washington, DC: US Department of Health and Human Services, Office of Planning, Research and Evaluation, Administration for Children and Families, 2015). Aprile D. Benner and Yijie Wang, "Adolescent Substance Use: The Role of Demographic Marginalization and Socioemotional Distress," *Developmental Psychology* 51, no. 8 (2015): 1086–97; Bridget K. Hamre and Robert C. Pianta, "Classroom Environments and Developmental Processes," in *Handbook of Research on Schools, Schooling, and Human Development*, ed. Judith L. Meece and Jacquelynne S. Eccles (London: Routledge, 2010), 25–41; David Osher and Julliette Berg, *School Climate and Social and Emotional Learning: The Integration of Two Approaches* (University Park: Edna Bennett Pierce Prevention Research Center, Pennsylvania State University, 2017).

4. Robert C. Pianta, "Classroom Processes and Teacher-Student Interaction: Integrations with a Developmental Psychopathology Perspective," in *Developmental Psychopathology, Volume 4: Risk, Resilience, and Intervention*, 3rd ed., ed. Dante Cicchetti (Hoboken, NJ: Wiley, 2016), 770–814.

5. National Center on Safe Supportive Learning Environments, *Creating a Safe and Respectful Environment in Our Nation's Classrooms: Creating a Supportive Classroom Climate* (Washington, DC: National Center on Safe Supportive Learning Environments, n.d.), https://safesupportivelearning.ed.gov/sites/default/files/sssta/20121108_20 120928ClsrmMod2HandoutsFINAL1.pdf.

6. Bridget K. Hamre and Robert C. Pianta, "Can Instructional and Emotional Support in the First-Grade Classroom Make a Difference for Children at Risk of School Failure?" *Child Development* 76, no. 5 (2005), 949–67.

7. Kate E. Norwalk et al., "Improving the School Context of Early Adolescence Through Teacher Attunement to Victimization," *Journal of Early Adolescence* 36, no. 7 (2016): 989–1009.

8. Claude M. Steele, *Whistling Vivaldi: How Stereotypes Affect Us and What We Can Do* (New York: Norton, 2010).

9. Cantor et al., "Malleability."

10. Allison Master, Lucas P. Butler, and Gregory M. Walton, "How the Subjective Relationship Between the Self, Others, and a Task Drives Interest," in *The Science of Interest*, ed. Paul A. O'Keefe and Judith M. Harackiewicz (New York: Springer, 2017).

11. Geneva Gay, *Culturally Responsive Teaching: Theory, Research, and Practice* (New York: Teachers College Press, 2010).

12. David Osher et al., "Issues of Cultural and Linguistic Competency and Disproportionate Representation," in *Handbook of Research in Behavioral Disorders*, ed. Robert B. Rutherford Jr., Mary Magee Quinn, and Sarup R. Mather (New York: Guilford, 2004), 54–77.

13. Kimberly Kendziora, David Osher, and Mary Anne Schmitt-Carey, *Say Yes to Education Student Monitoring System: Updated Literature Review* (Washington, DC: American Institutes for Research, 2014).

14. National Center on Safe Supportive Learning Environments, *Creating a Safe and Respectful Environment.*

15. Cantor et al., "Malleability."

16. "Physical Safety," National Center on Safe Supportive Learning Environments, https://safesupportivelearning.ed.gov/topic-research/safety/physical-safety.

17. Patricia A. Jennings and Mark T. Greenberg, "The Prosocial Classroom: Teacher Social and Emotional Competence in Relation to Student and Classroom Outcomes," *Review of Educational Research* 79, no. 1 (2009): 491–525, doi:10.3102 /0034654308325693; David Osher et al., "A Comprehensive Approach to Promoting Social, Emotional, and Academic Growth in Contemporary Schools," in *Best Practices in School Psychology V*, vol. 4, ed. Alex Thomas and Jeff Grimes (Bethesda, MD: National Association of School Psychologists, 2008), 1263–78.

18. Amrit Thapa et al., "A Review of School Climate Research," *Review of Educational Research* 83, no. 3 (2013): 357–85; Shannon Wanless, Dewey Cornell, and D. Davis, "Emotional and Physical Safety," in *Keeping Students Safe and Helping Them Thrive: A Collaborative Handbook on School Safety, Mental Health, and Wellness*, ed. David Osher et al. (Santa Barbara, CA: Praeger/ABC-CLIO, forthcoming).

19. Alexander J. Shackman et al., "Anxiety Selectively Disrupts Visuospatial Working Memory," *Emotion* 6, no. 1 (2006): 40–61; Cantor et al, 2018.

20. Benjamin Kutsyuruba, Don A. Klinger, and Alicia Hussain, "Relationships Among School Climate, School Safety, and Student Achievement and Well-Being: A Review of the Literature," *Review of Education* 3, no. 2 (2015): 103–35.
21. "Cyberbullying," National Center on Safe Supportive Learning Environments, https://safesupportivelearning.ed.gov/topic-research/safety/bullyingcyberbullying.
22. Thapa et al., "A Review of School Climate Research."
23. Ibid.
24. Michelle Birkett, Dorothy L. Espelage, and Brian Koenig, "LGB and Questioning Students in Schools: The Moderating Effects of Homophobic Bullying and School Climate on Negative Outcomes," *Journal of Youth and Adolescence* 38, no. 7 (2009): 989–1000; David Osher et al., "School Influences on Child and Youth Development," in *Advances in Prevention Science, Volume 1: Defining Prevention Science*, ed. Zili Sloboda and Hanno Petras (New York: Springer, 2014), 151–70.
25. Thapa et al., "A Review of School Climate Research."
26. National Center on Safe Supportive Learning Environments, *Creating a Safe and Respectful Environment*.
27. "Substance Abuse," National Center on Safe Supportive Learning Environments, https://safesupportivelearning.ed.gov/topic-research/safety/substance-abuse.
28. Clea McNeely and Christina Falci, "School Connectedness and the Transition Into and out of Health-Risk Behavior Among Adolescents: A Comparison of Social Belonging and Teacher Support," *Journal of School Health* 74, no. 7 (2004): 284–92.
29. US Department of Education, Office of Elementary and Secondary Education, Office of Safe and Healthy Students, *Guide for Developing High-Quality School Emergency Operations Plans* (Washington, DC: US Department of Education, Office of Elementary and Secondary Education, Office of Safe and Healthy Students, 2013).
30. Daniel J. Flannery et al., "The Scientific Evidence Supporting an Eight-Point Public Health–Oriented Action Plan to Prevent Gun Violence," in *Keeping Students Safe and Helping Them Thrive: A Collaborative Handbook on School Safety, Mental Health, and Wellness*, ed. David Osher et al. (Santa Barbara, CA: Praeger/ABC-CLIO, forthcoming).
31. "Emergency Readiness & Management," National Center on Safe Supportive Learning Environments, https://safesupportivelearning.ed.gov/topic-research/safety/emergency-readiness-management.
32. "Instructional Environment," National Center on Safe Supportive Learning Environments, https://safesupportivelearning.ed.gov/topic-research/environment/instructional-environment.
33. Cantor et al., "Malleability"; Thapa et al., "A Review of School Climate Research."
34. Steele, *Whistling Vivaldi*; Hamre and Pianta, "Classroom Environments and Developmental Processes," 25–41.
35. David Osher et al., "How We Can Improve School Discipline," *Educational Researcher* 39, no. 1 (2010): 48–58.
36. Lisa Flook, "Mindfulness for Teachers: A Pilot Study to Assess Effects on Stress, Burnout, and Teaching Efficacy," *Mind, Brain, and Education* 7, no. 3 (2013): 182–95; Patricia Jennings, Angela Minnici, and Nick Yoder, "Creating the Working Conditions to Enhance Teacher Social and Emotional Well-Being," in *Keeping Students Safe and Helping Them Thrive: A Collaborative Handbook on School Safety, Mental Health, and Wellness*, ed. David Osher et al. (Santa Barbara, CA: Praeger/ABC-CLIO,

forthcoming); Pianta, "Classroom Processes and Teacher-Student Interaction," 770–814.

37. "Physical Environment," National Center on Safe Supportive Learning Environments, https://safesupportivelearning.ed.gov/topic-research/environment/physical-environment.

38. "Why Healthy School Environments Are Important: Impact on Performance and Health at Schools," United States Environmental Protection Agency, https://www.epa.gov/schools/why-healthy-school-environments-are-important.

39. "The Role of States in Fostering Environmental Health Programs in K–12 Schools," United States Environmental Protection Agency, https://www.epa.gov/schools/role-states-fostering-environmental-health-programs-k-12-schools.

40. Catherine P. Bradshaw, Tracy Evian Waasdorp, and Sarah Lindstrom Johnson, "Overlapping Verbal, Relational, Physical, and Electronic Forms of Bullying in Adolescence: Influence of School Context," *Journal of Clinical Child & Adolescent Psychology* 44, no. 3 (2015): 494–508.

41. "Physical Environment."

42. "Physical Health," National Center on Safe Supportive Learning Environments, https://safesupportivelearning.ed.gov/topic-research/environment/physical-health.

43. Shannon M. Suldo et al., "The Impact of School Mental Health on Student and School-Level Academic Outcomes: Current Status of the Research and Future Directions," *School Mental Health* 6, no. 2 (2014): 84–98.

44. Erin Dowdy et al., "Enhancing School-Based Mental Health Services with a Preventive and Promotive Approach to Universal Screening for Complete Mental Health," *Journal of Educational and Psychological Consultation* 25, no. 2–3 (2015): 178–97; Kimberly Hoagwood and Jacqueline Johnson, "School Psychology: A Public Health Framework I: From Evidence-Based Practices to Evidence-Based Policies," *Journal of School Psychology* 41, no. 1 (2003): 3–21; James L. McDougal, Sheila Moody Clonan, and Brian K. Martens, "Using Organizational Change Procedures to Promote the Acceptability of Prereferral Intervention Services: The School-Based Intervention Team Project," *School Psychology Quarterly* 15, no. 2 (2000): 149.

45. National Center on Safe Supportive Learning Environments, *Creating a Safe and Respectful Environment.*

46. Christopher Boccanfuso and Megan Kuhfeld, *Multiple Responses, Promising Results: Evidence-Based, Nonpunitive Alternatives to Zero Tolerance* (Bethesda, MD: Child Trends, 2011), http://www.childtrends.org/wp-content/uploads/2011/03/Child_Trends-2011_03_01_RB_AltToZeroTolerance.pdf; Emily Morgan et al., *The School Discipline Consensus Report: Strategies from the Field to Keep Students Engaged in School and Out of the Juvenile Justice System* (New York: Council of State Governments Justice Center, 2014); Pamela Fenning and Jennifer Rose, "Overrepresentation of African American Students in Exclusionary Discipline: The Role of School Policy," *Urban Education* 42, no. 6 (2007): 536–59.

CHAPTER 12

1. Robert Blum, *School Connectedness: Improving the Lives of Students* (Baltimore: Johns Hopkins Bloomberg School of Public Health, 2005).

2. David Osher et al., "Drivers of Human Development: How Relationships and Context Shape Learning and Development," *Applied Developmental Science* (2018), forthcoming; Pamela Cantor et al., "Malleability, Plasticity, and Individuality: How Children Learn and Develop in Context," *Applied Developmental Science* (2018), forthcoming.

3. David M. Chavis and Kien Lee, "What Is Community Anyway?" *Stanford Social Innovation Review*, May 12, 2015, https://ssir.org/articles/entry/what_is_community_anyway.

4. Shirley N. Hord, *Learning Together, Leading Together* (New York: Teachers College Press, 2004).

5. Urie Bronfenbrenner, "Contexts of Child Rearing: Problems and Prospects," *American Psychologist* 34, no. 10 (1979): 844–50, doi:10.1037//0003-066X.34.10.844; Valerie Lee et al., *Social Support, Academic Press, and Student Achievement: A View from the Middle Grades in Chicago* (Chicago: Consortium on Chicago School Research, 1999), https://consortium.uchicago.edu/sites/default/files/publications/p0e01.pdf; Lang Ma et al., "The Development of Academic Competence Among Adolescents Who Bully and Who Are Bullied," *Journal of Applied Developmental Psychology* 30, no. 5 (2009): 628–44, doi:10.1016/j.appdev.2009.07.006.

6. Osher et al., 2018; Amrit Thapa et al., "A Review of School Climate Research," *Review of Educational Research* 83, no. 3 (2013): 357–85; https://safesupportive learning.ed.gov/sites/default/files/EDSCLS%20UserGuide_06202017.pdf.

7. Robert Blum, Clea McNeely, and Peggy Rinehart, *Improving the Odds: The Untapped Power of Schools to Improve the Health of Teens* (Cheshire, CT: CASCIAC, 2002), http://www.casciac.org/pdfs/ImprovingtheOdds.pdf; Carol Goodenow and Kathleen Grady, "The Relationship of School Belonging and Friends' Values to Academic Motivation Among Urban Adolescent Students," *Journal of Experimental Education* 62, no. 1 (1993): 60–71; Lee et al., *Social Support, Academic Press, and Student Achievement*; Karen Osterman, "Students' Need for Belonging in the School Community," *Review of Educational Research* 70, no. 3 (2000): 323–67; Kathryn R. Wentzel, "Student Motivation in Middle School: The Role of Perceived Pedagogical Caring," *Journal of Educational Psychology* 89, no. 3 (1997): 411–19; Anne Gregory and Dewey Cornell, "'Tolerating' Adolescent Needs: Moving Beyond Zero Tolerance Policies in High School," *Theory into Practice* 48, no. 2 (2009): 106–13; Patricia Houghton, "Finding Allies: Sustaining Teachers' Health and Well-Being," *Phi Delta Kappan* 82, no. 9 (2001): 706–12; F. Clark Power, Ann Higgins, and Lawrence Kohlberg, *Critical Assessments of Contemporary Psychology: Lawrence Kohlberg's Approach to Moral Education* (New York: Columbia University Press, 1989); Ming-Te Wang et al., "A Tobit Regression Analysis of the Covariation Between Middle School Students' Perceived School Climate and Problem Behavior," *Journal of Research on Adolescence* 20, no. 2 (2010): 274–86; Robert Croninger and Valerie Lee, "Social Capital and Dropping Out of High School: Benefits to At-Risk Students of Teacher's Support and Guidance," *Teachers College Record* 103, no. 4 (2001): 548–81; Ping Guo, "School Culture: A Validation Study and Exploration of Its Relationship with Teachers' Work Environment" (unpublished doctoral dissertation, Fordham University, New York, 2012), https://search.proquest.com/openview/42d14055d21f0 fbfefdcf80d2d9a2284/1?pq-origsite=gscholar&cbl=18750&diss=y; Ann Higgins-

D'Alessandro and Arnond Sakworawich, "Congruency and Determinants of Teacher and Student Views of School Culture" (paper presented at the Association for Moral Education annual conference, Nanjing, China, October 2011), http://www.amenetwork.org/ame2011nanjing; Jantine L. Spilt, Helma M. Y. Koomen, and Jochem T. Thijs, "Teacher Wellbeing: The Importance of Teacher–Student Relationships," *Educational Psychology Review* 23, no. 4 (2011): 457–77; Mary H. Shann, "Professional Commitment and Satisfaction Among Teachers in Urban Middle Schools," *Journal of Educational Research* 92, no. 2 (1998): 67–73.

8. Ron Astor, Nancy Guerra, and Richard Van Acker, "How Can We Improve School Safety Research?" *Educational Researchers* 39, no. 1 (2010): 69–78.

9. Bruce L. Wilson and H. Dickson Corbett, *Listening to Urban Kids: School Reform and the Teachers They Want* (Albany: State University of New York Press, 2001).

10. Kathleen Cotton, *Classroom Questioning* (Portland, OR: Northwest Regional Educational Laboratory, 1988), http://educationnorthwest.org/sites/default/files/ClassroomQuestioning.pdf.

11. Robert Felner et al., "Creating Small Learning Communities: Lessons from the Project on High-Performing Learning Communities About 'What Works' in Creating Productive, Developmentally Enhancing, Learning Contexts," *Education Psychologist* 42, no. 4 (2007): 209–21.

12. Douglas Reeves, "Of Hubs, Bridges, and Networks," *Educational Leadership* 63, no. 8 (2006): 32–7.

13. Hord, *Learning Together, Leading Together*; Alan M. Blankstein, Paul D. Houston, and Robert W. Cole, *Sustaining Professional Learning Communities*, Vol. 3 (Thousand Oaks, CA: Corwin Press, 2008).

14. Selena S. Blankenship and Wendy E. A. Ruona, "Professional Learning Communities and Communities of Practice: A Comparison of Models, Literature Review" (paper presented at the Academy of Human Resource Development International Research Conference in The Americas, Indianapolis, Indiana, February 28–March 4, 2007).

15. Eric Toshalis and Michael J. Nakkula, *Motivation, Engagement, and Student Voice Toolkit* (Boston: Jobs for the Future, 2013), https://jfforg-prod-prime.s3.amazonaws.com/media/documents/1_SATC_Motivation_Toolkit_051713.pdf.

16. Charles Ewing, "Sensible Zero Tolerance Protects Students," *Harvard Education Letter* 16, no. 1 (2000).
Anthony Biglan, *The Nurture Effect: How the Science of Human Behavior Can Improve Our Lives and Our World* (Oakland, CA: New Harbinger Publications, 2015).

17. G. Roy Mayer et al., "Preventing School Vandalism and Improving Discipline: A Three-Year Study," *Journal of Applied Behavior Analysis* 16, no. 4 (1983): 355–69.

18. APA Zero Tolerance Task Force, "Are Zero Tolerance Policies Effective in the Schools?" *American Psychologist* 63, no. 9 (2008): 852–62; Matthew P. Steinberg, Elaine Allensworth, and David W. Johnson, *Student and Teacher Safety in Chicago Public Schools: The Roles of Community Context and School Social Organization* (Chicago: Consortium on Chicago School Research, 2011); "Exclusionary School Discipline" (video file), American Institutes for Research, http://www.air.org/resource/exclusionary-school-discipline.

19. M. Amos Clifford, *Teaching Restorative Practices with Classroom Circles* (Santa Rosa, CA: Center for Restorative Process, 2015), https://www.ocde.us/HealthyMinds

/Documents/RP%20Resources/Teaching%20Restorative%20Practices%20with%20 Classroom%20Cirlces.pdf.

20. Ted Wachtel, "Defining Restorative," International Institute for Restorative Practices, https://www.iirp.edu/what-we-do/what-is-restorative-practices/defining -restorative.

21. Trevor Fronius et al., *Restorative Justice in U.S. Schools: A Research Review* (San Francisco: WestEd, 2016), https://www.wested.org/resources/restorative-justice -research-review/; "Ongoing Comprehensive School Safety Initiative Research," National Institute of Justice, https://nij.gov/topics/crime/school-crime/Pages /school-safety-initiative-components.aspx.

22. Wachtel, "Defining Restorative."

23. M. Amos Clifford, *Teaching Restorative Practices with Classroom Circles*.

24. Mark Bitel, *National Evaluation of the Restorative Justice in Schools* (London: Youth Justice Board for England and Wales, 2005).

25. M. Amos Clifford, *Teaching Restorative Practices*.

26. Opportunity to Learn Campaign, Advancement Project, American Federation of Teachers, and National Education Association, *Restorative Practices: Fostering Healthy Relationships & Promoting Positive Discipline in Schools: A Guide for Educators* (Cambridge, MA: Schott Foundation for Public Education, 2014), http://schott foundation.org/resources/restorative-practices-toolkit.

27. Howard Zehr, *Changing Lenses: A New Focus for Crime and Justice*, 25th anniversary ed. (Harrisonburg, VA: Herald Press, 2015); Howard Zehr with Ali Gohar, *The Little Book of Restorative Justice* (Brattleboro, VT: Good Books, 2003).

28. Margaret Thorsborne and Lisa Cameron, "Restorative Justice and School Discipline: Mutually Exclusive?" in *Restorative Justice and Civil Society*, ed. Heather Strang and John Braithwaite (Cambridge, UK: Cambridge University Press, 2001).

29. Kevin Dwyer and David Osher, *Safeguarding Our Children: An Action Guide Revised and Expanded* (Longmont, CO: Sopris West, 2005), https://www2.ed.gov/admins /lead/safety/actguide/action_guide.pdf.

30. International Institute for Restorative Practices, https://www.iirp.edu/.

31. Sonia Jain et al., *Restorative Justice in Oakland Schools: Implementation and Impact* (Oakland, CA: Oakland Unified School District, 2014), https://www.ousd.org /cms/lib/CA01001176/Centricity/Domain/134/OUSD-RJ%20Report%20revised %20Final.pdf.

CHAPTER 13

1. Angus J. MacNeil, Doris L. Prater, and Steve Busch, "The Effects of School Culture and Climate on Student Achievement," *International Journal of Leadership in Education* 12, no. 1 (2009): 73–84; Michael B. Ripski and Anne Gregory, "Unfair, Unsafe, and Unwelcome: Do High School Students' Perceptions of Unfairness, Hostility, and Victimization in School Predict Engagement and Achievement," *Journal of School Violence* 8, no. 4 (2009): 355–75; David Osher, Kevin Dwyer, and Shane R. Jimerson, "Foundations of School Violence and Safety," in *Handbook of School Violence and School Safety: From Research to Practice*, ed. Shane R. Jimerson and Michael J. Furlong (Mahwah, NJ: Lawrence Erlbaum, 2006), 51–71; David Osher, Susan Sandler, and Cameron Lynn Nelson, "The Best Approach to Safety Is to Fix Schools and Support Children and Staff," in *Zero Tolerance: Can Suspension and*

*Expulsion Keep Schools Safe? New Directions in Youth Development*, no. 92, ed. Russell J. Skiba and Gil G. Noam (San Francisco: Jossey-Bass, 2002): 127–54; Mary Magee Quinn et al., *Safe, Drug-Free, and Effective Schools for All Students: What Works!* (Washington, DC: Center for Effective Collaboration and Practice, American Institutes for Research, 1998).

2. Rebecca J. Collie, Jennifer D. Shapka, and Nancy E. Perry, "School Climate and Social-Emotional Learning: Predicting Teacher Stress, Job Satisfaction, and Teaching Efficacy," *American Psychological Association* 104, no. 4 (2012): 1189–1204; Jessica L. Grayson and Heather K. Alvarez, "School Climate Factors Relating to Teacher Burnout: A Mediator Model," *Teaching and Teacher Education* 24, no. 5 (2008): 1349–63.

3. Tracey G. Scherr and Shannon Snapp, "Gender Identity and Sexual Orientation," in *Keeping Students Safe and Helping Them Thrive: A Collaborative Handbook on School Safety, Mental Health, and Wellness*, ed. David Osher et al. (Santa Barbara, CA: Praeger/ABC-CLIO, forthcoming).

4. Amy Stuart Wells, Lauren Fox, and Diana Cordova-Cobo, *How Racially Diverse Schools and Classrooms Can Benefit All Students* (New York and Washington, DC: The Century Foundation, 2016).

5. Vincent J. Felitti et al., "The Relationship of Adult Health Status to Childhood Abuse and Household Dysfunction," *American Journal of Preventive Medicine* 14, no. 4 (1998): 245–58; Vanessa Sacks, David Murphey, and Kristin Moore, *Adverse Childhood Experiences: National and State-Level Prevalence* (Washington, DC: Child Trends, 2014), doi:10.13140/2.1.1193.8087.

6. Shannon M. Suldo et al., "The Impact of School Mental Health on Student and School-level Academic Outcomes: Current Status of the Research and Future Directions," *School Mental Health* 6, no. 2 (2014): 84–98.

7. Patricia Gándara and Jongyeon (Joy) Ee, "U.S. Immigration Enforcement Policy and Its Impact on Teaching and Learning in the Nation's Schools," Civil Rights Project, https://www.civilrightsproject.ucla.edu/research/k-12-education /integration-and-diversity/u.s.-immigration-enforcement-policy-and-its-impact -on-teaching-and-learning-in-the-nations-schools.

8. Suniya S. Luthar, Samuel H. Barkin, and Elizabeth J. Crossman, "'I Can, Therefore I Must': Fragility in the Upper-Middle Classes," *Development and Psychopathology* 25, no. 4 (2013): 1529–49.

9. David Osher et al., "Drivers of Human Development: How Relationships and Context Shape Learning and Development," *Applied Developmental Science* (2018), forthcoming.

10. "Understanding Child Traumatic Stress: A Guide for Parents," National Child Traumatic Stress Network, https://www.nctsn.org/sites/default/files/resources //understanding_child_traumatic_stress_guide_for_parents.pdf; Substance Abuse and Mental Health Services Administration (SAMHSA), *Trauma-Informed Care in Behavioral Health Services* (Treatment Improvement Protocol [TIP] Series 57, HHS Publication No. [SMA] 14-4816, Rockville, MD: SAMHSA, 2014).

11. SAMHSA, *Trauma-Informed Care in Behavioral Health Services*.

12. Ibid.

13. "Culture and Trauma," National Child Traumatic Stress Network, http://www .nctsn.org/resources/topics/culture-and-trauma.

14. Robert T. Carter, "Racism and Psychological and Emotional Injury: Recognizing and Assessing Race-Based Traumatic Stress," *Counseling Psychologist* 35, no. 1 (2007): 13–105; Thema Bryant-Davis and Carlota Ocampo, "Racist Incident-Based Trauma," *Counseling Psychologist* 33, no. 4 (2005): 479–500; Derald W. Sue et al., "Racial Microaggressions in Everyday Life," *American Psychologist* 62, no. 4 (2007): 271–86.

15. "Complex Trauma: Facts for Educators," National Child Traumatic Stress Network, https://www.nctsn.org/sites/default/files/resources//complex_trauma_facts_educators.pdf; Alexandra Cook et al., "Complex Trauma in Children and Adolescents," *Psychiatric Annals* 35, no. 5 (2005): 390–8.

16. William E. Copeland et al., "Traumatic Events and Posttraumatic Stress in Children," *Archives of General Psychiatry* 64, no. 5 (2007): 577–84;

17. David Finkelhor et al., "Prevalence of Childhood Exposure to Violence, Crime, and Abuse: Results from the National Survey of Children's Exposure to Violence," *JAMA Pediatrics* 169, no. 8 (2015): 746–54. As used here, *violence* includes assaults, sexual victimization, child maltreatment by an adult, and witnessed and indirect victimization.

18. Vincent J. Felitti and Robert F. Anda, "The Relationship of Adverse Childhood Experiences to Adult Health, Well-Being, Social Function, and Health Care," in *The Effects of Early Life Trauma on Health and Disease: The Hidden Epidemic*, ed. Ruth A. Lanius, Eric Vermetten, and Clare Pain (New York: Cambridge University Press, 2010; Carly B. Dierkhising et al., "Trauma Histories Among Justice-Involved Youth: Findings from the National Child Traumatic Stress Network," *European Journal of Psychotraumatology* 4 (2013): 10; Jennifer P. Edidin et al., "The Mental and Physical Health of Homeless Youth: A Literature Review," *Journal of Child Psychiatry and Human Development* 43, no. 3 (2012): 354–75; Katie Cyr et al., "Polyvictimization and Victimization of Children and Youth: Results from a Populational Survey," *Child Abuse & Neglect*, 37, no. 10 (2013): 814–20; Julian Ford et al., "Poly-Victimization Among Juvenile Justice–Involved Youths," *Child Abuse & Neglect* 37, no. 10 (2013): 788–800.

19. Ruth Pat-Horenczyk et al., "The Search for Risk and Protective Factors in Childhood PTSD," in *Treating Traumatized Children: Risk, Resilience and Recovery*, ed. Danny Brom, Ruth Pat-Horenczyk, and Julian D. Ford (New York: Routledge, 2009), 51–71; Ann S. Masten, *Ordinary Magic: Resilience in Development* (New York: Guilford Press, 2014); Christopher M. Layne, Ernestine C. Briggs, and Christine A. Courtois, "Introduction to the Special Section: Using the Trauma History Profile to Unpack Risk Factor Caravans and Their Consequences," *Psychological Trauma: Theory, Research, Practice, and Policy* 6, suppl. 1 (2014): S1–S8.

20. Pamela Cantor et al., "Malleability, Plasticity, and Individuality: How Children Learn and Develop in Context," *Applied Developmental Science* (2018), forthcoming; Osher et al., "Drivers of Human Development."

21. American Psychological Association, *Children and Trauma: Update for Mental Health Professionals* (Washington, DC: APA Presidential Task Force on Posttraumatic Stress Disorder and Trauma in Children and Adolescents, 2008), http://www.apa.org/pi/families/resources/update.pdf; National Scientific Council on the Developing Child, *Excessive Stress Disrupts the Architecture of the Developing Brain: Working Paper No. 3* (Cambridge, MA: National Scientific Council on the Developing Child

and Harvard University Center on the Developing Child, 2014), www.developing-child.harvard.edu; National Scientific Council on the Developing Child, *Persistent Fear and Anxiety Can Affect Young Children's Learning and Development: Working Paper No. 9* (Cambridge, MA: Author, and Center on the Developing Child, Harvard University, 2010), www.developingchild.harvard.edu; Michael D. DeBellis and Abigail Zisk, "The Biological Effects of Childhood Trauma," *Child and Adolescent Psychiatric Clinics of North America* 23, no. 2 (2014): 185–222.

22. Frank W. Putnam, "The Impact of Trauma on Child Development," *Juvenile and Family Court Journal* 57, no. 1 (2006): 1–11.

23. Michelle M. Perfect et al., "School-Related Outcomes of Traumatic Event Exposure and Traumatic Stress Symptoms in Students: A Systemic Review of Research from 1990 to 2015," *School Mental Health* 8, no. 1 (2016): 7–43.

24. Robert Kim, *A Report on the Status of Gay, Lesbian, Bisexual and Transgender People in Education: Stepping Out of the Closet, into the Light* (Washington, DC: National Education Association, 2009), http://www.nea.org/assets/docs/HE/glbtstatus09.pdf; Joseph G. Kosciw et al., *The 2015 National School Climate Survey: The Experiences of Lesbian, Gay, Bisexual, Transgender, and Queer Youth in Our Nation's Schools* (New York: GLSEN, 2016); Joseph G. Kosciw et al., *The 2013 National School Climate Survey: The Experiences of Lesbian, Gay, Bisexual and Transgender Youth in our Nation's Schools* (New York: GLSEN, 2014); Joseph G. Kosciw et al., *The 2011 National School Climate Survey: The Experiences of Lesbian, Gay, Bisexual and Transgender Youth in our Nation's Schools* (New York: GLSEN, 2012); Jeffrey M. Poirier et al., *A Guide for Understanding, Supporting, and Affirming LGBTQI2-S Children, Youth, and Families* (Washington, DC: American Institutes for Research, 2014).

25. Susan F. Cole et al., *Creating and Advocating for Trauma-Sensitive Schools: Helping Traumatized Children*, vol. 2 (Boston: Massachusetts Advocates for Children, 2013), https://traumasensitiveschools.org/tlpi-publications/download-a-free-copy-of-a-guide-to-creating-trauma-sensitive-schools; Ray Wolpow et al., *The Heart of Learning and Teaching: Compassion, Resiliency, and Academic Success* (Olympia: Washington State Office of the Superintendent of Public Instruction [OSPI] Compassionate Schools, 2009); Kathleen Guarino et al., *Trauma-Informed Organizational Toolkit for Homeless Services* (Rockville, MD: Substance Abuse and Mental Health Services Administration, Center for Mental Health Services, Daniels Fund, National Child Traumatic Stress Network, and W.K. Kellogg Foundation, 2009), http://www.air.org/sites/default/files/downloads/report/Trauma-Informed_Organizational_Toolkit_0.pdf.

26. Emily Morgan et al., *The School Discipline Consensus Report: Strategies from the Field to Keep Students Engaged in School and Out of the Juvenile Justice System* (New York: Council of State Governments Justice Center, 2014); Pamela Fenning and Jennifer Rose, "Overrepresentation of African American Students in Exclusionary Discipline: The Role of School Policy," *Urban Education* 42, no. 6 (2007): 536–59.

27. Christopher Boccanfuso and Megan Kuhfeld, *Multiple Responses, Promising Results: Evidence-Based, Nonpunitive Alternatives to Zero Tolerance* (Washington, DC: Child Trends, 2011), http://www.childtrends.org/wp-content/uploads/2011/03/Child_Trends-2011_03_01_RB_AltToZeroTolerance.pdf.

28. Avi Astor et al., *Welcoming Practices: Creating Schools That Support Students and Families in Transition* (New York: Oxford University Press, 2017).

29. National Center on Safe Supportive Learning Environments, *Creating a Safe and Respectful Environment in Our Nation's Classrooms: Creating a Supportive Classroom Climate* (workshop materials) (Washington, DC: National Center on Safe Supportive Learning Environments, n.d.), https://safesupportivelearning.ed.gov/sites/default/files/sssta/20121108_20120928ClsrmMod2HandoutsFINAL1.pdf.

30. Jonathan Cohen, Richard Cardillo, and Terry Pickeral, "Creating a Climate of Respect," *Educational Leadership* 69, no. 1 (2011), http://www.ascd.org/publications/educational-leadership/sept11/vol69/num01/Creating-a-Climate-of-Respect.aspx.

31. Adrienne Rich, *Blood, Bread, and Poetry: Selected Prose, 1979–1985* (New York: Norton, 1994); Ralph Ellison, *The Invisible Man* (New York: Random House, 1952); Dorothy M. Steele and Becki Cohn-Vargas, *Identity Safe Classrooms: Places to Belong and Learn* (Thousand Oaks, CA: Corwin Press, 2013).

32. Randy Ross, "School Climate and Equity," in *School Climate Practices for Implementation and Sustainability*, ed. Teri Dary and Terry Pickeral (New York: National School Climate Center, 2013), 40.

33. Linda Dusenbury et al., *What Does Evidence-Based Instruction in Social and Emotional Learning Actually Look Like in Practice? A Brief on Findings from CASEL's Program Reviews* (Chicago: CASEL, 2015).

34. Cohen et al., "Creating a Climate of Respect."

35. David E. Kirkland, Adriana Villavicencio, and Edward A. Fergus, *How Can We Improve School Climate and Discipline Practices? Schools Can Do It, but Not Alone* (New York: NYU Steinhardt Education Solutions Initiative, 2016).

36. The Annie E. Casey Foundation, *Race for Results: Building a Path to Opportunity for All Children* (Baltimore: The Annie E. Casey Foundation, 2014); Christy M. Byrd and Tabbye Chavous, "Racial Identity, School Racial Climate, and School Intrinsic Motivation Among African American Youth: The Importance of Person-Context Congruence," *Journal of Research on Adolescence* 21, no. 4 (2011): 849–60; Heejung Chun and Ginger Dickson, "A Psychoecological Model of Academic Performance Among Hispanic Adolescents," *Journal of Youth and Adolescence* 40, no. 12 (2011): 1581–94; Kusum Singh, Mido Chang, and Sandra Dika, "Ethnicity, Self-Concept, and School Belonging: Effects on School Engagement," *Educational Research for Policy and Practice* 9, no. 3 (2010): 159–75.

37. Christina Spears Brown, *The Educational, Psychological and Social Impact of Discrimination on the Immigrant Child* (Washington, DC: Migration Policy Institute, 2015).

38. Carola Suárez-Orozco, Marcelo Suárez-Orozco, and Robert Teranishi, *Pathways to Opportunities: Promising Practices for Immigrant Children, Youth & Their Families* (Los Angeles: Institute for Immigration, Globalization, and Education, 2016), http://ige.gseis.ucla.edu/PromisingPracticesWhitePaper4.25.16/#h.dpd2lmb0kcrk.

39. Ibid.

40. Institute of Medicine, *The Health of Lesbian, Gay, Bisexual, and Transgender People: Building a Foundation for Better Understanding* (Washington, DC: The National Academies Press, 2011); Poirier et al., *A Guide for Understanding, Supporting, and Affirming LGBTQI2-S Children, Youth, and Families*.

41. Stephen T. Russell, "Supportive Social Services for LGBT Youth: Lessons from the Safe Schools Movement," *Prevention Research* 17, no. 4 (2010): 14–16.

42. Kosciw et al., *The 2013 National School Climate Survey*; Pat Griffin et al., "Describing Roles That Gay-Straight Alliances Play in Schools," *Journal of Gay & Lesbian*

*Issues in Education* 1, no. 3 (2004): 7–22; Sarah E. Holmes and Sean Cahill, "School Experiences of Gay, Lesbian, Bisexual, and Transgender Youth," in *Gay, Lesbian and Transgender Issues in Education: Programs, Policies, and Practices*, ed. James T. Sears (Binghamton, NY: Harrington Park Press, 2005), 64–76; Ian K. Macgillivray, *Gay-Straight Alliances: A Handbook for Students, Educators, and Parents* (Binghamton, NY: Haworth Press, 2007); Melinda S. Miceli, *Standing Out, Standing Together: The Social and Political Impact of Gay-Straight Alliances* (New York: Routledge, 2005); Jeffrey M. Poirier, "Fostering Safe, Welcoming, and Supportive Schools for LGBT Youth," in *Improving Emotional & Behavioral Outcomes for LGBT Youth: A Guide for Professionals*, ed. Sylvia K. Fisher, Jeffrey M. Poirier, and Gary M. Blau (Baltimore: Brookes Publishing, 2012); James T. Sears, ed., *Gay, Lesbian, and Transgender Issues in Education: Programs, Policies, and Practices* (Binghamton, NY: Harrington Park Press, 2005).

## CHAPTER 14

1. Kent McIntosh and Steve Goodman, *Integrated Multi-tiered Systems of Support: Blending RTI and PBIS* (New York: Guilford Press, 2016).
2. Ibid.
3. National Center on Response to Intervention, *Essential Components of RTI—A Closer Look at Response to Intervention* (Washington, DC: US Department of Education, Office of Special Education Programs, National Center on Response to Intervention, 2010), https://rti4success.org/sites/default/files/rtiessentialcomponents_042710 .pdf.
4. National Center on Response to Intervention, *RTI Implementer Series: Module 3: Multi-Level Prevention System* (Washington, DC: US Department of Education, Office of Special Education Programs, National Center on Response to Intervention, 2012), 6–8, https://rti4success.org/sites/default/files/ImplementerSeries_Multi LevelManual.pdf.
5. National Center on Response to Intervention, *Using Fidelity to Enhance Program Implementation Within an RTI Framework* (Washington, DC: US Department of Education, Office of Special Education Programs, National Center on Response to Intervention, 2012), 11, 14, https://rti4success.org/sites/default/files/Using%20 Fidelity%20to%20Enhance%20Program%20Implementation_PPTSlides.pdf.
6. National Center on Response to Intervention, *RTI Implementer Series: Module 1: Screening* (Washington, DC: US Department of Education, Office of Special Education Programs, National Center on Response to Intervention, 2012), https:// rti4success.org/sites/default/files/ImplementerSeries_ScreeningManual.pdf, 4; National Center on Response to Intervention, *RTI—Implementer Series: What Is Progress Monitoring?* (Washington, DC: US Department of Education, Office of Special Education Programs, National Center on Response to Intervention, 2012), 6, https://www.rti4success.org/video/implementer-series-what-progress-monitoring.
7. National Center on Response to Intervention, *Progress Monitoring*, 6.
8. National Center on Response to Intervention, *Using Fidelity* to Enhance Program Implementation Within an RTI Framework, 10.
9. National Center on Response to Intervention, *Essential Components of RTI*, 7; National Center on Response to Intervention, *RTI Implementer Series Module 2: Progress Monitoring* (Washington, DC: US Department of Education, Office of Special Edu-

cation Programs, National Center on Response to Intervention, 2012), 10, https://rti4success.org/sites/default/files/RTI%20PM%20Manual_web_w_handouts.pdf.

10. Beth Harry, Maya Kalyanpur, and Monimalika Day, *Building Cultural Reciprocity with Families: Case Studies in Special Education* (Baltimore: Paul H. Brookes, 1999).

11. Jennifer Pierce and Dia Jackson, *Ten Steps to Make RTI Work in Your Schools* (Washington, DC: American Institutes for Research, Education Policy Center, 2017), 8.

12. National Center on Response to Intervention, *Using Fidelity*, 14.

13. National Center on Response to Intervention, *RTI Fidelity of Implementation Rubric* (Washington, DC: US Department of Education, Office of Special Education Programs, National Center on Response to Intervention, 2014), https://rti4success.org/sites/default/files/RTI_Fidelity_Rubric.pdf; National Center on Response to Intervention, *District RTI Capacity and Implementation Rubric and Worksheet* (Washington, DC: US Department of Education, Office of Special Education Programs, National Center on Response to Intervention, 2012), https://rti4success.org/sites/default/files/NCRTI_District_Rubric%20and%20Worksheet_061112.pdf.

14. Pierce and Jackson, *Ten Steps*, 8.

15. See https://dpi.wi.gov/sites/default/files/imce/sped/pdf/falleader16/19-Connections%20Fact%20Sheet%202016.pdf.

CHAPTER 15

1. Allison B. Dymnicki, Kimberly T. Kendziora, and David M. Osher, "Adolescent Development for Students with Learning Disabilities and Behavioral Disorders: The Promise of Social Emotional Learning," in *Classroom Behavior, Contexts, and Interventions (Advances in Learning and Behavioral Disabilities, vol. 25)*, ed. Bryan G. Cook, Melody Tankersley, and Timothy J. Landrum (Bingley, UK: Emerald Group Publishing Limited, 2012), 131–66.

2. William M. Reynolds and Kevin I. Coats, "A Comparison of Cognitive-Behavioral Therapy and Relaxation Training for the Treatment of Depression in Adolescents," *Journal of Consulting and Clinical Psychology* 54, no. 5 (1986): 653; John E. Lochman et al., "Treatment and Generalization Effects of Cognitive-Behavioral and Goal-Setting Interventions with Aggressive Boys," *Journal of Consulting and Clinical Psychology* 52, no. 5 (1984): 915–16; Frank M. Gresham and Richard J. Nagle, "Social Skills Training with Children: Responsiveness to Modeling and Coaching as a Function of Peer Orientation," *Journal of Consulting and Clinical Psychology* 48, no. 6 (1980): 718–29; Matthew K. Burns and Kimberly A. Gibbons, *Implementing Response-to-Intervention in Elementary and Secondary Schools: Procedures to Assure Scientific-Based Practices*, 2nd ed. (New York: Routledge, 2013).

3. National Center on Response to Intervention (NCRTI), *RTI Implementer Series Module 3: Multi-Level Prevention System* (Washington, DC: US Department of Education, Office of Special Education Programs, National Center on Response to Intervention, 2012), http://www.rti4success.org/sites/default/files/ImplementerSeries_MultiLevel_Notes.pdf.

4. OSEP Technical Assistance Center on Positive Behavioral Interventions and Supports, "FAQs," https://www.pbis.org/family/faqs.

5. PMHP is a program that is effective at reducing internalizing problems and attention disorders and symptoms, as well as improving social competence; Emory L.

Cowen et al., *School-Based Prevention for Children at Risk: The Primary Mental Health Project* (Washington, DC: American Psychological Association, 1996).

6. Joseph R. Jenkins, Roxanne F. Hudson, and Evelyn S. Johnson, "Screening for At-Risk Readers in a Response to Intervention Framework," *School Psychology Review* 36, no. 4 (2007): 582; Charles Hughes and Douglas D. Dexter, "Universal Screening Within a Response-to-Intervention Model," RTI Action Network, http://www.rtinetwork.org/learn/research/universal-screening-within-a-rti-model.

7. Centers for Disease Control and Prevention, *Web-Based Injury Statistics Query and Reporting System (WISQARS)* (Atlanta: Centers for Disease Control and Prevention, 2015), http://www.cdc.gov/injury/wisqars/index.html; Ruth Perou et al., "Mental Health Surveillance Among Children—United States, 2005–2011," *Morbidity and Mortality Weekly Report* 62, no. 2 (2013): 1–35, http://www.cdc.gov/mmwr/preview/mmwrhtml/su6202a1.htm?s_cid=su6202a1_w; US Department of Education, National Center for Education Statistics, *Digest of Education Statistics, 2015* (NCES 2016-014) (Washington, DC: National Center for Education Statistics, 2016).

8. Arthur J. Reynolds, Judy A. Temple, and Suh-Ruu Ou, "School-Based Early Intervention and Child Well-Being in the Chicago Longitudinal Study," *Child Welfare* 82, no. 5 (2003): 633–56; Kimberly T. Kendziora, "Early Intervention for Emotional and Behavioral Disorders," in *Handbook of Research in Behavior Disorders,* ed. Robert B. Rutherford, Mary Magee Quinn, and Sarup R. Mathur (New York: Guilford, 2004), 327–51.

9. Joseph R. Jenkins, "Candidate Measures for Screening At-Risk Students" (paper presented at the National Research Center on Learning Disabilities Responsiveness-to-Intervention symposium, Kansas City, Missouri, December 2003).

10. Todd A. Glover and Craig A. Albers, "Considerations for Evaluating Universal Screening Assessments," *Journal of School Psychology* 45, no. 2 (2007): 117–35.

11. Jenkins, Hudson, and Johnson, "Screening for At-Risk Readers."

12. "Screening Tools Chart," Center on Response to Intervention, American Institutes for Research, https://rti4success.org/resources/tools-charts/screening-tools-chart.

13. Donald L. Compton et al., "Selecting At-Risk First-Grade Readers for Early Intervention: Eliminating False Positives and Exploring the Promise of a Two-Stage Gated Screening Process," *Journal of Educational Psychology* 102, no. 2 (2010): 327–40.

14. Jay Gottlieb, "Attitudes Toward Retarded Children: Effects of Labeling and Behavioral Aggressiveness," *Journal of Educational Psychology* 67, no. 4 (1975): 581–5.

15. Samuel Messick, "Validity," in *Educational Measurement*, 3rd ed., ed. Robert L. Linn (New York: Macmillan, 1989), 13–103.

16. Scott P. Ardoin et al., "Application of a Three-Tiered Response to Intervention Model for Instructional Planning, Decision Making, and the Identification of Children in Need of Services," *Journal of Psychoeducational Assessment* 23, no. 4 (2005): 362–80.

17. Rob H. Horner, Caryn Blitz, and Scott W. Ross, "The Importance of Contextual Fit When Implementing Evidence-Based Interventions" (ASPE issue brief, Office of the Assistant Secretary for Planning and Evaluation, Office of Human Services Policy) (Washington, DC: US Department of Health and Human Services, 2014).

18. George Sugai, *School-Wide Positive Behavior Support: Getting Started Workbook* (Washington, DC: OSEP Center on Positive Behavioral Interventions and Supports,

2008), https://www.pbis.org/common/cms/files/pbisresources/0408gsgetting startedCO_CompatibilityMode.pdf.

19. "Planning Standards-Aligned Instruction Within a Multi-Tiered System of Supports," National Center on Intensive Intervention, http://www.intensiveintervention.org/sites/default/files/BasicFactsExample_508.pdf.

20. "Implementation Oversight for Evidence Based Programs," PEW Charitable Trusts, http://www.pewtrusts.org/en/research-and-analysis/issue-briefs/2016/05/implementation-oversight-for-evidence-based-programs; Roger Przybylski, *Implementing Evidence-Based Practices* (Washington, DC: Justice Research and Statistics Association (JRSA), Bureau of Justice Assistance, US Department of Justice (BJA), and National Criminal Justice Association (NCJA), 2014), http://www.jrsa.org/projects/ebp_briefing_paper2.pdf.

21. Edward S. Shapiro, "Tiered Instruction and Intervention in a Response-to-Intervention Model," RTI Action Network, http://www.rtinetwork.org/essential/tieredinstruction/tiered-instruction-and-intervention-rti-model.

22. NCRTI, *RTI Implementer Series Module 3*.

23. Kenneth A. Dodge, Thomas J. Dishion, and Jennifer E. Lansford, eds., *Deviant Peer Influences in Programs for Youth: Problems and Solutions* (New York: Guilford Press, 2007).

24. "Implementer Series: What Is Progress Monitoring?" (video), National Center on Response to Intervention, http://www.rti4success.org/video/implementer-series-what-progress-monitoring.

25. "I've Been Collecting Progress Monitoring Data, When Do I Know It's Time to Make an Intervention Change?" Center on Response to Intervention, http://www.rti4success.org/video/i%E2%80%99ve-been-collecting-progress-monitoring-data-when-do-i-know-it%E2%80%99s-time-make-intervention.

26. National Center on Response to Intervention, *Brief #3: Common Progress Monitoring Graph Omissions: Making Instructional Decisions* (Washington, DC: US Department of Education, Office of Special Education Programs, National Center on Response to Intervention, 2013), https://rti4success.org/sites/default/files/RTI%20Progress MonitoringBrief3-Making%20Instructional%20Decisions.pdf.

27. "Progress Monitoring Tools Chart," National Center on Response to Intervention, http://www.rti4success.org/resource/progress-monitoring-tools-chart.

28. NCRTI, *RTI Implementer Series Module 3*.

29. Ibid.

30. Mark D. Weist et al., "Challenges to Collaboration in School Mental Health and Strategies for Overcoming Them," *Journal of School Health* 82, no. 2 (2012): 97–105.

31. Kristin Anderson Moore and Carol Emig, *Integrated Student Supports: A Summary of the Evidence Base for Policymakers* (Bethesda, MD: Child Trends, 2014), http://www.childtrends.org/wp-content/uploads/2014/02/2014-05ISSWhitePaper1.pdf.

32. Ibid.

CHAPTER 16

1. Stephanie Al Otaiba and Douglas Fuchs, "Who Are the Young Children for Whom Best Practices in Reading Are Ineffective? An Experimental and Longitudinal Study," *Journal of Learning Disabilities* 39, no. 5 (2006): 414–31; Karen Bierman, "Evaluation of the First 3 Years of the Fast Track Prevention Trail with

Children At High Risk for Adolescent Conduct Problems," *Journal of Abnormal Child Psychology* 30, no. 1 (2002): 19–35; Kristen L. McMaster et al., "Responding to Nonresponders: An Experimental Field Trial of Identification and Intervention Methods," *Exceptional Children* 71, no. 4 (2005): 445–63; Jeanne Wanzek and Sharon Vaughn, "Students Demonstrating Persistent Low Response to Reading Intervention: Three Case Studies," *Learning Disabilities Research & Practice* 24, no. 3 (2009): 151–63.

2. Thomas J. Dishion and Kenneth A. Dodge, "Peer Contagion in Interventions for Children and Adolescents: Moving Towards an Understanding of the Ecology and Dynamics of Change," *Journal of Abnormal Child Psychology* 33, no. 3 (2005): 395–400; Thomas J. Dishion and Jessica M. Tipsord, "Peer Contagion in Child and Adolescent Social and Emotional Development," *Annual Review of Psychology* 62 (2011): 189–214.

3. Eric J. Bruns et al., "Adherence to Wraparound Principles and Association with Outcomes," *Journal of Child and Family Studies* 14, no. 4 (2005): 521–34; Jesse C. Suter and Eric J. Bruns, "Effectiveness of the Wraparound Process for Children with Emotional and Behavioral Disorders: A Meta-analysis," *Clinical Child and Family Psychology Review* 12, no. 4 (2009): 336–51; Bruce J. Kamradt, "The 25 Kid Project: How Milwaukee Utilized a Pilot Project to Achieve Buy-in Among Stakeholders in Changing the System of Care for Children With Severe Emotional Problems" (paper presented to the Washington Business Group on Health, October 1996).

4. Kimberly T. Kendziora et al., *Wraparound: Stories from the Field* (Washington, DC: Center for Effective Collaboration and Practice, American Institutes for Research, 2001).

5. L. Berry Kuchle et al., "The Next Big Idea: A Framework for Integrated Academic and Behavioral Intensive Intervention," *Learning Disabilities Research & Practice* 30, no. 4 (2015): 150–8.

6. Susan Barrett, Lucille Eber, and Mark Weist, eds., *Advancing Education Effectiveness: Interconnecting School Mental Health and School-Wide Positive Behavior Support* (Eugene, OR, and Baltimore, MD: Office of Special Education Programs Center on Positive Behavioral Interventions and Supports and the University of Maryland Center for School Mental Health, 2012), http://www.pbis.org/common/cms/files/Current%20Topics/Final-Monograph.pdf.

7. Ibid.

8. Krista Kustash and Al Duchnowski, "Understanding the Complexity of the Children and Families We Serve," in Barrett, Eber, and Weist, *Advancing Education Effectiveness*, 113–22.

9. Trina W. Osher, David Osher, and Gary Blau, *Shifting Gears to Family-Driven Care: Ambassadors Tool Kit* (Rockville, MD: Federation of Families for Children's Mental Health, 2006).

10. Mark Sander et al., "The District/Community Role in Advancing the Interconnected Systems Framework," in Barrett et al., *Advancing Education Effectiveness*, 73–82.

11. Ibid.

12. David Osher, "Creating Comprehensive and Collaborative Systems," *Journal of Child and Family Studies* 11, no. 1 (2002): 91–9; Trina W. Osher and David M. Osher,

"The Paradigm Shift to True Collaboration with Families," *Journal of Child and Family Studies* 11, no. 1 (2002): 47–60; Beth A. Stroul, Gary M. Blau, and Robert M. Friedman, *Updating the System of Care Concept and Philosophy* (Washington, DC: Georgetown University Center for Child and Human Development, National Technical Assistance Center for Children's Mental Health, 2010); Beth A. Stroul, Gary M. Blau, and Diane L. Sondheimer, "Systems of Care: A Strategy to Transform Children's Mental Health Care," in *The System of Care Handbook: Transforming Mental Health Services for Children, Youth, and Families,* ed. Beth A. Stroul and Gary M. Blau (Baltimore: Paul H. Brookes Publishing, 2008), 3–23.

13. Bazelon Center for Mental Health Law, *Way to Go: School Success for Children with Mental Health Care Needs* (Washington, DC: Bazelon Center for Mental Health Law, 2006).

14. Lucille Eber, Kelly Hyde, and Jesse C. Suter, "Integrating Wraparound into a School-Wide System of Positive Behavioral Supports," *Journal of Child and Family Studies* 20, no. 6 (2011): 782–90.

## CHAPTER 17

1. "What Is SEL?" Collaborative for Academic, Social, and Emotional Learning (CASEL), http://www.casel.org/what-is-sel/.

2. Ibid.

3. Mark Greenberg et al., "Enhancing School-Based Prevention and Youth Development Through Coordinated Social, Emotional, and Academic Learning," *American Psychologist* 58, no. 6–7 (2003): 466.

4. Niloofar Bavarian et al., "Using Social-Emotional and Character Development to Improve Academic Outcomes: A Matched-Pair, Cluster-Randomized Controlled Trial in Low-Income, Urban Schools," *Journal of School Health* 83, no. 11 (2013): 771–9; Stephanie M. Jones, Joshua L. Brown, and J. Lawrence Aber, "Two-Year Impacts of a Universal School-Based Social-Emotional and Literacy Intervention: An Experiment in Translational Developmental Research," *Child Development* 82, no. 2 (2011): 533–54; Sara Rimm-Kaufman et al., "Efficacy of the Responsive Classroom Approach: Results From a 3-Year, Longitudinal Randomized Controlled Trial," *American Educational Research Journal* 51, no. 3 (2014): 567–603; David Schonfeld et al., "Cluster-Randomized Trial Demonstrating Impact on Academic Achievement of Elementary Social-Emotional Learning," *School Psychology Quarterly* 30, no. 3 (2015): 406.

5. David J. Hawkins et al., "Effects of Social Development Intervention in Childhood 15 Years Later," *Archives of Pediatrics & Adolescent Medicine* 162, no. 12 (2008): 1133–41.

6. Richard F. Catalano et al., "Positive Youth Development in the United States: Research Findings on Evaluations of Positive Youth Development Programs," *Prevention & Treatment* 5, no. 1 (2002): 15a.

7. Robert W. Roeser et al., "Mindfulness Training and Reductions in Teacher Stress and Burnout: Results From Two Randomized, Waitlist-Control Field Trials," *Journal of Educational Psychology* 105, no. 3 (2013): 787; Patricia A. Jennings and Mark T. Greenberg, "The Prosocial Classroom: Teacher Social and Emotional Competence in Relation to Student and Classroom Outcomes," *Review of Educational Research* 79,

no. 1 (2009): 491–525; David Osher et al., "Building School and Teacher Capacity to Eliminate the School-to-Prison Pipeline," *Teacher Education and Special Education* 35, no. 4 (2012): 284–95.

8. Roeser et al., "Mindfulness Training," 787; Rebecca D. Taylor et al., "Promoting Positive Youth Development Through School-Based Social and Emotional Learning Interventions: A Meta-Analysis of Follow-Up Effects," *Child Development* 88, no. 4 (2017): 1156–71.

9. Martha B. Zaslow et al., "Federal Policy Initiatives and Children's SEL," in *Handbook of Social and Emotional Learning: Research and Practice*, ed. Joseph A. Durlak et al. (New York: Guilford, 2015), 549–65; Linda Dusenbury et al., "The Case for Preschool Through High School State Learning Standards for SEL," in Durlak et al., *Handbook of Social and Emotional Learning*, 532–47.

10. David Osher et al., "Advancing the Science and Practice of Social and Emotional Learning: Looking Back and Moving Forward," *Review of Research in Education* 40, no. 1 (2016): 644–81.

11. Theresa C. Lewallen et al., "The Whole School, Whole Community, Whole Child Model: A New Approach for Improving Educational Attainment and Healthy Development for Students," *Journal of School Health* 85, no. 11 (2015): 729–39.

12. Joseph Durlak et al., "The Impact of Enhancing Students' Social and Emotional Learning: A Meta-Analysis of School-Based Universal Interventions," *Child Development* 82, no. 1 (2011): 405–32; Joseph A. Durlak, Roger P. Weissberg, and Molly Pachan, "A Meta-Analysis of After-School Programs That Seek to Promote Personal and Social Skills in Children and Adolescents," *American Journal of Community Psychology* 45, no. 3–4 (2010): 294–309.

13. Jane Fortson et al., *Impact and Implementation Findings from an Experimental Evaluation of Playworks: Effects on School Climate, Academic Learning, Student Social Skills and Behavior* (Princeton, NJ: Mathematica Policy Research and Stanford, CA: John W. Gardner Center for Youth and Their Communities, Stanford University, 2013).

14. Dale Blyth, Brandi Olson, and Kate Walker, "Intentional Practices to Support Social & Emotional Learning" (Youth Development issue brief, University of Minnesota Extension, February 2015): 247–61, https://conservancy.umn.edu/bitstream/handle/11299/195178/issue-brief-intentional-practices-to-support-sel.pdf.

15. Eva Oberle et al., "Establishing Systemic Social and Emotional Learning Approaches in Schools: A Framework for Schoolwide Implementation," *Cambridge Journal of Education* 46, no. 3 (2016): 277–97.

16. Edward L. Deci and Richard M. Ryan, "The General Causality Orientations Scale: Self-Determination in Personality," *Journal of Research in Personality* 19, no. 2 (1985): 109–34.

17. Blyth et al., *Intentional Practices*, 247–61.

18. Collaborative for Academic, Social, and Emotional Learning (CASEL), *The 2013 Guide* (Chicago: CASEL, 2013); CASEL, *The 2015 CASEL Guide: Effective Social and Emotional Learning Programs—Middle and High School Edition* (Chicago: CASEL, 2015).

19. Daniel J. Flannery et al., "Initial Behavior Outcomes for the Peacebuilders Universal School-Based Violence Prevention Program," *Developmental Psychology* 39, no. 2 (2003): 292; Stephanie M. Jones and Suzanne M. Bouffard, "Social and Emotional Learning in Schools: From Programs to Strategies," *Sharing Child and Youth Development Knowledge* 26, no. 4 (2012), https://www.srcd.org/sites

/default/files/documents/spr_264_final_2.pdf; Joshua L. Brown et al., "The Resolving Conflict Creatively Program: A School-Based Social and Emotional Learning Program," in *Building Academic Success on Social and Emotional Learning: What Does the Research Say?*, ed. Joseph E. Zins et al. (New York: Teachers College Press, 2004): 151–69.

20. Rimm-Kaufman et al., "Efficacy of the Responsive Classroom Approach," 567–603.

21. Marc A. Brackett and Susan E. Rivers, "Transforming Students' Lives with Social and Emotional Learning," in *International Handbook of Emotions in Education*, ed. Patricia A. Alexander, Reinhard Pekrun, and Lisa Linnenbrink-Garcia (Abingdon, UK: Routledge, Routledge Handbooks Online, 2014); Greenberg et al., "Enhancing School-Based Prevention," 466.

22. Brackett and Rivers, "Transforming Students' Lives."

23. Rob Jagers, Brittney Williams, and David Osher, "Family Matters: Exploring the Role of Family Socialization and Parenting Practices in Promoting the Social and Emotional Learning of Children and Youth," in *Keeping Students Safe and Helping Them Thrive: A Collaborative Handbook on School Safety, Mental Health, and Wellness,* ed. David Osher et al. (Santa Barbara, CA: Praeger/ABC-CLIO, forthcoming).

24. Durlak et al., "The Impact of Enhancing Students' Social and Emotional Learning," 405–32.

25. CASEL, *The 2013 Guide*.

26. John Bridgeland, Mary Bruce, and Arya Hariharan, *The Missing Piece: A National Teacher Survey on How Social and Emotional Learning Can Empower Children and Transform Schools: A Report for CASEL* (Washington, DC: Civic Enterprises, 2013).

27. Nikki Pearce Dawes and Reed Larson, "How Youth Get Engaged: Grounded-Theory Research on Motivational Development in Organized Youth Programs," *Developmental Psychology* 47, no. 1 (2011): 259.

28. Kate Walker, Brandi Olson, and Margo Herman, *Social and Emotional Learning in Practice: A Toolkit of Practical Strategies and Resources* (St. Paul: University of Minnesota Extension, 2017), https://conservancy.umn.edu/bitstream/handle/11299/195764/sel-toolkit.pdf.

29. Kimberly Kendziora and Nick Yoder, *When Districts Support and Integrate Social and Emotional Learning (SEL): Findings from an Ongoing Evaluation of Districtwide Implementation of SEL* (Washington, DC: American Institutes for Research, Education Policy Center, 2016), https://www.collaborativeclassroom.org/wp-content/uploads/nodefiles/node-when-districts-support-and-integrate-sel-october-2016.pdf.

30. Elizabeth Hagen, "Resources for Measuring Social and Emotional Learning" (St. Paul: University of Minnesota Extension, 2014), https://conservancy.umn.edu/bitstream/handle/11299/195179/issue-brief-measurement-resource.pdf.

31. Joseph A. Durlak and Emily P. DuPre, "Implementation Matters: A Review of Research on the Influence of Implementation on Program Outcomes and the Factors Affecting Implementation," *American Journal of Community Psychology* 41, no. 3–4 (2008): 327–50.

CHAPTER 18

1. Raj Chetty, John N. Friedman, and Jonah E. Rockoff, "Measuring the Impacts of Teachers II: Teacher Value-Added and Student Outcomes in Adulthood," *American*

*Economic Review* 104, no. 9 (2014): 2633–79; Steven G. Rivkin, Eric A. Hanushek, and John F. Kain, "Teachers, Schools, and Academic Achievement," *Econometrica* 73, no. 2 (2005): 417–58; Jonah E. Rockoff, "The Impact of Individual Teachers on Students' Achievement: Evidence from Panel Data," *American Economic Review* 94, no. 2 (2004): 247–52.

2. Barbara Nye, Spyros Konstantopoulos, and Larry V. Hedges, "How Large Are Teacher Effects?" *Educational Evaluation and Policy Analysis* 26, no. 3 (2004): 237–57; National Association of Secondary School Principals and National Association of Elementary School Principals, *Leadership Matters: What the Research Says About the Importance of Principal Leadership* (Reston, VA, and Alexandria, VA: National Association of Secondary School Principals and National Association of Elementary School Principals, 2013), http://www.naesp.org/sites/default/files/Leadership Matters.pdf; Joseph A. Durlak et al. "The Impact of Enhancing Students' Social and Emotional Learning: A Meta-Analysis of School-Based Universal Interventions," *Child Development* 82, no. 1 (2011): 405–32; Pamela Cantor et al., "Malleability, Plasticity, and Individuality: How Children Learn and Develop in Context," *Applied Developmental Science* (2018), forthcoming, doi:10.1080/10888691.2017.13 98649; David Osher et al., "Drivers of Human Development: How Relationships and Context Shape Learning and Development," *Applied Developmental Science* (2018), forthcoming, doi:10.1080/10888691.2017.1398650.

3. Stephanie M. Jones and Suzanne M. Bouffard, "Social and Emotional Learning in Schools: From Programs to Strategies," *Sharing Child and Youth Development Knowledge* 26, no. 4 (2012): 3–22, http://www.ncflb.com/wp-content/uploads/2013/02 /Social-and-Emotional-Learning-in-Schools-From-Programs-to-Strategies.pdf.

4. Leib Sutcher, Linda Darling-Hammond, and Desiree Carver-Thomas, *A Coming Crisis in Teaching? Teacher Supply, Demand, and Shortages in the U.S.* (Palo Alto, CA: Learning Policy Institute, 2016), https://learningpolicyinstitute.org/sites/default /files/product-files/A_Coming_Crisis_in_Teaching_REPORT.pdf.

5. National Governors Association Center for Best Practices & Council of Chief State School Officers, *Common Core State Standards for Mathematics* (Washington, DC: National Governors Association Center for Best Practices & Council of Chief State School Officers, Student Achievement Partners, Common Core: ELA/Literacy, 2010), http://www.achievethecore.org/ela-literacy-common-core/shifts-practice/; Stephanie M. Jones and Jennifer Kahn, *The Evidence Base for How We Learn: Supporting Students' Social, Emotional, and Academic Development* (Washington, DC: Aspen Institute, National Commission on Social, Emotional, and Academic Development), https://assets.aspeninstitute.org/content/uploads/2018/03/FINAL_CDS -Evidence-Base.pdf.

6. K. Brooke Stafford-Brizard, *Building Blocks for Learning: A Framework for Comprehensive Student Development* (New York: Turnaround for Children, 2016), http://www .turnaroundusa.org/wp-content/uploads/2016/03/Turnaround-for-Children -Building-Blocks-for-Learningx-2.pdf.

7. John Bridgeland, Mary Bruce, and Arya Hariharan, *The Missing Piece: A National Teacher Survey on How Social and Emotional Learning Can Empower Children and Transform Schools* (Chicago: Collaborative on Social Emotional Learning, 2013), https:// casel.org/wp-content/uploads/2016/01/the-missing-piece.pdf.

8. Hillary Johnson and Ross Wiener, *This Time, with Feeling: Integrating Social and Emotional Development and College- and Career-Readiness Standards* (Washington, DC: The Aspen Institute, 2017), https://www.aspeninstitute.org/publications/this-time -with-feeling/.

9. David Osher and Juliette Berg, *School Climate and Social and Emotional Learning: The Integration of Two Approaches* (State College, PA: Edna Bennett Pierce Prevention Research Center, Pennsylvania State University, 2017), https://www.air.org/resource /school-climate-and-social-and-emotional-learning-integration-two-approaches; Nicholas Yoder, *Teaching the Whole Child: Instructional Practices That Support Social-Emotional Learning in Three Teacher Evaluation Frameworks* (Washington DC: Center on Great Teachers and Leaders, 2014), https://gtlcenter.org/sites/default/files /TeachingtheWholeChild.pdf.

10. Sheldon Berman with Sydney Chaffee and Julia Sarmiento, *The Practice Base for How We Learn: Supporting Students' Social, Emotional, and Academic Development* (Washington, DC: Aspen Institute, National Commission on Social, Emotional, and Academic Development), https://assets.aspeninstitute.org/content/uploads /2018/03/CDE-Practice-Base_FINAL.pdf.

11. Yoder, *Teaching the Whole Child.*

12. Joshua Brown et al., "Improving Classroom Quality: Teacher Influences and Experimental Impacts of the 4Rs Program," *Journal of Educational Psychology* 102, no. 1 (2010): 153–67; Elisabeth Davis et al., "Conditions for Learning and Academic Performance," *Keeping Students Safe and Helping Them Thrive: A Collaborative Handbook on School Safety, Mental Health, and Wellness,* ed. David Osher et al. (Santa Barbara, CA: Praeger/ABC-CLIO); Joseph E. Zins and Maurice J. Elias, "Social and Emotional Learning," in *Children's Needs III: Development Prevention and Intervention,* ed. George G. Bear and Kathleen M. Minke (Bethesda, MD: National Association of School Psychologists, 2006), 1–14.

13. Mark T. Greenberg, Joshua L. Brown, and Rachel M. Abenavoli, *Teacher Stress and Health: Effects on Teachers, Students, and Schools* (University Park: Edna Bennett Pierce Prevention Research Center, Pennsylvania State University, 2016), http://www.rwjf .org/en/library/research/2016/07/teacher-stress-and-health.html.

14. Patricia A. Jennings and Mark T. Greenberg, "The Prosocial Classroom: Teacher Social and Emotional Competence in Relation to Student and Classroom Outcomes," *Review of Educational Research* 79, no. 1 (2009): 491–525, doi:10.3102 /0034654308325693.

15. Greenberg et al., *Teacher Stress and Health;* Yoder, *Teaching the Whole Child.*

16. Yoder, *Teaching the Whole Child.*

17. Cantor et al., "Malleability, Plasticity, and Individuality."

18. National School Climate Center, *The School Climate Challenge: Narrowing the Gap Between School Climate Research and School Climate Policy, Practice Guidelines and Teacher Education Policy* (New York: National School Climate Center, 2007), https://www .schoolclimate.org/themes/schoolclimate/assets/pdf/policy/school-climate -challenge-web.pdf, 4.

19. Anne Podolsky et al., *Solving the Teacher Shortage: How to Attract and Retain Excellent Educators* (Palo Alto, CA: Learning Policy Institute, 2016), https://learningpolicy institute.org/sites/default/files/product-files/Solving_Teacher_Shortage_Attract

_Retain _Educators_REPORT.pdf; Jenny Demonte, Lynn Holdheide, and Paul Sindelar, *State Policy and Practice Portrait: Teacher Shortages: Meeting Demand Without Sacrificing Quality Preparation and Support* (Gainesville: University of Florida, CEE-DAR Center, 2016), http://ceedar.education.ufl.edu/wp-content/uploads/2016/10 /Teacher-Shortages-Policy-and-Practice-Portrait.pdf.

20. Matthew A. Kraft and John P. Papay, "Can Professional Environments in Schools Promote Teacher Development? Explaining Heterogeneity in Returns to Teaching Experience," *Educational Evaluation and Policy Analysis* 36, no. 4 (2014).

21. "ED School Climate Surveys," National Center on Safe Supportive Learning Environments, https://safesupportivelearning.ed.gov/edscls.

22. Osher et al., "Drivers of Human Development."

23. "State of America's Schools," Gallup, http://www.gallup.com/services/178709 /state-america-schools-report.aspx.

24. Dana Markow, Lara Macia, and Helen Lee, *The MetLife Survey of the American Teacher: Challenges for School Leadership* (New York: Metropolitan Life Insurance Company, 2013), https://www.metlife.com/content/dam/microsites/about /corporate-profile/MetLife-Teacher-Survey-2012.pdf.

25. Terry Salinger and David Osher, *Teacher Social Emotional Competency* (unpublished research memorandum) (Washington, DC: American Institutes for Research, 2012).

26. Leigh McLean and Carol McDonald Connor, "Depressive Symptoms in Third-Grade Teachers: Relations to Classroom Quality and Student Achievement," *Child Development* 86, no. 3 (2015), 945–54; Wendy L. G. Hoglund, Kirsten E. Klingle, and Naheed E. Hosan, "Classroom Risks and Resources: Teacher Burnout, Classroom Quality and Children's Adjustment in High Needs Elementary Schools," *Journal of School Psychology* 53, no. 5 (2015), 337–57; Anthony Bryk and Barbara Schneider, *Trust in Schools: A Core Resource for Improvement* (New York: Russell Sage Foundation, 2002).

27. Greenberg et al., *Teacher Stress and Health*.

28. Laura Goe, Lynn Holdheide, and Tricia Miller, *A Practical Guide to Designing Comprehensive Teacher Evaluations. A Tool to Assist in the Development of Teacher Evaluation Systems* (Washington, DC: Center on Great Teachers and Leaders, 2011), http://www.gtlcenter.org/sites/default/files/docs/practicalGuideEvalSystems.pdf; Lynn Holdheide, "Same Debate, New Opportunity: Designing Teacher Evaluation Systems That Promote and Support Educators in Practices That Support ALL Students' Learning," *Journal of Special Education Leadership: Special Issue on Special Education Teacher Evaluation in Practice: Voices from the Field* 28, no. 2 (2015): 74–81.

29. Laura Goe, Courtney Bell, and Olivia Little, *Approaches to Evaluating Teacher Effectiveness: A Research Synthesis* (Washington, DC: National Comprehensive Center for Teacher Quality, 2008), 8, http://www.gtlcenter.org/sites/default/files/docs /EvaluatingTeachEffectiveness.pdf.

30. Deborah Loewenberg Ball and Francesca M. Forzani, "What Makes Education Research 'Educational'?" *Educational Researcher* 36, no. 9 (2007): 529–40, doi:10.3102/0013189X07312896; Robert C. Pianta and Bridget K. Hamre, "Measurement and Improvement of Teacher-Child Interactions: Implications for Policy and Accountability Frameworks of Standardized Observation," in *Handbook of Education Policy Research*, ed. Gary Sykes, Barbara Schneider, and David N. Plank (New York: Routledge, 2009), 652–60.

31. Thomas J. Kane and Douglas O. Steiger, *Gathering Feedback for Teaching: Combining High-Quality Observations with Student Surveys and Achievement Gains* (Seattle: Bill & Melinda Gates Foundation, 2012), http://files.eric.ed.gov/fulltext/ED540960.pdf.

32. Goe et al., *Approaches to Evaluating Teacher Effectiveness*; Thomas L. Good, Caroline R. Wiley, and Ida Rose Florez, "Effective Teaching: An Emerging Synthesis," in *International Handbook of Research on Teachers and Teaching, Book 21*, ed. Lawrence J. Saha and A. Gary Dworkin (2009), 803–16.

33. Holdheide, "Same Debate," 74–81.

34. Tish Jennings, Angela Minnici, and Nick Yoder, "Creating the Working Conditions to Enhance Teacher Social and Emotional Well-Being," in *Keeping Students Safe and Helping Them Thrive: A Collaborative Handbook for Education, Mental Health, Child Welfare, Safety, and Justice Professionals, Families, and Communities*, ed. David Osher et al. (Santa Barbara, CA: Praeger/ABC-CLIO, forthcoming).

35. David Strahan, "Promoting a Collaborative Professional Culture in Three Elementary Schools That Have Beaten the Odds," *Elementary School Journal* 104, no. 2 (2003): 127–46, http://www.journals.uchicago.edu/doi/abs/10.1086/499746; Susan M. Kardos, "The Importance of Professional Culture in New Teachers' Job Satisfaction" (paper presented at American Education Research Association, Montreal, Canada, 2005), 6, https://projectngt.gse.harvard.edu/files/gse-projectngt/files/kardos_rev_4_webversion.pdf.

36. David Osher et al., *Addressing the Root Causes of Disparities in School Discipline: An Educator's Action Planning Guide* (Washington, DC: National Center on Safe Supportive Learning Environments, 2015), https://safesupportivelearning.ed.gov/sites/default/files/15-1547%20NCSSLE%20Root%20Causes%20Guide%20FINAL02%20mb.pdf; Thomas Rudd, *Racial Disproportionality in School Discipline: Implicit Bias Is Heavily Implicated* (Columbus: The Ohio State University, Kirwan Institute for the Study of Race and Ethnicity, 2014), http://kirwaninstitute.osu.edu/wp-content/uploads/2014/02/racial-disproportionality-schools-02.pdf.

## CHAPTER 19

1. Julie E. Learned, "'Feeling Like I'm Slow Because I'm in This Class': Secondary School Contexts and the Identification and Construction of Struggling Readers," *Reading Research Quarterly* 51, no. 4 (2016): 367–71; Julie E. Learned, "Becoming 'Eligible to Matter': How Teachers' Interpretations of Struggling Readers' Stress Can Disrupt Deficit Positioning," *Journal of Adolescent and Adult Literacy* 59, no. 6 (2016): 665–74; Julie E. Learned, "'The Behavior Kids': Examining the Conflation of Youth Reading Difficulty and Behavior Problem Positioning Among School Institutional Contexts," *American Educational Research Journal* 53, no. 5 (2016): 1271–1309.

2. Danielle S. McNamara, Matthew E. Jacovina, and Laura K. Allen, "Higher Order Thinking in Comprehension," in *Handbook of Individual Differences in Reading: Reader, Text, and Context*, ed. Peter Afflerbach (New York: Routledge, 2016), 164–77.

3. Urie Bronfenbrenner and Pamela A. Morris, "The Ecology of Developmental Processes," in *Handbook of Child Psychology, Volume 1: Theoretical Models of Human Development*, ed. Richard M. Lerner (New York: Wiley, 1998), 993–1028.

4. Megan Gunnar and Ronald Barr, "Stress, Early Brain Development, and Behavior," *Infants & Young Children* 11, no. 1 (1998), 1–14, doi:10.1097/00001163

-199807000-00004; David Benton and Pearl Y. Parker, "Breakfast, Blood Glucose, and Cognition," *American Journal of Clinical Nutrition* 67, no. 4 (1998): 772S–8S.

5. Dorothy M. Steele and Becki Cohn-Vargas, *Identity Safe Classrooms: Places to Belong and Learn* (Thousand Oaks, CA: Corwin Press, 2013), 10.

6. Ibid.

7. Ibid., 93.

8. Ibid.

9. Gordon Wells, *The Meaning Makers: Children Learning Language and Using Language to Learn* (Portsmouth, NH: Heinemann, 1985).

10. Catherine E. Snow, Peg Griffin, and M. Susan Burns, *Knowledge to Support the Teaching of Reading: Preparing Teachers for a Changing World* (New York: John Wiley, 2005).

11. Timothy Shanahan, *The National Reading Panel Report: Practical Advice for Teachers* (Naperville, IL: Learning Point Associates, 2005).

12. Steele and Cohn-Vargas, *Identity Safe Classrooms*, 104–109.

13. Pedro Noguera, Linda Darling-Hammond, and Diane Friedlaender, "Equal Opportunity for Deeper Learning," in *Rethinking Readiness: Deeper Learning for College, Work, and Life*, ed. Rafael Heller, Rebecca E. Wolfe, and Adria Steinberg (Cambridge, MA: Harvard Education Press, 2017).

14. Steele and Cohn-Vargas, *Identity Safe Classrooms*, 106.

15. Lisa S. Blackwell, Kali H. Trzesniewski, and Carol S. Dweck, "Implicit Theories of Intelligence Predict Achievement Across an Adolescent Transition: A Longitudinal Study and an Intervention," *Child Development* 78, no. 1 (2007): 246–63, doi:10.1111/j.1467-8624.2007.00995.x; Jeni L. Burnette et al., "Mind-Sets Matter: A Meta-Analytic Review of Implicit Theories and Self-Regulation," *Psychological Bulletin*, 139, no. 3 (2013): 655.

16. Steele and Cohn-Vargas, *Identity Safe Classrooms*, 125.

17. Martin E. P. Seligman, ed., *Learned Optimism: How to Change Your Mind and Your Life* (New York: Random House, 2006).

18. Harri Daniel, "Benefits of Multicultural Education," November 29, 2010, Benefits Of.net, http://benefitof.net/benefits-of-multicultural-education/; Norman Garmezy and Ann S. Masten, "Stress, Competence, and Resilience: Common Frontiers for Therapist and Psychopathologist," *Behavior Therapy* 17, no. 5 (1986), 500–21, doi: http://dx.doi.org/10.1016/S0005-7894(86)80091-0; J. Bruce Overmier, "On Learned Helplessness," *Integrative Physiological & Behavioral Science* 37, no. 1 (2002): 4–8; Joseph Murphy, *The Educators Handbook for Understanding and Closing Achievement Gaps* (Thousand Oaks, CA: Corwin, 2010).

19. Steele and Cohn-Vargas, *Identity Safe Classrooms*, 125.

20. Adapted from Linda Darling-Hammond et al., "Science of Learning and Development: Implications for Educational Practice," *Applied Developmental Science* (under review).

21. Noguera et al., "Equal Opportunity for Deeper Learning."

22. Magdalene Lampert, "Ambitious Teaching: A Deep Dive," in Heller et al., *Rethinking Readiness*, 160.

23. Ibid.

24. Ibid.

25. Ibid.

26. Ibid.
27. See https://readingapprenticeship.org/our-approach/our-framework/.
28. Noguera et al., "Equal Opportunity for Deeper Learning."
29. Bruce M. Mitchell and Robert E. Salsbury, *Multicultural Education in the United States: A Guide to Policy and Programs in the 50 States* (Westport, CT: Greenwood Press, 1998).
30. Steele and Cohn-Vargas, *Identity Safe Classrooms.*
31. Terry Salinger, Myra Thomas, and Alejandra Martin, *Scholastic Balanced Literacy Tools Development and Pilot Testing* (Washington, DC: American Institutes for Research, 2017).
32. Kris D. Gutiérrez, P. Zitlali Morales, and Danny C. Martinez, "Remediating Literacy: Culture, Difference, and Learning for Students from Nondominant Communities," *Review of Research in Education* 33, no. 1 (2009), 212–45.
33. Martin L. Blank, Reuben Jacobson, and Atelia Melaville, *Achieving Results Through Community Partnerships: How District and Community Leaders Are Building Effective, Sustainable Relationships* (Washington, DC: Center for American Progress, 2012), https://cdn.americanprogress.org/wp-content/uploads/issues/2012/01/pdf /community_schools.pdf; Joseph F. Murphy, *The Educator's Handbook for Understanding and Closing Achievement Gaps* (Thousand Oaks, CA: Corwin, 2009).
34. Margary Martin, Edward Fergus, and Pedro Noguera, "Responding to the Needs of the Whole Child: A Case Study of a High-Performing Elementary School for Immigrant Children," *Reading and Writing Quarterly* 26, no. 3 (2010): 195–222.
35. Noguera et al., "Equal Opportunity for Deeper Learning," 97.
36. Marie-Andrée Somers et al., *The Enhanced Reading Opportunities Study Final Report: The Impact of Supplemental Literacy Courses for Struggling Ninth-Grade Readers*, NCEE 2010-4021 (Washington, DC: National Center for Education Evaluation and Regional Assistance, Institute of Education Sciences, US Department of Education, 2010), https://ies.ed.gov/ncee/pubs/20104021/pdf/20104021.pdf.
37. "How to Choose High School Electives," College Board (n.d.), https://bigfuture .collegeboard.org/get-in/your-high-school-record/how-to-choose-high-school -electives.
38. *Weekly Reader* is no longer published, but the *New York Times*, Scholastic Publishers, *National Geographic*, and many other associations publish high-quality print and digital magazines for students at all grades. See the *Bluford* series of young adult novels at https://www.bluford.org/.

CHAPTER 20
1. Gerald J. Langley et al., *The Improvement Guide: A Practical Approach to Enhancing Organizational Performance* (San Francisco: Jossey-Bass, 2009); Anthony S. Bryk et al., *Learning to Improve: How America's Schools Can Get Better at Getting Better* (Cambridge, MA: Harvard Education Press, 2015); Shelley H. Billig, "Progress Monitoring: Evidence from the Research," in *Progress Monitoring: Supporting Research* (St. Paul, MN: National Youth Leadership Council, 2010), 2, http://lift.nylc.org/pdf/PM _SupportingResearch.pdf.
2. "CBAM: The Concerns-Based Adoption Model," American Institutes for Research, https://www.air.org/resource/concerns-based-adoption-model-cbam.

3. Kathryn P. Boudett, Elizabeth A. City, and Richard J. Murnane, *Data Wise: A Step-by-Step Guide to Using Assessment Results to Improve Teaching and Learning* (Cambridge, MA: Harvard Education Press, 2013).

4. Julie Kowal and Joe Ableidinger, *Leading Indicators of School Turnarounds: How to Know When Dramatic Change Is on Track* (Charlottesville, NC: University of Virginia's Darden/Curry Partnership for Leaders in Education, 2011).

5. Todd Rose, *The End of Average* (New York: HarperCollins, 2015).

6. Michael Scriven, "The Methodology of Evaluation," in *Perspectives of Curriculum Evaluation*, vol. 1, ed. Ralph W. Tyler, Robert M. Gagné, and Michael Scriven (Chicago: Rand McNally, 1967), 39–83.

7. Monica Hargraves and Jennifer Brown Urban, "Evaluation Partnerships and the Systems Evaluation Protocol: The Role of Stakeholder Analysis," *NFOCUS Solutions Blog*, October 29, 2015, http://www.nfocus.com/blog/evaluation-partnerships -systems-evaluation-protocol-role-stakeholder-analysis/.

8. David Osher and Kimberly Kendziora, "Building Conditions for Learning and Healthy Adolescent Development: Strategic Approaches," in *Handbook of Youth Prevention Science*, ed. Beth Doll, William Pfohl, and Jina Yoon (New York: Routledge, 2010), 121–40.

9. David M. Fetterman, "Empowerment Evaluation: Building Communities of Practice and a Culture of Learning," *American Journal of Community Psychology* 30, no. 1 (2002): 89–102.

10. Stafford Hood, Rodney K. Hopson, and Karen E. Kirkhart "Culturally Responsive Evaluation: Theory, Practice, and Future Implications," in *Handbook of Practical Program Evaluation, 4th ed.*, ed. Kathryn E. Newcomer, Harry P. Hatry, and Joseph S. Wholey (Hoboken, NJ: Wiley/Jossey-Bass, 2015); Vivian Louie, "Identifying Responses to Inequality: The Potential of Qualitative and Mixed-Methods Research," *William T. Grant Foundation Digest* 1 (June 2016), http://wtgrantfoundation .org/library/uploads/2016/06/The-Value-of-Qualitative-and-Mixed-Methods -Research.pdf.

11. David Osher, Kimberly Kendziora, and Marjorie Chinen, *Student Connection Research: Final Narrative Report to the Spencer Foundation* (Washington, DC: American Institutes for Research, 2008).

12. "School Climate Improvement Resource Package," National Center on Safe Supportive Learning Environments, https://safesupportivelearning.ed.gov/scirp /about.

13. http://teachstone.com/class/

14. Public Profit, *Dabbling in the Data: A Hands-on Guide to Participatory Data Analysis* (Oakland, CA: Public Profit, 2015).

15. Matthew B. Miles, A. Michael Huberman, and Johnny Saldaña, *Qualitative Data Analysis: A Methods Sourcebook*, 3rd ed. (Thousand Oaks, CA: Sage Publications, 2013).

16. Mark H. Bornstein, "Fostering Optimal Development and Averting Detrimental Development: Prescriptions, Proscriptions, and Specificity," *Applied Developmental Science* (2018), forthcoming; David Osher and Michael Kane, *Describing and Studying Innovations in the Education of Children with Attention Deficit Disorder. A Series of Papers on the Federal Role in Improving Practice in Special Education* (Washington, DC:

Directed Research Branch, Division of Innovation and Development, Office of Special Education Programs, US Department of Education, 1993).

17. Andrew P. Swanlund and Samantha Neiman, "Intraclass Correlations and Other Variance Estimates for Designing School-Climate Research Studies" (paper presented at the annual meeting of the Association for Public Policy Analysis and Management, Chicago, Illinois, November 2, 2017).

# Acknowledgments

The editors would like to gratefully acknowledge the many individuals who contributed to this volume, who share a common mission to provide the most up-to-date resources to foster equity and create excellent schools. First, we would like to thank those individuals who shared their day-to-day stories to help illuminate the practices outlined in this volume. It was an honor to learn from them while we crafted the book. They are: Mary Catherine Ricker from American Federation of Teachers; Tiffany Pruitt and Lisa Coney from Saginaw Public Schools (Michigan); Gene Chasin from Say Yes to Education in Syracuse; Jessica Juarez from Communities In Schools of Chicago; Dia Jackson from American Institutes for Research (AIR); Kristine Hensley from Hillsborough County Public Schools (Florida); Derrick Bushon from Swartz Creek Community Schools (Michigan); Matthew Holloway from the Massachusetts Department of Elementary and Secondary Education; Lauren Degiulio from Bernhard Moos Elementary School, Chicago Public Schools; David Gillis from New Haven Community Schools (Connecticut); Nicole Bucka, Ellen Reinhardt, and Michele Walden-Doppke from Northern Rhode Island Collaborative; Chuck Holland, Donna Teuber, and Tom Cranmer from Richland School District Two (South Carolina); Kevin Dwyer and Bill Stencil from Cleveland Metropolitan School District; Sasha Rabkin from Equal Opportunity Schools; and Mark Sander from Hennepin County and Minneapolis Public Schools (Minnesota). We could not have captured these important voices without the diligence and active listening of Kellie Anderson (AIR), who served as interviewer and documentarian for this effort. We also would like to thank AIR's publications team, who worked to ensure the quality of our work. We were so happy to have the tireless partnership of Phil Esra, Emma Ruckley, Kim O'Brien, and Sharon Wallace. We would also like to thank Zaretta Hammond and Abe Wandersman for critical chapter reviews.

Twenty chapters, three editors, and multiple contributors and reviewers is a lot to manage, and we are so grateful to have the early help from SooYun Chung and Jessy Newman (AIR) and the phenomenal dedication and over-the-finish-line coordination from Amanda Mitchell (AIR). We had a terrific and collaborative team. We couldn't be more grateful for the guidance, good humor, and reflective partnership provided by Nancy Walser from Harvard Education Press. Nancy was with us from the conception of the book through production, and helped to share our thinking and to ensure the book would be accessible to a wide audience of readers. Finally, we would like to thank the many in-school- and out-of-school time leaders, professionals, and para-professionals; family members; youth; advocates; researchers; funders; and systems builders who have taught us, shared with us, and partnered with us to foster conditions for teaching, learning, and development for all students. We are honored to work alongside you in the education movement.

Throughout this volume, you will read stories from the field, exemplifying the strategies and innovations described by the authors. To gather these real-life scenarios, we scanned the field to compile a list of people doing good work to support safe, equitable, and engaging schools. We then interviewed these people—to share their stories, and to confirm what we know from the research. Kellie Anderson conducted hours of interviews and authored the stories, which are an important contribution to this volume.

# About the Editors

**David Osher, PhD,** is an Institute Fellow at American Institutes for Research. He is an expert on school safety, conditions for learning and school climate, social and emotional learning, youth development, violence prevention, supportive school discipline, cultural competence, family engagement trauma vulnerability, cultural responsiveness, and collaborative research. He has led numerous evaluations of initiatives and programs, systematic reviews, expert panels, and projects that supported schools, districts, and states in promoting school safety and addressing disciplinary disparities.

Osher coauthored *Safe, Drug-Free, and Effective Schools: What Works!* and led the expert panel that produced *Early Warning, Timely Response: A Guide to Safe Schools*, which was released by President Clinton, as well as two related products for the Departments of Education, Justice, and Health and Human Services, *Safeguarding Our Children: An Action Guide* and *Safe and Supportive Schools Step by Step*. He was also the lead author of *Addressing the Root Causes of Disparities in School Discipline: An Educator's Action Planning Guide*, which was released by the White House in July 2015. Osher helped the US Department of Education develop the National Agenda for Improving Results for Children and Youth with Serious Emotional Disturbance, served as senior advisor in the development of the Department of Education School Climate Surveys, chaired the expert panel convened for the Coordinating Council on Juvenile Justice on the relationship between disability and involvement in the juvenile court and correctional systems, and led the What Works Clearinghouse review of character education.

Osher serves on numerous expert panels and editorial boards and has authored or coauthored over 390 books, monographs, chapters, articles, and reports, as well as 185 peer-reviewed papers and invitational presentations. He has served as dean and taught at a liberal arts college and two professional schools of human services.

**Deborah Moroney, PhD,** is a Managing Director at American Institutes for Research, and is Director of the Youth Development and Supportive Learning Environments practice area. Moroney's research and practice experience is in social and emotional learning and youth development. She is the architect of a collaborative method for the design of dual-purpose (improvement and demonstration) evaluation frameworks for national multisite youth development programs. Additionally, she serves as the principal investigator of evaluations and research studies in youth development programs. Moroney has consulted with intermediaries, foundations, associations, and universities on their conceptualization of youth development resources and evaluation strategies. Her work provides a bridge between research and practice.

Moroney currently serves on the editorial board of Afterschool Matters and is on the publication committee of the *Journal of Youth Development*. She has authored numerous chapters, peer-reviewed publications, and organizational guides using both research findings and practitioner input on youth development and social and emotional learning, including *Ready to Assess*. She was a coauthor of the fourth edition of the seminal resource *Beyond the Bell: A Toolkit for Creating Effective Afterschool and Expanded Learning Programs*. Prior to joining AIR, Moroney was a clinical faculty member in educational psychology at the University of Illinois at Chicago in the Youth Development Graduate Program.

**Sandra Williamson, MEd, CAGS,** is a Vice President for Policy, Practice, and Systems Change at American Institutes for Research. She has over forty years of experience working to improve services for students with special learning or behavioral needs. She was a special education administrator at the district level early in her career, and has provided technical assistance and training for the last eighteen years through nationally funded projects. She has led the National Center on Safe Supportive Learning Environments since 2010 for the US Department of Education, providing technical assistance to states and districts on improving school climate. She has also led the National Center for Mental Health Promotion and Youth Violence Prevention funded by the Substance Abuse and Mental Health Services Administration, focused on improving access to school- and community-based mental health services. She serves as principal investigator for projects related to developing multitiered social-emotional supports in schools and accessing school-based mental health services and community-based programs, and for district evaluations of implementations of evidence-based programs, including programs that incorporate positive behavioral supports and programs focused on school discipline.

Williamson has contributed to multiple publications, including *School-Based Mental Health Services in Systems of Care, Inclusion Strategies for Students with Learning and Behavioral Problems, Collaboration with Other Agencies: Wraparound and System of Care for Children and Youth with EBD, A Comprehensive Approach to Promoting Social, Emotional, and Academic Growth in Contemporary Schools,* and *Focusing on the Whole Student: An Evaluation of Massachusetts' Wraparound Zone Initiative.*

# About the Contributors

**Kellie Anderson, MPH,** is an Online Learning, Publications, and Communications Consultant at American Institutes for Research. Anderson has been working in the fields of public health and health communication for twenty years. She has particular expertise in school-based behavioral health and social and emotional learning initiatives, children's health promotion, youth substance abuse and violence prevention, and college health and safety. She is an experienced instructional designer and writer who creates online trainings and related materials for school-based administrators and staff.

**Catherine Barbour, MEd,** is a Principal Consultant at American Institutes for Research. Barbour has worked in K–12 education for thirty years, focusing her efforts on turnaround leadership and school improvement. She has expertise in developing the capacity of state and local education agencies in identifying, recruiting, developing, and supporting turnaround leaders, and in providing support to states and districts to implement successful turnaround and school improvement services.

**Juliette Berg, PhD,** is a Senior Researcher at American Institutes for Research. Her work focuses on understanding how to build the conditions and opportunities necessary to support the development of social-emotional and academic competencies in children and youth. She has methodological expertise in research design, program evaluation, implementation science, and advanced quantitative methods.

**Ilene Berman, EdD,** is a Senior Associate at the Annie E. Casey Foundation, where she works to help public systems, schools, and communities partner to improve child well-being. Her career in education spans more than twenty years, during which she has focused on improving education policy and expanding the availability and use of evidence-based programs and practices.

**Aaron R. Butler, PhD,** is a Principal TA Consultant at American Institutes for Research. Butler has worked in the field of educational leadership for twelve years. He has particular expertise in leadership coaching, strategic planning, resource allocation, and development of progress monitoring systems. He is also involved in training school leaders on the effective use of data, curriculum and standards mapping, and district and school improvement planning and budgeting.

**Vanessa Coleman, PhD,** is a Principal TA Consultant at American Institutes for Research. Coleman is a seasoned change management consultant, with a particular focus on cross-system and broad stakeholder engagement. She uses an equity approach to guide her work with foundations, national nonprofits, education systems, and community-based organizations. She designs equity frameworks with organizations and systems, and facilitates processes to implement equity in policies, cultures, structures, strategies, and processes.

**Greta Colombi, MA,** is a Senior Researcher at American Institutes for Research. Colombi has been providing technical assistance, program monitoring and reporting, and research in both the education and the health and human services fields for twenty years. She has particular expertise in working with states, districts, and schools to improve school climate. She also focuses on advancing supportive school discipline, including addressing persistent disparities.

**Kevin Dwyer, MA, NCSP,** is a retired Associate Principal Research Scientist at the American Institutes for Research. Dwyer has been working in the field of school psychology and education reform for over fifty years. He has particular expertise in social-emotional resilience, primary prevention, school climate, systemic change, and interagency collaboration. He is also involved in the effective measurement of interventions needed to ensure positive emotional, mental health, and academic student outcomes.

**Allison Dymnicki, PhD,** is a Senior Researcher at American Institutes for Research. Dymnicki has worked in the fields of social and emotional learning, positive youth development, and prevention research for thirteen years. She has particular expertise in conducting research on school- and community-based programs that aim to promote positive youth development and prevent engagement in problem behaviors. She is also involved in developing the best ways to translate research findings to different audiences, including practitioners and staff working in federal agencies, and in developing the best methods for assessing the effectiveness of comprehensive school- or community-based interventions.

**Edward Fergus, PhD,** is Assistant Professor of Urban Education and Policy at Temple University. Fergus has worked in the field for over twenty years. His current work is on the intersection of educational policy and outcomes, with a specific focus on black and Latino boys' academic and social engagement outcomes, disproportionality in special education and suspensions, and school climate conditions.

**Karen Francis, PhD,** is a Principal Researcher at American Institutes for Research. Francis is a medical sociologist, and has grounded her work in the principles of cultural competence and a commitment to address disparities across social, health, juvenile justice, and educational service systems. Her expertise spans a variety of issues, including children's behavioral health, gender-responsive programming, rural behavioral health, youth violence prevention, safe and supportive learning environments, health disparities, disproportionality in juvenile justice, cultural and linguistic competence, and diversity and inclusion.

**Elizabeth V. Freeman, MSW,** is a Senior TA Consultant at American Institutes for Research. Freeman has worked in the field of school mental/behavioral health for twenty-five years. She has particular expertise in building collaborations among schools and community groups, using evidence-based practices, and developing mechanisms to finance and support community efforts to build sustainable comprehensive programs. She is also involved in research and measurement of school-based programs—related to students' social and emotional learning, behavior, and mental health—that promote effective conditions for students' learning and healthy development in schools.

**Allison Gruner Gandhi, PhD,** is a Managing Researcher and Director of the Special Education Practice Area at American Institutes for Research. Gandhi, who has worked in the field for over twenty years, has extensive knowledge about special education policy and practice, especially related to identifying and communicating about evidence-based practices to support improved outcomes for students with disabilities. Since 2005, Gandhi has led the knowledge development work for the federally funded National Center on Response to Intervention and National Center on Intensive Intervention.

**Kathleen Guarino, MA,** is a Senior TA Consultant at American Institutes for Research. Guarino has worked in the field of trauma for sixteen years. She has particular expertise in developing tools and curricula and providing training and consultation to support child-serving systems in adopting a trauma-informed approach. She also provides training and technical assistance to help schools and districts increase their capacity to identify, assess, and serve students exposed to pervasive violence.

**Lynn Holdheide, MS,** is a Managing TA Consultant at American Institutes for Research. Holdheide has more than twelve years of experience in providing technical assistance of the highest quality to state education agencies, educator preparation programs, and regional comprehensive centers. With experience as a special education teacher and as an education consultant at the Indiana Department of Education, Holdheide is sensitive to the needs of students with disabilities and the challenges educators face in closing the achievement gap, and has a deep understanding of evidence-based practices for students with disabilities.

**Stephanie Jackson, PhD,** is a Managing Researcher at American Institutes for Research. Jackson has worked in the education field for more than forty years. She has particular expertise in special education policy and practice. She is also involved in helping states, districts, and schools implement evidence-based practices to improve outcomes for all students, including students with disabilities.

**Jessica Johnson, MPP,** is a Senior Vice President of Policy, Practice, and Systems Change at American Institutes for Research. Johnson is a leader in developing and implementing evidence-based services for states and local districts targeted at improving outcomes for low performing schools. Her areas of expertise include statewide systems of support, school and district improvement, and systems change. Under her leadership, AIR's partnerships with states, districts, and schools have led to better systems and improved outcomes for students.

**Jason Katz, MA,** is a Researcher at American Institutes for Research. Katz has been working in the fields of program evaluation and implementation science for over ten years. He has particular expertise in evaluating training and technical assistance to support implementation of programs and practices in community settings. He is also involved in the measurement of readiness, including school- and district-level readiness for implementing social and emotional learning.

**Kimberly Kendziora, PhD,** is a Managing Researcher at American Institutes for Research. Her work focuses on the evaluation of school-based student support initiatives—particularly programs related to students' social and emotional learning, behavior, mental health, and health. Kendziora has also been involved in the measurement of school climate, or the conditions for learning, in schools.

**R. Jason LaTurner, PhD,** is a Principal Consultant at American Institutes for Research. LaTurner has worked in K–16 evaluation and research for over fifteen years, focusing his efforts on educator preparation and assessment. He has expertise in developing the capacity of state and local education agencies in program evaluation, with a particular emphasis on change management.

**Fausto Alejandro López, MA,** is a Senior TA Consultant at American Institutes for Research. López has been in the field of educational psychology and youth development for fifteen years. He provides technical assistance, training, and professional development to diverse audiences in the education and out-of-school time sectors. López has particular expertise in working with educators on youth program quality and youth development, school climate, social and emotional learning, restorative practices, and afterschool and expanded learning initiatives. He is also an adjunct professor in the education department at the University of Illinois at Chicago. In his role at AIR, he facilitates national educational workshops that bring the most up-to-date research to the field in collaborative and relatable formats.

**Amy Mart, PhD,** is a Researcher at American Institutes for Research. She has over a decade of experience working at the intersection of research, policy, and practice to promote positive outcomes for young people. She has experience working in K–12 education systems, applying empirical and practical evidence to continuously improve conditions that support students' social-emotional and academic development. She currently leads research, evaluation, and consultation projects that focus on social and emotional learning and supportive learning environments.

**Robert V. Mayo, PhD,** is a Senior TA Consultant within the Policy, Practice, and Systems Change group at American Institutes for Research. Mayo has worked in the education field in various capacities for over twenty-five years. He has particular expertise in the provision of technical assistance and professional development to district- and site-level leaders, in learning-centered family involvement, and in public charter school policy and practice. He is also involved in developing, implementing, and evaluating data-driven decision-making systems, holistic student support service-delivery systems, progressive school culture and climate initiatives, and outcomes-oriented accountability mechanisms.

**Sam Neiman, MA,** is a Senior Researcher at American Institutes for Research. Neiman has been in working in the field of large-scale surveys for more than ten years. She has particular expertise in survey design and data use related to school crime, violence, discipline, safety, school climate, and social and emotional learning. She is also involved in examining measurement properties of school climate survey data, and has expertise in bullying, trends and clusters of school crime, adolescent drug use, and issues of survey nonresponse.

**Jessica Newman, MA,** is a Researcher at American Institutes for Research. She has been in the field of social and emotional learning and youth development for ten years. Newman has particular expertise in the structures and settings that support a young person's growth and development. Through ongoing research, evaluation, and practice work, she endeavors to connect the dots in the field by conducting rigorous research and evaluations to create meaningful resources that ultimately promote high-quality programming for youth.

**Trina Osher, EdD,** has forty years of experience as an educator, special educator, and teacher educator, administering education policy at the state level and analyzing it nationally. Moreover, she is a parent of two adopted children with special needs whose mental health suffered from lack of coordination among the many systems providing services to them. As a well-recognized leader in the movement for family-driven care, she advocates for children's behavioral health care to be integrated with education, health, and safety.

**Jill Pentimonti, PhD,** is a Principal Researcher at American Institutes for Research. Pentimonti has been in working in the field of reading development for ten years. She has particular expertise in intervention research designed to support children's reading skills. She is also involved in developing and synthesizing knowledge on intensive interventions and assessments to be used within the Multitiered Systems of Support framework.

**Jeffrey M. Poirier, PhD,** is a Senior Research Associate at the Annie E. Casey Foundation, where he leads research and evaluation investments. Poirier has worked in the education field for seventeen years. He has particular expertise in youth well-being, conducting research, and applying data and evidence to improve outcomes for underserved populations, including young people who are LGBTQ. His current work also addresses issues related to adolescent science, child welfare, employment, homelessness, and juvenile justice.

**Frank Rider, MS,** is the Senior Human Services Financing Specialist at American Institutes for Research. Rider managed service systems for individuals with developmental and intellectual disabilities, for child victims of maltreatment, and for children and youth with behavioral health needs in Arizona for more than two decades. He has been a trainer and TA consultant for federal programs in more than thirty states since 2006, specializing in human service integration, financing, and public policy. Rider is involved in the development and sustainability of school and community mental health and health-care services for children, youth, and families.

**Terry Salinger, PhD,** is an Institute Fellow and Chief Scientist for Reading Research at American Institutes for Research. Salinger has worked in the field of reading since her early days as a first-grade teacher in Brooklyn. Throughout her career, she has studied reading development, teacher knowledge about reading, and valid assessment of the reading skills of both students and adults, especially those who struggle to master the skills they need for success. She is especially interested in the effects of K–12 reading difficulties in adulthood, and their impact on adult self-efficacy and civic engagement. She is also involved in providing conceptual and technical guidance on the development of measures of social-emotional skills and learning environments.

**Manolya Tanyu** is a Senior Researcher at American Institutes for Research. She has been working in the field of educational research and evaluation for more than fifteen years. She has particular expertise in evaluating school and community initiatives to promote social and emotional learning, positive youth development (e.g., youth mentoring), violence prevention, and alternatives to the juvenile justice system, and works on projects examining the effects of prevention strategies on youth outcomes.

**Roger P. Weissberg, PhD,** is a Distinguished Professor of Psychology and Education and NoVo Foundation Endowed Chair in Social and Emotional Learning at the University of Illinois at Chicago, where he is Chair of the Community and Prevention Research Program and directs the Social and Emotional Learning Research Group. He is also Board Vice Chair and Chief Knowledge Officer for the Collaborative for Academic, Social, and Emotional Learning (CASEL), a national organization committed to making evidence-based social, emotional, and academic learning an essential part of preschool through high school education. For almost four decades, Weissberg has trained scholars and practitioners on innovative ways to design, implement, and evaluate family, school, and community interventions.

**Lacy Wood, MLIS,** is a Principal TA Consultant at American Institutes for Research. Wood has over eighteen years of experience in the field of family and community engagement in education. She also has expertise in state-level education policy, expanded learning opportunities, and support systems for school improvement. Wood chairs the Family Engagement State Leaders Network. She also serves as vice chair of the National Association of Family, School, and Community Engagement policy committee, and is a founding board member of the association.

**Sara Wraight, JD,** is a Policy Principal at American Institutes for Research. Wraight has been in the field of education for thirteen years. She has particular expertise in state education governance and policy. She is also involved in supporting state education agencies in developing and implementing school improvement initiatives.

**Nick Yoder, PhD,** is a Senior TA Consultant at American Institutes for Research. Yoder has worked in the field of education for thirteen years as a teacher, instructional coach, preservice instructor, researcher, and consultant. He has particular expertise in research and technical assistance on school-based programs and practices that support students' social-emotional development. He is also involved in advocating schoolwide practices that support the conditions for teaching and learning, including the use of data for continuous improvement.

# Index